FORENSIC
PSYCHOLOGY

THEORY, RESEARCH, POLICY AND PRACTICE

JENNIFER BROWN
YVONNE SHELL
TERRI COLE

Los Angeles | London | New Delhi
Singapore | Washington DC

Los Angeles | London | New Delhi
Singapore | Washington DC

SAGE Publications Ltd
1 Oliver's Yard
55 City Road
London EC1Y 1SP

SAGE Publications Inc.
2455 Teller Road
Thousand Oaks, California 91320

SAGE Publications India Pvt Ltd
B 1/I 1 Mohan Cooperative Industrial Area
Mathura Road
New Delhi 110 044

SAGE Publications Asia-Pacific Pte Ltd
3 Church Street
#10-04 Samsung Hub
Singapore 049483

Editor: Luke Block
Production editor: Shikha Jain
Copyeditor: Elaine Leek
Proofreader: Jill Birch
Marketing manager: Michael Ainsley
Cover design: Wendy Scott
Typeset by: C&M Digitals (P) Ltd, Chennai, India
Printed in India at Replika Press Pvt Ltd

Library of Congress Control Number: 2014959447

British Library Cataloguing in Publication data

A catalogue record for this book is available from the British Library

MIX
Paper from responsible sources
FSC® C016779

ISBN 978-1-4739-1193-2
ISBN 978-1-4739-1194-9 (pbk)

At SAGE we take sustainability seriously. Most of our products are printed in the UK using FSC papers and boards. When we print overseas we ensure sustainable papers are used as measured by the Egmont grading system. We undertake an annual audit to monitor our sustainability.

This book is dedicated to Elizabeth Campbell who conceived the original idea with me but who was unable to begin work on the project because of her untimely death from cancer.
Jennifer Brown

I dedicate this book to my immediate family – my husband, Rob, children, Lily and Alfie, and of course my Mum. For putting up with me, my crazy career choice and understanding my need to work; for making me eternally happy; and for keeping me grounded and (relatively) sane.
Terri Cole

To my son, Marcus, without whose love, laughter and patience this book would never have been written. Also to my late parents, Tony and Marion Shell, who supported my choices always and who I like to think taught me laughter, compassion and a sense of fairness in equal measure.
Yvonne Shell

CONTENTS

ABOUT THE AUTHORS

Jennifer Brown is a visiting professor and Co Director of the Mannheim Centre for Criminology at the London School of Economics. She has previously directed a Masters programme in Forensic Psychology at the University of Surrey and was formerly the research manager for the Hampshire Constabulary. She co-edited the *Cambridge Handbook of Forensic Psychology* with the late Elizabeth Campbell and most recently edited a forensic psychology collection in the critical concepts in psychology series, published by Routledge.

Yvonne Shell is currently a forensic clinical psychologist working in the fields of addictions and sex offender treatment. Her career has previously included working in both medium and maximum security settings for the Ministry of Justice, and also in medium and maximum security psychiatric establishments such as Broadmoor Hospital, specializing in the assessment and treatment of sexual offenders and working with those diagnosed with personality disorders. She has also worked as an expert witness and worked directly with police services to develop initiatives to address local areas of identified need. Yvonne has also held a senior academic post at Canterbury Christ Church University and honorary posts at the University of Surrey, University of Portsmouth and Canterbury University.

Terri Cole has worked nationally alongside the police advising on behavioural aspects of serious crime investigation for 17 years. Firstly working as a placement student at the National Crime Faculty alongside investigators and clinicians, then as an assistant and serious crime analyst in the Serious Crime Analysis Section and for the past 13 years as a behavioural investigative adviser (BIA). Her specialism is in relation to behavioural analyses of murder, rape and sexual offences committed by strangers. She has advised and provided reports to investigations in relation to offender profiling, offence linkage, crime scene assessment and prioritization of persons of interest. She also worked for a number of years as a Victim Support volunteer. Terri is now working as a Senior Lecturer in Forensic Psychology at Bournemouth University. She has a first class undergraduate degree in Psychology with Criminal Justice from the University of Plymouth, and a PhD from the University of Surrey, which explored a pragmatic psychological approach to the provision of behavioural investigative advice for difficult-to-detect murder investigations in the UK. Other research interests have included offender signature in serial rape, what senior investigators want from BIAs, when such advice should be delivered, and offender post-offence behaviour in homicide. She has spoken at numerous conferences and as a guest lecturer on many undergraduate and postgraduate courses. She is a member of the British Psychological Society.

LIST OF FIGURES AND TABLES

Figures

Tables

LIST OF BOXES

FOREWORD

In the days before everybody knew everything, I believed that most criminals fell into one of two camps. They were either something like Robert de Niro in a Martin Scorcese movie, or they were like one of those men who is 'irresistible to women' on the Jeremy Kyle Show – all toothless, tattooed, disagreeable and disruptive. That was enough to make me curious however and I followed my tried and tested strategy of stumbling through life and ended up on a Forensic Psychology Masters programme. I shouldn't even have really been studying psychology at undergraduate level in the first place as I saw myself heading for the certainties of rock stardom (a dream which has not yet disappeared, I should add). It was happenstance, the unappreciative delusions of everyone else in the world and a tendency towards tone deafness which led me through a variety of endeavours, eventually to psychology.

So there I was being bashed around from one thought to another within the science as if I was in a psychedelic, psychological pinball machine until an interest in clinical and abnormal psychology developed in my third year of University leading to an assistant post. I had always harboured an interest in the more extreme ends of human behaviour and personality – possibly due to nefarious associates in my nefarious youth – and only realized fairly late that this was even an existing area of study. That in itself shows how far the profession has moved in the last 15 years – nowadays if you were to ask a psychology undergraduate, they would likely know something about 'forensic psychology' – hopefully something more than that which they have gleaned from second rate TV fiction or a dodgy Morgan Freeman movie.

Following the MSc and a spell of travelling where I lost my found self, I began working as a community Forensic Mental Health Practitioner. And I suppose that is where it really began. The course had been fascinating, touching on all of the areas of interest I had been developing and conducting my research into the assessment of psychopathy at Broadmoor was an experience which sailed my already floating boat. But the nuts and bolts of forensic psychology began for me when I started seeing 'real life offenders.' And that is where all this background stuff became relevant. The amount of our own lives we bring into these jobs has always been an area of interest for me. Whether it be some crazy experience in a far off country, hanging out with friends from a variety of backgrounds, coming from a diverse and eclectic socio-cultural background on a personal level and indeed having one's own array of life experiences and significant events – it all seemed to find its way into my personal and professional toolbox. And just as I did during my first green days as an unqualified, untrained and wary junior to the point I am at now – as an Expert Witness, consultant and Chair of the National Division – I still rely on those life experiences to inform my practice. This happens from the point of engagement and developing a relational dynamic in an assessment or therapeutic context, or providing a normative context and sense of appropriateness in the social functioning and pragmatic risk determinations when working with offenders. I have found the integration and objective appraisal of my own life experiences vital to my practice. These jobs are not for the faint hearted and I am always one to promote such life experience and intuition as fundamental tools to good practice or rather, to being a good practitioner.

My first job, working for a charity in partnership with the Probation Service in London was fairly new at the time and this meant that I was well supported in carving out the role and fashioning the job into one which would allow me the opportunity to apply for my Chartership. This set the tone for the future of similar roles to some degree as I was the first person in this position to do so and this team has grown hugely, successfully pioneering new strategies for Court Diversion and community working with offenders, fitting well into the current 'Transforming Rehabilitation' model, with partnership working as the cornerstone of its success. I was pleased to end up managing that team and am still involved as a specialist independent external clinical supervisor.

I have come from a background of 15 years working in Forensic Mental Health, programme design and delivery, assessment and Expert Witness work in Independent Practice. I have also worked part time running MSc courses in Forensic Psychology and at the time of writing I am current Chair of the Division of Forensic Psychology and Chair of the DFP Training Committee – I have been told that I am the first person in the history of the Division of Forensic Psychology to hold these two positions at the same time. I also sit on the Expert Witness Advisory Group of the BPS and it is this rather eclectic mix of experience which has informed my motivation for the progression of the discipline.

Forensic Psychology has come a long way in the time I have been involved but so have forensic psychologists. The understanding of good practice is distinct from being a good practitioner to some degree. A good practitioner for example, must understand where they can be vulnerable, where they must be assertive, where the line is to be drawn between empathic sentiment and collusive interaction and indeed where the limits of their skills lie. A good practitioner must find their balance in bringing aspects of their own life experience to an open-minded approach to working with offenders. They must utilize supervision as the safe place to be vulnerable, be stupid and be safe. Good practice, for me is understanding the theory behind assessment and intervention approaches, keeping abreast of developments through CPD and understanding how best to implement knowledge, understanding and theory into practice. This becomes more than the simple understanding of CBT based intervention programmes which may be of limited utility. Indeed, this is more than learning how to run a group through a manual and understanding how to interpret psychometrics. While it might be stretching it to say a monkey could do those things, I'm fairly sure that with a little help, Tarzan would be able to and he hung around with monkeys.

Often, professionals can forget what it means to be a psychologist or indeed a human being who is subject to a string of events which influence behaviour and decision making. In my view, we must flatten any sense of hierarchy between practitioners and offenders. Broadly speaking, we employ the same decision making processes which are subject to the same life experience influence and the skills we employ are derived from the same levels of theory as poor decisions made by offenders. The sooner we realize there is little between 'us and them' the sooner we can become more efficient practitioners. Forensic Psychology is moving on at a pace now and it is important that we move on from the old school mentality of professional insecurities and an understanding of ourselves as 'softies' delivering CBT programmes in prisons to offenders who have done bad things, viewing them from a pedestal being held up by intervention manuals. In my career, I have worked with some very high profile and dangerous individuals (that includes some colleagues as well as offenders!). I have moved through criminal clinical work into working in family law and child protection. This is some of the hardest, most emotionally taxing and professionally challenging work I have ever done. To have a key role through one's assessment in determining whether a child remains with a family plays on one's own sense of family, fairness and emotional stability unlike any criminal work I have ever done. To place the long-term welfare of the child as central where the result may indeed be detrimental to the adults one has assessed is a complex dynamic I had never considered in the early days where I was bumming around the world, listening to Led Zeppelin and still deciding what to do with my life and the responsibility weighs seriously and heavily on my shoulders. The distinct lines of professional responsibility are continually drawn for me and at times it does become too much. Understanding your limits and the values of self-protection, supervision, distraction and a bit of gallows humour becomes essential at times like these.

But in line with my own professional development, the profession itself is also developing and it is a genuine privilege for me to have a role in fashioning this through my work at the British Psychological Society/DFP. For me, Forensic Psychology needs to hold its head high and I hope to encourage practitioners and academics in the field to work closely together to promote and shout loudly about the dynamic, integrative and uniquely focused discipline that Forensic Psychology is. We are not consigned to a unidimensional measure of understanding risk but rather a tripartite model of understanding risk of harm, deteriorating mental health and recidivism and fully considering the impact of one on the other and the interaction between these dimensions is central and identifying for forensic psychology. We should all be in a position to robustly define and defend who we are and what we do in the face of greater challenges – those that are judicial, political, financial and professional. It is a credit to the authors of this book that the developing range of professional expertise and functioning is reflected in an honest and challenging manner. I believe it is the duty of all forensic psychologists to challenge the status quo, push the boundaries of professional development, utilize our skills as project managers and explore the applied nature of our expertise across psychological domains – including organizational psychology, clinical psychology, counselling psychology and other traditionally perceived fields of psychology. The chapters in this book and the range of professionals engaged with this discussion are reflective of this ongoing dialogue and process of development for psychology in general and not just forensic psychology.

Those who have a vested interest in forensic psychology will see that stage one has undergone a significant change in recent years. Stage two is also developing fast and is in the process of transformation to reflect the principles of expansive working and skill development and it is clear to me that the discussions in this book and the motivation for us to challenge previously scripted roles for forensic psychologists underpins the writing which follows and is central to the profession flourishing in the future. It is our role now to nurture the potential for future generations to be dissatisfied with what they are told and create new scripts, new boundaries and new challenges for the profession. We are moving towards a 'cross-divisional' approach and stage two is embracing the advent of professional doctorates, a model of 'pseudo-apprenticeship', selection on the basis of merit and potential with transparency in achieving core role competencies. This change is significant and reflective of an ongoing evolution in our understanding of the discipline and it is notable that key individuals involved in this process are also contributory authors in this book.

Psychology as a whole is in the process of change. We are likely to see a more valued profession, higher profile, contributing to policy development at the highest level and the British Psychological Society itself is at the advent of significant transformation with a 'Member Network Review' of society structures and processes. As the individual responsible for representing all Divisions within the Society in this process of change, I am able to witness first hand and indeed contribute to directly influencing the way psychology is seen and used in the United Kingdom. The applied nature of psychological practice underpinned by academic rigour impacts wider than the classically understood protected titles and Divisions and hence change is necessary and is beginning. That a forensic psychologist is now in such a representative position to challenge the way psychology is accessed and understood is testament to how the profession itself has developed over the years. That this person is me is testament to how easy it is to hoodwink people even in this day and age! It would be my contention and one which is reflected in the authors' own voices here, that we should question, challenge, explore but also seek to develop answers to some of these questions and not sit back and accept restrictions to practice and understanding.

I believe it is essential to understand the aspects of forensic psychology driven by understanding core psychological principles and that we should consider ourselves psychologists first, before considering ourselves as experts or specialists in forensic psychology. This will allow us to grow dynamically as a profession with a clear understanding of the range of skills we have and help us to identify areas in which we can ethically develop ourselves and best utilize our skill base. Misconceptions about offending behaviour and indeed offenders can have the potency to create a whirlwind of public opinion which can influence sometimes knee-jerk reactions from the media and politicians as well as impacting our own conscience and ability to carry out our daily work. It is important for us as individuals, citizens and professionals, in my view to challenge myths about such things, but also as a profession to take issue with some of these and have a direct influence on such reporting and possibly more importantly, to have an audible, pragmatic, informed and professional voice in the *right* places.

It is true that we face challenging times. It is true that we must be responsive, alert and flexible in our reaction. However, it is also my view that we should not be alarmed or threatened by change. Rather we should attempt to influence that change where necessary but also retain pride and confidence in our own skills to adapt and evolve our profession with the highest focus on professional standards. It may be the case that we cannot prevent the public from believing that all sex offenders should be named, shamed and dealt with by amateur surgery, that prisoners should never be released from prison but that prisons should be nowhere near anybody's house, that those with a substance misuse problem are as bad as any criminal and we are only kept safe by Fake Sheikhs and redtops. But we can and should take responsibility for furthering knowledge and responsible practice, educating where necessary and developing the profession promoting the science of psychology along the way.

Dee Anand BSc, MSc, C.Psychol, AFBPsS

Chartered Psychologist, Forensic Psychologist
Chair – Division of Forensic Psychology
Chair – Division of Forensic Psychology Training Committee
Deputy Programme Director – MSc Forensic Psychology University of Portsmouth

ACKNOWLEDGEMENTS

I am truly grateful to my friends and colleagues Terri Cole and Yvonne Shell who came on board and helped me re-think and complete this project drawing on their many years of experience to make this book speak to truth. You did so with huge enthusiasm and great generosity. It's been hard work and fun working with you both.

Jennifer Brown

Firstly I acknowledge the often unrecognized efforts of my BIA colleagues Lee Rainbow, Adam Gregory and Pippa Gregory, for their peer support and continual dedication to assisting investigations. I am also indebted to my constant mentors Paul Lobb, Adrian West and Jennifer Brown, for their advice and encouragement. Finally to my own partner in crime, Clare Bowie, who thankfully has been here through thick and thin, sharing the journey with me. I would not have wanted to have done it without you.

Terri Cole

Finally, we would like to acknowledge the truly brave contributions to this book by those who have had histories of criminal behaviour and who have without a doubt created new identities for themselves. We wanted you, our readers, to hear and understand those we call offenders.

Yvonne Shell

To our professional colleagues Dee Anand, Laurence Alison, Anthony Beech, Ray Bull, Rebecca Campbell, Gavin Collett, Leam Craig, Theresa Gannon, Gisli Gudjonsson, Carys Hamilton, Sean Hammond, Clive Hollin, Andy Inett, Jan Jordan, Kerry Joy, Barbara Krahé, Paul Lobb, Mary McMurran, Adrian Needs, Derek Perkins, Lee Rainbow, Betsy Stanko, Tania Tancred, Martyn Underhill, Tony Ward, Paul Williamson, Pam Wilson, Danielle Wunsch, to Setanta and Steve, and two anonymous contributors we want to say a particular thank you and we hope that in encountering their narratives it offers those reading this book a taste of the depth and richness of the experiences when working as a forensic psychologist. We hope too their insights will make for better practice, and more fundamentally increased compassion and understanding of those whose behaviours we study and work alongside in therapy.

We are also grateful to SAGE for keeping the faith with this project, in particular Michael Carmichael, Luke Block, Keri Dickens, Shikha Jain and Elaine Leek.

We thank two anonymous reviewers of the manuscripts who made some helpful comments to allow us to improve. Of course any remaining shortcomings are our responsibility.

Jennifer, Terri and Yvonne

1
SCENE SETTING

KEY CONCEPTS

This introduction sets out the framework for the book and provides some markers whereby the reader can locate coverage of particular topics in the forthcoming chapters. Areas covered include content of the British Psychological Society's stage one and stage two training requirements. A definition of forensic psychology is provided. The reader is also introduced to several key concepts to be found in greater detail in subsequent chapters.

Knowledge concepts	Practice considerations
Andragogy	Accreditation
Capacity	Continuing professional development
Competency	(CPD)
Credibility	Health and Care Professions Council
Learning styles	(HCPC)
New Public Management (NPM)	Specialty Guidelines
Reflective practice	
Risk	
Treatability	
Veracity	

Having read this introduction you should have a road map to guide you through the subsequent chapters of the book, and have an overall sense of the requirements of the knowledge part one and core skills part two practice requirements of the British Psychological Society's criteria to become qualified as a forensic psychologist. You should also get a 'feel' for the subject areas that forensic

(Continued)

psychologists are interested in and an appreciation of why it is useful and important to have an understanding of the wider policy and political contexts that underpin forensic psychology's practice settings.

Questions addressed

What is different about this book?

What is forensic psychology?

What are the objects of interest to forensic psychologists?

What is the criminal justice system?

What is the legal system?

How have government policies impacted forensic psychology?

What is the difference between criminology and psychology?

What are the knowledge and skills sets needed to be a forensic psychologist?

What is reflective practice?

What is the emotional toll of working as a forensic psychologist?

How does forensic psychological expertise develop over time?

How do you train to be a forensic psychologist?

WHAT IS DIFFERENT ABOUT THIS BOOK?

> I find television very educational. The minute somebody turns it on, I go to the library and read a good book. (Groucho Marx)

Today we should probably substitute the internet for television in this quotation. Whilst the internet undoubtedly is the source of much knowledge, it is still very satisfying to have a compact digest of what you need to know about a subject in the pages of a good book. We hope the present volume is a good book, with much of what is relevant when studying forensic psychology or developing your career as a practitioner. What you need is to:

- have an understanding of the different contexts in which forensic psychologists work;
- develop an appreciation of the importance of theory;
- apply a critical lens when thinking about victims and offenders;
- be exposed to some of forensic psychology's essential tools (i.e. research and assessment);
- become aware of the different approaches to interventions and rehabilitation.

There is a range of available texts that fulfil these requirements so what is different about this one? The aim of this book is to explain some of forensic psychology's key concepts in a way that will assist trainees through their stage one and two training requirements as set out by the British Psychological Society. Additionally, we think it highly desirable that this book provides:

- knowledge about the political context both of organizations and also the politicization of crime and punishment (actually as engaged citizens as well as forensic psychologists);
- assessment of the contribution of forensic psychology and some engagement in how the discipline should develop;
- an awakening for some critical thinking and generation of ideas, especially when choosing research topics.

In this way, we hope the concepts we touch on will also be of relevance to a wider audience of practitioners wishing to maintain their continuing professional development (CPD). The book is also aimed at our colleagues in allied professions working inter-disciplinarily and as a generic background for forensic professionals in other jurisdictions as well as interested lay readers wishing to be informed about forensic psychology.

In particular, we wish to cover three noticeable omissions from the array of currently available references. The first is the general absence of a discussion of the wider political and socio-economic contexts. We feel knowledge about these issues will give trainees and early career practitioners the necessary backcloth against which they can:

- help choose career pathways;
- learn about developing policy;
- have the necessary awareness of the working climate of a variety of forensic settings;
- become mindful of the performance requirements and realities of different professional occupational cultures;
- develop a discerning critical view of the purpose of interventions.

The second is to present an examination of the more subjective impacts of being involved in forensic psychological work, its paradoxes and dilemmas, and also the developmental aspects of a potential career. This is to assist in establishing some of the issues to think about over a career lifespan of being a reflective practitioner. We want to alert our readers to the ethics of emotion. By this we mean the potential for difficult material, such as hearing about instances of sexual violence and being involved in the assessment and treatment of sex offenders or researching an emotionally laden topic. As human beings we cannot but be affected by the things we see and hear, and this book tries to make this explicit within an ethical framework, and present ways of coping with these issues.

Thirdly, we want to provide a pragmatic take on practice-relevant issues. Many of the current texts present an idealized version of practice. Whilst this guidance sets out the highest ideals, sometimes practice has to be 'good enough' and we present a discussion of the limitations to what is possible whilst maintaining the interests of clients.

This then is a book providing different perspectives: we pull back to have a look at the wider policy context within which forensic psychology is practised and we narrow the focus to look at specific details of professional life. We are suggesting in this book that research and practice are symbiotically inter-twined and rest on three pillars: ideology, politics and theory, which we detail in Chapters 4, 5 and 6, respectively. Suffice to say here:

- by *ideology* we mean the implications of neo-liberalism (the common label given to an economic doctrine that has become embedded in policy both in the UK and actually most of the rest of the world and underpins both private and public sectors);
- by *politics* we mean the way decisions are made about the allocation of resources and how choices are derived, and how to operationalize policies and evaluate outcomes;
- by *theory* we mean developing our understanding of causation.

We also detail the settings in which forensic psychologists work (Chapter 2) and include a detailed description of the legal setting (Chapter 3). We lay out issues and considerations when researching (Chapter 7). We deal with more specific practice skills of assessing (Chapter 10), intervening through treatment and rehabilitation (Chapter 11) and report writing (Chapter 12). We also have chapters focusing on victims (Chapter 8) and profiling offenders (Chapter 9). Our final chapter reviews the status of forensic psychology and asks not only what good the discipline has achieved but also how it may further develop. Here, to be rather grand, we are asking not so much what forensic psychology can do for you, but what you can do for it.

At the head of each chapter is a brief steer outlining what the chapter is about and also listed are some of the key ideas, both knowledge-based concepts and practice-based considerations. At the beginning we set out the questions the chapter addresses and at the end of each chapter we provide some indicative references as well as highlighting source journals. We also set readers a reflective task in each chapter to get you thinking about the issues we are discussing. In addition, we wanted to introduce you to some well-known forensic psychology colleagues whose work has informed the development of the discipline over the past two decades. They, together with the more newly qualified, offer some reflections on their career paths and positioning within forensic psychology. These short vignettes offer some insights from real-world settings on what it is like working and researching as a forensic psychologist over the course of a career.

WHAT IS FORENSIC PSYCHOLOGY?

Blackburn (1996) draws our attention to the semantic disagreements that pre-vailed about the remit and definitional precision of forensic psychology. For Blackburn, forensic psychology is 'the application of psychological knowledge for the purpose of the courts' (p. 4). It is not 'a specific branch of psychological knowledge comparable, for example, to social, developmental or abnormal psychology' (p. 8). Rather, it is a branch of applied psychology that cuts across educational, occupational and other applied psychology boundaries. Heilbrun and Brooks (2010: 221) also tackle the definition question. They call for a broadening of the field and accepted the Specialty Guidelines for Forensic Psychology position that forensic psychology is 'professional practice by psychologists, within any sub-discipline of psychology (e.g. clinical, developmental, social, experimental) when engaged regularly as forensic psychologists' (American Psychology-Law, 1991: 656).

Definitional issues remain a continuing source of debate (Brown and Campbell, 2010; Needs, 2008). Historically, forensic psychology tended to be concerned with applications of practice within courts of law (Howitt, 2009). However, in more recent times this has broadened to include 'any topic even remotely connected with crime' (Hollin, 2007: 43). Others (such as Bartol and Bartol, 2008) place some limits on the scope of forensic psychologists to those who examine aspects of criminal and civil cases. So why does terminology matter? Roesch and Rogers (2011) suggest this is an important question because it affects training models and practice standards. Lack of clarity also creates confusion in professionals from other disciplines with whom forensic psychologists interact (Brigham, 1999). Definitions say something about the claim forensic psychology has for being a coherent, autonomous discipline. Is it a 'raider' in the sense used by Loader and Sparks (2010) that simply borrows from other disciplines to see what it can get out of them or does it form a 'bridge' between disciplines, psychology and law for example, as suggested by Carson (2003)?

We opt for a definition where forensic psychology includes consideration of the entirety of the legal process from the commission of crime, by whom and why, how this is investigated, processed through a trial and the assessment, treatment and management of those found guilty. We include in our considerations offenders, victims, justice professionals and different communities within the general public.

WHAT ARE THE OBJECTS OF INTEREST TO FORENSIC PSYCHOLOGISTS?

Blackburn (1997) identified central interests of forensic psychology as: behaviour within the legal arena that includes offender, victim, police, counsel, judge, jury and administrators of the penal systems, which provide the frame of reference to look at decision making and its outcomes. He groups these under the heading of psycho-legal studies. He employed the term 'criminological psychology' to cover empirical research incorporating public attitudes, interventions with offenders and crime prevention. He confined the term 'expert evidence' to mean the direct contribution of psychologists to aid in legal decision making, including the giving of expert testimony and using findings from psycho-legal studies (any branch of psychology) in providing assessments of defendants. Rather than listing all the crimes, types of civil cases and the topics that forensic psychologists currently write about, we can represent the overall objects of interest in terms of our clientele under four broad headings: inner life, experience and influences, behaviour, and dispositions and traits, as detailed in Figure 1.1.

Inner life	**Overt behaviour**
Learning	Anti-social
Memory	Compliance
Reasoning	Imitative
Attitudes	Coercive
Beliefs	Violence
Emotion	Anger
Motivation	Sexual
Locus of control	Acquisitiveness
Decision-making	Harassing
Self esteem	Victimization
Empathy	**Covert behaviour**
Perspective taking	Deception
Resilience	Fraud
Readiness to change	Delusional
	Self injurious behaviour
Experience/influences	Drinking
Early life	Drug taking
Family life	Self harm
Role models	Suicide ideation
School and education	
Demographics	
Peers	**Dispositions/traits**
Media	Personality
Genetic/biological	Risk taking
Environment	Violent
Employment histories	Aggressive
Trauma	Anxious
Abuse	Learning disability
Culture	Suggestibility

Figure 1.1 Objects of interest of forensic psychology in external clienteles

These objects of interest are subjected to scrutiny through research and practice by means of the variety of tools at the forensic psychologist's disposal, such as assessments, psychometric instruments, physiological measurement and the whole panoply of research methods. More often than not, questions are asked about:

- credibility, i.e. judgement concerning the quality and veracity of evidence (Kebbell, 2010: 153);
- capacity, e.g. parental capacity to provide a child with a safe and nurturing environment (Puckering, 2010: 242); or impairment of intellectual or social functioning (Taylor and Lindsay, 2010: 195);
- treatability, i.e. amenability and suitability to engage in change interventions (McMurran, 2010: 118);
- risk management, i.e. minimizing the likelihood and risk of offending behaviour for potential victims (Hall, 2010: 411).

Blackburn also refers to more introspective interests where the focus is the forensic psychologist her/himself. In other words, issues of competency. In Blackburn's example this is courtroom familiarity. We provide below a more detailed specification of competencies required by the BPS and in Chapters 2 and 3, there is a detailed account of the various arenas such as prisons, probation, police and the courts and tribunals where forensic psychologists may work or appear.

Blackburn also highlights ethical issues and, as discussed below, matters to do with training and professional practice. Our chapter on courts and tribunals gives some attention to the role of the Health and Care Professions Council (HCPC), which is the body responsible for upholding the standards of the profession within the UK. The ethical dilemmas outlined by Blackburn remain as salient today. Blackburn asks 'who is the client?' when a psychologist is providing information about a person for legal purposes. Clearly codes of ethics place a powerful obligation on the psychologist to hold the welfare and well-being of the client as paramount. Yet a psychological assessment may be instrumental in depriving a person of their liberty or declining a parole when the psychologist is acting at the request of legal officials, where the client is the state. We especially reflect on these issues in Chapter 11 when discussing rehabilitation.

WHAT IS THE CRIMINAL JUSTICE SYSTEM?

This book explores forensic psychology within the broader societal trends that profoundly shape the settings within which forensic psychologists work – mostly the criminal justice system (CJS) – as well as affecting us as citizens. By and large, the CJS refers to the delivery of justice, and includes the legal framework that specifies the penalties and consequences of committing crime, incapacitation of known criminals, crime investigation and prevention (Hudson 2001: 66; Laycock, 2005: 9).

The criminal justice system has three stages: pre-trial, dominated by investigation; trial, dominated by prosecution; and sentencing, which involves the disposition of the person if found guilty (Bekerian and Levey, 2005). There are many participants, paid and voluntary, within it, and many others are affected by it either as a witness, victim or offender at some stage in their lives. When a crime is committed, ideally it gets reported and recorded, hopefully it gets detected, and then the case may go to court. As such, police officers, prosecutors, judges, magistrates, solicitors, barristers, witnesses, victims, experts (including forensic psychologists), volunteer organizations (victim support, court witness service), ushers, recorders and other court personnel are amongst the multitude of individuals involved. If the offender is found guilty then disposal may involve probation, social services, prison or special hospital services. However, the respective priorities of all of these individuals can conflict, and specifically the relationships between psychology and the law are not always harmonious. Eastman (2000) writes about two countries, 'Legaland' and the subservient 'Mentaland', explaining how each has a different culture, language and history, with different overriding goals and purpose. The discussion in this book takes us into this territory and maps a terrain perhaps less familiar to forensic psychologists.

A key feature of the CJS is the avoidance, minimization or mitigation of harm, which increasingly scrutinizes professionals if things go wrong and, driven by particular catastrophes, subjects them to formal inquiries (Carson, 2012). As Barbara Hudson (2001: 144) opines, justice seems to have been subordinated to the concept of risk as a singular preoccupation of justice professionals.

WHAT IS THE LEGAL SYSTEM?

The CJS exists within the broader framework of 'the legal system'. This encompasses both civil and criminal matters. In brief, civil law tends to deal with disputes, degrees of liability and the potential awarding of compensation. Claimants are private parties and the standards of proof required are balance of probabilities. Criminal law rests on a standard of proof that is beyond reasonable doubt and cases are brought by the state in order to determine guilt or innocence of an individual accused of breaking the law. Also included within the purview of the legal system are the courts, a plethora of tribunals and a range of professionals and key institutions that will be described in later chapters. For now, we will briefly lay out the macro and micro functions of law.

Generally speaking, law is about the means to secure order, i.e. public, political, social and economic, international and moral order, and the protection of civil liberty (Partington, 2006: 13–21). Unusually, the United Kingdom does not have a written constitution as such, so that many practices arise from unwritten conventions, for example the collective responsibility of government by cabinet and individual ministerial responsibility. In addition, politicians may use law to solve social problems by regulating conduct. An example here would be the legislation defining and penalizing anti-social behaviour and introducing the anti-social behaviour orders (ASBOs). Law relating to sexual conduct sets the limits to what is considered acceptable, for example the minimum age of consensual sexual activity. There is also an educative or ideological function of law. Partington (2006) gives by way of example drinking and driving, where attitudes of acceptability are reflected in legislation. Equality legislation also creates means to redress discriminatory practices. As Partington (p. 23) declares, the 'rule of law' limits the power of the state and asserts individual citizens' rights by creating opportunities to challenge decisions that are thought unfair or wrong.

The micro functions of law include the regulation of human behaviour, not just that which is deemed criminal but also if contracts and agreements are broken, or a person acts negligently. Law also regulates conduct of those who provide services to the public though tribunals, such as the HCPC, and provides mechanisms such as judicial reviews (JR) to prevent abuses of power.

As Partington (2006: 27) concludes:

- functions of law are contingent upon the stage in the development of society and the pressures and challenges that it faces;
- law is not always consistent and may in fact be in conflict, such as the preservation of social order and the maintenance of civil liberties;
- the existence and use of laws are dependent on ideology and politics, such as a country's ideas about social justice and equality;
- not all activity is subject to legal regulation, e.g. activity on the internet;
- law also relates to values, e.g. the limits of tolerance to religious practices or the curtailment of freedom of expression.

HOW HAVE GOVERNMENT POLICIES IMPACTED FORENSIC PSYCHOLOGY?

In relation to our ideological pillar, we think it helpful to get below the surface and explain where the policies that have impacted forensic psychology settings originate. We contend such an analysis is important because the seismic forces that political ideas have unleashed are instrumental in criminal justice reforms that have taken place over the past three decades and have dramatically changed the world in which we live, research and practise. The 'politicization' of crime and penal policy within an ideology of neo-liberalism has been particularly critical in developments such as New Public Management (NPM), which in turn spawned privatization, performance regimes and multi-agency partnerships that have been such a feature of criminal justice over the past 30 years, not just in Britain, but also elsewhere (Lacey, 2013; McLaughlin et al., 2002). These policies and practices have had profound effects on the sites within which forensic psychologists work, such as prisons (Bell, 2013; Thomas-Peter, 2006), probation (Mair and Burke, 2012) and the police (Leishman et al., 1996; Savage, 2007). As Needs (2008) hints, developments in our discipline have not necessarily been internally driven by some benign intellectual flowering but rather a consequence of government policies. We attempt in this book to situate developments in forensic psychology within the political framework and the economic realities of the last several decades. We deconstruct ideas embedded in neo-liberalism and show how the policies that flow from this have impacted all agencies working within the CJS. We take a look at the world-wide phenomenon of falling crime notwithstanding economic austerity and the rising prison population. We also try to get a grip on the rehabilitative–punitive debate that bedevils the penal system.

As David Garland puts it, 'it is easy to live in the immediacy of the present and to lose all sense of the historical processes out of which our current arrangements emerged' (Garland, 2001: 1). He goes on to describe the rapid and far-reaching transformation that has literally turned the professional worlds of probation officers, prison officials, prosecutors, judges, police officers and researchers upside-down. As he says, 'hierarchies shifted precariously, settled routines were pulled apart, objectives and priorities were reformulated, standard working practices were altered, and professional expertise subject to challenge and viewed with increasing scepticism' (p. 4). He articulates 12 indices of change:

- The decline of the rehabilitative ideal towards target risk reduction of individuals
- Re-emergence of punitive sanctions and expressive justice, i.e. 'just desserts' retributive justice
- Changes in the emotional tone of crime policy manifest in the incantations about fear of crime and stereotypic depictions of unruly youth and dangerous sexual predators
- The return of the victim, illustrated by Megan's Law in the United States and Sarah's Law in the UK, which introduced rules for disclosing the whereabouts of released sex offenders
- Concerns about public safety with prison becoming a means of incapacitating violent offenders and a reinvention of probation from its social work origins towards controlling and managing risk
- Politicizing and popularizing crime and crime policy making
- The rise in custodial sentencing against the view that 'prison works'
- Shifts in intellectual thinking from causes of crime linked to deprivation and mental health issues with crime being an abnormal state of affairs towards the normalization of crime and the need to impose societal restraints and controls
- Expanding infrastructure of crime prevention and community safety at local levels to address crime and disorder
- Commercialization of criminal justice providers to include the private sector
- New management styles and working practices – notable managerialism and cost-effectiveness
- A perpetual sense of crisis in a disenchantment with traditional arrangements for controlling crime, which are seen as ailing and failing.

Thomas-Peter (2006: 25) argues, and we agree, it is imperative that forensic psychologists understand the influences of social trends and political fashion because, as implied above, these define, direct and even limit what we can do. They create the climate within which we work and guide the channelling of resources, for example to fund (or not fund) research investigations and programmes of interventions. We need to widen the scope of our knowledge. As a psychologist working for the UK Prison Service highlighted:

psychologists need more than just psychological skills. To know your psychology is not enough. You have to know the prison system and what everyone in it does. You also have to know how bodies like the parole board operate ... you have to be able to speak with clarity and authority. (Pakes and Pakes, 2009: 129)

WHAT IS THE DIFFERENCE BETWEEN CRIMINOLOGY AND PSYCHOLOGY?

Throughout the book we aim to ground forensic psychology on a wider base than is normally the case in texts and also introduce some new literature and references to forensic psychology researchers and practitioners. We will draw on the work of our criminology colleagues because, as does Clive Hollin, we believe there is a 'juxtaposition' between psychology and criminology (Hollin, 2007: 43). Whereas Canter (2010) distinguishes between criminology as studying patterns and causes of crime, for example correlating poverty and crime, and psychology, which studies criminals themselves and why some in poverty commit crime, like Hollin we see huge value in a rapprochement between the two disciplines to the advantage of furthering our understanding of mutual areas of concern. We would venture further than Hollin and align forensic psychology to 'public' criminology. Loader and Sparks (2012) explain that changing economic, social and cultural conditions impacts the way crime and punishment are understood, discussed and acted upon. Further that there is interplay between the governance of crime, competing political ideas and electoral politics. Thus public criminology as they define it examines how those who produce knowledge about crime might engage with and influence public debate and policy making. They suggest that such an enterprise is not unique to criminology but raises questions about the production of knowledge and its uses across the social sciences and involves the scrutiny of the context in which knowledge is commissioned, championed, abused or disregarded. We think this approach resonates with ideas from critical psychology (Fox et al., 2009) and political psychology (Fine, 2012), both of which share with public criminology the lofty aim of seeking a better world through attention to values and a more active engagement in influencing policies. This is why we give considerable attention to context and provide a political analysis. We try to bring all this together in our discussion in the final chapter as to the future direction of forensic psychology.

WHAT ARE THE KNOWLEDGE AND SKILLS SETS NEEDED TO BE A FORENSIC PSYCHOLOGIST?

We look at the intellectual knowledge needed and the practice skills necessary to carry out the roles of a forensic psychologist in different settings and examine not only the theories but also the reality of working within real-world environments. Multidisciplinary working is now the norm, hence it is no longer feasible to exist in our own 'bubbles' without at least being aware of the other parts of the justice system and the roles and responsibilities of other professionals within it. Throughout the book we therefore also try to think about and incorporate the nature of the work of forensic psychologists in real-life settings and the impact that this may have throughout a career. This involves giving consideration to the salience of theory, the findings from research, the ability to manage others, giving strategic direction and developing policy, as the requirements of a career evolve and develop. We want to give a practical reality to the job of a forensic psychologist, for example the pragmatic necessity of distinguishing between a non-negotiable aspect of service and delivering what is 'good enough' in a given set of often pressurized circumstances.

Many books discuss in detail the history, different settings and skill requirements of forensic psychology practice and theoretical underpinnings (e.g. Adler and Grey, 2010; Brown and Campbell, 2010; Carson and Bull, 2003; Gavin, 2014; Hollin, 2013; O'Donohue and Levensky, 2004; Towl and Crighton, 2010; Weiner and Hess, 2006). There have been some texts that have incorporated views of practitioners (e.g. Ashmore and Shuker, 2014; Clarke and Wilson, 2012; Ireland and Fisher, 2010; Needs and Towl, 2004; Pakes and Pakes, 2009). In this book we have attempted to bring the theoretical and practical together.

WHAT IS REFLECTIVE PRACTICE?

What appears to be missing from currently available texts are reflections on what it is actually like, and more directly what it *feels* like, to work in different practice settings. The present book will be interspersed with rich descriptions, drawing upon not only experienced practitioners and trainees from different settings and disciplines but also offenders and victims, and will include personal reflections of the current authors. For example, as an early career behavioural investigative adviser (BIA), T.C. was asked to speak at a large conference and her reactions are given in Box 1.1.

Box 1.1   Terri Cole's reflection on giving a conference paper

I was seated on a panel on stage alongside some very senior personnel and people whom I greatly admired and whose books I had read at university. Before me was a large number of round tables at which were seated professional psychologists from all over the country. I felt like an imposter at an awards ceremony I had gate-crashed. I was nervous. I was a fake. I wondered why on earth I had 'agreed' to go. I gave my input, received a few direct questions and realized that in actual fact I did know more than most of the audience about my specific topic area. Today if presented with a similar situation, whilst I would still feel (a little, but less) nervous, I would spend a few less hours preparing – though I still would thoroughly prepare; I would find out who is in the audience – it is always good to know if it is going to be psychologists or police officers, what rank and roles, to ensure I targeted the talk appropriately; I would have water at the ready – in case of a dry throat or to give thinking time in order to answer a difficult question; and rather than merely want to 'get through it' I would also use it as an opportunity to network, invite interaction and where appropriate promote the need for relevant applied research.

In this book we hope readers may share the learnt experiences of others, identify highs, lows, difficulties and concerns, and have those involved explain the issues and how they dealt with them.

The concept of reflection is central both to training and CPD once in practice (Millward, 2005: 97). Millward suggests that the concept of andragogy is one way to describe and explain self-evaluation aspects of reflective practice. Andragogy is self-directed learning (as opposed to pedagogy which is instructor-centred learning) and assumes the learner is motivated to become increasingly independent and engage in self-diagnosis. Whilst there may be formal requirements to acquire certain knowledge and principles that are pedagogic, the learning for the practitioner to maintain the currency of their knowledge once in practice is encouraged by means of self-reflection. What is interesting is there are individual differences in reflective tendencies; Kolb (1984), for example, argues that gathering and processing experiences conforms to particular learning styles: e.g. 'divergers' reflect on specific experiences from different perspectives; 'assimilators' develop theoretical ways of thinking; 'accommodators' use active experimentation as their basis for new learning.

Critical psychology offers us a chance to push out the limits of reflexivity. Bullock and Limbert (2009) ask us to think particularly about class. Many of the participants in experimental research are university students, thus skewing findings to an overrepresentation of the educated white middle class. Similarly, they suggest that psychology tends to approach the issue of poverty through a deficit model reflecting a deficiency of cultural values, norms and behaviours that represent a 'risk' to 'others.' So Bullock and Limbert extol us to adopt a critical reflexivity that examines our own class and norms. Further, they advise we should continually consider the ways in which our own social identity impacts the research we do, the questions we ask, the findings we chose to emphasize and play down, and the outcomes we seek for those we treat.

WHAT IS THE EMOTIONAL TOLL OF WORKING AS A FORENSIC PSYCHOLOGIST?

We also want to consider the emotional toll and professional support necessary when making decisions, for example about assessments, treatments or research options. Crego, Alison, Roocroft and Eyre (2008) suggest that the role of emotion has largely been overlooked in models of decision making and in particular how a negative emotion may result in bias in information processing or avoiding making a decision at all. An aim of this book is to describe what it is actually like to be a producer and user of forensic psychological knowledge on the one hand and on the other hand being a consumer of that knowledge as a client. Thus we look at the importance of supervision and peer support to provide assistance for the practitioner in their assessments and decision making. In Chapter 7 we examine the potential emotional toll and ways to mitigate this when undertaking research. Of necessity, the subject matter, and interactions, may involve distressing material or difficult and sometimes violent clients. Notwithstanding the necessity for professionalism, researchers and practitioners are not immune from potentially adverse impacts of these encounters. We look in some detail at the clientele, offenders and victims, as well as commissioners of the services of experts.

HOW DOES FORENSIC PSYCHOLOGICAL EXPERTISE DEVELOP OVER TIME?

What also appears to us as having been largely ignored in previous literature is how our expertise develops and changes over time. Otto and Heilbrun (2002) suggest three levels described as:

1. 'legally informed', i.e. a basic education in law relevant to practice – for example issues surrounding confidentiality and note taking;
2. 'proficient clinician', i.e. a middle-level expert with extended knowledge of publication, procedures and ethics, who has received more training, supervision and attained more experience; and
3. 'clinician', i.e. one who apart from formal training has in-depth understanding of the law, procedures and issues relevant to their role.

We wish to expand on this idea and be sensitive to needs of individuals just beginning to study forensic psychology as a trainee, the newly qualified, those in early or mid-career, or someone later in their career about to retire or post retirement.

HOW DO YOU TRAIN TO BE A FORENSIC PSYCHOLOGIST?

Blackburn clearly identified forensic psychology as a professional specialism. At the time he was writing use of experts in UK courts mostly related to the care and protection of children, compensation claims following industrial injury and use of experimental evidence in, for example, trade disputes. Blackburn presaged the professionalization of forensic psychology which he thought was premature and was likely to foreclose the dialogue between psychology and law.

Looking first at training and accreditation, the British Psychological Society had established a Division of Legal and Criminological Psychology in 1977 but it was not until the late 1980s and early 1990s that its training subcommittee, at which time J.B. was a member, developed accreditation criteria and agreed curriculum requirements. The early forensic psychologists were made members of the Division through 'grand-parenting' arrangements where their experience was recognized and they became the first generation of chartered forensic psychologists, who accredited the next generation.

Box 1.2   Pam Wilson's reflections on a career as a forensic psychologist in HM Prison Service, 1982-2009

I will simply give my view on a number of issues/changes observed over my career. Hopefully readers will relate to some of these, whereas others might see this as ancient history.

When I first started, personal computers were a new innovation. I wrote my MSc on a typewriter, and my PhD on a tape-based Commodore 64. In the office we played Pacman (obviously only at lunchtime) and I recall a fairly straightforward principal components analysis taking about six hours to compute and then the printer jamming.

I started out at HMP Grendon, running small groups within the therapeutic community. Formal training was limited, but support from older, wiser and vastly more experienced colleagues was always at hand. I moved to become head of department at HMYOI Aylesbury, finding it a very 'hard' environment by comparison. At one point I ran learning and development sessions for newly joined staff, alongside sessions for some problematic young offenders. Many times we looked separately at the same issues from the different points of view – it always seemed to me that it would have been better to get the parties together! Then, at Feltham, I had a very wide-ranging role, including a great deal of organizational change management, which whetted my appetite for the consultancy work I still engage in today.

I became chartered under a 'grandparent' arrangement, recognizing my prior work, and am glad not to have had to face the extensive requirements today. Training and regulation of psychologists has become a great deal more rigorous, both in respect of academic qualification and supervised practice. Roles have narrowed, some professional autonomy has been lost, but evidence-based practice has overall, I believe, ensured greater impact in respect of interventions aimed at reducing the likelihood of reoffending. I never delivered a single session of an accredited programme. But then neither was I guilty of

(Continued)

putting someone on a programme to make the numbers up, rather than based on need. In this respect, Key Performance Indicators (KPIs) have a lot to answer for.

Assessment has now developed into case formulation; motivational report disclosure is viewed as essential, having come through a period in which the offender was not really involved in the process at all. Psychologists now spend a great deal of time dealing with litigation and defending their practice in court, which was simply unheard of when I started out.

Managerialism and privatization have impacted on the prison environment. Whilst ideologically against privatization, I am of the view that its introduction did a great deal in raising standards for prisoners. It also seems right that prisons have become more accountable, although I believe that too much attention to counting and checking and the loss of what had been an emerging understanding of the value of psychologically minded practice means that the soul of an essentially people-focused organization has been lost.

The British trajectory is to see forensic psychology as drawing from 'a wide range of areas within psychology' to be applied in 'the police, the courts, prisons, secure units and hospitals, probation and other community-based services, and academia' (Needs, 2008: 75). In 2000 the Board of Examiners for forensic psychology was established through which means trainees become chartered members of the renamed (in 1999) Division of Forensic Psychology, which in the UK enables them to officially label themselves a 'forensic psychologist'. The training is generic and there is no specific requirement to be clinically qualified.

In the United States and Australia it is more likely that forensic psychologists have clinical backgrounds and are required to have a licence to practise (Brown and Campbell, 2010). In the mid 1990s the 'Villanova Conference' held in Philadelphia set out an agenda that was a training continuum for psychology and law and a specification for undergraduate and postgraduate education (Bersoff et al., 1997). Building on the scientist–practitioner model, the vision for those constructing this agenda was to abate the stereotype in US courtrooms of psychology being 'seen as a mysterious, inexact discipline populated by hired guns who will switch sides and proffer opinions for the right fee and greatest notoriety' (p. 1302).

Recognized training in forensic psychology within the UK comes under the purview of the British Psychological Society, which provides curricula guidelines and accreditation for courses at masters and doctoral levels. At present there are 6,134 student members, 24,885 graduate members and 18,822 chartered members (BPS, 4 July 2014). Of the 10 divisions, forensic psychology makes up 9% (2,590) of chartered psychologists (Figure 1.2). (For more detail on the divisions see the BPS website.)

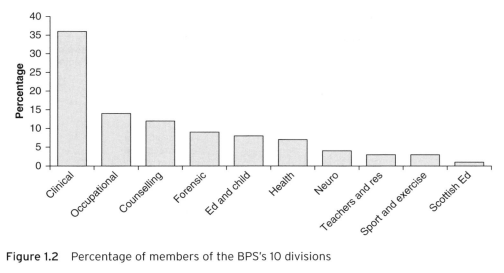

Figure 1.2   Percentage of members of the BPS's 10 divisions

From 2009, the role of mandatory regulator of all practitioner psychologists, including forensic, came under the jurisdiction of the Health Professions Council, now called the Health and Care Professions Council (HCPC).

For UK practitioner forensic psychologists there is a requirement to have a first degree in psychology to provide a general background in psychological theory and principles together with some basic research skills. Secondly, a stage one masters-level training covers three broad areas: knowledge, research and practice. The BPS accredits programmes and requires course providers to ensure that trainees develop core skills within eight curriculum areas. These are set out in Table 1.1 (drawn from BPS guidelines).

Table 1.1   Stage one curriculum requirements

Legal and criminal justice context	Assessment and formulation	Interventions	Research methods	Advice and consultancy	Development and training
Theory Legal frameworks Processes of investigation Processes of detention Working with litigant appellants	Different approaches to assessment and formulation Tools of assessment	Range of interventions **Client groups** Patients Offenders At-risk individuals Victims Professionals	Range of techniques – qualitative and quantitative Data collection Analysis	Understanding of theory Evidence relevant to working in organizations Contribute to practice guidance and policy	Principles of reflective practice Responsibility for conducting own CPD Understanding principles, theories and evidence underpinning the training of others

(Continued)

Table 1.1 (Continued)

Legal and criminal justice context	Assessment and formulation	Interventions	Research methods	Advice and consultancy	Development and training
Arbitration Mediation Multi-disciplinary working **Forensic settings** Hospitals Mental health Police Courts Community settings NGOs				Principles/ procedures when evaluating practice of organizations and conducting consultancy	

CPD, continuing professional development; NGO, non-governmental organization.

Thirdly, there is the stage two supervised practice within four core role competencies: conducting applications and interventions; research; communicating with other professionals; and training other professionals. Practitioner doctorate programmes may combine stage one and two training. Table 1.2 describes these in a little more detail.

Table 1.2 Stage two supervised practice

Conducting psychological applications and interventions	Research	Communicating psychological knowledge and advice	Staff development and training
Planning assessments and interventions Establishing working relationships Evaluating interventions Supervising an intervention	Designing Conducting Evaluating	Awareness of contribution of forensic psychology Contribution of psychological advice in problem solving Formulation and implementation of policy Preparing and presenting evidence Feedback to clients	Identify, analyse needs to improve job performance Planning, designing training programmes Implementing programmes Planning assessments Evaluating training

This detailed requirement maps onto the HCPC standards of proficiency, which require practitioner forensic psychologists to understand:

- the application of psychology to the legal system;
- how to apply theory in the case of socially and individually damaging behaviours;
- development of criminal and anti-social behaviours;
- effective assessment approaches;
- consultation models of service delivery;
- theory and its application in the provision of psychological therapies to both offenders and their victims;
- psychological interventions with different client groups.

The BPS criteria were built on a problem-based learning approach whereby students develop appropriate capabilities to review current knowledge, theory and the evidence base; identify and develop appropriate skills; apply these within an ethical framework; evaluate and reflect on practice applications; and communicate appropriately (Anand, 2014).

A course provider develops the curriculum around these requirements but often provides optional courses or in-depth knowledge depending on the course team's interest. For example, at the University of Liverpool there is a particular emphasis on police investigative skills and critical incident decision making. The University of Kent draws on its history and tradition of social psychological theorizing and research, whilst the University of Huddersfield has a rich seam of investigative psychology as its emphasis.

Stage two requirements include assessments, formulation, interventions, advice and consultancy in situ. This is a formal process of supervised practice which involves the trainee completing and submitting a portfolio of written evidence to demonstrate their competency and includes the keeping of a practice diary, competence logs and undertaking some research. The process of completing stage two can be quite arduous, as the following trainee observes.

Box 1.3   Steve on the difficulties of securing stage two supervised practice

Prior to undertaking the MSc, I worked in a medium secure unit and also the police. My hope, on completion of the course, was to become a chartered forensic psychologist in the Prison Service. Having completed the MSc in 2004, however, there were limited opportunities to follow this career path and the chartership process was difficult to undertake in a clear and effective way without such positions and support. As a result I pursued a different psychological career path in mental health. While I don't for one minute regret undertaking the course, I do feel that better clarity and support at the post-qualification stage would have been helpful and would have supported me to follow my original hoped-for career path.

There is also an academic practitioner doctorate route to chartership which combines stages one and two, and several universities (e.g. Birmingham, Nottingham and Cardiff Metropolitan) now offer this.

Once stages one and two have been successfully completed, a trainee can apply for full membership of the Division of Forensic Psychology and is entitled to call themselves a chartered forensic psychologist.

What we set out to do in this book is to address the learning requirements (see Table 1.3) and identify the critical concepts associated with developing a career in forensic psychology. We have also tried to incorporate our own reflections about the state of the discipline and provide some ideas and provoke some reactions in addressing the future developments of forensic psychology.

Table 1.3   Chapter map for learning areas

Stage 1	Stage 2	Chapters
Legal and CJS context and FP settings		1, 2, 3, 4, 5
Assessment formulation	Assessment, formulation and intervention	6, 10
Interventions		6, 11
Research methods	Research	7
Assessment and consultancy	Communicating psychological knowledge	2, 11
Development and training	Staff development and training	4, 5, 13

CJS, criminal justice system; FP, forensic psychologist.

RESOURCES

For curriculum details and core roles see the BPS website, www.bps.org.uk/.

For short descriptive accounts of the key concepts of credibility, competence, risk and treatability see entries by Kebbell, Puckering, Taylor and Lindsay, Hall and McMurran respectively, in *The Cambridge Handbook of Forensic Psychology* edited by Brown and Campbell (2010).

Helen Gavin has a recent general text on criminological and forensic psychology which includes details of how to become a forensic psychologist (see pages 10–17).

The *Dictionary of Forensic Psychology* edited by Graham Towl and colleagues (2008) is a good starting point for key definitions.

Forensic Update for April 2014 contains an account of the requirements and routes to full Division of Forensic Psychological membership and the acquiring of chartered status.

Key journals

Behavioural Sciences and the Law

British Journal of Criminology

Criminal Behaviour and Mental Health

Journal of Forensic Psychiatry

Journal of Law and Society

Law and Human Behaviour

Legal and Criminological Psychology

Psychology Crime and Law

2
PLACE SETTINGS

KEY CONCEPTS

This chapter discusses the roles played by forensic psychologists and describes the different settings in which forensic psychology research and practice takes place, i.e. academia, police, probation, prison (probation and prisons are now amalgamated into the National Offender Management Service - NOMS), special hospitals, Community Forensic Services, and the private sector.

Knowledge concepts	Practice considerations
Hostage negotiation Professional-personal dialectic Therapeutic community (TC) Treatability	Behavioural investigative advisers (BIAs) Broadmoor Community Forensic Mental Health Service (CFMHS) Community Rehabilitation Companies (CRCs) Crime analysts High Security Psychiatric Services Commissioning Board (HSPSCB) Medium secure units (MSUs) National Intelligence Model (NIM) National Offender Management Service (NOMS) Research commissioning Youth Justice Board (YJB)

This chapter introduces you to the main arenas within which forensic psychologists work and distinguishes broadly between practitioners and academics. The material covers stage one aspects of knowledge of forensic settings, organizational cultures and how recent policies have influenced working practices in different settings and the context for staff development and training for stage two.

Questions addressed

What is academic forensic psychology?

What do forensic psychologists do who work for the police?

What do forensic psychologists do who work in the prison and probation services?

What do forensic psychologists do who work in special hospitals and medium secure units?

What are community forensic services?

Can forensic psychologists work in private practice?

In what way can forensic psychologists assist the courts?

WHAT IS ACADEMIC FORENSIC PSYCHOLOGY?

Much, but not all, research and theorizing is conducted in academia and research centres, both private and public. Within the academy it is likely that a senior member of staff will have one or several areas of interest. They may have a team or work independently. They are likely to supervise research, probably at masters and doctoral levels. They may also be the principal investigator in funded research, won through a competitive bidding process. Research is funded by government, e.g. the Research Councils in the UK, or directly commissioned by government departments. Charitable foundations also support research, as do private companies. Research may also be conducted unfunded and be the product of collaboration with supervised students or on a pro bono basis.

The research commissioning process sometimes seems impenetrable. One of the present authors (J.B.) was involved in a funding application to evaluate a prison therapeutic community (TC). She and a team from the University of Surrey prepared and submitted a research proposal. Below is Roland Woodward's account of the letting of the contract and the tendering process. He was the first director of therapy at the prison, where he established the therapeutic regime in 2001 which was the subject of the research bid.

> Whilst all the practical preparations had been going on, one of my tasks was to tender and award the research contract. In the original prison contract we had negotiated a ring-fenced sum of money for a seven year research contract to be undertaken by an independent body. The original research specification was similar to the work undertaken by Genders and Player (1995) at Grendon Prison and published in their book. The work was done from a mainly sociological perspective by participant

observation with the addition of some analysis of the routine psychometrics that had been collected over the years by the Psychology Department. The research specification at Dovegate TC was focused mainly on social processes and a description of the TC process. I thought that this was an inadequate specification and rewrote it to include a reconviction study, a personal change study and a study of the therapeutic process as it related to individuals reaching a point of psychological change readiness.

The project was put out to tender and as it was worth a total of £750,000 it attracted several good calibre bids. After what felt like a long process in which I was pleased to receive the support from several people, but particularly Ron Blackburn, Emeritus Professor of Clinical Psychology at Liverpool University, whose expertise and good sense were indispensable to the process, we awarded the contract. Professor Jennifer Brown and her team from Surrey University won and the process of integrating them into the life of the TC began. (Woodward in Cullen and Mackenzie, 2011: 147–8)

Roland wrote in his preface to the book arising from the project (Brown et al., 2014: xv)

What was also clear was that by the nature of the TC, the research team would recognise the need to do the work collaboratively with the men. In modern parlance the service users need to be involved in the process of design and delivery of the research project. These men were to become experts by experience and had a lot to offer the process. It also reflects the TC ethos that things happen by consensus and democratic process not by enforcement of a rigid set of rules. In thinking about these issues whilst drafting the tender documents it began to give us an idea of what criteria we might look for in the research proposals that would be submitted. We would certainly be looking for teams that were proposing high levels of resident participation and collaboration.

A pen portrait of the life of an academic forensic psychologist is given in Wrightsman and Fulero's (2005) textbook. They profile American psychologist Gary Wells explaining that his training was actually in social psychology and his area of specialism is eyewitness identification. He publishes on this topic in learned journals, teaches classes and mentors graduate students. Dr Wells also appears as an expert witness in criminal cases and appears before congressional committees to provide expert testimony about witness identification when changes in the law are being considered. He frequently works with law enforcement officers in respect of live cases. Such a profile of activity would encapsulate the work of key figures in the forensic psychology field within the UK such as Gisli Gudjonsson, Ray Bull, David Canter, the late Lionel Haward, Clive Hollin, Anthony Beech, Theresa Gannon, Elizabeth Gilchrist, Jane Ireland, Joanna Adler, Mary McMurran and many others working within British universities. Box 2.1 has a reflection by Professor Mary McMurran on her career.

Box 2.1   Reflection by Mary McMurran

I began my career as a prison psychologist in a borstal. To save you the trouble of looking it up, borstals were replaced in 1982 by youth custody centres, which became young offender institutions a few years later. In those very early days, I was told to 'run an alcohol group' because that's what the previous psychologist had done. I hadn't a clue where to start! In those days, the 'what works' evidence-based practice movement hadn't yet taken off and we were working largely from an empty book. There were opportunities to study the characteristics of offenders, design interventions to suit them and evaluate outcomes. Most of this research was carried out within resources and, rather shockingly, line management approval rather than ethical approval was all that was required. Over the years, practitioners' workloads have grown, leaving little room for ad hoc post-qualification research activities. Additionally, research governance frameworks have evolved to control research standards and practices. Essentially, research is now done by those paid to do research, whether in-service, such as the Ministry of Justice's (MOJ) Offender Management and Sentencing – Analytical Services (OMSAS), by researchers who win tenders to conduct projects on behalf of the MOJ, or by researchers who are lucky enough to secure funding from grant-awarding bodies. Only the latter offers opportunities for researcher-led research projects. For a while, we were lucky enough to have the Department of Health's National Programme on Forensic Mental Health Research and Development, but this was short-lived (1999–2007). Now, the main source of responsive funding for applied research is the National Health Service's (NHS) National Institute for Health Research (NIHR). The NIHR, not surprisingly, is mainly interested in health outcomes. One problem for forensic psychologists is that, while they deliver treatments that improve the nation's health by reducing violence, victimization and imprisonment, funding is not forthcoming for crime outcomes. As a researcher, I'm not sure that I count myself as a forensic psychologist any more (but see my footnote on terminology!). What funding I have been successful in acquiring has drawn me away from forensic psychology. I have spent the past few years evaluating treatments for personality disorder. There is relevance to offender populations in that the prevalence of personality disorder is high among offenders, but I have not recently been working on projects aiming to reduce crime. Helping people to function better is worthwhile in itself, and very satisfying work. Nonetheless, through no fault of my own, I do feel I've ended up somewhere I didn't plan to be.[1]

Research centres are also a feature of life for an academic psychologist, and an example is given here of Forensic Psychological Services at the University of Middlesex:

Forensic Psychological Services (FPS) at Middlesex University is directed by Professor Joanna Adler with Dr Miranda A.H. Horvath as her deputy. They are guided by an advisory board consisting of leading practitioners and researchers from the criminal and civil justice fields and have a pool of over 20 freelance consultants with whom they work closely to deliver a range of services and projects. FPS is based in the Psychology department of the university and has close links with colleagues in other departments including Criminology, Sociology and Social Policy. We contribute significantly to the MSc in Forensic Psychology, the Forensic Psychology Research Group and supervise a number of PhD students. FPS undertake evaluations of various programmes such as the impact of The Forgiveness Project (TFP) in prisons which is a broadly restorative intervention aimed at working with offenders at early stages of their sentence and with short-term sentence servers. We have adopted a mixed-methods, prospective, matched-control design with a small sample of interviews to be conducted retrospectively. The evaluation is based in two adult prisons and one mixed adult and youth institution. (extract from Mannheim Matters, November 2011)

Other examples are David Canter's International Research Centre for Investigative Psychology at the University of Huddersfield;[2] Centre for Forensic Interviewing at the University of Portsmouth directed by Dr Becky Milne;[3] the University of Birmingham's Centre for Forensic and Criminological Psychology,[4] which incidentally is amongst the first in the UK to offer a practitioner doctorate in forensic psychology; or the Police Research Laboratory run by Craig Bennell at Carlton University in Alberta, Canada.[5] Here primary research is conducted around the leading academics' interests and there is often a direct link to law enforcement by way of specialist courses and students may undertake their doctoral studies.

A considerable amount of research activity has been involved in evaluating interventions and treatment programmes within prisons. This initially gave rise to the 'nothing works' position after a key paper 'What Works? Questions and Answers about Prison Reform' was published by Martinson (1974). His conclusion that education and psychotherapy, at their best, cannot overcome, or 'even appreciably reduce, the powerful tendency for offenders to continue in criminal behaviour' (p. 49) found a ready acceptance in the political climate of the 1970s and 1980s (Howells and Day, 1999). However, with better statistical techniques such as meta-analyses, new studies (e.g. Gendreau and Ross, 1987) proposed that effective treatment of offenders was possible and moreover could be measured. The 'what works' approach has since resulted in a huge output, recently reviewed by McGuire (2013).

As alluded to above, evaluation methods have had their share of controversy. Peter Raynor for example (2004, 2008) has been very critical about research evaluating the Probation Service's Pathfinder programmes. He says:

In a country where the failures of trains can be blamed on the wrong kind of snow, or the wobbliness of bridges on the wrong kind of walking, it was predictable that one explanation for the 'failure' of the pathfinders to demonstrate success would be that we did the wrong kind of research. (2004: 31)

There is a current debate about the place of randomized controlled trials as the preferred method of evaluation (Hope, 2009; Tilley, 2009). We address the arguments in Chapter 5.

WHAT DO FORENSIC PSYCHOLOGISTS DO WHO WORK FOR THE POLICE?

The police are responsible for upholding the law, reassuring the public, maintaining public order and national security, preventing and investigating crime, and bringing those responsible to justice (Independent Police Commission, 2013). Many police officers themselves have qualifications in psychology (for example, the late Tom Williamson was instrumental in developing the cognitive interview and John Grieve was involved in formulating practice applications of offender profiling).

Forensic psychologists undertake work in relation to policing in a number of ways. They may be directly employed by the police to conduct research on their behalf, which was the experience of J.B. from 1986 to 1994 when working for the Hampshire Constabulary. The larger metropolitan police forces still have research departments and some aspects of the work they undertake is described in Box 2.2.

Box 2.2 Danielle Wunsch on working in the Metropolitan Police Service

I have never had the kind of job that makes it easy to answer the question 'so, what do you do?' Over the years I have been a 'strategic researcher', a 'strategy development manager' and a 'research officer'. My job titles usually conjure up some confusion and I tend to have to follow it up with an explanation of what my job actually entails. What I set out to be, however, was a 'Forensic Psychologist'. So I studied Forensic Psychology because I wanted to work within a hospital or a prison setting. As it happened, I fell into a slightly different career – that of a social researcher within the police.

During the course of my master's degree I became interested in policing and ended up undertaking a dissertation with a policing focus. I absolutely loved

(Continued)

doing the research: collating data and analysing it – finding common themes and the somewhat geeky excitement of identifying statistical significance – and then relating it back to what this may actually mean in the real world. It just so happened that at the time the Metropolitan Police was putting together a small in-house team of social researchers. And that is how I ended up working for the police – in many ways down to nothing more than sheer coincidence and luck.

I started my career as a policing researcher at a time when neighbourhood policing had just taken off (again) and there was a lot of appetite to understand the views and needs of the public. I began with mainly qualitative research, such as observations of Safer Neighbourhoods Teams, and focus groups with Londoners about how they wanted the police to communicate with them. Over the years the type of research I have been conducting has changed. My team now undertakes more evaluation work, including randomized controlled trials – very much with a focus on demonstrating 'what works', often in the context of evidencing value for money. In this sense, austerity is indeed reflected even in the research we do.

What has not changed, though, is the challenge of reporting findings of academic research to a practitioner audience. Recommendations may not always support assumptions or expectations, indeed they may well challenge existing 'but this is how we have always done it' mind sets. The recent rise in evidence-based policing[6] has given us researchers a little bit of 'back up' in making sure we are being heard. It has also brought additional responsibilities and remits. My team has been managing an internal programme of work designed to routinely embed evidence-based ways of working in the police. This has made me not 'just' a researcher, but also lecturer, lobbyist and change manager. This goes beyond reporting findings and recommendations – this is about affecting a more fundamental change towards evidence-based decision making as 'business as usual'.

I did not plan on becoming a police researcher and I would now not really describe myself as a forensic psychologist. But my work is varied and challenging and I know it impacts on policy and practice – and thereby directly onto policing and criminal justice improvements.

Since time of writing the Metropolitan Police Service has moved its main research activity to the Mayor's office (see https://www.london.gov.uk/priorities/policing-crime/about-mopac for details).

Forensic psychologists may also undertake the role of crime analysts and be involved in providing intelligence 'analytical products' within the framework of the National Intelligence Model (NIM) (see Bullock, 2014, for a detailed explanation of NIM). As Bullock explains, the increased sophistication of data sharing and analytic software has tended to have moved employment of former police officers in the role of intelligence officers towards social science graduates (including those with forensic psychology qualifications). Their role may include producing charts of an offender's known associates, looking for patterns in financial transactions or communications data or identifying hot spots where crimes congregate in time or location in order to prioritize police patrols and resources. It would be fair to say, however, that the Police Service has struggled to introduce specific training and a career structure for this new 'breed' of intelligence officer.

Another option is for graduates to become civilian investigators. Schedule 4, part 2 of the Police Reform Act 2002 provides powers to a Chief Constable to designate investigating officers who are not police officers. The newly established College of Policing and the Association of Chief Police Officers (ACPO) jointly sponsored the Professionalizing Investigation Programme (PIP) through which both police officers and civilian staff may become investigators to varying levels of proficiency.

There are five recognized tiers of interviewers depending on levels of training received. These are:

- Tier 1 – Student officers and support staff responsible for interviewing in cases of volume and minor crimes
- Tier 2 – Investigators or detectives responsible for interviewing in more serious cases, including volume crime child witnesses
- Tier 3 – Specialist interviewers and detectives responsible for interviewing in serious or complex categories of crime or other incidents including murder/manslaughter, child sexual abuse, serious sexual assaults and fatal road traffic crashes
- Tier 4 – Interview supervisors responsible for quality assuring interviews at Tiers 1, 2 and 3
- Tier 5 – Interview advisers, managers and coordinators of the interview functions at Tier 3.

As Bullock mentions, there is no specific career structure identified and non-police officers rarely proceed beyond Tier 3. Rather as the analysts, retention is a problem as progression routes are unavailable.

The Behavioral Research and Instruction Unit of the FBI employs psychologists as crime scene consultants. They work in multidisciplinary teams to examine a crime scene to see what can be inferred about behaviour from physical clues. The psychologist may speculate about the psychological makeup of the possible offender. In the United States the crime scene consultant often testifies about his or her findings in court. The FBI also uses civilians as pre-trial investigators.[7] They would, for example, listen to defendant testimonies, comment on any indications of deception or advise in matters such as jury selection, and assess factors such as defendant ability to understand what was happening and their ability to stand trial, and their mental competency to appreciate that the behaviour they are accused of is wrong.

The provision of behavioural investigative advice is another key feature of psychological expertise being harnessed to assist in the investigative work of the police within the UK. Rainbow and Gregory (2011: 28–33) outline the contributions that behavioural investigative advisers (BIAs) make to police investigations. This includes crime scene assessment, whereby careful analysis of the physical traces and circumstances generate hypotheses about possible lines of enquiry. BIAs may also look for common features and consistencies between offences and suggest whether or not they may be linked. They can develop likely characteristics of an unknown offender, often based on statistical regularities of previous offences from various databases such as the Violent Crime Linkage Analysis System (ViCLAS) held by the Serious Crime Analysis Section (SCAS). From these predictions, a prioritization matrix may be constructed where individuals are scored and ranked to determine the most promising lines of enquiry and indicate the most likely persons of interest for further investigation. Specially selected forensic clinical psychologist consultants may also conduct risk assessments of continued or escalating seriousness of offending, and give additional media or interview advice in relation to a particular suspect. More on the role, underlying theory and a critique of this area of work is given in Chapters 6 and 10.

Forensic psychologists may act as consultants, be in receipt of funding to undertake a specific piece of research or run a bespoke training programme within the Police Service. Y.S. for example ran a series of workshops for various police forces offering a diversion programme as an alternative to court in the case of kerb crawling, i.e. cruising through a town's red light district in order to pick up a prostitute (see Box 8.2).

Psychological concepts have also been adopted to assist in public order policing. Clifford Stott and Hugo Gorringe (2014) describe their involvement in helping to develop, train and evaluate a new method of crowd control within public order policing requirements. By drawing on the literature about the behaviour of people in crowds, the concept of police liaison teams (PLTs) was developed. This represented a major 'break with the past' (p. 247) in terms of policing protests. Officers were trained in crowd psychology and protest liaison skills and their primary role was 'to enhance police communications at street level, facilitate peaceful protest and build trust and confidence by enhancing perceptions of police legitimacy among protestors' (p. 247). In addition to being good communicators, the PLTs were also trained as problem solvers who resolved issues as they arose and helped to inhibit tension building in the crowd. The evaluation indicated their successful deployment by promoting self-regulating behaviours amongst the protest participants. The use of PLTs is now part of a national strategy.

There are other roles played and functions performed by psychologists working within or for the police (Ainsworth, 1995; Brown, 2000; Scrivner, 2006; Wrightsman and Fulero, 2005). It is here we come up against some of the definitional boundary issues discussed earlier. Some of the work is clinical, as in fitness for duty evaluations, stress and trauma counselling services, resilience and suicide prevention. Other work involves recruitment selection and job evaluations which are the province of occupational psychology. Yet other work has been to provide operational advice, as in hostage negotiations or training in the use of the cognitive interview, which is not exclusively within the purview of the forensic psychologist.

WHAT DO FORENSIC PSYCHOLOGISTS DO WHO WORK IN THE PRISON AND PROBATION SERVICES?

In the UK, the Probation Service was formally set up through the 1907 Probation of Offenders Act. Its early role was as a befriender of offenders and was closely allied to social work. Over the last several decades the Service has been through considerable upheavals, which we discuss in more detail in the next chapter. In 2000 the Criminal Justice and Courts Services Act created 42 local probation areas within a National Probation Service (NPS) corresponding with the police and Crown Prosecution Service (CPS) boundaries (Mair and Burke, 2012: 165). This Act also introduced Multi-Agency Protection Panels (MAPPs) through which police and probation were to collaborate to manage the risks posed by sexual and other high-risk offenders.

Psychologists were first employed in the Prison Service in 1946 to assist in preparing reports to courts (Marcus, 1982) and by the 1980s there were 85 psychologists and 35 psychological assistants working within the prison estate in England and Wales and they were heavily involved in training of prison staff. Towl and Crighton (2008) describe the growth in numbers and increased professionalization of psychologists working within prisons. Most recently, in 2004, a National Offender Management Service (NOMS) was created which amalgamated the two services. Intended as a single correctional service, NOMS oversees end-to-end management of offenders and delivers interventions and services. From 1 June 2014 the Probation Trusts were replaced by the new National Probation Service (NPS) and 21 Community Rehabilitation Companies (CRCs). The NPS is responsible in the community for carrying out risk assessments of all offenders and for the direct management of those offenders who pose the highest risk of serious harm to the public and who have committed the most serious offences. The CRCs are responsible for delivering community requirements for medium- and low-risk offenders.

Box 2.3 Tania Tancred on being a forensic psychologist who works in probation

I think I get most satisfaction from working in a community context where the people I work with are living their lives. I used to work for HM Prison Service and it always felt as though a lot of the work I was doing was hypothetical, as people were living in an institution. Getting to work holistically with people and their families

(Continued)

whilst they reintegrate back into the community is very rewarding. A main area of my work is with individuals who are managed by Multi-Agency Public Protection Arrangements (MAPPA). MAPPA include probation, police and prison service as statutory partners who assess and manage the highest-risk offenders in the community. As a forensic psychologist working for probation I provide a consultation service and am frequently tasked with individual work and liaison with mental health services. I greatly enjoy working with a number of different agencies including police, social services, housing providers and volunteers such as those working with Circles of Support and Accountability. This brings together a lot of different perspectives about the same person and enables thorough assessment.

In addition to the wide range of other agencies I work with, my job involves a broad range of work with clients and staff. I deliver individual and group work interventions, risk assessment and a lot of staff consultation and training. I get to work in many different environments such as court, approved premises and home visits to clients. This means there is great variety in my role and no two days are the same. Probation has a strong focus on rehabilitation and therefore there has always been a lot of support for my role and my work from probation colleagues.

There have been many changes in probation over the years and most recently 'Transforming Rehabilitation', which has meant a split into the publicly owned National Probation Service (NPS), which is responsible for high and very high risk of harm offenders, and the privately run Community Rehabilitation Companies (CRCs), who will manage medium- and low-risk cases. This may bring a wider range of opportunities for forensic psychologists whose skills could be well utilized. Recently the community personality disorder strategy has brought about a lot of new roles for psychologists to assist staff in working in a psychologically minded way with clients. I hope that in the future more forensic psychologists will contribute to this work and the work of the NPS and CRC.

A recent statement by the Ministry of Justice describes the present arrangements for NOMS (see https://www.gov.uk/government/publications/noms-annual-report-and-accounts-2013-2014), which is described as an

Executive Agency of the Ministry of Justice (MOJ), responsible on behalf of the Secretary of State for Justice for commissioning and delivering prison and probation services in England and Wales. We are committed to protecting the public and reducing reoffending. During 2013–14 we delivered our services through:

Probation Trusts – 35 Trusts responsible for the delivery of probation services at a local level;

Public sector prisons – 106 prisons which provide around 82 per cent of prison places;

Private sector providers – operating 14 prisons under contract and pro-viding other significant services including prisoner escorts and electronic monitoring (EM) of offenders;

Partnerships – with a range of public and social sector partners, including police, local authorities, health and education providers, and with a wide range of organisations in the voluntary and social enterprise sector;

Providing contracted services – the Agency is contracted by the Youth Justice Board to provide 1,120 commissioned beds for young people (under 18) and by the Home Office to provide 850 places at three Immigration Removal Centres.

Our Headquarters (HQ) functions provide corporate and operational sup-port services for the Agency and undertake the work required to meet our responsibilities to Parliament.

The prison estate comprises eight maximum security prisons holding the most high risk – Category A prisoners. Category B prisoners are those who do not need to be held in the highest security conditions but their potential for escape should be made very difficult. Category B establishments may also function as remand prisons, holding prisoners appearing before the courts for either trial or sentence, whilst Category C are training prisons, and Category D open or resettlement prisons. Prisoners serving sentences of less than 12 months usually remain in remand or local prisons.

There are 13 women's prisons in England. These are:

Askham Grange, York – Yorkshire & Humberside

Bronzefield*, Middlesex – Greater London

Downview, Surrey – Greater London

Drake Hall, Staffordshire – West Midlands

East Sutton Park, Kent – Kent & Sussex

Eastwood Park, Gloucestershire – South West

Foston Hall, Derbyshire – East Midlands

Holloway, Greater London – Greater London

Low Newton, Durham – North East

New Hall, West Yorkshire – Yorkshire & Humberside

Peterborough*, Cambridgeshire – East of England

Send, Surrey – Greater London

Styal, Cheshire – North West

*privately operated establishments

Young women offenders aged between 18 and 21 are known as young adult women. In the women's estate they reside in designated accommodation within women's prisons, but depending on risk assessment, may take part in the full range of activities available to all prisoners. Young women aged under 18 are held in young women's units, which are separate units within women's prisons. There are three dedicated units – the Josephine Butler Unit at Downview, the Mary Carpenter Unit at Eastwood Park and the Rivendell Unit at New Hall.

Young offender institutions (YOIs) were introduced under the Criminal Justice Act 1988, although special centres for young offenders have existed since the nineteenth century, the first opening in 1902 at Borstal Prison in Kent, whose name was lent to similar institutions. The Criminal Justice Act 1982 abolished the borstal system, replacing it with a network of youth custody centres. Young people may be detained in secure children's homes (SCH), a secure training centre (STC) or a young offender institution such as Cookham Wood (Kent), Feltham (Greater London), Hindley (Greater Manchester), Parc (Wales), Warren Hill (Suffolk), Werrington (Staffordshire) and Wetherby (West Yorkshire).

Box 2.4   Kerry Joy on working in a young offender institution

Currently I am employed as a forensic psychologist as part of a regional psychology team. This enables me to have wider opportunities and experiences within my career. The regional approach allows me to move between prisons where the high priority work is located, thus completing tasks in both male and female prisons, with young offenders, Indeterminate Sentenced Offenders, and working in different security categories of prison. My role is varied and requires all the skills demonstrated across the four core roles from the British Psychological Society forensic training route. For example; I often provide psychological risk assessments for the parole board and give verbal evidence at oral hearings. I complete intervention through group work with high-risk offenders. There is the opportunity to complete research on emerging areas or trends within the service. The consultancy role is crucial for the Offender Management Model and advising on sentence planning for offenders. This aspect of the role also requires advice to be given as the Negotiation Adviser at serious incidents. As forensic psychologists working within a prison setting we are often involved in training staff in specialist areas of knowledge.

During my career I have received the most satisfaction from working with offenders and seeing the positive impact of rehabilitation. A particularly rewarding time, was when I was working with young people. I spent time working with males who were between 15 and 18 years old. I found them fun and engaging. Often the young people had complex backgrounds that impacted on their attachment styles. Through this work, trying to build up trust in professional working relationships was challenging. When they did respond and I saw change it was really rewarding. This client group is also very unique. As a practitioner you are always thinking of new ways in which to introduce the learning and keep their attention. I found that I was able to be far more creative, which is another aspect of my work that I enjoy.

The route to becoming chartered with the British Psychological Society and registered with the Health Care and Professions Council can be a long and challenging one. It is crucial that you are organized, motivated and have a good Co-ordinating Supervisor. Alongside this you need to take responsibility for your training and be driven to achieve the targets on the route. Having registered status requires the ability to use defensible decision making, effective communication, safe and ethical practice, confidence in your own ability and good psychological knowledge. Being a Registered Forensic Psychologist carries a lot of responsibility as ultimately you are often commenting on people's risk of harm to others and themselves.

Some of the challenges to working in this field can be the day-to-day challenges of working in a secure environment and how the very nature of the environment can impose restrictions on your working practice. The client group often have at least one personality disorder and working with clients with this diagnosis can be demanding, so being very resilient is key both to your own psychological survival and effective practice.

One thing I have realized from working for HMPS/NOMS for 15 years is that things are always developing and changing. This is an important part of improving the service and our work as psychologists. One of the most recent changes in practice has been the review of the open estate and how psychologists can help to advise on how to manage risk in open prisons and the community. This has provided me with an opportunity to complete more work in the open prisons but also to refine my risk management skills.

The Youth Justice Board for England and Wales (YJB) is an executive non-departmental public body. Its board members are appointed by the Secretary of State for Justice. In April 2000, the YJB was given statutory responsibilities for the secure estate for children and young people. In their plans the YJB stated as their five working principles:

- The secure estate for children and young people should be distinct from adult provision and specialist in its focus on children and young people.
- Commissioned services should recognize diversity and promote equality proactively.
- Commissioned services should maintain the safety and well-being of children and young people placed in custody and actively incorporate the views of young people.

- Interventions to address offending behaviour should be based on evidence of effectiveness and their delivery informed by thorough assessment and individualized sentence planning processes.
- Service providers should recognize and promote children and young people's potential, enabling them to lead healthy, crime-free lives on release.

The numbers of young people in secure environments has been declining and correspondingly there has already been a decommissioning of under-18 YOIs. It is predicted that further decommissioning will take place in secure training centres (STCs) and secure children's homes (SCHs).

Another area of work the YJB has been involved with is preventing violent extremism in young people. To that end they published a process evaluation (Hirschfield et al., 2012) and commissioned a systematic review of the literature (Christmann, 2012).

Crighton and Towl (2008) describe the work undertaken in UK prisons whilst Brunswig and Parham (2003) provide an overview of correctional psychology in the United States. The latter, for example, enumerate the following roles: management/supervision; working in multidisciplinary teams; personnel selection; staff counselling and employee assistance; risk assessment; end of sentence assessments; parole; intake assessments; substance abuse assessments; suicide prevention; isolation placement; sexual assault assessment; malingering; crisis intervention and hostage negotiation; individual and group therapy; sex offender treatment; family counselling and research co-ordinator. From this list, we can see the same definitional boundary issues arise as with psychologists who work within the police setting. Clearly some of these roles are clinical, others are occupational. A forensic psychology training, for example, may not accredit the practitioner to administer personal selection psychometric tests or undertake a critical job analysis. Much activity with the prison setting involves group work and the delivery of structured programmes. Basically aimed at reducing reoffending, many are cognitive-behavioural in approach. Cognitive skills, sex offending and violent offending are amongst programmes that are delivered. Immersive therapies such as delivery of therapeutic communities are also undertaken. (See Brown et al., 2014 for a detailed account of such a programme.) Brunswig and Parham's managerial and supervisory role involves overseeing the work of interns and practicum students as well as participating in organizational committees such as staff well-being and labour relations. Towl (2003) notes that within the UK prison setting psychologists have been caught up in the New Public Management (NPM) regimes and have also contributed to change management implementation. We describe this more fully in Chapter 4.

The Probation Service in particular engages with health, housing and employment services and both services work extensively with the third sector voluntary agencies. Psychologists within both arms of NOMS (probation and prison) engage in risk assessments and management strategies for offenders. Psychologists within this sector may be involved with probation and assist the police in obtaining a sexual prevention order to stop an individual being with certain categories of people (e.g. children) or in particular locations at certain times (e.g. school finishing times) or involved in the managements of prison hostage taking incidents or other disturbances.

Box 2.5   Yvonne Shell on a hostage taking experience

Approximately 18 years ago, I worked as a forensic psychologist in a special unit within the prison estate – a unit that was deemed to hold a maximum of 18 of the most difficult and dangerous men in the prison system, so described as a result of not only the behaviour that led to their imprisonment but also their continued behaviour in prison. This behaviour included the murder of other inmates and of prison staff, assaultive behaviour, disruptive behaviour, including rooftop protests, and hostage taking. Indeed, many of the men on the unit had histories of taking other inmates and staff hostage.

I hold a story in my head from my days on the unit, one that is readily recalled and triggered by hearing of such events taking place even now. It is one that, oddly, makes me smile on recollection of it. I'm sure at this stage you are thinking I am decidedly strange in saying that, but let me tell you the account of the day that I was threatened by a known hostage taker to be his next hostage.

The inmate in question was a man who I had spent over three years trying to engage in assessment and treatment on the unit. The dynamic that existed between us went something like this. I would walk onto the wing every morning and he would be waiting on the landing, hurling abuse at me, with a smile on his face. My response over the entire three years never altered, or faltered. On each occasion I entered the wing and was in receipt of this 'greeting' I would respond with a smile and shout 'good morning' back. Over this time, the offender – who was a life sentence prisoner – refused all interviews with me, the only man on the unit to do so. Despite his unrelenting refusal, I unrelentingly offered and he would tell me in a forceful manner that he declined my kind offer. It became a dance of sorts. A dance in which we carefully stepped around each other, myself being careful not to tread on his toes!

And so to the day in question. It may surprise readers to know that there were very few incidents on the unit. The reasons for this were most likely a combination of the following. Each prisoner was acutely aware of the reputation of other prisoners, and their potential, and as such a rather healthy, or perhaps unhealthy, respect was one of the reasons for few incidents. Furthermore, proactive management, excellent communication and an exceptional Personal

(Continued)

Officer Scheme were significant in this also. Therefore, when an alarm was raised on the unit, all knew that it was potentially a very serious incident. On this occasion, an alarm went off at the other end of the wing to where my office was located. My office was an old cell, and at all times an officer sat in an outer office, gate-keeping (for want of a better word) the entry to mine, the wing governors' and psychiatrists' offices. However, when this alarm sounded, in the panic to respond, the outer office was unwittingly left unmanned and this particular inmate, the one I was doing a rather slow dance with, took the opportunity presented to slip through unnoticed, arriving at my door, all other offices being empty in the area.

I had been sitting in my office writing a report when the alarm had sounded. I remained working, oblivious to the fact that the outer office was unmanned. The first I knew of this was when I became aware of someone standing in the doorway of my office, leaning against the doorframe. It was the offender I previously mentioned. He had his hands in his pockets and was staring at me, a smile playing on his lips. I realized that this was a very dangerous scenario for me. Thoughts flew through my head. I knew I was alone and that no one would realize he was here with me. I also knew that if I pressed my panic button, located on the underside of my desk, the response would be slow and that it would only serve to escalate the situation I found myself in. It took all my strength to hold my nerve, remain seated and not press the alarm. Instead, I put down my pen and leant back in my chair and said the offender's name. His response was to smile and say, 'I could take you hostage now'. I knew before he said the words that this was coming. At that precise moment I knew I had to use whatever I had in terms of the 'relationship' I had built over the three years with this man to hopefully extricate myself from this situation. I also knew that whatever I did might just not work at all.

'I could take you hostage now' ringing in my ears, I forced myself to relax, smile and acknowledge the truth in his statement. And so I heard myself say, in the slowest delivery possible, to buy time, 'Well that's true, XXX, you could take me hostage. But you know what ... I have to tell you if you do that, I will talk to you, XXX, and you have spent the last three years avoiding doing just that.' I swear the world stood still momentarily. I'm sure I held my breath, tried to keep an open expression on my face and to remain seated. For what seemed the longest time, he considered my response. He then let out a bark of laughter, shook his head and said, 'You're f***ing right', turned and walked away.

I believe that on another day, used by another person, this same strategy may not have worked. However, I also believe that over the three years that we had built a form of therapeutic relationship, a dance, that gave me some limited insight into how I might survive this encounter. Now when I reflect on the events of that day I do smile. I also feel afresh the fear and consider the 'what if's' of that moment in time. A moment that could very easily have ended very differently. And in case any of you are wondering, the following day when I walked onto the wing I was greeted in exactly the same way as I had been for the previous three years and I surprised myself by responding in the same way back.

Forensic psychologists within a prison may provide counselling to assist the offender in coping with existing or new issues the prison environment may induce, such as separation from family, depression, anxiety, being bullied, substance misuse or self harm. They advise upon which skills courses or treatment may be appropriate and develop and monitor individual or group treatment programmes such as anger management, enhanced thinking skills or sex offence courses. They may also be involved in staff training, researching an intervention or conducting a regime evaluation, and may testify or write reports for tribunals, courts or to parole boards. They will be involved in risk assessment evaluating the likely risk of harm to self and others, for example advising upon the likely risk of an individual reoffending if released.

Research into risk assessments, development of psychometric measurement and programme evaluations has proliferated (see the edited collection by McMurran, Hollin, Craig, Dixon and Gannon 2010). Other more specialized topics have also received attention. Prison suicide research has increased in recent years as its occurrence is greater than in the general population (Towl, 2010b). Towl points out the importance of particular skills that are necessary for involvement in this type of work and the need to first minimize depersonalization rituals of prison life and normalize feelings of depression and anxiety that accompany periods of incarceration.

Paul Gendreau and his colleagues (key players in refuting the nothing works position) discuss the underlying philosophies of punitive and rehabilitative ideals (Gendreau et al., 2006). Their treatise anticipates a more detailed discussion in this present book's Chapter 4.

Forensic psychologists may work with specific categories of prisoners. Mention has already been made of YOIs. Alternatively, they may engage with prisoners committed to a life sentence and be involved in interventions that help them to adapt to the prison environment. 'Lifers' are especially prone to suicide attempts, so when assessing prisoner risk it is important to look at potential harm to self as well as to others.

Lea, Auburn and Kibblewhite (1999) highlight a particular tension amongst professionals working with sex offenders. They encapsulate this in their notion of the 'professional–personal dialectic' which is a potential dilemma between having to treat and engage with offenders notwithstanding a personal revulsion towards the offences they have committed. We discuss this further in Chapters 10 and 12. This research played an important part in developing the ambition of Terri Cole towards becoming a forensic psychologist.

Box 2.6   Terri Cole's reflection on assisting with Susan Lea's research

I needed a summer job whilst at university and was living a short commute away so thought I would ask the lecturers of subjects I was interested in if they needed any (paid) assistance. I was asked if I could type and luckily I could. Tim Auburn and Susan Lea were conducting research looking at the narratives of rapists, and needed someone to transcribe their recordings of a sex offender treatment programme. I was pleased to have an interesting paid job, and felt privileged not only to be working with lecturers I respected but also to gain access to such raw data which would give me an insight as to what treatment in prison actually involved. I probably did not realize it at the time but it also gave me an immense insight and passion for qualitative research, which as an under-graduate I had limited previous exposure to. They were using discourse analyses, so not only was I required to listen and type every word verbatim, but each individual who spoke had to be identified by their voice, and every detail of speech (e.g. pause - including length, interruption, raised voice etc.) accu-rately recorded. 'Attention to detail' has been the mantra and wise words from a persistent mentor throughout my work in psychology, and it was no truer than here. Anyone who has ever conducted qualitative research soon realizes it is certainly never the easy option, and my eyes were opened as I learnt the time required in transcribing, let alone analysing the vast amount of data amassed. Although I literally typed all summer, rather than being bored with the mun-daneness of the exercise, I was fascinated listening to the content and learning the methodology. In addition, although I considered myself somewhat of a 'lay' person at that time, even I could elicit patterns in the offender discourses and recognize themes such as denial, justification and minimization. So that sum-mer certainly inspired me: this area of work was interesting, exciting, intelligent (using different methods depending upon the research focus) and could be applied in the real world, was new and innovative, and one day I hoped I would be able to play an even greater part in it.

WHAT DO FORENSIC PSYCHOLOGISTS DO WHO WORK IN SPECIAL HOSPITALS AND MEDIUM SECURE UNITS?

If the courts decide there is an issue with an individual's mental health, the person may be detained in a special secure hospital rather than prison. Predominantly forensic clinical psychologists are based in secure units in order to work with, assess and treat patients who have mental health problems. For example, they may interview, observe, assess and treat someone who has com-mitted an offence but is suffering from schizophrenia or a personality disorder. Forensic psychologists in such settings may also work in conjunction with psychiatrists specializing in the treatment of mental disorders.

In the UK there are four 'special' hospitals that house offenders deemed to be mentally ill. Broadmoor was built as a Victorian asylum and housed its first patient, a woman admitted for infanticide, on 27 May 1863. The first male patients arrived the following year. Daniel M'Naghten was held in Broadmoor in 1864. M'Naghten had shot a civil servant, possibly thinking he was the prime minister, Sir Robert Peel, because 'The Tories in my native city [Glasgow] have compelled me to do this. They follow, persecute me wherever I go, and have entirely destroyed my peace of mind ... That is all I have to say.' It was indeed all he had to say. He never spoke about the assassination again (Diamond, 1956). This crime, apparently committed for an irrational reason (M'Naghten had a bank receipt for £750 on him when he was arrested, so theft was an unlikely motive), led to the establishment of the Rule bearing his name which indicates that a person is not criminally responsible if

> at the time of the committing of the act, the party accused was labouring under such a defect of reason from disease of the mind, as not to know the nature and quality of the act he was doing, or if he did know, it, he did not know what he was doing was wrong. (Howitt, 2006: 327)

The equivalent in the United States is the Bonnie Rule which states 'a person is mentally ill (for the purposes of a prosecution) if as a result of mental diseases or defect he was unable to appreciate the wrongfulness of his conduct at the time of the offence' (Howitt, 2006: 328). The M'Naghten and Bonnie Rules constitute the basis for a plea of insanity or diminished responsibility and is invoked as a defence, often in the case of murder, and will determine a disposal in a secure hospital or prison. However, there is a 'third' category of offender, i.e. those suffering from a dangerous and severe personality disorder (DSPD). A personality disorder is not considered to be a mental disorder but rather a dispositional tendency and as such the question of treatability arises (Howitt, 2006).

Treatability is an important concept because patients can be admitted involuntarily as long as appropriate medical treatments are available. The 'appropriate treatment test' means that those deemed dangerous due to severe personality disorder can be detained without their consent, if a particular intervention is available, even if it may not be effective for that person. Thus being 'mad' or 'bad' may result in a stay in a special hospital, serving a sentence in a prison or being consigned to a DSPD unit (Blackburn, 1995). The Paddocks Centre at Broadmoor was established to house and treat those suffering from DSPD, but was subsequently closed in April 2012 following the Coalition government's Green Paper and invention of Offender Personality Disorder Pathways, which seeks to revert housing prisoners previously classified as DSPD to prison establishments (O'Loughlin, 2014).

Eventually, Broadmoor found difficulty in accommodating the number of patients sent to it, so Rampton and Ashworth were also designated special hospitals as spill-over institutions. Carstairs is the equivalent institution in Scotland.

Administratively, the Special Hospitals Service Authority had been responsible for the organization and governance from 1989 to 1996 with an operational brief to:

- ensure the continuing safety of the public;
- ensure the provision of appropriate treatment for patients;
- ensure a good quality of life for both patients and staff;
- develop the hospitals as centres of excellence for the training of staff in all disciplines in forensic and other branches of psychiatry, psychiatric care and treatment;
- develop closer working relationships with local and regional NHS psychiatric services;
- promote research into fields related to forensic psychiatry.

The Authority was abolished in 1996, when its commissioning functions passed to the High Security Psychiatric Services Commissioning Board, which is responsible for approximately 7,719 inpatient beds (795 in high security, 3,192 in medium security and 3,732 in low security). These beds account for almost one-fifth of NHS spending on mental health services in England (NHS Commissioning Board, 2013).

Neurological and psycho-physical research began at Broadmoor with the arrival of Tony Black, who built a research laboratory there in 1959 (Black, 2013). As Black says, the polygraph, which measures changes in cardiovascular, respiratory and skin conductivity, was used as a device to compare autonomic responses to various sensitive stimuli related to a patient's offence compared with neutral ones and not, as some critics protested, as a means to detect deception in Broadmoor patients. Not without doubts about its accuracy, the polygraph nevertheless has since successfully been applied to post-conviction sex offending testing (Grubin, 2008).

Box 2.7 Derek Perkins' reflections on Broadmoor Hospital

Prior to taking up my post at Broadmoor in 1986, quaintly titled Top Grade Clinical Psychologist in those days, I worked for a number of years in the Prison Service in the Midlands and at Prison HQ on the training programme for entrant prison psychologists, as well as in the community forensic psychiatric services through what was then the Midland Centre for Forensic Psychiatry in Birmingham. It was through there that we began the first community follow-up of sex offenders who had received treatment in prison.

My move to Broadmoor high secure psychiatric hospital was a new venture and one which I entered with both excitement and trepidation. Part of my induction was to take part in a number of NHS management courses as well as to receive induction visits and guidance from the other heads of the UK high secure services, which I look back on with appreciation for what I learned at that time.

As well as being Head of Department at Broadmoor, a post which was then interestingly only three management steps to the junior minister, my duties included being team psychologist for two clinical teams – I worked on pretty much all wards from intensive care to pre-transfer rehabilitation – and contributing to research at the hospital: my research was mainly linked to the Department's psycho-physiological assessment 'lab', mainly with sex offenders, some procedures from which became incorporated into the Prison Service sex offender treatment programmes (SOTPs) during the 1990s. For a period, I was one of the prison SOTP advisers along with my friends and colleagues Karl Hanson, Bill Murphy and Bill Marshall (recently awarded a lifetime achievement award by the International Association for the Treatment of Sexual Offenders), during which brainstorming and friendly heated arguments took place in various hotels around the country.

A major psychology development at Broadmoor, in my view, was the gradual joining together of the psychology, psychotherapy, arts therapies (art, drama and music) and nurse therapists in the hospital into one coordinated psychological services directorate, a period of great enthusiasm, mutual learning and creativity. The development of the (multidisciplinary) centralized group work service around 2000 was I believe another important milestone in psychological treatment, for which a dedicated area of the hospital was set up (Newbury Therapy Unit), which enabled the running of an increasing number of themed groups to meet patients' needs as they moved through the hospital. There are now a number of groups addressing psycho-education and cognitive skills; mental health restoration, such as CBT for psychosis and DBT (dialectical behaviour therapy); and offence-related themes of violence, sexual offending, fire setting and homicide.

Over the years we were able to move from a good but patchy psychology service provision into a much more streamlined and comprehensive service, which I think played its part in gradually reducing patients' lengths of stay down to the current 5–6 years.

I also look back with affection on a long collaboration with the University of Surrey MSc Course in Forensic Psychology, which Graham Powell and I set up in the 1990s in which Broadmoor psychologists delivered the more clinical lectures on the course, on assessing and treating violence and sexual offending, and which provided Broadmoor research placements and supervision for the trainees. The course, which is now coming to an end after more than 20 successful years, has seen most of its graduates moving into work in forensic psychology within the criminal justice system and forensic mental health services.

Having now moved on from Head of Psychological Services, in which I was so ably succeeded by Dr Estelle Moore, I look back on the enormous developments that have taken place over the years. We have moved from an overcrowded institution where care staff presented more as prison officers than nurses (even in the same uniforms), in which security and therapy were often unhelpfully pitted against one another, and where there was a lack of coordination between different areas of patient care, to a hospital in which services are now much more patient-focused, comprehensive and integrated. The forthcoming redevelopment of the hospital for patients will complement and further enable the development of clinical services for this most challenging and needy group of patients.

Medium secure units (MSU) provide patients with a level of intensive care within a secure environment (Coid et al., 2001). Some patients are transferred from prison and subsequently return to complete their sentences. Others return to a lower level of secure services. Patients usually graduate from a number of programmes designed to reduce their likelihood of reoffending and whose risk is sufficiently minimized to permit a return to the community. MSUs have physically secure perimeters, secure practices, such as restricting or banning patients from certain items, searches and high staff to patient ratios. There are about 50 MSUs in England and Wales and the main sources of referral are prison, the courts, special hospitals or NHS psychiatric hospitals. Reasons for referral include discovery of or deteriorating mental states during judicial proceedings, aggressive behaviour or non-compliance in other custodial settings. Patients present a serious but not immediate risk to the public.

Forensic psychologists are involved in the administration of programmes such as reasoning and rehabilitation as well as engaging in evaluations of such programmes (Young et al., 2008).

WHAT ARE COMMUNITY FORENSIC SERVICES?

The Community Forensic Mental Health Service (CFMHS) provides or facilitates case management of a defined caseload of service users in the community who present a significant risk of serious harm to others related to their mental disorder, particularly those leaving secure care, for whom the risk is best managed by specialist forensic mental health services. Service users under the care of the CFMHS include those discharged from secure care from restricted hospital orders (or equivalent) or community treatment orders, and those who have transferred from other community mental health services (Kenney-Herbert et al., 2013).

The CFMHS provides:

- liaison, advice, specialist interventions, educational and skills development to mental health services and other agencies; service users, carers and families;
- care pathway management, into and out of secure settings and prisons, for appropriate individuals – this may be direct involvement for service users on the team caseload or through facilitating and advising those under the care of other teams;
- clinical liaison and a resource for Multi-Agency Public Protection Arrangements (MAPPA) and associated processes in the area;
- liaison with local criminal justice liaison/court diversion services, with written protocols;
- court diversion or criminal justice liaison services;
- aftercare for people discharged from secure care who will often be subject to Conditional Discharges or Community Treatment Orders under mental health legislation.

Specialist interventions include those related to the management of criminogenic needs emphasizing harm reduction, for example structured personality disorder assessment and the use of evidence-based structured professional judgement risk assessment tools (such as HCR-20, RSVP, SAM, SARA).

Community forensic services frequently comprise a multidisciplinary team consisting of forensic psychiatrists, community psychiatric nurses, forensic and clinical psychologists, social workers, occupational therapists and clinical pharmacy.

Box 2.8   Andy Inett on working in community forensic services

I am a forensic psychologist working in the NHS, in a community-based forensic psychology service for people with intellectual disabilities (ID) in Kent. The service offers case consultation and training to Community Learning Disability Team (CLDT) practitioners, individual service user risk assessments using tools such as the HCR-20 and START, and specially adapted group-based interventions for sex offending, fire setting and thinking skills.

Whilst the criminogenic needs of ID offenders are broadly similar to mainstream offenders, one of the key concerns for the service is responsivity. Service users vary widely in their cognitive abilities, communication skills and ability to internalize coping strategies, making the use of manualized programmes difficult, and necessitating a closely person-centred approach to delivering treatment. Complex concepts, such as victim empathy or perspective taking, need to be simplified, using less complex language and pictorial enhancement to improve understanding. Small group work, with facilitators scaffolding learning, and more interactive approaches to treatment are essential, to offer experiential learning, with less didactic work and more activities using the physical space, role plays and drama therapy techniques. Positive outcomes have been observed, such as post-group reductions in offence supporting attitudes, and a follow-up study looking at recidivism rates is planned.

Managing risk with ID offenders is fraught with ethical and moral dilemmas. They are often vulnerable individuals, who may be more easily coerced into offending by more able anti-social peers, or more likely to have been victims of crime or abuse themselves. Concepts such as capacity, criminal responsibility and 'mens rea' are difficult issues for teams to assess and achieve a consensus view. The line between 'challenging behaviour', rooted in maladaptive strategies to communicate distress or avoid/escape difficult situations, and more anti-social offending behaviour is a difficult one to draw with any great certainty. This increases the risk of inconsistency in Criminal Justice System (CJS) response, a

(Continued)

possible lack of convictions, and a subsequent lack of a legal framework to manage risk, such as a probation order, or placement on the sex offender register. Effective risk management tends to rely on external support from family members, support workers and Community Team for Learning Disabilities (CTLD) members, because of the increased risk of impulsivity, and impaired consequential thinking and problem solving skills. Service users are not always accepting of such support, perhaps lacking insight, and lacking capacity to act in their own best interests. National policy initiatives such as Valuing People Now (2009) rightly encourage greater inclusion for people with ID, but what if less support and increased independence in the community leads to increased risk to the public? This is a paradox that can prove difficult for CTLD care managers to overcome. The role of the forensic psychologist is to offer a risk formulation and risk management plan that is achievable within this context, thereby sharing the responsibility for containing the risk.

The Bradley Report on offenders with ID in the CJS (2009) highlighted the need for more joint working. The service is working to address this in several ways, including developing close links with local police Violence and Sex Offender Register (ViSOR) units, providing training and consultation for CJS staff, and the co-facilitation of an adapted Sex Offender Treatment Programmes (SOTP) with Kent probation staff, recently rewarded with a Howard League Award nomination. The service also works closely with Community Mental Health Teams.

CAN FORENSIC PSYCHOLOGISTS WORK IN PRIVATE PRACTICE?

There are now an increasing number of forensic psychologists who work either as sole independent practitioners or who work commercially in a forensic psychology consultancy.

They will receive commissions from those requiring forensic psychology services, such as risk assessment, interview training or various forms of profiling. They may run accredited continuing professional development (CPD) training days or organize conferences.

Box 2.9   Leam Craig on working in private practice

I work as a Consultant Forensic and Clinical Psychologist and Managing Partner at a private psychology practice and have worked in private practice for over 18 years now. I hold Honorary Professorial positions at the University of Birmingham and Birmingham City University in Forensic and Clinical Psychology. The challenges working in private practice are varied and at times pressured, but always enjoyable. So, where did it all begin?

During my undergraduate days I was recruited into the Royal Air Force University Air Squadron. I lived on the air base and trained as a pilot whilst studying for a psychology degree at Keele University. After graduating, I was in a position of choosing between two careers, that of aviation or psychology. My interest in understanding extreme behaviours led me to enrol onto the MSc in Forensic Psychology at the University of Surrey. This degree opened my eyes to the complexities of human behaviour and forensic research and my passion to learn more and contribute to the world of forensic psychology practice was born.

After completing the MSc I stayed at the University for a short period working as a Research Assistant at the Human Psychopharmacological Research Unit, before joining Forensic Psychology Practice Ltd. The early part of my career here focused on the assessment of risk to children and capacity of parents in child protection cases heard in County Courts throughout England and Wales. Before long I was giving evidence in my first court case in Cardiff, which can only be explained as a baptism of fire. I have since gone on to become a partner of the practice and have been involved in over 250 child protection cases, including domestic violence, non-accidental injury and child homicide and over 300 cases in the criminal courts.

Although private practice brings with it freedom and autonomy, this is tempered by the need to secure contracts and search out new business opportunities. While this can sometimes make for a nervous time, it also brings with it a varied working model. For example, I have worked in four forensic psychiatric hospitals, consulted with five different probation services, three NHS Trusts, HM Prison Service (England and Wales) and the Northern Ireland Prison Service, all on a contracted basis. I have acted as a Consultant Lead to three independent community low secure hospitals for people with personality disorder and challenging behaviours and completed Approved Clinician training with the Royal College of Psychiatrists.

My early training in clinical practice emphasized the importance of evidence-based practice and I started to pursue a research profile, walking the line between academia and practice. I have been privileged to have the intellectual companionship of a number of world-renowned practitioners and researchers in the field of violent and sex offender assessment, treatment and research, both in the UK and overseas. These collaborations have led to an active research profile focusing on the assessment of sexual and violent offenders, offenders with intellectual disabilities and personality disorder. This has resulted in over 70 publications, including seven books, with research papers translated into five languages. My research into sexual offenders has opened further work opportunities where I have consulted with the Catholic diocese, Salvation Army, the US Army Attorney's Office in Germany on the risk assessment of service personnel, and UK police forces on crime scene evidence.

(Continued)

Looking back at my career choices then, my interest in understanding extreme behaviours took over from my passion in participating in them. I scratch this itch at the weekends now! Any regrets? No. I have been in the fortunate position of helping people struggling with life crises and I hope I have made some small positive difference in their lives while at the same time contributing to forensic research and practice.

Private practice is not a single job but several different jobs all rolled into one. Flexibility, adaptability and resilience are essential. While there are undoubtedly challenges in running a successful psychology practice in an increasingly competitive market, the work opportunities are varied, exciting and unique.

IN WHAT WAYS CAN FORENSIC PSYCHOLOGISTS ASSIST THE COURTS?

Psychologists have appeared in court as experts since the 1890s. One early example was Albert von Schrenck-Notzing who testified in a case of a triple murder in a Munich court in 1896. There had been a huge amount of sensational media coverage in the months leading up to the trial. Schrenck-Notzing suggested that as a consequence of this publicity, which had been widely read, witnesses would not be able to distinguish details from the coverage with their own recollections (Bartol and Bartol, 2006 [1987]). They note the early work of an American psychologist who testified in a Belgian court case in 1911 examining the veracity of child witness statements. Appearances in the American courts by psychologists in the 1920s were in the area of visual perception experiments trying to resolve trademark infringements. Their appearance in criminal cases was inhibited because then only medical experts, i.e. those licensed by law to practise, could testify on matters of fitness to plead. By the later 1920s American psychologists were appearing in court but it was not until 1958 that this prohibition was breached in courts in the UK. Lionel Haward describes how the breakthrough came because of the hearsay rule. The occasion was a pre-trial conference at which a psychiatrist was trying to explain a psychologist's (Haward's) report of the defendant but was unable to do so. The defence barrister raised the matter with the judge, who concluded that the psychiatrist's attempt to explain findings drawn from a third party was indeed an infringement of the rule of hearsay and that Professor Haward should appear himself to explain his own report in court (Gudjonsson and Haward, 1998: 15). Elizabeth Loftus provides an account of her experiences as an expert witness in the American courts (Loftus, 1986). She testified in relation to her research on human perception, recollection and eyewitness accounts. She lists the other areas, such as typical behaviour of domestically abused women, effects of bilingualism on children, impact of television on behaviour, typical behaviour of rape victims, where psychologists were providing expert testimony. Interestingly, in part, her own involvement was motivated by research findings that there were a high number of wrongful convictions based on faulty eyewitness testimony.

Loftus explains that the purpose of expert evidence, or any evidence come to that, offered in a trial is to 'supply knowledge that will aid the judge or jury in reaching a final determination' (Loftus, 1986: 245). Expert testimony is opinion evidence given by someone who has some qualification to hold the relevant expertise. It does not necessarily have to be an academically qualified person; a taxi driver, for example, might be considered an expert in matters relating to licensed hackney cab driving. As Michael Carlin explains:

> an expert witness is an individual who appears before the court or a tribunal. The purpose is to provide information not discernible by ordinary means, about matters not within the ken of persons other than those familiar with the science surrounding the issue about which they will speak and concerning which they have special knowledge by reason of their learning, experience and particular skill. (Carlin, 2010: 723)

An expert usually appears in courts designated the first tier trier of facts, in other words criminal and civil courts together with regulatory discipline panels, employment tribunals, other bodies such as parole board hearings and mental health tribunals, which is the first level of judicial proceedings hearing evidence and coming to some view. Carlin lists the kinds of things an expert in a criminal trial might be asked to give an opinion on, such as intellectual functioning of a defendant and their ability to take part in a trial, capacity of an individual to understand a police caution administered before an interview, vulnerability of a witness in interrogations, risk of violent recidivism. Civil matters may include personal injury cases (Powell and Powell, 2010) or parental capacity in custody hearings (Herbert, 2010).

Carlin explains that the subject matter of the testimony of a forensic expert must relate to issues that require knowledge of, for example, psychological theory, results of psychometric testing, interpretation of psychometric data, efficacy of a treatment programme, that would be thought of as special knowledge and beyond that of the ordinary person on the street. The 'Clapham Omnibus Test' is the term used to describe what might be expected from the testimony of a, hypothetical, ordinary reasonable person; an expert's opinion would have to be beyond that.

Box 2.10   Gisli Gudjonsson on being an expert witness

My first experience of court work in the UK was during 1975 and 1977, when I was a trainee clinical psychologist at the University of Surrey. The late Professor Lionel Haward was the head of the course and he was at the time actively involved in high-profile court cases and discussed the cases in class. I was inspired by his interesting presentations and enthusiasm. In March 1980, shortly after taking

(Continued)

up a lecturer position in clinical psychology at the Institute of Psychiatry, Lionel and I first worked on a case together and gave evidence at the Old Bailey in a fraud case. At the time forensic psychology was in its infancy and there was scepticism about the real value of psychology in court proceedings (Tunstall et al., 1982). The cross-examination during two trials was lengthy and hostile and almost discouraged me from further forensic practice. In December 1981, I was to give my first evidence for the prosecution; it was a landmark case and involved assessing the capacity of a moderately learning disabled woman to give evidence in court (Gudjonsson and Gunn, 1982). Suggestibility was the one issue I was asked to evaluate and I discovered that no suitable instrument was available. As a result, I developed the Gudjonsson Suggestibility Scale (Gudjonsson, 1984), which is now in common international use.

Lionel Haward informed me in the late 1980s that he had never given evidence in the Court of Appeal during his lengthy career as a forensic psychologist. Part of the problem was that until the 1980s most cases were referred by doctors who then incorporated the psychological findings into their report and the psychologist did not have to give evidence in court. I objected to this practice, and in fact this was not a problem I encountered with my psychiatrist colleagues at the Maudsley Hospital and Institute of Psychiatry. My first appeal case involved a man who had been arrested suspected of drunken driving, but had failed to provide a blood sample for testing. He was convicted and appealed on the basis that he was genuinely blood injury phobic, which was supported by the psycho-physiological evidence I provided in court and which resulted in his acquittal (Gudjonsson and Sartory, 1983). In 1991, I gave my first evidence in the Court of Appeal in a major murder case and the criteria for determining the admissibility were broadened to include borderline IQ, and tests of suggestibility and compliance. Since that case I have testified in a large number of appeal cases in the UK and abroad, and in one case my psychological evidence was successfully used in the House of Lords to overturn a conviction (Gudjonsson, 2003a, 2010). Clinical and forensic expert evidence has come a long way since the 1980s and I am pleased to have had the opportunity to contribute to that development. I have treated each case as a learning experience and incorporated the knowledge gained into my research and practice.

American psychologists have been associated with amicus curiae briefs whereby relevant research is summarized for the presentation of psychological issues to appeals, legislative committees or in civil proceedings (Wrightsman and Fulero, 2005: 40). A high-profile case was that of Ann Hopkins, who was, by all accounts, a competent, committed and effective professional in the accountancy firm Price Waterhouse. When she was denied a partnership, she alleged gender stereotyping. The company claimed she overcompensated for being a woman in a male environment and needed a course in charm school.

She was apparently advised 'to walk more femininely, talk more femininely, dress more femininely, wear make-up and have her hair styled and wear jewellery' (Fiske et al., 1991). Fiske testified on her behalf, presenting research findings. The claimant won her case and the company appealed, claiming the psychological testimony was 'sheer speculation' having no evidentiary value. Price Waterhouse lost again. Eventually the US Supreme Court reviewed the case. The American Psychological Society (APA) entered an amicus curiae brief in order 'to disabuse the court of the notion that sex stereotyping was not an identifiable and legally cognizable source of sex discrimination' (Fiske et al., 1991). The Supreme Court was not persuaded that Fiske's expert testimony was 'gossamer evidence' based on 'intuitive hunches'.

This case is important for several reasons. Its appearance in the Supreme Court was the first time psychological evidence on sex stereotyping had been examined in this way. A key distinction was made that the claimant's mental status was not the purpose of the psychological evidence; rather it was drawing on research to demonstrate the conditions that evoked the stereotyping. Finally, the case drew criticism because it was argued that the brief slanted the evidence and forfeited the APA's impartiality and scientific credibility (Barrett and Morris, 1993). Around this time a landmark judgment (*Daubert* v *Merrell Dow Pharmaceutical*) resulted in what have become known as the Daubert Principles (Campbell, 2010). These state that experts should rely on peer-reviewed evidence based on testable theories that are regarded as acceptable by the scientific community and judges should bear these principles in mind when ruling on the admissibility of an expert's evidence.

We have been describing psychologists providing opinion evidence. Psychologists may also become witnesses of fact because their notes or reports about a client could be subject to disclosure (Morgan and Palk, 2012). In some cases a client's documentation could be subpoenaed, which is a court mandated requirement of disclosure.

Box 2.11 Reflective exercise

David Canter (2013) writes:

> For many people 'offender' or 'criminal' or 'personality' profiling implies everything that psychologists and other behavioural and social scientists contribute to law enforcement.

Write down all the activities you can think of that a forensic psychologist might undertake.

Of all of the things you listed, which interests you most?

Identify the forensic setting that most closely matches your interests.

CONCLUSION

This chapter has described various settings in which a forensic psychologist may work. In doing do a number of controversies have been alluded to, including the preferred use of particular kinds of evaluation methodologies, the threats to impartiality, the role as an expert witness.

As well as picking up these themes in subsequent chapters, we spend Chapter 3 describing in more detail the range of courts and tribunals where a forensic psychologist may give evidence. There has been a progressive shift of psychologist involvement in civil cases. Gudjonsson (in Gudjonsson and Haward, 1998) describes results of a survey conducted in 1984 when 51% of cases involved civilian proceedings, rising to 55% in a survey conducted in 1995. By 2007, in a further survey, Gudjonsson found 60% involved reports in civil cases (Gudjonsson, 2008). This perhaps demonstrates that not all activity involves criminal cases.

RESOURCES

The British Psychological Society (BPS) has produced a number of relevant publications, including: *Statements on the Conduct of Psychologists Providing Expert Psychometric Evidence to Courts and Lawyers* (2007), *Guidelines on Memory and the Law* (BPS, 2010a) and *Psychologists as Expert Witnesses: Guidelines and Procedures for England and Wales* (BPS, 2010b).

The Law Society of Scotland (undated) has published a code of practice relating to solicitors engaging expert witnesses (www.expertwitnessscotland.info/code-pract.htm).

The Ministry of Justice website (www.justice.gov.uk/) has a wealth of reports and publications providing details about prison establishments.

Future plans for developing secure estate for children and young people can be found at http://yjbpublications.justice.gov.uk/en-gb/scripts/prodView.asp?idproduct=502&eP.

David Crighton and Graham Towl's book *Psychology in Prisons* (2008) presents a full account of working within the UK prison service and their 2005 edited collection on psychology in probation services provides a useful description of working in this environment.

Peter Ainsworth's *Psychology and Policing in a Changing World* (1995) details the role of psychology within policing.

Key journals

British Journal of Forensic Practice

Criminal Justice and Behaviour

Criminal Behaviour and Mental Health

International Journal of Prisoner Health

Probation Journal

Policing

The Prison Journal

The Probation Journal

NOTES
1 Of course, I never did call myself a forensic psychologist, but rather a criminological psychologist. About 15 years ago there were heated debates in what was then the British Psychological Society's Division of Criminological and Legal Psychology about a possible name change to the Division of Forensic Psychology. The protagonists felt that 'forensic' was a snappier title and more readily understood by the media and the general public. The antagonists knew that 'criminological and legal' was the more accurate terminology. The pragmatists won; the purists lost.
2 www.hud.ac.uk/research/researchcentres/ircip/.
3 www.port.ac.uk/centre-of-forensic-interviewing/.
4 www.birmingham.ac.uk/research/activity/psychology/forensic/cfcp/index.aspx.
5 carleton.ca/policeresearchlab/research/.
6 Evidence-based policing is an approach that believes that all policing practice should be informed by robust and objective evidence of 'what works'. It has gained a lot of support in recent years, particularly through the College of Policing and their drive to professionalize the police.
7 http://work.chron.com/careers-forensic-psychology-fbi-16383.html.

3
THE LEGAL SETTING

KEY CONCEPTS

This chapter describes the key players and settings in which legal proceedings take place. Attention is also drawn to research on aspects of especial interest to forensic psychologists such as witness testimony and statement credibility. Mention is also made of the special status of the role of the expert witness.

Knowledge concepts	Practice considerations
Actus reus	Barristers
Adversarial system	The Bench
Cognitive interview	Coroners
CSI effect	Crown Prosecution Service (CPS)
Fitness to plead	Expert witness
Inquisitorial system	Health and Care Professions Council (HCPC)
Mens rea	
Standards of proof (beyond reasonable doubt	Her Majesty's Inspectorates (HMIs)
and balance of probability)	Judges
'Ticking bomb' problem	Juries
'Weapon focus' effect	Litigants in person
	Procurators fiscal (PFs)
	Protected characteristics

Here you are given a 'Cook's tour' of the legal system in England and Wales and a description of the main courts and tribunals, including Coroners' courts.

There is also an account of the disciplinary body that regulates forensic psychologists, the Health and Care Professions Council (HCPC). Attention is drawn to equalities legislation that should alert you to issues both as an employee and manager delivering services in the public sector.

Questions addressed

What are the key legal concepts and considerations relevant to forensic psychologists?

How are police powers, investigative interviewing and human rights concerns of interest to forensic psychologists?

What is the Crown Prosecution Service?

How are forensic psychologists involved in the prosecution process?

How are courts and tribunals organized in England and Wales?

What are the key roles in the British judicial system?

What systems are used to inspect the major criminal justice agencies?

WHAT ARE THE KEY LEGAL CONCEPTS AND CONSIDERATIONS RELEVANT TO FORENSIC PSYCHOLOGISTS?

It is important that as a forensic psychologist you understand the legal terrain within which you will be working. David Canter (2014) argues that because in the past 40 years psychological aspects of crime have become part of a professional discipline, there is considerable overlap of roles in a variety of legal, investigative, correctional and therapeutic settings therefore 'the influence of legal context and culture as well as local institutional frameworks ... need to be kept in mind' (p. 1). This means being aware of the key institutions, roles and courts in which either potential clients or you yourself as an expert witness may appear. In this brief introduction several legal concepts are explained. It is also important that you are aware of discrimination legislation and the obligations this places on you, especially working with disadvantaged groups and being in the public sector. Finally, as a practitioner you are likely to be or need to be registered with the Health and Care Professions Council (HCPC). The workings of this body are explained.

However, the first thing we want to briefly discuss is the UK's political arrangements – it is a constitutional monarchy, hence the idea of 'the Crown', as in Minister of the Crown. Prosecutions are undertaken on behalf of the state in the name of the monarch by the Crown Prosecution Service. You will see the expression Regina (or Rex) versus Smith in criminal proceedings (Regina for a queen, Rex for a king), which is often abbreviated to R v Smith.

In the UK there is a separation of powers between the legislature, executive and judiciary. Laws are enacted through Parliament. An Act of Parliament starts life as a Bill. Often there is a consultation process in the form of a Green Paper, which sets out what the government of the day is proposing, and a White Paper, which sets out the proposals decided upon having taking representations into account; Malleson and Moules, 2010: 51). A Bill has a number of amending stages through the two Houses of Parliament before receiving royal assent and becoming law. The executive is made up by the officials who implement the requirements of law and includes public bodies such as the prison, police, probation and prosecution services. The courts and judges uphold the law but, as has been seen lately, the government and judiciary may be at odds, such as the protracted amount of time taken to extradite Abu Hamza to face terrorist charges in the United States.

The Ministry of Justice, created in 2007, is responsible for the courts, prisons, probation and constitutional affairs whilst the Home Office retains responsibility for the police and national security. The Minister of Justice is also the Lord Chancellor, a role that dates back to the eleventh century. After the Constitutional Reform Act (2005), the Lord Chancellor no longer takes the role as head of the judiciary or presiding officer of the House of Lords, although the office holder retains responsibility for appointing judges and has a statutory duty to uphold judicial independence and the rule of law.

There are two other important political appointments made by the government of the day: the Attorney General and deputy, the Solicitor General. Both provide legal advice to government. This can be controversial, as in Lord Goldsmith's advice to Prime Minister Tony Blair on the legal basis for declaring war on Iraq. The Attorney General oversees the Crown Prosecution Service and appoints its head, the Director of Public Prosecutions.

There has been in perhaps the past 40 years an increasing tension between the government and the institutions of the criminal justice system (CJS). On the one hand, since 1979, as Chapter 4 documents, there have been drives to seek cost efficiencies in the administration of justice and management of offenders. By 2010 the CJS accounted for £14 billion in public expenditure and major reductions in budgets across the criminal justice system were required to be implemented (Malleson and Moules, 2010). On the other hand there has been an increased political influence on the courts especially through the process of judicial review. This is a procedure that allows challenges to the decisions made by public bodies, including the government. During the 1990s the Conservative government then in power faced numerous judicial reviews and the numbers of challenges have been rising ever since (see Figure 3.1). Berlins and Dyer (2000: 81) express a view that judges are more 'adventurous' than they used to be, especially in their treatment of judicial review applications, many of which are highly critical of government policy. The recent Coalition government (to May 2015) sought to limit recourse to judicial review, which has met with strong criticism (Human Rights Joint Committee, 2014). Annison (2014: 340) argues that 'the British senior judiciary are thoughtful participants in British politics, seeking to affect the course taken by criminal justice and sentencing policy'.

Further reform, such as the funding of legal aid, has also provoked fierce debate about whether saving money in this way is at the expense of access to and quality of justice.

As we discuss in Chapter 5, there has been a politicization of crime and justice issues. Malleson and Moules (2010) note that since 1997 over 20 major criminal justice statutes have been passed and there has been 'an almost constant stream of official reviews' (p. 109). Sentencing has been a particular area of public debate. The Attorney General can instruct that cases where sentences

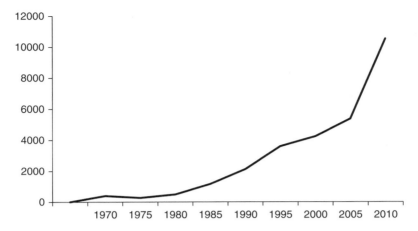

Figure 3.1 Numbers of applications receiving permission for judicial review, 1970-2010. (Source: Ministry of Justice Judicial and Court Statistics for individual years)

are considered too lenient can be referred back to the courts. This happened in the case of the broadcaster Stuart Hall whose 15 months' jail sentence for sexual assaults was doubled by the Court of Appeal. Often such cases attract considerably heated media commentary (Frost, 2010).

Another important concept to introduce here is the adversarial or accusatory legal system, as opposed to an inquisitorial one (Malleson and Moules, 2010: 11–12). The former system, adopted in the UK, is based on a 'contest' in which lawyers present the case for and against the accused, the defendant. Examining witnesses to support their case is called giving evidence in chief; the respective defence and prosecution barristers cross examine witnesses called by their opponent. This questioning is governed by strict rules, with the judge acting as 'umpire' to ensure the procedures are adhered to. The initial presumption is that the accused is innocent until proved guilty so that the prosecution's duty is to present a compelling case demonstrating guilt whilst the defence challenges the soundness of the case against the defendant; they do not have to 'prove' innocence. The threshold for determining the outcome is called the burden of proof and to secure a guilty verdict in a criminal case this has to be beyond reasonable doubt, whilst in civil cases it is on the balance of probability. As will be seen later, the directions given by judges to juries, most notoriously in rape cases, have given rise to controversy.

The inquisitorial system, more common in other European countries, is one in which the judge plays a greater role in deciding which witnesses to call and asking them questions. As lawyers play a more secondary role, there are fewer procedural rules. Judges in inquisitorial systems act as investigating magistrates and can direct police to gather evidence. Scotland has the interesting hybrid role of procurators fiscal (PFs), who investigate all sudden and suspicious deaths. The PF undertakes preliminary investigations, takes written statements from witnesses (known as precognition) and is responsible for the investigation and prosecution of crime, which includes the power to direct the police in their investigation. The PF also presents cases for the prosecution. The independence of the role and functions of the PF was a feature of reforms that brought about the Crown Prosecution Service under the Prosecution of Offences Act 1985.

Finally, before detailing the various locations and institutions of note, the legal concepts of *mens rea* and *actus reus* are defined. A fundamental principle of criminal law is that there has to be both a state of mind, i.e. intention and awareness that the act to be committed is criminal (*mens rea*), and the actual physical committing of the criminal act (*actus reus*). A Court of Appeal case (details given in Box 3.1) illustrates how both have to be present. In the case in question, a Mr Fagan drove onto a police officer's foot when required to stop and park his car. He was requested to reverse the car and declined to do so immediately. He was charged and found guilty of an assault even though he claimed his initial action of driving onto the officer's foot was an accident and therefore unintentional (i.e., no *mens rea*). He appealed. Although the initial action may have been unintentional, as soon as Mr Fagan realized the car's wheel was on the officer's foot, the act became a criminal assault when he chose not to reverse the car, i.e. he intentionally chose to leave the car on the officer's foot thereby causing an injury. So the *mens rea* might not have been present when the accidental driving onto the officer's foot first occurred (that being the *actus reus*) but there was *mens rea* in not reversing and thereby causing an intentional harm.

Box 3.1 *Fagan v Metropolitan Police Commissioner*

Divisional Court 31 July 1968 [1968]3 W.L.R. 1120 [1969] 1 QB 439

On 31 August 1967, the appellant [Mr Fagan] was reversing a motor car in Fortunegate Road, London, NW10, when police Constable Morris directed him to drive the car forwards to the kerbside and standing in front of the car pointed out a suitable place in which to park. At first the appellant stopped the car too far from the kerb for the officer's liking. Morris asked him to park closer and indicated a precise spot. The appellant drove forward towards him and stopped the car with the offside wheel on Morris's left foot. 'Get off, you are on my foot,' said the officer. 'F**k you, you can wait,' said the appellant. The engine of the car stopped running. Morris repeated several times, 'Get off my foot.' The appellant said reluctantly 'Okay man, okay,' and then slowly turned on the ignition of the vehicle and reversed it off the officer's foot.

For an assault to be committed both the elements of *actus reus* and *mens rea* must be present at the same time. The *actus reus* is the action causing the effect on the victim's mind. The *mens rea* is the intention to cause that effect. It is not necessary that *mens rea* should be present at the inception of the *actus reus*; it can be superimposed upon an existing act.

HOW ARE POLICE POWERS, INVESTIGATIVE INTERVIEWING AND HUMAN RIGHTS CONCERNS OF INTEREST TO FORENSIC PSYCHOLOGISTS?

Parliament and the courts try to strike a balance between the police's ability to prevent and detect crime and the rights of the citizen. A key piece of legislation setting out police powers in England and Wales is the Police and Criminal Evidence Act of 1984, commonly referred to as PACE. Malleson and Moules (2010) suggest that the balancing of police powers and citizen rights rather depends on the political mood at the time, and in recent years politicians have sought to extend police powers such as ending the right of silence to suspects being questioned by the police and restricting rights to bail. To counter this, the Human Rights Act of 1998 incorporated the European Convention on Human Rights into domestic UK law. Four particular sections of this legislation relate to the exercise of police powers: right to a fair trial; freedom from arbitrary detention; freedom from inhumane and degrading treatment; right to privacy.

Human rights considerations have exercised forensic psychologists, not least because of the potential of dual role conflicts (Blackburn, 1996; Birgden and Ward, 2009). Thus as a treatment provider, there may be conflicts if the forensic psychologist also has to provide an assessment of an offender for legal purposes or has to provide advice to management about safe practices for staff. Ward and Birgden (2007) discuss the human rights of offenders. They acknowledge that offenders' personal liberty is restricted by incarceration, but they ask to what extent do offenders forfeit other human rights because of the offences they have committed? Human rights violations can occur because of abuses of power, client vulnerability, blurred role boundaries and a lack of respect for an individual's rights and dignity. We touched on the professional–personal dialectic dilemma earlier, i.e. where the provider of treatment to an offender is in conflict with their personal distaste for the crime committed. Ward and Birgden (2007) extend human rights concerns to the area of assessment and monitoring of offenders as well as treatment. They counsel that extreme care should be taken when gathering information about an individual's criminogenic needs so that any decisions affecting the offender's freedom and well-being are rationally justified. Moreover, risk assessment may be strongly influenced by public anxiety and the interest of the community, such that 'political and social agendas strongly influence the process' (p. 639). They make the point that the forensic psychologist provides an opinion about the probability of risk and it is for courts or tribunals to decide about the acceptability of that risk. Finally, they suggest that there may be pressure to subsume the human rights of an offender to serve the interests of other members of the community and propose that offenders' rights should not only be acknowledged but also counted 'equally' in any assessment process. This can be in tension with the growth in the movement of victims' rights we discuss later.

Forensic psychologists are also involved in providing advice during suspect interviewing and the interrogation of suspected terrorists. Birgden and Ward

(2009) draw attention to allegations of psychologists' involvement in torture or at least acting as consultants who help develop and teach such interrogation strategies. The dilemma this presents is the 'ticking bomb' problem. If there is a possibility that coercive means may reveal information to disarm a device that otherwise could result in mass killing is the discomfort of the one justified in the protection of the many? Keegan (2011: 98) puts the dilemma thus:

> [t]he basis for torture as a means of protecting human rights relies on a calculus in which the initial violation is essentially cancelled out by the security gained, a security in which a wider scale of human rights can be enjoyed.

Box 3.2 Reflective exercise

Philosophers use thought experiments to get us to think about moral dilemmas. Philippa Foot (1967) uses this example.

Suppose you are the driver of a runaway tram which you can only steer from one narrow track to another. Five men are working on one track and one man is working on the other. Whichever track the tram enters will plough through and kill whoever is working there. Do you switch to the track with one or five workmen?

Foot argues that most of us would choose the death of one rather than five. Foot then applies this dilemma to a medical and legal examples. Do we keep dangerous lunatics confined in order to preserve public safety?

What do you think is the moral justification for the indeterminate sentences that keeps those categorized as having DSPD incarcerated beyond the tariff of the offence they committed?

Take another of Foot's dilemmas:

Suppose a judge is faced with a riotous mob demanding that a culprit be found for a certain crime otherwise they will exact a bloody revenge on a particular section of the community. The real culprit is unknown. The judge sees that he/she may be able to prevent wide-scale bloodshed only by framing some innocent person and having him/her executed to satisfy the mob.

She suggests that there is an additional feature implied in the second example. What do you think this additional aspect is?

The doctrine of double effect as explained by Foot (1967) is based on the distinction between what a person foresees as the consequences of a voluntary act and what is intended, even if the means to achieve a good end are regrettable. The double effects referred to are the twin effects an action may produce, the potential good which is the intention and the other foreseen but undesired outcome. The added dimension to the legal conundrum in Box 3.2 is that it involves the corruption of the rule of law and potentially undermines the principles of justice. Do we, for example, usurp the rule of law by summarily executing extremists in our fight against terrorism.

Keegan (2011) argues in his paper that not only is torture morally unacceptable, but also pragmatically – the information gained is likely to be unreliable – and its occurrence will have the unintended consequence of radicalizing the victims' associates and wider population.

Gudjonsson (2010) raises the issue of suspect vulnerability more generally within police interviewing and the role of forensic psychologists in exploiting potential vulnerabilities to secure admissions. These areas may involve human rights violations and be in contravention of ethical codes of practice.

A huge amount of forensic psychology interest has been spent in developing techniques to enhance investigative interviewing (Bull et al., 2009; Köhnken et al., 1999; Memon et al., 2010; Milne and Bull, 1999, 2003). In the aftermath of various miscarriages of justice, the Home Office and Police Service initiated research (Baldwin, 1992) that revealed police interviews often lacked preparation, and were riddled with poor interviewing techniques and general ineptitude. This review led to the creation of an ethos (such as keeping an open mind, and acting fairly) that was to underpin investigative interviewing and the PEACE training model. An acronym for planning and preparation, engage and explain, account, closure and evaluation, PEACE offered two approaches, one derived from conversation management (Shepherd, 1993), which was thought particularly useful when interviewing resistant suspects, and the cognitive interview (CI), which proved useful when interviewing cooperative witnesses (Milne and Bull, 1999).

Developed from some original work by Fisher and Geiselman (1992), the CI comprises a series of memory retrieval and communication techniques designed to increase the amount of information that can be obtained from a witness. It is based upon a psychological understanding of the factors that affect memory, such as stress levels or the involvement of the witness in the events in question and memory recall factors such as interference and degrading effects of delay (Milne and Bull, 1999). Memon, Meissner and Fraser's (2010) meta-analysis suggested that previous critiques of policing interviewing methods resulted in revision to the PEACE training, which has now been incorporated within the Professionalizing Investigation Programme (PIP) since 2009.

WHAT IS THE CROWN PROSECUTION SERVICE?

The Crown Prosecution Service (CPS) was created in 1986 as a consequence of the Philips Royal Commission on Criminal Procedure. The view was formed by the Commission that a counterbalance was needed to the increased powers given to the police through the provisions of PACE. Prior to that in England and Wales the decision to prosecute, or not, was taken by the police.

As explained above, the head of the CPS is the Director of Public Prosecutions (DPP), who is appointed by and responsible to the Attorney General. The Criminal Justice Act of 2003 established that the CPS could be involved in determining the charges to be brought against a person. Once a person is charged with an offence, the CPS prepares papers for a trial and presents the case in court. The decision to prosecute is based on two tests: the realistic prospect of success, and public interest. A code for prosecutors sets out guidance as to what should be taken into account and progressively this has made more reference to the position of the victim. Decisions are made to discontinue or proceed with the prosecution.

HOW ARE FORENSIC PSYCHOLOGISTS INVOLVED IN THE PROSECUTION PROCESS?

Fitness to plead is a fundamental principle in British law (Rogers et al., 2008) and is reflected in the human rights discussion above, i.e. when a defendant declares whether they are guilty or not guilty of the crime they have been accused of, they should be competent to make such a declaration. This is related to the desire to ensure that those who are mentally ill, have learning disabilities or are suffering a mental disorder receive treatment rather than punishment. Forensic psychologists can be involved in fitness to plead assessments. Rogers and colleagues outline five assessment criteria:

- Ability to plead
- Ability to understand evidence
- Ability to understand court proceedings
- Ability to instruct a lawyer
- Knowing that a juror can be challenged.

The CPS may discontinue legal proceedings if a person's mental health considerations outweigh the interests of justice. It is considered unjust for someone to stand trial if they are unfit to plead or lack the capacity to understand the proceedings (Murphy and Clare, 2003). There is no standardized test of fitness to plead (for a review of a variety of instruments see Rogers et al., 2008), including the audit tool developed by Catherine Dooley and others issued as guidance by the British Psychological Society (2010c).

HOW ARE COURTS AND TRIBUNALS ORGANIZED IN ENGLAND AND WALES?

CRIMINAL AND CIVIL COURTS

Courts hear both criminal and civil matters. County Courts, also referred to as small claims courts, deal with matters such as debt repayments, breach of contract and housing disputes. All criminal cases start life in a magistrates' court. The seriousness of the offence will determine if the case can be dealt with by the magistrate or needs to be sent to the Crown Court. Serious offences such as murder and rape are classified as 'indictable only' whereas motoring offences or criminal damage and such like are classified as summary offences. The former are dealt with by Crown Courts and the latter by magistrates' courts. There is a class of offences termed 'either way' which may be dealt with in either court. Cases heard in magistrates' courts have a panel of two or three magistrates or a district judge and there is no jury. At Crown Court, cases are heard by a judge in front of a jury.

Most cases are dealt with in magistrates' courts where, more often than not, defendants plead guilty and the magistrate's role is to decide on a sentence. Contested cases are relatively rare. Mostly, young people under the age of 17 are tried by magistrates in youth courts. The Crown Court hears the more serious cases and also appeals of decisions made by magistrates. Appeals from the Crown Court are heard by the Court of Appeal and thereafter the Supreme Court. Civil cases also have a route to the Supreme Court. (See Figure 3.2)

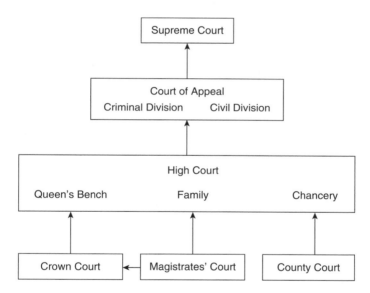

Figure 3.2   Organizational diagram of the main courts in England and Wales

More recently, an interesting body of research has looked at (criminal) courtroom architecture and the spatial practices adopted (Mulcahy, 2007, 2010, 2013). Mulcahy makes the suggestion that space and its control within the courtroom is an exercise in power. Thus the elevation of the judge, sitting in front of a royal coat of arms, is symbolic of the authority and legitimacy of the proceedings. Carlen (1976) previously suggested that the exploitation of courtroom space can be intimidating to those not used to the court system. The court is a segregated space with the advocates, witnesses and spectators not only having designated areas but also different entrances. In particular, the placement of the defendant in 'the dock' argues Mulcahy (2013), is redolent with meaning. Secure docks are not only physically elevated but have a protective screen which makes communication between the defendant and advocate difficult. As Mulcahy argues, the use of the dock implies that the defendant should remain silent and passive and could interfere with the presumption of innocence, with some research even suggesting it may impact jurors' assessments. Docks continue to be used in some European courts, although they are absent in Holland and Denmark.

Special measures introduced to assist vulnerable witnesses include the use of a screen so that the witness cannot see the defendant in the dock. Live TV links were introduced in England and Wales through provisions of the 1999 Youth Justice and Criminal Evidence Act (Bull, 2010).

CORONERS' COURTS AND INQUESTS

A Coroner is an independent judicial official who is paid for by the local authority in which he or she serves. Coroners are either lawyers or doctors or sometimes both. They are charged with looking into violent or unnatural deaths, sudden deaths of unknown origin and deaths that occur in prison. The Coroner presides over an inquest to determine the identity of the deceased, when and where their death came about. Inquests do not apportion blame, they are fact-finding exercises. Usually a death is referred to a Coroner by the police or possibly some other body such as the Health and Safety Executive, the prison authorities, the Care Quality Commission or the Independent Police Complaints Commission (Ministry of Justice, 2010a).

A death may be reported if, for example:

- a doctor did not attend during the last illness;
- it was the result of an industrial accident;
- it was unexpected or sudden or unnatural;
- was due to neglect or violence;
- occurred in the custody of the police or prison services;
- occurred during an operation, before recovery from or from the effects of an anaesthetic.

The Coroner may request a post-mortem (and does not need the consent of relatives to do so). If a person has been charged with causing the death, the inquest is adjourned until the criminal trial is over. Most inquests are held in the absence of a jury, but juries are called if the death occurred in prison or a police cell or was the result of an accident at work.

A Coroner may give a number of possible verdicts, such as death due to natural causes, accident or misadventure, suicide, unlawful killing, lawful killing, industrial disease and an open verdict where there is insufficient evidence to come to a view. Coroners may also provide a narrative verdict which sets out the facts in more detail and explains the verdict reached.

Box 3.3 Example of a narrative verdict from the Worcestershire Coroner's Court

INQUEST TOUCHING THE DEATH of: Dana Louise BAKER

Narrative verdict

At approximately 5 p.m. on the 3rd of March 2011 Dana Baker hanged herself with the clear and deliberate intention of ending her own life. She did so following the breakdown of her relationship with her foster carers to whom she was profoundly attached. Her death was contributed to by a failure to have in place adequate measures to protect her from a known, present and continuing risk that she would kill herself.

G U Williams
H M Senior Coroner
County of Worcestershire
Date 29 May 2014

Most verdicts conclude that the death was from natural causes or was an accident. In 2013, of the total number of deaths recorded, 45% (227,984) were reported to a Coroner. Of these, about 30,000 (13%) were the subject of an inquest. Fewer than 1% of these (154) were recorded as a homicide. Figure 3.3 shows the verdicts by gender for the year 2013.

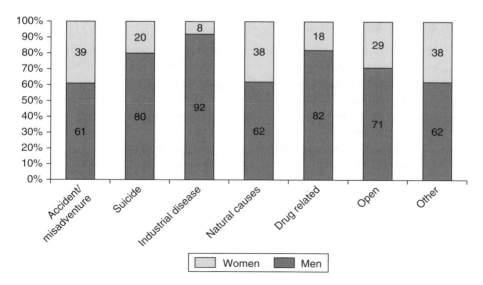

Figure 3.3 Conclusions recorded at inquests by gender in England and Wales, 2013. (Source: MOJ, Coroners' statistics)

TRIBUNALS

There is a parallel system of tribunals, which are also courts of law dealing with employment, health, education, immigration and other issues. These are referred to as first tier. Mental health comes under the jurisdiction of the Health, Education and Social Care Chamber. Appellate hearings, i.e. when the decision of a lower tribunal or body is appealed, are exemplified by the Employment Appeal Tribunal (EAT) or the Police Appeals Tribunal (PAT) and these are referred to as second tier or upper tribunals. The Administrative Appeals Chamber is an upper tribunal where mental health appeal cases are heard.

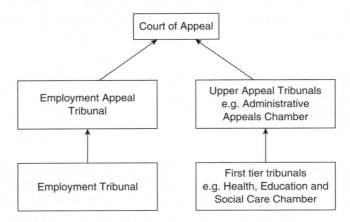

Figure 3.4   Organizational structure of tribunals in England and Wales

EMPLOYMENT TRIBUNAL AND EQUALITY LEGISLATION

It is important to know about Employment Tribunals and discrimination law for three reasons. As an employee yourself you should know how you are protected from discrimination, and as a manager you need to know the rights of people you are responsible for. You also need to be aware of the general public sector equality duty that pertains to many of the forensic settings where you may work in the delivery of services.

The 2010 Equalities Act consolidated previous discrimination legislation and in sum it is unlawful to discriminate on grounds of any of the following: age, being a transsexual person, being married or in a civil partnership, being pregnant or having a child, having a disability, on grounds of race, nationality or ethnic origin, religion, belief or lack of religion or belief, sex, sexual orientation. All of these are referred to as 'protected characteristics'. Discrimination can be direct, for example, treating someone less favourably because they have one of the protected characteristics, or indirect, where someone with a protected characteristic is put at a particular disadvantage even though the rules apply to everyone.

The criminal justice system is demographically unequal in that there are many more men in the law than women, and certainly the police and prison services have a greater proportion of men to women serving as officers. Such structural inequalities can give rise to discrimination and harassment. This has led to a considerable body of research that examines occupational cultures and its impact on the experiences of women, ethnic minorities and those having a non-heterosexual orientation (see chapters by Dick, Silvestri and Westmarland, by Jones, and by Rowe, respectively, in the edited collection by Brown (2014) for reviews of gender, sexual orientation and race discrimination issues respectively in the Police Service).

Equality legislation makes provision for positive action where there are demographic disparities such that training, encouragement or other arrangements can be made for underrepresented groups, for example, a police force may hold a recruitment day specially for women and ethnic minority recruits (Equality and Human Rights Commission, 2009). Positive action is different to positive discrimination, which is when a person is given preferential treatment on the basis of a protected characteristic and is unlawful. However, employers can use a preference in a tie-break situation. Supposing two candidates are equivalent in most respects in their ability to do a job, a preference can be exercised in favour of a candidate who is from an underrepresented group. In practice it is quite difficult to determine equivalence.

Employment tribunals hear claims of unequal treatment if these have not been resolved in the organization or through a mediation process. There have been a number of important cases: for example, within the Police Service, Alison Halford, Sarah Lockyer and more recently Carol Howard brought attention to harassing and discriminatory treatment against women and those from an ethnic minority. In the latter case Police Constable Howard was a member of the Metropolitan Police's Diplomatic Protection Group (DPG), which required her to be an authorized firearms user. She successfully claimed before an Employment Tribunal that she had been treated differently and discriminately on grounds of her gender and race.

Box 3.4   Employment Tribunal judgment in the case of Carol Howard

Howard v Metropolitan Police Service (2014) Case no. 2200184/2013 & 2202916/2013

The picture that emerges when one puts all the above incidents together is that within a few weeks of becoming the Claimant's [Carol Howard] line manager, [Inspector] Al Kelly formed a view, without any sound basis for doing so, that the Claimant was dishonest and not up to the standard required by DPG [Diplomatic Protection Group]. Linked to that was another view, equally without foundation, that his colleagues were frightened to deal with these issues

(Continued)

because the Claimant was black and female and might complain of discrimination. Thereafter he embarked on a course on conduct that was designed to, and which in fact did, undermine, discredit and belittle her – every absence was assumed not to be genuine and was probed and investigated, shooting sessions were booked for her, her commitment was challenged in front of two sergeants, her sergeants were instructed to investigate her on spurious grounds.

DPG was at the relevant time, and probably still is, an almost exclusively male and predominantly white unit. The Claimant stood out in the unit because she was different from almost everyone else in it because she was black and she was female ... There was no evidence that the negative perception that Al Kelly had of the Claimant was based on any knowledge that he had of her from other sources. One is therefore driven to the conclusion that the negative perception must have been based on what he saw – a black woman.

The Police Service, as are other public sector bodies bound under section 149 of the Equalities Act (2010), is directed to eliminate unlawful discrimination, harassment and victimization, and actively advance equality of opportunity and foster good relations between people who share protected characteristics. Police Services in particular have been accused of institutional racism (i.e. the collective failure of an organization to provide an appropriate and professional service to people because of their colour, culture or ethnic origin; it can be seen or detected in processes, attitudes and behaviour that amount to discrimination through unwitting prejudice, ignorance, thoughtlessness and racial stereotyping) in the aftermath of the Stephen Lawrence shooting and Lord Macpherson's subsequent inquiry (see, e.g., Rowe, 2007 which discusses the implications of the 1999 Macpherson Report).

HEALTH AND CARE PROFESSIONS COUNCIL

In 2012 the Health and Care Professions Council (HCPC) was established. Its predecessor organizations were the Council for the Professions Supplementary to Medicine (CPSM) and the Health Professions Council (HPC). The HCPC regulates 16 professions, including psychologists. The total number of professionals who come under the jurisdiction of the HCPC is around 322,305 as at 10 July 2014 (HCPC, 2014). Of these 20,057 (6%) are psychologists. The majority of registrants are clinical psychologists, with about 4% having a forensic psychology designation. The HCPC's primary function is protection of the public, which it fulfils by setting and publishing standards of proficiency for each of the registered professions as well as standards of conduct, performance and ethics that apply to all registrants, and by considering complaints against registrants. It is required reading that you look at the relevant documents (standards of performance and standards of performance ethics and conduct, available from the HCPC website – see Resources below). This is a regulatory body which is different from but works with the professional body, in this case the British Psychological Society and in particular the Division of Forensic Psychology.

In its fitness to practise function, the HCPC adopts the same test as most other healthcare regulators. The HCPC definition of fitness to practise is that practitioners

> have the skills, knowledge and character to practise their profession safely and effectively. However, fitness to practise is not just about professional performance. It also includes acts by a professional which may affect public protection or confidence in the profession. This may include matters not directly related to professional practice. If a professional's fitness to practise is 'impaired', it means that there are concerns about their ability to practise safely and effectively. This may mean that they should not practise at all, or that they should be limited in what they are allowed to do. (HCPC, 2013)

Impairment can be alleged on the grounds of misconduct, lack of competence, physical or mental health, criminal conviction or caution or a determination of impairment by another health or social care regulator. The HCPC also has powers to investigate allegations of fraudulent or incorrect entry on the register. Complaints may arise from clients, service users, employers or former employers of the registrant in question. Once a complaint is made it is referred to an Investigating Committee Panel which will consider whether there is a case to answer. If there is, the case is referred to either the Conduct and Competence Committee or the Health Committee, depending on the nature of the allegation. Once investigated, a panel of the relevant committee will be convened to hear the complaint. Investigations may take a few months but also can last several years. The hearing is a formal procedure and often a registrant is legally represented. The outcome may be no case to answer, a caution, a conditions of practice order or expulsion from the register, i.e. striking off, which inhibits the person from continuing to practise.

A tiny fraction of HCPC registrants, about 0.5% on average, are subject to disciplinary hearings, although the number is rising and of these, practitioner psychologists figure significantly (see Figure 3.5).

Per capita, psychologists are the third largest group of health practitioners subject to concern (0.93%) and in volume were the third largest number of registrants (179). The types of problems that take a psychologist registrant to a hearing included inadequate record keeping, inappropriate relationship with a service user, or breaching of service user confidentiality. Maintaining professional standards is clearly a significant issue and is there to protect the public. Being caught up in a disciplinary process is stressful and an experience to be avoided.

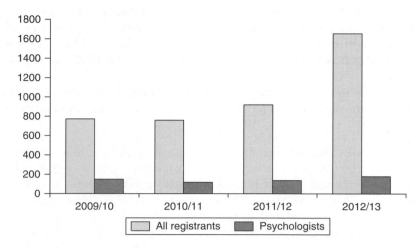

Figure 3.5 Number of fitness to practise cases heard by the HCPC, 2009–2013, (Source: HCPC, 2013)

Box 3.5 Commentary on the disciplinary process

Disciplinary issues in terms of professional misconduct and fitness to practise are the remit of regulatory bodies. Whilst some disciplinary matters can be identified and dealt with at organizational level, there is still a requirement to inform the relevant regulatory body as to the presenting issue and the outcome. A decision is then made as to whether they need to enact any further investigation. In general terms the disciplinary procedure is applied where a practitioner's decisions and/or behaviours are considered to have breached the code of professional conduct, and include concerns relating to fitness to practise by way of ill-health. Codes of conduct, such as those of the HCPC, are designed to ensure that we offer the best services to our clients, and where courage can be required to deal with difficult issues as opposed to simply avoiding or turning away from them. It further focuses on educating and inspiring best practice in its members.

I have previously spent a number of years being a member of an Investigatory Committee as well as workplace investigations. As part of this, there are always the obvious instances where a code of professional practice has clearly been broken, and where penalties are then introduced. These penalties can be varied, including implementation of supervision, provision of training, a temporary period of suspension or even expulsion. These are the obvious cases that most individuals would easily determine as wrong and which clearly bring the profession into disrepute. These can include a significant breach of professional boundaries or engagement in a serious criminal act. Yet others require more detailed consideration, and where there can be much debate as to whether a code has been breached, where the quality of the presenting evidence is brought into question, or where the matter may be more of a professional difference in opinion as opposed to a breach of any code of practice.

What is important to appreciate, is that when working in a professional capacity there is always the presentation of ethical considerations and dilemmas in our work, and which require us to make choices. If it is felt that an individual has breached their professional code, then the first step is always to inform the regulatory body. Once it is clear as to which part of the code is alleged to have been potentially breached, then a process begins whereby the parties involved present written evidence, and which is managed and coordinated by the regulatory body. However, once it is felt that there is sufficient evidence to at least pursue an allegation this is then orchestrated by the regulatory body, in this instance the HCPC, as opposed to the initial instigator of the allegation. There can be a number of stages at which such allegations can progress, and where at each stage there can be a decision to discontinue. This may be at the initial stage when the allegation/s are made, or there can be an initial meeting by the regulatory body to discuss the principles of the case. If it is felt there is sufficient evidence (prima facie) in terms of the allegation then this will proceed to an oral hearing, where both sides present their cases. This can also be true where it is felt that the allegations are of sufficient gravity that it is in the public interest to proceed to a hearing in any event, and where such smaller pre-meetings may be felt to be insufficient as a result. Examples may be those that have been met with a certain degree of media or political interest. As such, the procedure of determining if misconduct has taken place is not a simple one. It can take a number of years to reach a resolution (the last two I was involved in lasted over two years from the point of allegation to its resolution), and where the oral hearings can be public. As such, this can have a significant detrimental impact on the individual who is the subject of the allegation(s), both professionally and personally. This is irrespective of whether allegations are found to have been true or not. Professionals who have had their conduct questioned have often reported to me over the years that they feel their life is on hold, their resilience is tested and that they are unable to make significant career decisions until a resolution is reached. As such, I would encourage individuals to consider carefully the impact on those where misconduct has been queried. Such allegations not only question their working roles but can also pose questions as to the type of individuals they view themselves to be and how this contrasts to any allegations made. This is not to say that such allegations of misconduct should not be made; of course they should if the evidence is sufficient and it clearly fits a breach of a code.

(Continued)

I would always implore professionals to think carefully about using such procedures. In terms of regulation, they are designed to protect the public and keep them safe, and are not a forum by which to play out any other intentions or motivation. For example, I would on occasion review cases as part of investigations where it was simply a difference of professional opinion, not a case of misconduct. I also observed allegations where they appeared more emotionally driven, seeming to form part of a more complex dynamic. This would be noted in the arguments presented as part of the allegations, and where rationality would appear to have become lost.

If you are in a position where an allegation is made against you, it is always helpful to remove the emotion from any response and to address each point carefully, with evidence, and in the timeframes set. I have seen some clinicians choose not to engage in the process as they feel it is unfair. In such circumstances the consideration of the allegations will simply take place in their absence, which should never be the preferred route. I have also noted responses that have been driven by determining the motives of the individual/s who have placed the allegation/s; again this simply distracts from the focus of the process and can prolong it.

All allegations are serious and can have far-reaching implications for those involved, both psychologically and in terms of general career paths, even if such allegations are eventually dismissed. As part of this, I am strongly of the view that professionals need to be supported when allegations are made. This is irrespective as to whether we form the view that misconduct has taken place or not. In much the same way as any legal representative would support their client, the same must be said of those who have had complaints made against them. Unless they openly admit to misconduct, we must always regard allegations as allegations. In my experience those who have had complaints made against them require emotional and professional support. It can lead some individuals to question their own abilities and confidence can be shaken. An approach of empathy toward a difficult circumstance must be undertaken, and which is not necessarily one of sympathy. Yet, I have seen such allegations made in the early careers of some clinicians which has then damaged their confidence and self-esteem in the longer term, even when such allegations were not supported and no misconduct was found. Such support is clearly not the remit of the regulatory body, yet an identified other should undertake this role, to support and guide, and to ensure a careful, considered and rational approach is encouraged.

My experience of the HCPC, such as giving evidence and supporting clinician's through the process, would be similar to my experience of other professional bodies. This focuses on the appreciation that ethical dilemmas form part of our daily professional role, and where there may be more than one solution. The important factor is the attempt to work through ethical dilemmas with clear ethical decision making. If as part of this it can be considered that a clinician should clearly have made a different choice, then an acknowledgement of this is regarded more positively than simply arguing that their initial decision was correct. The very nature of our profession is to reflect on our decisions and to recognize when things could have been done differently. It is no different when there are questions in terms of alleged misconduct. This is not to concede that you have done something wrong when you feel this is not the case, but to give consideration to the possibility that some things could have been done differently. This shows a regulatory body that you are an individual who can reflect on your actions, which is an expectation of our profession. Doing so can instil faith within the regulatory body that you have the potential to reflect and then act on these considerations.

My general thoughts in regard to the HCPC is that it is a significantly more drawn out process compared to my other experiences. I appreciate the need to gather information in a clear manner. Yet, I am less clear when this can take a number of years, and with the passage of time the very information that is required can begin to get lost or become eroded. Little attention is paid toward the impact of this on the professional whose conduct is brought into question, and who can feel their 'life is on hold'. Whilst I would not expect the HCPC to offer any level of support in regard to this – it is not their role – I do think more could be done toward recognizing the potential impact. I have often experienced the HCPC process to be a chaotic one in terms of some procedures, processes and timeframes, with long periods of silence and then a flurry of activity. As such, I would always suggest that legal support is utilized as part of liability insurance for any clinician, and to help guide them through the process.

In summary and as a general rule of working to our codes of conduct, I would always be mindful of the work of Francis (2009). This includes the consideration that where a career has been tarnished by an ethical breach, in almost every case, the breach has been preventable. Further, you should always interact with your client as though your professional relationship is going to be a long-term one and ethics is a skill that can be taught. Codes of conduct, including those of the HCPC, offer us guides to inform our practice, overarching principles and where we should aim to work to the letter of the code as well as its spirit. Ultimately, as long as the work we undertake can demonstrate evidence-based practice, ethical decision making and that we are fit to undertake the work, then disciplinary processes are unlikely to take place, and if they do, they are less likely to proceed to misconduct.

THE PAROLE BOARD

The Parole Board of England and Wales was established in 1968 as a provision of the Criminal Justice Act (1967), becoming an executive non-departmental independent public body by virtue of the Criminal Justice and Public Order Act of 1994. The Parole Board carries out risk assessments on prisoners and manages:

- early release of prisoners serving fixed-length sentences of four years or more;
- release of prisoners who are serving life sentences or indeterminate sentences of imprisonment for public protection (IPPs);
- re-release of prisoners who have been given life or an IPP and were then re-imprisoned;
- recommendations of suitability for transfer to open prisons.

The risk assessments have the primary aim of protecting the public but also contribute to the rehabilitation of the offender (Parole Board, 2014). Typically the Parole Board receives a dossier containing the judge's sentencing remarks, reports from prison and probation staff (typically offender supervisors or managers) and details of the prisoner's offending history. There is also likely to be a formal risk assessment based on static features (e.g. prior convictions) and dynamic features (e.g. behaviour in prisons) as well as courses completed whilst incarcerated. There may also be a victim impact statement (see Chapter 8). Parole Boards have a (paper) panel to consider the file or may refer the case to a full oral hearing.

The oral hearing usually takes place in prison and may also be heard via a video link. Usually there are three Parole Board members on the panel and often there is a psychologist or psychiatrist present. The prisoner can be legally represented. Victims may attend as well as witnesses on behalf of the prisoner, such as their offender manager or prison psychologist. The issue at stake is whether the prisoner continues to pose a risk.

One of the troubling aspects of IPPs is that these offenders may be disadvantaged at parole hearings because they have been unable to attend courses whilst in prison that may demonstrate a lessening of their risk. Another problem is the dilemma posed by a person declaring their innocence (see Box 3.6 for an example).

Box 3.6 *R v Mohammed Hanif Khan*

[2012] EWCA Crim 2361, 9 October 2012

An IPP sentence was replaced with a determinate sentence with an extended licence where a prisoner maintaining innocence was unlikely to secure future release.

Mr Khan appealed a conviction of child sex offences for which he was given an IPP sentence with a minimum tariff of 8 years based on the judge's finding in relation to dangerousness. Because he maintained his innocence, he was ineligible for admission to an accredited sex offender treatment programme and hence unlikely to be able to demonstrate a reduction in his risk in order to secure his release at a future Parole Board hearing, notwithstanding a pre-sentence report confirming that he would be suitable for offending behaviour courses on licence, some of which are compatible with a denial of guilt. The Appeal judges concluded that Mr Khan 'would then never be regarded by the Parole Board as being eligible for release on licence and he will be "stuck in the system"'. The Court of Appeal quashed the IPP sentence and imposed a custodial determinate sentence of 16 years with a 5-year extended licence.

THE SENTENCING GUIDELINES COMMISSION

The Coroners and Justice Act of 2009 established the Sentencing Guidelines Commission whose purpose is to set authoritative guidance on the sentences available to judges in Crown Courts as well as to magistrates. The Commission also has a general remit to raise public awareness and understanding of sentencing issues.

WHAT ARE THE KEY ROLES IN THE BRITISH JUDICIAL SYSTEM?

JUDGES

Judges in the UK tend to be appointed from the ranks of practising barristers or solicitors and appointments are scrutinized by the Commission for Judicial Appointments. Collectively judges are also termed 'the Bench'. The make-up of the judiciary is still predominantly male (see Figure 3.6) and white, although some inroads are being made in the magistracy and upper tier courts.

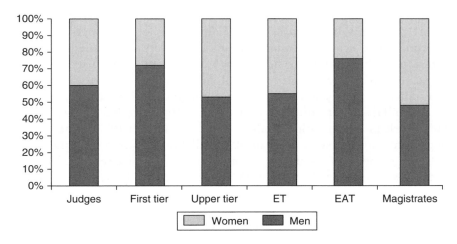

Figure 3.6 Gender distribution of the judiciary, 2012–2013. (Source: Ministry of Justice)

The proportion of judges across the different courts and tribunals from visible ethnic minorities is only between 6 and 14%. Given that appointments tend to made from experienced lawyers, that increases the average age (only recently were judges required to retire at the age of 70) leading to charges that judges are out of touch. One judge famously was said to have asked who The Beatles were during a trial.

Judges' decision making has been the subject of empirical study (e.g. Dhami, 2003; Spohn, 1991). An important aspect of the judge's role is giving directions to juries. Comments may, for example, be made about the way evidence is approached and in cases of rape about why a victim may have delayed in reporting. Ellison and Munro (2009) used a mock jury study to examine the relative impact of judges' directions and experts' explanations about the demeanour of the victim, whether she resisted or not and whether she delayed in reporting a rape. Whilst these researchers caution extrapolation from role play experimental conditions to the real courtroom, they did find that judicial instruction was a mechanism 'to disavow jurors of their ignorance or biased assumptions in regard to what constitutes "credible" rape complainants' behaviour' (p. 374). Dhami (2008) showed experimentally that although she too cautions about the general applicability of the results given her study respondents were student mock jurors, she established that lay judgments of reasonable doubt differed to the standards generally adopted by judges.

Relatively few studies are undertaken looking at actual judges' real decision making. Langevoort (1998) suggests that there is an association between more liberal interpretations of evidence and the political leanings of judges in the United States.

BARRISTERS

The legal profession is broadly divided into two branches: solicitors and barristers. The latter by and large are self-employed and work collectively in a set of chambers. In England and Wales they must be members of one of four Inns of Court (Lincoln's Inn, Gray's Inn, Middle Temple and Inner Temple). On completing their academic qualifications, barristers are 'called to the Bar' which is a formal ceremony held in whichever Inn of Court the person is attached to. Often you will see 'year of call' attached to a barrister's details which indicates their years of experience. Once called, a barrister must complete a pupillage before offering their services to represent clients. Solicitors usually work in partnerships. Malleson and Moules (2010) say that the UK's arrangements are unusual, as in most jurisdictions lawyers undertake a common training and then specialize in commercial work or advocacy. In terms of presenting a case at court, most often this is done by a barrister, but solicitors also have what is called 'rights of audience'. A defendant of course may also represent themselves as a 'litigant in person'. Usually a person requiring legal representation seeks advice from a solicitor who then 'instructs' a barrister to present the case in court. With recent cuts in legal aid, there has been a rise in the number of people attempting to represent themselves.

Collectively the term 'the Bar' refers to barristers. As with judges, it is still a largely male profession with about one-third of the 15,000 or so barristers in England and Wales being women and about 9% are from an ethnic minority. About 10% of the Bar is made up of Queen's Counsel (QC), also known as 'Silks'. 'Taking silk' designates a barrister as a senior advocate and appointments are made by an independent selection panel. Box 3.7 provides greater detail of the role of the barrister and some differences when presenting a case for the prosecution or defence in criminal cases.

Box 3.7   Gavin Collett on the role of a barrister

Having studied Law and Social Sciences at Sussex University I attended the Inns of Court School of Law (the only Bar school in those days). Twenty-eight dinners eaten and a lot of exams passed saw me called to the Bar in 1993. A year of pupillage and 21 years of practice has left me experienced in the law but continuously flummoxed by human nature.

A barrister has to foremost assist the court and the judge, then to fight for his or her client, try to keep their instructing solicitor happy and above all (as far as possible), ensure that justice is not only done but seen to be done. While this seems a complete contradiction in some respects actually it's not, as very few people would argue with a just result. This does, however, sometimes mean that the barrister must stand up to a judge if that judge is being misled or worse being misleading! However, such occasions are very rare. More commonly the conflict arises from the client and the way the case is presented in court.

A barrister can never mislead (or worse lie to), a court. Indeed perhaps the most two commonly asked questions are how can you defend the guilty and how can you defend someone when the evidence is completely against them? Well, firstly, if the client says they are guilty then you cannot argue their innocence (unless they have a defence in law that they are unaware of, and that has only happened once in 20 years to me and normally it's less frequent than that). If they have admitted their guilt you can mitigate but never defend.

The second question is more common: how can I defend someone who claims that he or she is innocent when all the available evidence points to their guilt. In my view this is precisely when an accused needs a good advocate. The fact that all the 'prosecution' evidence points to their guilt is expected – that is the purpose of prosecution evidence. If it pointed to their innocence then hopefully the charges would have been dropped. It is for the professional advocate to review the evidence, to consider what evidence can be brought to challenge the prosecution case and how to present that evidence. If I accept the prosecution evidence at face value and believe my client to be guilty then I have ceased to

(Continued)

be his or her advocate and have become their judge and jury, roles that are already filled within the court system. If I prejudged my client's guilt (or innocence for that matter), then I am not their advocate and I should withdraw from their case immediately.

Finally one is often asked how can you defend 'that' man or woman? Normally this is where there is a considerable amount of press interest over a particular crime. It may be that the offence involves children or other vulnerable people, or the crime is particularly violent or cruel, or simply the views of the accused are unpopular at the time. In these circumstances the role of the independent advocate is crucial. If the accused has no voice and cannot defend himself, then how can the just verdict be obtained? It is imperative that any case is properly argued before judge and jury so that the right verdict can be reached, and in the case of those found guilty, so that they cannot argue that they did not have a fair trial or have been victimized by the stigma of popular opinion. Worse still, if an innocent defendant is convicted not only is that unjust but it means that the real criminal is free to offend again!

So irrelevant of how bad the case looks against an accused, the barrister must approach his or her task fearlessly. I sometimes wonder when reading about 'fat cat' lawyers interfering with justice whether those accusers would equally have condemned the few lawyers who stood up for the minority oppressed in 1938 Germany against the fascist majority who had equal condemnation for such fearless advocates.

Is there a difference in approach to presenting a prosecution case and a defence case?

In a typical lawyer fashion the answer to this question is yes and no! In a prosecution case the barrister will present the prosecution evidence and then challenge any evidence brought forward by the defence. The defence barrister will do the reverse and to that simple extent the answer is no.

However, this is far from the end of the story. In the case of the prosecution barrister it is not his or her job to 'persecute' merely to present the evidence. If the prosecution case is well founded the facts should speak for themselves. Clearly the evidence has to be presented in a form and manner that a jury will understand and be able to follow. To that extent there is a skill to prosecution and it is sometimes overlooked that the best case can be lost if the barrister is not careful and confuses the court or presents evidence in a disjointed way.

A defence barrister has to challenge this evidence but in doing so he or she cannot create evidence or mislead the court. Often the defence barrister will have to challenge the evidence of vulnerable or confused witnesses, and this takes a particular skill in itself. Often when lay people are asked to emulate a barrister they will ask a series of questions aggressively; often, not even waiting for a reply. Rarely does this ever happen in court and in any event such an approach would be pointless. It is the witnesses' answers to questions that will make or break a case not the questions they were asked. If you take an aggressive approach you risk reducing the witness to tears, stopping any useful evidential points and losing the sympathy of the court. As is so often ignored by popular fiction, cross-examination does not mean you have to be 'cross' when conducting it. A gentle but firm line of questions will often illicit far more useful information and evidence than a few barked orders.

Perhaps the only answer to this question is that in every case it will need a different approach on a case-by-case basis by both prosecution and defence barristers and probably it is just as well that it is that way.

Research into barristers has looked at their emotional stress load (Healy, 2014) and also gender differences in advocacy (Smyth and Mishra, 2014). The latter examined transcripts of cases presented to the High Court in Australia and reported that appellants represented by a woman barrister were less likely to receive a High Court justice's vote than when represented by male colleagues. Having panels with more women justices was associated with greater likelihood of voting for cases represented by women barristers. Research has also been undertaken of defendants' satisfaction with their lawyers (Raaijmakers et al., 2014). Looking at Dutch defendants, they found high levels of satisfaction, although this was greater if the advocate was a privately hired lawyer rather than a court appointed lawyer. Overall, defendants are more satisfied with their interactions with the criminal justice system if they feel they can participate, and they are treated with dignity and respect.

WITNESSES

There are two kinds of witnesses: a witness of fact and an expert witness. The first is a person who has direct knowledge of some aspect of the events in question and could be an 'eye' witness or indeed an 'ear' witness. There has been a great deal of forensic psychology interest in eyewitnesses and the reliability of their evidence (for a review see Bull, 2004; Howitt, 2006; Ghetti et al., 2004, and a short accessible chapter by Memon, 2008). Much of the research effort has been directed at accuracy and generally speaking people are good at being able to identify gender, eye shape, hair colour but are more equivocal about race, height and age (Van Koppen and Lochun, 1997). Witness confidence has also been an issue of interest and linked to potential miscarriages of justice. Ainsworth (2000: 166) describes the case of Patrick Murphy by way of an example. In 1992, a London taxi driver was stopped, threatened with a gun and told to drive to the Prime Minister's residence in Downing Street, a bomb having been placed in the cab. The driver was able to abandon the taxi and shout a warning before the bomb exploded. An Irishman, Patrick Murphy, was arrested by the police as the bomber and in an identity line-up Mr Murphy was recognized by three different people. Fortunately for Mr Murphy he was able to prove that he had been attending an Alcoholics Anonymous meeting at the material time and all charges were dropped. This is one of many examples of confident identification that was actually mistaken (Davies, 1996).

Memon (2008) describes some of the variables that influence accuracy of eyewitnesses. These include visibility, distance from the person, or trauma associated with the events witnessed. The 'weapon focus' effect is a term given to the impact an emotionally arousing stressor such as the presence of a gun has on accuracy, particularly the face of the perpetrator. In addition, there are a host of demographic characteristics such as the race of the identifier and the perpetrator that may impact accuracy. A witness is more likely to recognize a person from their own race. Older witnesses tend to be less accurate. A considerable amount of research effort has gone into identification procedures. Evidence is variable as to accuracy and Memon concludes that mistaken identification is still a cause of miscarriages of justice.

Ray Bull (2004) has taken a particular interest in earwitness testimony, i.e. voice identification. He notes (pp. 169–70) that

- voice identification is more difficult than visual;
- identifying a stranger's voice is particularly difficult;
- voice identification is wrong more often compared to visual identification.

In courts in England and Wales, following a number of miscarriages of justice based on identification evidence, guidance known as the Turnbull Directions made distinctions between good- and poor-quality identifications (the former being when there has been a relatively long exposure to seeing the suspect and the latter when this was only fleeting). Judges' directions contain cautions to the jury about reliance placed on identification evidence.

The expert witness is someone who provides an opinion based on their particular expertise. Psychologists did not present evidence as expert witnesses until the late 1950s (see Coleman and Mackay, 1993 and Gudjonsson and Haward, 1998 for a brief history). Psychologists may present expert testimonies in civil as well as criminal courts and also in other tribunals such as mental health and employment tribunals, and in parole hearings. As has been mentioned earlier (see Chapter 2 and 7), in the United States there are specific rulings as to the standards of expert evidence (Frye and Daubert tests).

The expert's role is to assist the court over a technical matter and he or she may be asked to prepare a report by either side, i.e. defence or prosecution. Wrightsman and Fulero (2005: 35) point out the risk of becoming a 'hired gun', in which the expert works in the interest of the side that employed them rather than in the interests of presenting their findings objectively. Box 3.8 details a lawyer's perspective of some of the requirements of expert testimony.

Box 3.8   An expert from a lawyer's point of view, by Gavin Collett

Sometimes the facts of a case will call for an expert witness to give evidence. In the United Kingdom such evidence can only be introduced with leave of the court, in other words, a judge has allowed it. This also means that both prosecution and defence teams will be aware if such evidence is going to be used so that neither side can 'ambush' their opponents. Frequently, in more recent times, a joint expert is instructed so that costs are not wasted and hopefully a definitive answer can be reached, but this is not always possible. This is particularly true where the subject of the enquiry cannot be reviewed, such as psychology evidence as opposed to broken glass or skid marks on a road. Where two experts are called, often the court will hear their evidence back to back so that the jury, or judge, can appreciate the variance between the opinions and the reasons for it. (Clearly if there is no disagreement between the experts they will not be called but a prepared statement will probably simply be read.)

Calling an expert witness the barrister will be expecting him or her to meet criteria in three main skill areas.

Education (degrees and training)

- Specific knowledge of the subject area.
- Practical experience (if possible).
- Publications and/or teaching.
- Any required licensing or certification.
- A history as an expert witness or consultant.

Educate counsel

- Evaluate the client's position and assist in the case development.
- Provide testing or experiments to assist counsel with what the other side's evidence means.
- If need be, suggest or obtain other expert witnesses.

Give evidence at the trial

- Provide written statements.
- Have sufficient presentation skills for the courtroom.
- Prepare demonstrations or explain complex results in understandable terms.
- Have a balanced approach to the case.

The first of these areas is obvious. An expert must be just that. Informed amateurs can be found in any public bar but to be able to be a credible expert witness

(Continued)

you must understand and be at the forefront of your field. It is worth noting that expert witnesses are the only people other than direct witnesses of fact that are allowed to give their 'opinion' as to what the correct evidential position should be. So they have to be 'expert' in their field. It is better that they wrote the leading textbook rather than merely read it. Nobel prizes also help, but so will 30 years of experience!

The second requirement is perhaps less well known. Before a barrister can present evidence he or she must be able to understand it. The expert has therefore to educate counsel in their area of expertise, not only to the degree where counsel understands it, but also so that they can cross-examine the other side's expert as well. This may involve experiments or tests, either to recreate the alleged circumstances or to disprove them. Finally it may be that one expert realizes that they do not have the necessary knowledge base and will need to recommend another expert. It would be a foolish person that tries to bluff their way through a cross-examination in the full glare of the court on a subject they are not utterly familiar with.

The third requirement is that an expert is also a good witness. They first have to provide a comprehensive written statement; simply stating facts is not enough. The methodology used has to be understood, transparent and, of course, right. Once the expert is in court he or she has to make themselves understood. A poor speaking style, mumbling or simply being incomprehensible through overuse of jargon or technicalities all means that the evidential value is reduced, or worse, lost. We can all remember teachers that brought subjects alive, or alternatively, those that drained the interest from a subject to the point of boredom.

Finally, and in all respects, the expert witness must take a balanced view of the case. If he or she becomes too involved in the case and cannot see alternatives, even when demonstrated, they have lost their impartiality and have become the judge or jury themselves. In these instances their evidence becomes worthless, even if it is right.

Of some interest is the role of 'offender profilers' as experts. Freckelton (2008) notes that whilst the insights of profilers (BIAs – behavioural investigative advisers) and forensic psychologists are increasingly being used at the investigative stage, the question arises as to whether this material should be admissible in court. By and large Anglo-American and Australian courts have shown a disinclination to permit profiling evidence, partly because of its speculative nature. One particular form of profiling is the psychological autopsy (Ogloff and Otto, 1993), which is an attempt to discern the state of mind of a deceased person in cases of suicide or equivocal death and has been used in Coroners' courts in the United States.

In the UK there are two cases of particular interest in relation to the limits of admissibility of psychological evidence: the appeal case of Eddie Gilfoyle and the criminal case against Colin Stagg (Norris and Petherick, 2010; Wilson et al., 1997).

In the Gilfoyle case (Gilfoyle [2001] 2 Cr App R 57) Mr Gilfoyle had been convicted of the murder of his pregnant wife, who was found hanging in the garage of their home. A suicide note was found next to her body. An analysis was presented in court to suggest that the note did not contain the 'hallmarks of Paula Gilfoyle's own writings and further it was not consistent with a woman who planned on taking her own life' (Norris and Petherick, 2010: 41). The Court of Appeal declined to accept the expert evidence on the following grounds:

> while psychological evidence relating to the state of mind of a victim or defendant that fell short of mental illness could be admitted in certain cases if derived from medical records or established criteria, the existing academic standing of psychological autopsies was not sufficient to allow their admittance as expert evidence ... it was apparent that the psychologist, whilst an expert in the field, had not previously attempted the task required of him in the instant case. Moreover the psychological reports were speculative and could not be validated quantitatively or by previous established research.

In the Colin Stagg case, he was indicted for the murder of Rachel Nickell on Wimbledon Common in 1992. Paul Brittain provided a psychological profile and advice to an undercover officer in an attempt to reveal Stagg's supposed sexually violent behaviour (Alison and Rainbow, 2011). The profile indicated that the sexual predilections of the likely offender were highly idiosyncratic such that the chances of two people on the Common having these characteristics were highly unlikely. In the event, the case against Mr Stagg was dismissed and Robert Napper was subsequently convicted of the murder. Alison and Rainbow (2011: xv) noted that Mr Stagg made a complaint about the profile on the grounds that as a consequence of it he had been prioritized as a suspect. Norris and Petherick (2010: 46) write of this case that despite much in the profile being correct, in the absence of reliable statistics on the prevalence of the behaviours in question there remained uncertainty about rates of occurrence. Thus:

> [t]he fact that Robert Napper and Colin Stagg were both present on the common the day Rachel Nickell was murdered and they both had a predilection for violent sexual behaviour is a good example of the prosecutor's fallacy. We have assumed because the incident rate for this behaviour is so small ... that the chances of this occurring are so minute that it renders the defendant almost 'automatically' guilty in the eyes of the average juror.

Norris and Petherick conclude (2010: 31) from a legal perspective there remains some scepticism in the case of profiling evidence being presented in court. Wilson, Lincoln and Kocsis (1997: 8) raise the question of professional competence and suggested that the problems arising from the Stagg case 'should not be used to condemn profiling outright'.

JURORS

Within an adversarial system, juries comprise members of the public who are chosen to assess the evidence presented during a trial and come to a view – usually guilty or not guilty of the charges. Scotland in addition has a 'not proven' verdict, which is tantamount to an acquittal. In England and Wales there are 12 members of a jury (15 in Scotland) and verdicts may be cast with a majority (ten to two in England and Wales).

The decision making and behaviour of actual juries are difficult to study because of legal restrictions in accessing jurors' deliberations. Thus mock jury experimental studies, often with student participants, and documentary analyses of actual cases outcomes are employed to study decision making processes (see Penrod et al., 2011 for a review of the different methods employed). One particular criticism of mock jury studies is the ecological validity problem, i.e. the potential methodological artefacts that may be present in simulations such as the lack of any consequence for the decision reached in the experimental setting. Much of the research has paid attention to potential biases in decision making (see Hope, 2010 for a brief review) and in the United States there has been considerable effort expended on jury selection strategies (Davis and Follette, 2004).

As mentioned above, judges' directions can influence juries' decisions and there is research to suggest that jurors struggle to understand judges' instructions (Bornstein and Hamm, 2012). They report findings from mock jury studies that show jurors may be influenced by judges' non-verbal behaviours if the judge either believes or does not believe the defendant to be guilty. Judges' directions can also influence perceptions of liability in civil cases. Their series of studies concluded that modifying instructions to jurors did not necessarily sensitize them to pertinent issues.

The influence of pre-trial publicity has interested psychologists from the advent of its involvement in law. Schrenck-Notzing, a graduate of Wundt's Leipzig laboratory, was asked about the impact of extensive and sensational press coverage in the case of a defendant accused of a triple murder. Schrenck-Notzing presented the results of laboratory experiments in suggestibility and errors in recall due to a process he termed 'retroactive memory falsification' to the court (Bartol and Bartol, 2006 [1987]). He concluded that witnesses were unable to distinguish between what they had seen and what they had read in the press coverage. More up-to-date experiments conclude that pre-trial publicity does have an influence on mock jurors rendering a guilty or not guilty verdict (Kovera and Greathouse, 2009).

The other area causing some concern is the so-called 'CSI effect'. There have been several series of a TV show, *Crime Scene Investigation*, in which the appliance of forensic science techniques seems to render infallible evidence as to the guilt or innocence of suspects. Schweitzer and Saks (2007) found that *CSI*-viewing mock jurors tended to be more critical of forensic evidence compared to non-viewers. More non-*CSI* mock jurors would convict (29%) compared to *CSI* viewers (18%), although this was not statistically significantly different. *CSI* viewers were also more confident in their verdicts compared to non-viewers.

WHAT SYSTEMS ARE USED TO INSPECT THE MAJOR CRIMINAL JUSTICE AGENCIES?

The criminal justice system is inspected for its standards and efficiency by:

- Her Majesty's Inspectorate of Constabulary (HMIC)
- Her Majesty's Crown Prosecution Service Inspectorate (HMCPSI)
- Her Majesty's Inspectorate of Prisons (HMI Prisons)
- Her Majesty's Inspectorate of Probation (HMI Probation).

They produce annual reports, a wealth of statistical data and also undertake thematic and joint inspections on a number of topics. HMIC was established in 1856 to ensure the efficiency of police forces in England and Wales. The Royal Commission on Policing in 1962 recommended that a Chief Inspector of Constabulary be appointed to coordinate strategic planning. The Royal Commission also recommended the establishment of a research unit within the Home Office under the direction of the Chief Inspector. The inspectorate conducts base-line inspections of all police forces in England and Wales and also undertakes thematic inspections of a small number of forces on topics such as equal opportunities and diversity. It also looks at national policy, such as the management of counter-terrorism, and was responsible for a major project on modernizing the workforce. The inspectorate can be directed by the Home Secretary to look into specific matters, such as the policing of domestic violence. Their report (Her Majesty's Inspectorate of Constabulary, 2014) came to the stark conclusion that the police's response was 'not good enough'.

More recently there has been some adjustment to the work of the HMIC because of the advent of Police and Crime Commissioners (PCCs) and the establishment of the College of Policing. Martyn Underhill describes the role of a PCC (see Box 3.9).

Box 3.9   Martyn Underhill on being a Police and Crime Commissioner

I retired from the police, having been an SIO, and having used psychologists such as Terri in real-life cases. As postgraduates, you enter this world at a time of unprecedented change. The 'chess board' I call the criminal justice system has seen many, many changes in a small period of time; some pieces have arrived and some have disappeared – PCCs, the College of Policing, the National Crime Agency, the National Police Council have all replaced other agencies or authorities.

The role of Police and Crime Commissioner is a controversial and exciting change in police accountability. PCCs don't run the police operationally, the

(Continued)

Chief Constable does that. PCCs set direction, they create Police and Crime Plans the police work to, and they govern the police, scrutinize their activity and make them more accountable to the public.

Since my arrival, I have reversed decisions made by Dorset Police that the public found unacceptable, such as disbanding the marine policing unit. I have held them to account and made them change procedures in relation to the 101 non-emergency number, closure of police station enquiry desks and speed camera enforcement.

The hardest part of my role is reaching the public, all of them! I hear a lot about hard-to-reach communities, and I always say that there are no hard-to-reach groups, just hard-to-reach services. Engagement is key to my role.

I was delighted and flattered to win the national COPAC 'Community Engagement Award' earlier this year, suggesting we are getting some of the engagement right.

I always say that the clue to the role of the PCC is in the name, and the largest part of my role is actually the 'and crime' bit of the title. I am busy directing resource and commissioning money into community projects, early intervention in schools, providing youth cybercrime advice, funding mental health triage and liaison and diversion, and expanding street pastors. In short, I fund issues that help keep communities safe.

This is a huge role, covering a vast area, and if the politicians are to be believed, the role will morph and change dramatically in the next two years. I am very relaxed about that, as long as the public accountability remains, I welcome change and new direction. Police Authorities were invisible and ineffectual; we must never return to that model.

I am often asked – Would I do it all again? Absolutely!

HMI Probation looks at the effectiveness of work with adults, children and young people. The inspections examine a representative sample of offender cases to assess whether each aspect of work was done efficiently and effectively. HMI Prisons reports on the conditions and treatment of those in prison, young offender institutions, secure training centres, immigration detention centres and court custody suites, customs custody facilities and military detention. There is a Chief Inspector, some of whom in recent years have been outspoken about the state of prisons, particularly David Ramsbotham and Anne Owers, and most recently Nick Harwicke.

HMCPSI assesses the work of the Crown Prosecution Service, again by examining a selection of cases. The inspectorate ensures the Code for Crown Prosecutors is applied correctly, notably that prosecutions are undertaken both in the public interest and with a reasonable chance of securing a conviction. Systemic problems are identified, such as failures to weigh the strength of identification or forensic evidence (noted in the latest annual report). They too undertake thematic reviews, for example on youth offender casework, and they evaluate pilot schemes such as the early guilty plea.

An important series of joint inspections was undertaken by HMIC and HMCPSI on the conduct of rape enquiries by the police and prosecutions by the CPS. The Police and Justice Act of 2006 established the Criminal Justice Joint Inspection to coordinate the activities of the four inspectorates.

RESOURCES

Clive Hollin's book *Psychology and Crime* (2013) has highly readable chapters on police practice and the courts.

David Faulkner's chapter on the justice system in England and Wales in Towl and Crighton's edited collection *Forensic Psychology* (2010) is a useful succinct summary of the major tribunals and courts.

Practice standards and ethical conduct documents are available from the HCPC website at: www.hcpc-uk.org.uk/assets/documents/10002963SOP_Practitioner_psychologists.pdf and www.hcpc-uk.org.uk/assets/documents/10003B6EStandardsofconduct,performanceandethics.pdf.

An historic account of Old Bailey cases is well worth viewing at: www.oldbaileyonline.org.

Her Majesty's Inspectorates have websites that contain a wealth of information, reports and statistics at: www.justiceinspectorates.gov.uk.

The Ministry of Justice website also has information about courts tribunals and the Coroner's service at: www.gov.uk/government/organisations/ministry-of-justice.

Lorraine Hope (2013) provides a detailed overview of interviewing in forensic settings.

Key journals

Equal Opportunities Review

Journal of Forensic Psychiatry and Psychology

Journal of Law and Society

Psychology Public Policy and Law

4
IDEOLOGICAL CONTEXT

KEY CONCEPTS

As explained in the introductory chapter, here we give an account of the last three decades of government thinking and policy that sets out the requirements for working within the criminal justice system. We introduce readers to a number of relevant concepts.

Knowledge concepts	Practice considerations
Best value (BV)	Acts of Parliament
Big Society	Green Papers
Neo-liberalism	Private finance initiative (PFI)
New Public Management (NPM)	What Works centres
Payment by results (PbR)	White Papers
Rehabilitation revolution	
Value for money (VFM)	

This chapter provides the backcloth to the stage one legal and criminal justice context and forensic settings curricula requirements as well as explaining how policies were derived as precursors to designing staff development and training within core role 4 of stage two.

Questions addressed

What has political philosophy got to do with us?

What is the origin of government policies that impact the working environments of forensic psychologists?

What is New Public Management?

How was the rehabilitation revolution idea born from the Big Society idea?

What are the different financial models driving government policies?

What impact has government policy had on criminal justice agencies?

WHAT HAS POLITICAL PHILOSOPHY GOT TO DO WITH US?

Crime and imprisonment are the 'stuff' of forensic psychology, with much of its thinking and interventions revolving around these twin pillars. Over the last three decades or so there have been two strong undercurrents directing the shape of criminal justice policies and practice, one ideological the other more political. This chapter tackles the first of these and the next chapter takes on the second. In particular, the chapter explains the concept of 'neo-liberalism' and its practical manifestation, New Public Management (NPM), which dramatically changed the way criminal justice services (police, prison, probation and the Courts) are organized and managed. These next two chapters describe the rise and practice implications of managerialism and explain the background to the debates this has engendered.

Criminologists and sociologists have argued that not only has political life come to play an increasing role in shaping the agencies within which forensic psychologists work, it has also infiltrated the consciousness of citizens (Loader and Sparks, 2012). Downes and Morgan (2012) suggest that law and order has, since the 1979 general election, certainly in Great Britain, become a much more potent force, with slogans such as 'prison works', adopted by Michael Howard when he was the Conservative Party's Home Secretary, and 'tough on crime and tough on the causes of crime', an election mantra of Tony Blair when shadow Home Secretary. Crime rates, particularly as recorded crime began to rise 'exponentially' through the 1980s and into the 1990s, became a politicized issue (Loveday, 1996: 77). Sentencing, incarceration rates and the hearts and minds battle over punitiveness versus rehabilitation have been topics of considerable debate over the past 30 years (Ward and Maruna, 2007). This chapter looks at why this became so and some of the subsequent ramifications.

WHAT IS THE ORIGIN OF GOVERNMENT POLICIES THAT IMPACT THE WORKING ENVIRONMENTS OF FORENSIC PSYCHOLOGISTS?

In the opening chapter we suggested that forensic psychologists should be aware of the context within which they work. To do this in some depth requires an appreciation of the political philosophy underlying much economic policy that has been developed over the past 40 years. In 2010, the UK's Coalition government published its programme aimed at converging

> Conservative plans to strengthen families and encourage social responsibility, and add to them the Liberal Democrat passion for protecting our civil liberties and stopping the relentless incursion of the state into the

lives of individuals; you create a Big Society matched by big citizens. This offers the potential to completely recast the relationship between people and the state. (Her Majesty's Government, 2010: 8)

Included in the document were plans to reform the police, introduce a 'rehabilitation revolution' whereby independent providers will be paid based on their success in reducing reoffending, explore alternative forms of secure, treatment-based accommodation for mentally ill offenders, and carry out a fundamental review of legal aid. These policies were subsequently implemented and are having a profound effect on the sites where forensic psychologists work, e.g. probation (Deering, 2014), special hospitals, particularly in reference to the treatment of dangerous and severe personality disorder (DSPD) offenders (O'Loughlin, 2014), and in the police (Independent Police Commission, 2013). These policies are the inexorable culmination of the practical implementation of a political philosophy called neo-liberalism.

Neo-liberalism is the common label given to an economic theory postulating the benefits of freeing markets to maximize efficiency and prosperity by enabling consumers to make choices about which producers of services they wish to use. Reiner (2007: 1–2) defines neo-liberalism as a

> theory of political economic practices that proposes that human well-being can best be advanced by liberating individual entrepreneurial freedoms and skills within an institutional framework characterized by strong private property rights, free markets, and free trade.

Services managed by the state in the form of the public sector, in accordance with this thinking, are converted into markets, either by privatizing provision or introducing internal markets within monopolies that remain in state ownership, or by de-regulating private industry. Once this is done the state withdraws from being the sole provider, instead creating a plurality of means to deliver these services.

Harvey (2005: 6) goes on to say

> [t]he process of neo-liberalism has, however, entailed much 'creative destruction' not only of prior institutional frameworks and powers ... but also divisions of labour, social relations, welfare provisions, technological mixes, ways of life and thought, reproductive activities, attachments to the land and habits of the heart.

Thus, goes the neo-liberal argument, social good will be achieved by maximizing the mechanisms of the market and bringing all human transactions within its purview. Harvey argues that the adoption of some version of the policies deriving from neo-liberalism has been virtually a world-wide phenomenon. This was because the political consensus that dominated the reconstruction of nations after the Second World War broke down. That consensus accepted a blend of state, market and regulatory institutions to guarantee peace and prosperity, at least in Western industrialized nations. By the 1960s both international and domestic economies were under pressure, exacerbated by the oil crisis of 1973. In Harvey's view, neo-liberalism was the 'potential antidote' to economic melt-down (p. 19).

Although it was neo-liberalism that prevailed, this was by no means uncon-tested, and the 'creative destruction', mentioned by Harvey, has not gone unnoted (Reiner, 2007, 2012, 2013). Reiner proposes that civil disorder, simpli-fication of the role of justice agencies, particularly the police and partiality in the use of evidence can be laid at the door of the 'neo-liberal hegemony' of the past 40 years (Reiner, 2012: 136). He argues (Reiner, 2007: 3–8) that free mar-kets are prone to generating concentrations of power, create greater inequalities and promote consumption by the rich rather than responding to human needs. He also suggests that, in turn, inequality produces social consequences, nota-bly poor health, social conflict and violence. As well as exhibiting these social consequences there is also an ethical deficit, in that neo-liberalism tends to cultivate egoism, and short termism, with little concern about the wider rami-fications for future societal needs. His proposed alternative is a form of social democracy, which we will return to in Chapter 13.

But if we take the UK as a case example, we can show how neo-liberalism and its accoutrements came to be adopted. In the latter part of James Callaghan's Labour government (1976–9), they were forced to impose stringent cuts in public expenditure as a condition of their acceptance of financial assistance from the International Monetary Fund (IMF). This sparked a breakdown in industrial rela-tions and created the 'winter of discontent' marked by strife and strikes. The economy was in crisis, crime was rising and the Conservative opposition declared that the country had become 'ungovernable' (Downes and Morgan, 2012).

The restoration of law and order became a hotly contested political issue. So, by 1984, the Conservative Thatcher government announced a series of redundancies and pit closures thereby provoking a year-long strike of coal miners. This was an emblematic confrontation partly because the National Union of Miners tended to be in the vanguard of pay settlements and partly because this dispute contributed to a process called the politicization of the police (Reiner, 2010: 78–80). As Savage (2007: 171) explains, a previous Conservative government had been wounded by a miners strike in 1972 and a plan had been formulated to build up stocks of coal and strengthen the police to help in a future confron-tation with the miners. To civil libertarians, the policing of the miners' strike and later civil disorder compromised the police's impartiality and stimulated calls for greater accountability. Reform of the Police Service was to be a par-ticular feature of government over the next three decades.

Once the miners had lost their political struggle with the government, the stage was set to introduce market disciplines into the public sector, including the agencies of criminal justice. The state shifted from being a sole provider to a regulator and supervisor of services (McLaughlin and Murji, 2001). The Audit Commission was established to help introduce devolved budgeting, perfor-mance management and a market approach (Savage and Charman, 1996). Together with the activities of think tanks such as the Adam Smith Institute, and the Institute of Economic Affairs, innovations developed that collectively bore the title of New Public Management (NPM), whose purpose was to alter the formulation and delivery of public service (McLaughlin and Murji, 2001).

WHAT IS NEW PUBLIC MANAGEMENT?

A critical concept in the management and organization of public services in general and those within which forensic psychologists in particular work is New Public Management (NPM). McLaughlin and Osborne (2002: 1) suggest that 'the UK has played a pivotal role in the development of the New Public Management paradigm and can arguably claim to have been its "birthplace" ... However the impact of NPM has spread far beyond [the UK] and it has become one of the dominant paradigms for public management across the world, and in particular in North America, Australasia and the Pacific Rim.'

Given this view that it was within the UK that the seeds of NPM were sown, we use this experience to show how the approach fared and more specifically how this has impacted forensic psychology settings. The ground into which the embryonic NPM became planted was made fertile by a number of factors from the late 1970s: economic crisis, a right-wing political critique of the welfare state and the dependency culture this was said to instigate in citizens, and a particular Conservative (party political) castigation of both the professional cadre and public officials who were said not only to be inefficient and ineffective, but also to put their needs above those of the users of the services (Osborne and McLaughlin, 2002: 8). Thus, as Maddock (1999: 131) characterizes it, hierarchical public sector organizations were to be radically reformed; there was to be no more 'buck' passing or operating within a culture of inertia with staff neither coming into direct contact with their clients nor taking responsibility for the consequences of their decisions or hiding behind and positively revelling in 'red tape'.

This critique – of bureaucracy, attacks on the energy-sapping dependency of the welfare state, the patrician attitudes of professional elites and the trades unions' self-interest – would, it was claimed, if unchecked, see 'unacceptable growth in tax bills, an increasingly dissatisfied electorate and declining standards in public services' (Dawson and Dargie, 2002). The drive was to contain costs and improve performance by imposing market disciplines and terms such as 'downsizing', 'hollowing out', 'privatization', 'internal markets' and 'workforce modernization' entered the lexicon. The client became the customer and charters for passengers, patients, victims and pupils proliferated, laying out rights and expectations for standards of service in transport, hospitals, criminal justice and education respectively.

McLaughlin and Murji (2001) observed two waves of NPM in the UK; the first during the Thatcher and Major Conservative administrations and the second during the Blair–Brown Labour administrations. As we shall see in later sections, NPM profoundly changed the ways that agencies of justice were managed and organized. McLaughlin and Murji (2001) itemize some NPM mechanisms and techniques:

- appointment of professional managers to be held accountable for the management of resources and to extract the maximum value from them;
- setting of clear, measurable standards and targets;
- explicit costing of activities;
- development of performance indicators to measure efficiency;
- increased emphasis on outputs rather than processes;
- rationalization of purpose through identification of core tasks and competencies;
- creation of a competitive environment and a split between providers and purchasers of services;
- reconfiguration of recipients of services from clients to customers;
- overhauling of work cultures to improve accountability and productivity.

As they say, NPM is important because it represents 'the post-neo-liberal means through which the public sector is to be managerialized so that it becomes performance-oriented' (p. 109). But NPM was not simply the introduction of market disciplines and private sector managerial practices into the public sector, it was much more. Osborne and McLaughlin (2002) argue that NPM shifted the provision of public services by permitting the creation of the plural providers of these services and a withdrawal or 'rolling back' of the state.

As NPM gained ascendancy, it was not without its critics. NPM's implicit assumption is that private sector management and market disciplines are superior to the model of the old style service ethos of public administration (Osborne and McLaughlin, 2002). Holding that NPM was more about cost-cutting than necessarily introducing efficiencies, a growing body of work disputed its delivery of improvement (Lynn, 1998; Pollitt, 2000). Others have questioned NPM's universal applicability, especially as an apparent panacea to the somewhat different problems faced in the Third World (McCourt, 2002). NPM has also been suggested to erode the vocational element of working in the public service and undermine the social capital and organizational citizenship that this engenders.

When the period of Conservative government ended in 1997, whether New Labour enthusiastically embraced both the principles and policies of neo-liberalism or established a distinctive 'Third Way' is the subject of considerable academic debate (Downes and Morgan, 2012; McLaughlin and Murji, 2001). Nevertheless, NPM became central to New Labour's workforce modernization project. It pursued public–private partnerships and extended private finance initiatives (PFIs), introduced in 1992 by the Conservative government led by John Major. These policies progressively extended into the criminal justice arena as the UK engaged in major reforms of police, prisons and probation over the next two decades. As McLaughlin and Murji (2001) explain, the modernization of criminal justice involved establishment of consistent and mutually re-enforcing aims and objectives, installation of what works/best practice culture, development of an evidence-based approach to the allocation of resources and institutionalizing of performance management to improve productivity. The private sector was to have a greater role in delivery of services that used to be the monopoly of the public sector. Performance regimes, managerialism and fiscal restraint have all had an impact in defining policy and also the working environment.

HOW WAS THE REHABILITATION REVOLUTION IDEA BORN FROM THE BIG SOCIETY IDEA?

The global fiscal crisis triggered by the subprime mortgage collapse in the United States and subsequent bank failures in the United Kingdom characterized the last years of the Brown New Labour administration. Once again the economy was a critical driver of the election. The two key government departments affecting the administration of justice in the UK are the Ministry of Justice (MOJ) and the Home Office. In 2007 there was a major constitutional change which split responsibilities between the Home Office, to concentrate on counter terrorism, policing, asylum and immigration, whilst a new Ministry of Justice was created to take on other criminal justice functions including the National Offender Management Service (i.e. probation and prison) (House of Commons Constitutional Affairs Committee, 2007). As Labour departed office, the incoming Conservative and Liberal Democrat Coalition declared reducing the deficit as a priority. Haldenby et al. (2012) noted that the two justice departments were expected to cut their budgets by 23% before 2014/15 with further cuts of 3–4% in 2015/16 and 2016/17. Prior to this, criminal justice services had enjoyed an extended period of increased funding. In the decade beginning 2000 these increases were averaging 3.3% per annum or a rise of 36% over the decade. From 2010 in an effort to meet targets imposed by the reduction in budgets, there have been cuts in staffing levels. Thus between 2010 and 2012 there was a drop by 10% in police officer numbers, 4% in probation and 3% in operational prison staff – a total loss of 26,061 personnel.

Accompanying the budgetary cuts, the government also set out a reform agenda aiming to transform the administration of justice as mentioned at the opening of this chapter. This included the Big Society idea. As Reiner observes, neo-liberalism is said to promote not only economic efficiency but also personal responsibility (Reiner, 2006). The Big Society agenda was designed to further open up public services, empower local communities and promote greater volunteering and civic participation (Ishkanian, 2014). Although not necessarily promoted as a continuation of the Thatcher neo-liberal policies, Ishkanian argues that since the latter were intended to roll back the state and infiltrate the market into public service delivery, and propounding an emphasis on individual initiative and enterprise, the Big Society agenda does at least resemble neo-liberal policies. This was to involve an even greater diversity of provision of public services, including the voluntary sector, through the mechanism of payment by results.

Rodger (2012) suggests that as part of the Big Society concept the 'rehabilitation revolution' was conceived. In the Green Paper 'Breaking the Cycle' (Ministry of Justice, 2010b) Kenneth Clarke, then Secretary of State for Justice, argued for a 'radically different approach to punishment and rehabilitation', proposing to use the payment by results approach as a mechanism to involve commercial, voluntary and community sector organizations in the delivery of offender management objectives.

Before we proceed to show how these policies developed and impacted the key justice agencies, it is probably helpful, firstly, to chart which political party

Table 4.1 Parties in government, Prime Ministers, Home Secretaries and key events and documents, 1976–2013

Prime Minister/ time period	Political party/ Home Secretaries	Key issues/event/publications/legislation
James Callaghan April 1976–May 1979	**Labour** Merlyn Rees	International Monetary Fund (IMF) settlement 1975/6 'Winter of discontent' – breakdown of industrial relations 1978
Margaret Thatcher May 1979–Nov 1990	**Conservative** William Whitelaw Leon Brittan Douglas Hurd David Waddington	Brixton riots 1981, 1985 HO Circular 114/83 Manpower, effectiveness and efficiency Audit Commission established 1983 Miners' strike 1984/5 Statement of National Objectives and Priorities (SNPO) 1984 HO Circular 106/88 Green Paper 'Punishment, Custody and the Community' 1988 Privatization programme Green Paper 'Supervision and Punishment in the Community' 1990
John Major Nov 1990–May 1997	**Conservative** Kenneth Baker Kenneth Clarke Michael Howard	1990s recession Black Wednesday 1992 Continuation of privatization agenda Criminal Justice Act 1991 National Criminal Intelligence Service 1992 White Paper on police reform 1993 Sheehy Inquiry 1993 Posen Inquiry 1993 Police and Magistrates' Courts Act 1994 Criminal Justice and Public Order Act 1994
Tony Blair May 1997–June 2007	**Labour** Jack Straw David Blunkett Charles Clarke John Reid	Human Rights Act 1998 White Paper 'Modern Local Government' 1998 Local Government Act 1999 Green Paper 'Managing Dangerous People with PD' 1999 Criminal Justice and Courts Services Act 2000 White Paper 'Policing a New Century: Blueprint for Reform' 2001 Criminal Justice and Police Act 2001 Sexual Offences Act 2002 Anti-Social Behaviour Act 2003 Carter Review 2003 White Paper 'Building Communities and Beating Crime' 2004

(Continued)

Table 4.1 (Continued)

Prime Minister/ time period	Political party/ Home Secretaries	Key issues/event/publications/legislation
		National Offender Management Service created 2004 Serious Organized Crime and Police Act 2005 London bombings 2005 Police and Justice Act 2006
Gordon Brown June 2007–May 2010	**Labour** Jacqui Smith Alan Johnson	Financial crisis 2007–10 Policing and Crime Bill 2008
David Cameron May 2010–2015	**Conservative– Liberal Democrat Coalition** Theresa May	Programme for Government 2010 Austerity Comprehensive Spending Reviews Green Paper 'Breaking the Cycle' 2010 Winsor Review 2010/11 Riots summer 2011 Police Reform and Social Responsibility Acts 2011 Closure of NPIA announced 2011 White Paper 'Swift and Sure Justice' 2012 Formal opening of the College of Policing 2013 Audit Commission disbanded 2013 Legal Aid, Sentencing and Punishment of Offenders Act 2013

Table 4.2 Definitions of Parliament's documents

Document	Definition
Green Paper	Consultation document produced by the government, especially when a department is considering introducing a new law. The aim of this document is to allow people both inside and outside Parliament to debate the subject and give the department feedback on its suggestions.
White Paper	A document produced by the government setting out details of future policy on a particular subject. A White Paper will often be the basis for a Bill to be put before Parliament and allows the government an opportunity to gather feedback before it formally presents the policies as a Bill.
Bill	A proposal for a new law, or a proposal to change an existing law, that is presented for debate before Parliament. Bills are introduced in either the House of Commons or House of Lords for examination, discussion and amendment. When both Houses have agreed on the content of a Bill it is then presented to the reigning monarch for approval (known as Royal Assent). Once Royal Assent is given a Bill becomes an Act of Parliament and is law.
Act of Parliament	Part of the work of Parliament is to make laws. These are called Acts of Parliament. Usually the House of Commons and the House of Lords both debate proposals for new laws called Bills. If both Houses vote for the proposals then the Bill is ready to become an Act. It can only be described as an Act when it has received Royal Assent from the monarch.

Document	Definition
Select committee reports	Select committees are set up by either House, usually for a whole Parliament, to look at particular subjects. In the House of Commons the select committees examine the expenditure, administration and policy of each of the main government departments and associated public bodies. Select committees have the power to take evidence and issue reports. In the House of Lords, select committees do not mirror government departments but cover broader issues, such as science and technology, the economy, the constitution and the European Union.
Comprehensive Spending Reviews	Governments hold spending reviews to determine how much money each department will have to spend in coming years. These decisions used to happen annually, but Gordon Brown introduced a system of three-year spending reviews to bring more certainty to long-term planning.
Home Office circulars	Guidance and information providing updates and details on policy and procedures. The Home Office states 'they are useful to people who work for, or with, the Home Office or who need to know the latest policy updates'. Home Office guidance is advice only. It has no element of compulsion, and recipients may disregard the advice, providing that in so doing they do not disregard the law.

Source: http://www.parliament.uk/site-information/glossary/

was in power at Westminster over the 30 years or so we are considering and identify the serving Home Secretary.

In the course of outlining the various trends and pressures, this chapter will draw on and explain the key events and documents listed in Table 4.1. In addition, in order to appreciate how the UK government goes about its business, a number of documents and processes are referred to and are defined in Table 4.2. These documents, such as the consultation papers (Green and White) as well as the reports of the select committees and ministerial statements, contain a wealth of useful information, often including up-to-date statistics, and have been the source material for various analyses, for example on the development of the anti-social behaviour order (ASBO) legislation (Macdonald, 2007) and discrimination issues (Gray, 2001).

WHAT ARE THE DIFFERENT FINANCIAL MODELS DRIVING GOVERNMENT POLICIES?

As described above, the neo-liberalism project covered changes in government, the shifting fortunes of the economy and a programme of public sector reform that may be encapsulated in three styles of thinking termed value for money (VFM), best value (BV) and payment by results (PbR).

VALUE FOR MONEY

Value for money (VFM), simply put, is about achieving the best results ('effectiveness') at the lowest cost ('efficiency' and 'economy') (Savage, 2007: 83). Savage sketches the context in which the VFM movement emerged. NPM was seen as the way to maximize VFM in the public sector. In brief, NPM assumes the superiority of markets over state monopolies as service providers and market forces, such as competition, are held to drive up efficiencies and reduce costs. There is a separation between making policies and setting budgets, those responsibilities being retained by government, and delivering services, through not just public bodies, but also private companies and voluntary agencies. An essential idea was that by these means the provider was brought closer to the consumer of services. And thus arrived mission statements, league tables of performance and the application of business models, all of which, as we show in a later section, affected the police, prison and probation services as well as health providers.

One innovation was the introduction of Compulsory Competitive Tendering (CCT), resulting in modest amounts of privatization for services such as cleaning, catering and vehicle maintenance. Another important aspect of this re-alignment was an increasing role of inspection, audit and regulation. Just as responsibility for delivery of public services was being de-centralized and localized, accountability for delivery was being placed in the hands of agencies such as the Audit Commission, Her Majesty's Inspectorates for Police, and Prisons. Thus, as Savage suggests (Savage, 2007: 96), central control of public services is maintained through the regulatory machinery rather than through direct provision of the services. Both the inspectorates and the Audit Commission were highly influential in changing ways of working within criminal justice agencies and the latter also had responsibilities in relation to the National Health Service, including the issuing of national performance indicators.

BEST VALUE

With the advent of the New Labour government in 1997, whilst there remained curbs on public spending, there was a definite shift of emphasis. Rather than give free rein to unfettered market forces, the Labour government's 'Third Way' sought to facilitate and encourage wealth creation through private enterprise but alongside ideas of social cohesion and social justice. The government introduced its concept of best value (BV) as a way to achieve its modernization project. In the White Paper 'Modern Local Government: In Touch with the People', issued by the Department for the Environment, Transport and the Regions in 1998, the Deputy Prime Minister, John Prescott, said in the introduction 'We want local communities where everyone can participate in society, and effective care is available to those who need it.' The White Paper goes on to explain how this was to be done through BV:

- by planning a programme of fundamental performance reviews of every service, and developing means of consulting and involving the public in the improvement of service provision and cost (2.26)
- consultation ... will be a key feature of the approach to producing a community plan and achieving best value through performance review and the development of local performance plans (4.6)
- the most efficient possible use of resources in the delivery of all public services, while keeping the overall burden of taxation as low as possible (5.3).

As Martin and Davis (2001) say, BV did not sweep away the previous government's reforms, rather they built on and extended them. BV extended the limited remit of CCT within the public sector and now there was a duty to review all of their services over five years to determine whether a service was still needed and if so, how it may be more efficiently and effectively provided, focusing particularly on partnership arrangements. The essential idea of BV was of continuous improvement to be secured through published performance plans (Savage, 2007: 109). Best value reviews were also to be published and contain an action plan. These were accompanied by a national set of Best Value Performance Indicators (BVPIs) and a modernization project to ensure public sector organizations were equipped to manage their services. To achieve the desired modernization, the Audit Commission and relevant inspectorates (HMIs) were to promote 'what works' derived from evidence-based practice and public service agreements (PSAs) were formulated to ensure commonly agreed standards and inter-departmental cooperation.

PAYMENT BY RESULTS

In 2010 the United Kingdom had its first coalition government in over 50 years, made up of the Conservatives and Liberal Democrats. The Big Society idea was intended to open up provision of services, not just to private enterprise but also to non-governmental organizations (NGOs). The payment by results approach (PbR) would, it was argued, incentivize a range of independent providers, including the charitable sector, to participate in reducing reoffending through greater efficiencies, lowering costs by innovative practice (Fox and Albertson, 2011: 37).

Paying on receipt of results was an attractive proposition during a period of austerity when, as indicated above, savings were being sought from ministries involved in criminal justice services. Fox and Albertson (2011) note that a major challenge to PbR is the raising of working capital because payment only occurs after the outcome is known. One mechanism is the Social Impact Bond (SIB) which will be used to raise the start-up money. Public, private or social investors (such as a philanthropist or charitable trusts) would agree to pay for a specific outcome and this income would meet the up-front costs of a programme.

The advantages of PbR are seen to be:

- greater efficiency by extending the range of providers and greater variation in modes of delivery by allowing successful organizations to share in the benefits achieved;
- more innovation by minimizing prescription as to how outcomes are to be achieved and 'micro management' by commissioners of services;
- transfer of risk from government to service provider.

This would seem to be a move away from the NPM approach which was focused on creating more business-oriented public sector organizations in favour of increasing new, particularly private, organizations, to enter the market as suppliers of services. PbR signals the speeding up of the proportionate share that the private sector is to have in delivering services previously undertaken by the public sector.

PbR relies on measuring outcomes and determining whether the return is worth the investment. Measurement is not always straightforward and as Fox and Albertson (2011) rightly point out, not only is the existing evidence on 'what works' patchy, there is a lively debate about what evaluative methods are best employed to evidence success. One way the government seeks to address this problem is by setting up a 'what works network', which is explained in a later section.

How then has all of this affected the agencies within the criminal justice system? In broad terms, this has been a story of the attempts by respective governments to change the ethos and culture of public sector professionals and in the following section we provide a synopsis of this process.

Box 4.1   Reflective exercise

Key to the NPM initiatives has been the identification of consumers of public services as 'customers' and their 'right to choose their preferred provider'.

What considerations might parents make in choosing a school for their children?

What are the constraints of parents being able to send their children to their school of choice?

Should a prisoner, say a sex offender, be able to choose the prison they serve their sentence in because:

(a) It came top in the league table for the effectiveness of its sex offender treatment programme?
(b) A sibling is serving in that prison?
(c) It is in the most convenient location?

If you said no (or yes) to this question, what are your reasons?

WHAT IMPACT HAS GOVERNMENT POLICY HAD ON CRIMINAL JUSTICE AGENCIES?

THE POLICE SERVICE

One of the first interventions of Margaret Thatcher's government to impact agencies of criminal justice was policing. Several Home Office Circulars were issued marking the beginning of the three 'E's revolution: efficiency, effectiveness and economy. Circular 106/88 encouraged the process of civilianization, whereby roles and functions previously undertaken by police officers would be done more cheaply by civilian employees allowing officers to concentrate on operational tasks. One of the authors (J.B.) was an early beneficiary of this process, becoming the research manager for the Hampshire Constabulary in

1985 and was able to instigate a programme of professional research within that police force (Reiner, 1994).

Savage (2007: 173) notes that it was not until John Major's administration in the early 1990s that police reform really began to bite and more radical changes were proposed (Farrall and Hay, 2010). Kenneth Clarke, previously initiating NPM in Education and Health, became Home Secretary and set about the police by means of: an inquiry into roles and responsibilities (the Sheehy Inquiry); a White Paper on police reform; a review by Ingrid Posen (1994) on core tasks; and the Police and Magistrates' Courts Act (PMCA). All these were in line with NPM agenda as suggested by McLaughlin and Murji (2001) above. A pattern of civilianization and outsourcing were well established by the time the Labour Party came to power in 1997. David Blunkett as Home Secretary issued a White Paper in 2001, 'Blueprint for Reform', which extended the civilianization project and incidentally created more openings for forensic psychology graduates. The White Paper included a proposal of substituting police operational officers by 'support staff' with civilian investigators being able to function as a full member of a police investigating team. Box 4.2 provides a description of a forensic psychologist graduate who took up this opportunity.

Box 4.2   Carys Hamilton on being a civilian investigator

My journey could be described as the 'road less travelled' compared to many of my fellow Chartered Forensic Psychologists. I completed my masters degree at Surrey University in 2004 and chose to take up a position as a civilian investigator in Surrey Police. Although I had heard about the challenges of undertaking Chartership (mainly from those in the NHS, the Prison Service and Probation Service), I decided to register for stage two knowing that I was not in a 'Trainee' position, and would in all likelihood, not be supported financially or otherwise by the police. I gained valuable experience working in high volume crime in the first two years at Surrey Police, and had ample opportunity to use the knowledge I had gained in forensic psychology. In 2006, I moved to major crime (i.e. the investigation of serious offences including kidnap, stranger rape, murder and extremism), where I spent the next very exciting but frustrating six years.

Whilst on major crime, I took every opportunity to use my forensic psychology skills to progress enquiries and develop multidisciplinary practice. I did this in an effort to both complete my Chartership, and also to prove myself as a competent practitioner in an inflexible working environment. This said, I pushed the boundaries, and was one of the first civilians to be trained as a family liaison officer (FLO). I found working with the families of deceased victims, and families

(Continued)

who had lost infants to sudden infant death syndrome (SIDS) both demanding and rewarding. In 2011, I was chosen to represent Surrey Police FLOs at Clarence House, where I met Prince Charles and the Duchess of Cornwall. In the wake of the 7/7 bombings, the Royal Family wanted to recognize the excellent and trying work FLOs undertook over and above their day jobs.

Working in the police as a civilian investigator brought many challenges and obstacles. With variable success, I constantly challenged bureaucratic practices and tried to promote the many skills forensic psychologists could offer the Police Service. I am proud to say that despite the many challenges, I was able to use my skills to some effect. During my time in the police, I initiated improvements to the initial crime investigation process through policy development and training, improved service delivery at all levels in relation to high volume crime, undertook research on matching specialist investigative interviewers to suspects to get the best evidence in serious crime enquiries, and set up a forum between five police forces to encourage improved and standardized training and practice in the area of specialist interviewing. It was individuals rather than the 'police organization' that provided me with the opportunities and mentoring I required to complete my Chartership (which I must add, I completed entirely over and above my day job, and at my own expense). Following a number of core role completions based on work within the police and the Youth Justice Service, in 2012, I was finally awarded my Chartership as a forensic psychologist.

Years previously, I had accepted a secondment for 18 months to another police force to work with officers from all over the country; investigating and prosecuting a number of domestic extremists. I found both the area of work and the individual perpetrators very interesting, and it fostered my interest in terrorism. In 2013, I received a Chief Constable's commendation for my contribution to this enquiry. In 2012, I left the police, and started consulting privately to an organization affiliated with the Ministry of Defence to further develop my interest in terrorism, and seek opportunities to learn and specialize.

The other move in the White Paper was to strengthen front line policing by introducing police community support officers (PCSOs) empowered to carry out basic patrol functions. These are literally 'civilians in uniform' as they have limited powers and do not hold a warrant that authorizes them to arrest and detain. BV was enshrined in legislation and the application of the four 'Cs' – challenge, comparison, continuous improvement and competition – was initiated. The final plank was instigated through the Crime and Disorder Act of 1998 which required the police to work in partnership and develop local crime reduction strategies through the Crime and Disorder Reduction Partnerships.

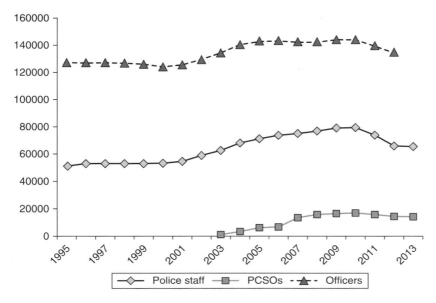

Figure 4.1 Numbers of warranted police officers, support staff and community support officers, 1995–2013. (Source: Police workforce statistics, Home Office)

In the aftermath of the financial crisis 2007–10, the newly elected Coalition government made it clear in the 2010 Comprehensive Spending Review (CSR) how the deficit was to be reduced by reduction in public sector spending. In 2012 Her Majesty's Inspectorate of Constabulary indicated that the Police Service faced a 20% cut across England and Wales with a need to save £2.1 billion by 2014–15. One way to achieve this has been to cut numbers of staff, as the downturn in the graph in Figure 4.1 shows, which represents a loss of 21% of support staff, 19% of police and community support officers and 11% of police officers between 2010 and 2013.

Some commentators (e.g. Brogden and Ellison, 2013) are both critical and sceptical of the private sector's involvement in 'policing-for-profit' as they term it. Their claim is that accountability becomes blurred in the 'convergence' of private enterprise and the state (p. 17), a criticism also levelled at privatization initiatives within the prison service (Andrew, 2007).

The other trend discernible throughout the last 30 years has been the move towards evidence-based practice and scientific methods of evaluation not least to demonstrate worth of outcomes. A key element was the Financial Management Initiative (FMI), setting targets, measuring outputs and performance against those targets, specifying resources and identifying the individuals responsible for those resources (Cabinet Office, 1983). As the raft of quantitative performance indicators crept up, the Police Service moved toward more qualitative measurements, such as satisfaction with aspects of service (Waters, 1996).

This generated more psychologically interesting data, including analysis of fear of crime (which we discuss in more detail in Chapters 5 and 8.).

David Blunkett's police reform agenda, published in the 2001 White Paper 'Policing a New Century: Blueprint for Reform', also included the establishment of a National Centre for Policing Excellence to:

> cover all aspects of operational policing, and to promote evidence-based practices. Working with the Association of Chief Police Officers (ACPO), the Centre will produce a specification of theory and practice of investigation. The work will form part of the programme of good practice codes and guides co-ordinated by [a] Standards Unit. (p. 4)

The National Intelligence Model (NIM) was a product of the commitment to BV (James, 2013: 86) and derived from the 'what works' evidence-based logic then beginning to prevail. As a consequence there was a stimulus towards more systematic crime pattern analysis, offender profiling and a growing body of work on eyewitness identification and investigative decision making (see Tong et al., 2009 for an overview of this body of research). The next White Paper, 'Building Communities and Beating Crime', and the subsequent Police and Justice Act (2006) endorsed the NIM approach and established the National Policing Improvement Agency (NPIA). This agency was incidentally, abolished by the next government. In a written ministerial statement on 15 December 2011, the Conservative Home Secretary, Theresa May, announced the wind down of the NPIA and the establishment of a 'police professional body [which] will develop policing as a single profession'. That professional body was the College of Policing, which was announced and elaborated in a further ministerial statement on 16 July 2012:

> The College of Policing will protect the public interest, enhance policing standards, identify evidence of what works in policing and share best practice. It will support the education and professional development of staff and officers and it will motivate the police and partners to work together to achieve a shared purpose, including taking a major role in shaping the work of the higher education sector to improve the broader body of evidence on which policing professionals rely.

The College hosts the What Works Centre for Crime Reduction, which involves collaboration with academics and a university consortium as well as commissioning research and setting up regional networks. The Coalition government gave an undertaking to create a 'what works network' (Cabinet Office, 2013). The National Institute for Health and Care Excellence (NICE) was the first centre, followed by the Education Endowment Centre. Four new areas include crime reduction, early intervention, ageing better and early economic growth.

Box 4.3   Core functions of What Works centres

Each What Works centre will be independent of government, with a clear and relevant policy focus. Each will:

Generate evidence synthesis

1. Undertake systematic assessment of relevant evidence and produce a sound, accurate, clear and actionable synthesis of the global evidence base which:

   - Assesses and ranks interventions on the basis of effectiveness and cost-effectiveness;
   - Shows where the interventions are applicable;
   - Shows the relative cost of interventions;
   - Shows the strength of evidence on an agreed scale.

Translate the evidence

2. Produce and apply a common currency for comparing the effectiveness of interventions.
3. Put the needs and interests of users at the heart of its work.

Evidence absorption

4. Publish and disseminate findings in a format that can be understood, interpreted and acted upon.

Promote good evidence

5. Identify research and capability gaps and work with partners to fill them.
6. Advise those commissioning and undertaking innovative interventions and research projects to ensure that their work can be evaluated effectively.

Clearly, for those forensic psychologists researching in academia, this move to evidence-based practice opens up opportunities for greater engagement with policing.

THE PRISON SERVICE

Bell (2013: 79) argues that neo-liberalism is 'of vital importance in explaining punitive trends in recent years, not just in the British context but also in a global one'. In October 1993 the Conservative Home Secretary, Michael Howard, gave his 'prison works' speech, which included a 23-point programme to tackle crime. In his speech Mr Howard said his measures might mean more people going to prison but he was unrepentant: 'I do not flinch from that. We shall no longer judge the success of our system of justice by a fall in our prison population ... Let us be clear. Prison works. It ensures that we are protected from murderers, muggers and rapists, and it makes many who are tempted to commit crime think twice.'

Significant in its programme was leave for six new prisons to be financed, built and run by the private sector. As part of its reforms, in 1992 the Conservative government created the private finance initiative (PFI) as a way to encourage private financing of public sector infra-structure. This was extended to prison provision after successful lobbying by the Adam Smith Institute so that progressively over the next 25 years private companies came to own and manage a total of 14 prisons in England and Wales. In Cullen and Mackenzie's (2011: 44) view, 'perhaps, inevitably, private prisons began in the USA' and the idea migrated to the UK. Delivering punishment was no longer to be the prerogative of the state, and currently just over 13% of the prison population are held in privately run institutions. Cullen and Mackenzie (2011) note the concerns that the adoption of privatization in the UK raised, notably that private management may put a motive for profit ahead of the public interest, inmate welfare or rehabilitation. They mention the 'abiding' concern of the ethics of private imprisonment and catalogue a number of successful court actions by prisoners in the United States suing private companies for ill-treatment and assaults. They argue that the case for private prisons can be made on grounds of cost, creativity and innovation, and accountability through contractual scrutiny. The case against is made by Elaine Genders (2002, 2003, 2007) who is pessimistic that the public interest is always served by the involvement of the private sector. Moreover, for some, making profit from incarceration is held to be morally repugnant (Andrew, 2007: 898). Andrew summarizes the widely accepted view that the fundamental motivation for prison privatization was that this would reduce operating costs by providing faster and cheaper capacity. However, she also highlights that such arguments are not politically neutral. In the case of Australia, she cites a significant report that includes an appeal to the market to solve the persistent failures of the (Australian) prison sector, which, as in the UK, was represented as a difficult, problematic and unionized workforce resistant to more flexible working practices.

Bell (2013) documents the rise of managerialist values within the prison estate, which seeks to measure success against 'objective' management targets. Crighton and Towl (2008: 4–8) itemize the NPM regime as including measurable standards of performance, pre-set output measures, creation of cost centres to control budgets, introduction of competition and sub-contracting as well as the dis-aggregation of public services by increasing the separation of the role of purchaser and provider. Crewe, Bennett and Wahidin (2008: 5–7) document the impacts of NPM on prison staff, which included:

- specialization, i.e. focus on the core role for each post and the growth of the operational support grade who carry out tasks formerly conducted by prison officers, e.g. gate work and prisoner escorts;
- professionalization, i.e. increases in professional staff such as psychologists;

- decentralization, i.e. delegation of finance and human resource management to each establishment;
- individualization, i.e. the move to break down the collective representation of groups, which attempts to by-pass the unions and industrial relations mechanisms and instead engage in an employee-relations culture through which means employees are directly consulted and managed.

Around the late 1990s, consistent with pre-set output targets that were potentially easy to measure, psychologically based manualized programmes, particularly cognitive behaviour approaches and structured group-based interventions, flourished. It was relatively easy to monitor completers of such programmes and to compare a battery of psychometric scores against some pre-engagement baseline. But, as Crighton and Towl (2008) point out, problems were soon encountered, such as the perverse incentive to select prisoners who would complete their programme rather than those for whom it was necessarily appropriate. An added dimension was ethical concerns that inappropriate selection through pressures to meet completion targets or maintain numbers may actually result in harm for some prisoners. Furthermore, overuse of psychometric testing to demonstrate 'successful' completion in Crighton and Towl's view has led to some dubious professional practices. They suggest pressures to meet management targets may well be in tension with professional judgements. Thomas-Peter (2006) goes further and proposes creating a market approach to service delivery, contributes to a decrease in the power of the professions to regulate services and manualized programmes can be run by lower-cost competence-based workers who replace more highly skilled and expensive professionals.

During Tony Blair's Labour administration Patrick Carter recommended there should be a unitary system focused on the end-to-end management of offenders throughout their sentence; that there be a risk-assessed use of scarce resources, through the use of a system based on improved information; and more effective service delivery through greater contestability, by using providers of prison and probation from across the public, private and voluntary sectors. He proposed the creation of a unified prison and probation service called the National Offender Management Service (NOMS). A national director supported by regional managers would then fund the delivery of specified contracts – based on evidence of what reduces reoffending. NOMS was created in 2004 becoming an Executive Agency of the Ministry of Justice in July 2008, very much on the lines that Carter suggested. This paved the way for the Coalition government, which took power in 2010, to introduce its 'rehabilitation revolution', which included the payment by results scheme. Doncaster, a privately run prison, was amongst the first to pilot a PbR scheme in 2011.

THE PROBATION SERVICE

Over the past three decades, the Probation Service has been under 'constant pressure' to change its culture and practices (Deering, 2014). The origins of the service can be found in a combination of evangelical religious rescue missions, the Temperance movement, the activities of pressure groups and philanthropic ventures of the Victorian era, so that by 1897 there was a formal recognition of full-time missionaries working to support prisoners and their families through and after court (Mair and Burke, 2012). The newly emerging sciences of criminology, eugenics, statistics and psychology also played a role. The latter in particular moved arguments about the reasons for offending towards dispositional characteristics of the offender. The Probation of Offenders Act of 1907 set the groundwork for the modern Probation Service whereby, with the consent of an offender, under certain conditions, they would be remitted under a probation order and supported to lead an honest and industrious life. From its inception probation was seen as a diversionary option distinct from punishment. Psychology continued to play a role in the development of the Probation Service. In the 1940s industrial psychologists were consulted to help select suitable individuals to become probation officers. This paralleled the role of psychology in helping to screen recruits to enter the Police Service (Brown, 2000; see also Chapter 9 in this volume). Psychology contributed to the development of case work and this specialized knowledge was thought necessary to enable officers to recognize those who would be responsive to assistance. This involved being more aware of the offenders' emotional as well as material needs. Research also began to play a role.

With the advent of community service arising from the Wootton Report and supervision of those on suspended sentences, Mair and Burke (2012) identify that this moved probation away from its more social work orientation. The introduction of day training centres (DTCs) required attendance, and was seen by some in the Probation Service to undermine the consent element of a probation order. By the 1970s probation was moving even further from its rehabilitation ethos towards diversion from custody, in part driven by prison overcrowding and partly as a consequence of the 'nothing works' debate which suggested that probation orders were not particularly effective at reducing reoffending.

The 1982 Criminal Justice Act made some significant changes to probation:

- powers to attach a requirement to attend a day centre for a maximum of 60 days or refrain from specified activities;
- community service orders of between 60 and 120 hours were extended to 16-year-olds;
- social enquiry reports would have to be prepared for offenders not having previously served a prison sentence.

Mair and Burke (2012: 138) suggest these provisions were intended to add rigour to a probation order to make them more appealing to the public as an alternative to prison, rather than being thought of as a 'soft' option. Probation's incorporation into the three Es (economy, efficiency and effectiveness) began in the second Thatcher Conservative administration with the publication in 1984 of the Statement of National Objectives and Priorities (SNOP).

The SNOP declared that the key objective was the supervision of offenders in the community, especially those who otherwise might have been given a custodial sentence. Probation was enjoined to work with other agencies, be involved in new tasks such as mediation, and to use its resources efficiently. According to Mair and Burke (2012), SNPO was a marker for the consolidation of probation geographic areas and by the setting of national objectives eroded the power and autonomy of local chief probation officers. The introduction of computerization and standardization of record keeping and data entry was another trend towards a national approach and modernization of the service.

FMI applied to resource management and the setting of performance indicators for probation followed, and in 1989 the Home Office introduced a national standard for community service orders, a more comprehensive set of standards covering pre-sentence reports, probation and supervision orders, and the management of hostels.

Towards the end of Mrs Thatcher's period of office there were a number of consultative Green Papers (e.g. 'Punishment, Custody and Community', 1988; 'Supervision and Punishment in the Community', 1990) encouraging each probation area to allocate a proportion of its expenditure on partnership working. A Green Paper in 1990 proposed a major re-organization of the Probation Service, summarized by Mair and Burke (2012: 144) as including:

- amalgamation of probation areas;
- Home Office control over senior appointments;
- greater emphasis on criminal justice in training;
- 100% funding by the Home Office;
- removal of the requirement for probation officers to hold a social work qualification;
- introduction of a national probation service.

The Audit Commission (Audit Commission, 1989: 2) made it clear that an NPM regimen was to be introduced:

> The probation service ... to give value for money ... must target its activities, coordinating them with other agencies within the criminal justice system, and it must develop and apply new ways of working with more difficult offenders. These changes in turn require it to be managed differently.

As a result of the introduction of the day centres (subsequently renamed probation centres) and a desire to better target offenders at risk of custodial sentences, predicting risk of custody became a preoccupation of probation, which extended into risk of re-conviction. Rather than the clinical judgement approach used by many probation officers, the government adopted a computer-based computation, the Offender Group Reconviction Scale (OGRS). Other developments include greater engagement with community probation work, crime prevention and panel assessment schemes to divert mentally disordered offenders away from the criminal justice system.

The use of electronic monitoring of offenders was a further innovation. Another idea borrowed from the United States, tagging was seen as a way to enhance community supervision as a means of containing the prison population (Smith, 2001). The first British experiments began in 1989, although they were not deemed very successful. More successful trials took place in 1995 and a further expansion began under provisions of the Crime and Disorder Act 1998. Commercial contracts were let to monitor the supervision of offenders. Interestingly, in 2013 the Minister of Justice announced in the House of Commons significant anomalies in billing practices by two private companies, Serco and G4S, and their conduct was to be subjected to a criminal investigation by the Serious Fraud Office (Hansard, 2014). The two companies have since withdrawn from the next generation of electronic monitoring contracts thus denting the assumption that private contractors are necessarily more effective and efficient.

As explained previously, the development of evidence-based practice grew out of the 'what works' movement and probation alongside other agencies became involved in New Labour's Crime Reduction Programmes. In 1999, investment in 'what works' dramatically increased (Raynor, 2008). Several 'Pathfinder' projects were designed covering offender behaviour, basic skills, community punishment and re-settlement of short-term prisoners. These were centralized and accredited programmes. As a result of this top-down style, spiralling workloads and increasing pressure to meet targets and to implement and evaluate programmes, probation experienced considerable difficulties and setbacks (Raynor, 2004).

The move towards even more central control and national programmes coalesced in 2000 with the Criminal Justice and Court Services Act which created a National Probation Service (NPS). Jack Straw, the Labour Home Secretary, had previously announced a new probation officer training scheme which broke its traditional link with social work and its welfarist ethos, replacing it with a criminal justice orientation. This together with the creation of the NPS effectively turned probation into an agency of criminal justice. The Act also required probation to participate in Multi-Agency Public Protection Agency (MAPPA) to manage the risks presented by sex and other high-risk offenders.

The newly established NPS struggled to reorganize itself, deliver and provide data for the evaluation of the Pathfinder programmes, develop MAPPA collaborations and get up to speed with new Drug Treatment and Testing Orders (DTTOs). Thus, as outlined above in relation to prisons, following the critical review by Patrick Carter and a consultative paper, radical proposals paved the way for the amalgamation of prisons and probation to form the National Offender Management Service, an 'end to end' service (Hough, Allen and Padel, 2006). Further, the idea of 'contestability' was similarly introduced to create competition from the private and voluntary sectors as a way to improve services and provide better value for money (Mair and Burke, 2012).

The National Association of Probation Officers (NAPO) was opposed to the proposals on the grounds that they risked:

- dismantling the Probation Service by splitting it into a purchaser as well as provider;
- losing the relationship with local communities;
- having a confused governance model;
- creating even more confusion by hurrying through the changes.

Legislation nevertheless was passed (Offender Management Act 2007) and as Mair and Burke (2012: 175) concluded: 'The probation service as (effectively) the monopoly provider of community interventions for offenders – a situation that had lasted for 100 years ... was gone.' Probation boards were replaced with 35 more business-like trusts that could commission as well as provide services. Twenty-one Community Rehabilitation Companies (CRCs) have been created to deliver the Coalition's rehabilitation revolution by means of PbR schemes which are designed to attract a fee on delivery of a statistically significant reduction in reoffending against a baseline (House of Commons Committee of Public Accounts, 2014).

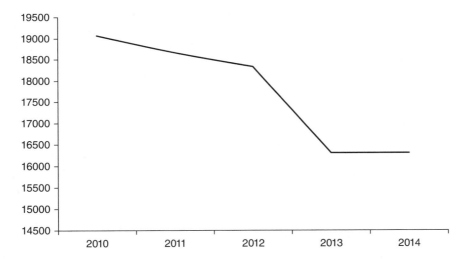

Figure 4.2 Numbers working in the Probation Service, 2010–2014. (Source: Ministry of Justice)

In the space of 30 years, probation has been transformed in terms of its mission, organization and numbers (see Figure 4.2). Historically it had been an autonomous, locally facing service working with the consent of clients to support and rehabilitate with a social services orientation. Now it is an agency of criminal justice focusing on risk and desistance. No longer being a monopoly supplier of service and in danger of being swamped by its larger prison partner in NOMS, probation is feared by some to have lost its identity (Deering, 2014; Mair and Burke, 2012). One way for probation to preserve an identity and its professional standing is to create, like the Police Service, a college to set and maintain professional standards (Shepherd, 2013). Shepherd's idea of a Royal College of Probation and a companion set of university-based research institutes integrated with probation trusts could return probation to its rehabilitation ideals. Deering (2014: 4) is more pessimistic and sees as a future scenario probation as 'a mere "sequencer" of interventions delivered by others, rather than having any form of constructive role with offenders', or alternatively probation could virtually disappear, being left with an assessment and risk management role.

MENTALLY DISORDERED OFFENDERS

'Treatment is the fundamental justification for separate provision for mentally disordered people who have committed offences' writes Peay (1994: 1143). However, she points out that not only is it unclear what is meant by treatment but also there is a lack of clarity about what the treatment is attempting to do, particularly its target, i.e. the criminal behaviour or the underlying disorder.

Take the example of dangerous and severe personality disorder (DSPD). This was an invention of 'politicians and civil servants' (Maden, 2007). Described as 'the Third Way' to deal with individuals who are at the boundary between the health and criminal justice systems, Howells, Krishnan and Daffern (2007) explain DSPD is not a 'clinical diagnosis or classification' rather it arises from a working definition originating from the Department of Health and denotes an individual who 'presents a significant risk of serious physical and psychological harm from which it would be difficult or impossible for the victim to recover'. This intervention arose as a political imperative because of a particular event. The backcloth had been the evolving debate about what was believed to be the public's tolerance of risk in general and the threats posed by individuals with personality disorders in particular. In 1998 Michael Stone murdered a mother and child, with another child surviving the attack. Stone was thought to have had a personality disorder but was considered untreatable and hence could not be detained under mental health legislation. The murder and the ensuring acrimonious media coverage is what stimulated a political intervention rather than it being a forensic psychology initiative. O'Loughlin (2014) explains how a later government in the UK felt able to 'abolish' the DSPD label and is currently dismantling DSPD units in hospitals and moving facilities to prisons.

COURTS

The administration of justice and the management of the courts were not immune from NPM. The Police and Magistrates' Courts Act (PMCA) 1994 provided powers to impose mergers of magistrates' courts committees and established a new justices' chief executive. This resulted in an administrative officer working alongside justices' clerks, thereby separating administrative and legal functions. The administrative officer is charged with meeting efficiency targets such as listing cases, and managing the magistrates' rotas (Fitzpatrick et al., 2001). Justices' clerks provide legal advice to magistrates. In addition, the PMCA established the Magistrates' Courts Service Inspectorate (MCSI), which was incorporated into Her Majesty's Court Service (HMCS) in 2005 and merged with the Tribunals Service to form Her Majesty's Courts and Tribunals Service in 2011.

Fitzpatrick et al. (2001) suggest that MCSI introduced a management information system, performance targets and mission statements. Accompanying these were concerns for judicial independence, and (rather as the potential clash between the exercising of clinical judgements by doctors and achieving value for money savings by managers within the NHS) critics have argued that cost saving has primacy over professional judgement. The main role of the private sector has been in the 'tooling up' of the courts with the necessary information technology.

In the 2010 Comprehensive Spending Review, the Ministry of Justice was required to save two billion pounds. Proposals to save money included the closing of 103 magistrates' courts and 54 County Courts to save £15.3 million a year. Other proposed changes include deviations to the way criminals are sentenced, such as giving shorter sentences to defendants who make an early guilty plea, as well as cuts in the use of remand. More controversially, the government proposed to radically reform and cut its funding. In April 2012, the Legal Aid, Sentencing and Punishment of Offenders Act (LASPO) came into force, with the aim of reducing the civil legal aid budget by a quarter (£320m) within a year. Again, concerns have been expressed about the impact of these cuts (Byrom, 2013).

CONCLUSION

We have argued in this chapter that it is important for forensic psychologists to have an appreciation of the political context that influences policies and in turn steers practice in all the settings in which we work. We are living in an era that is seeing a diminishing of the public sphere wrought by budget cuts in a period of particular economic austerity. The role of the private sector in providing forensic psychology services provokes questions about accountability, which in turn has a number of ethical and moral concerns. Key to the care of people within our criminal justice system is accountability. This requires access to information, which is needed if institutions are to be kept under review and challenged about the quality of their services, and having an open culture in which to improve. Professional judgements sometimes come into conflict with commercial imperatives.

RESOURCES

Arianna Silvestri (2012) has edited a collection of reflective essays on the first year of the 2010 Coalition government's policies for the justice system.

House of Commons select committee reports, particularly of the Accounts and Home Affairs committees, have useful reviews of developing government policies.

Jane Andrew (2007) has a very thoughtful essay outlining some of the moral and ethical concerns that arise from the application of neo-liberal economics to the criminal justice system.

Mike Brogden and Graham Ellison (2013) provide a very lively, if somewhat partial, political analysis of policing under conditions of austerity.

Mike Hough, Rob Allen and Una Padel's edited collection (2006) provides a recent and thorough account and analysis of the thinking behind and setting up of the National Offender Management Service.

Key journals

Behavioral Sciences and the Law

British Journal of Criminology

Journal of Judicial Administration

Law and Contemporary Problems

5

POLITICAL CONTEXT

KEY CONCEPTS

This chapter discusses contextual factors of three inter-related issues, those of crime, risk and punishment/rehabilitation, as a precursor to appreciating the theoretical accounts outlined in the chapter that follows and the practice implications discussed in Chapters 10 and 11. This continues our exploration of legal and criminal justice contexts of the BPS's stage one training and conducting interventions of stage two. A discussion is presented that unpicks the idea of the politicization of these concepts and provides the background to crime trends, rise of risk consciousness and the punishment–rehabilitation debate, thus filling an important comprehension gap when looking at all aspects of stage two core roles.

Knowledge concepts	Practice considerations
Debut crimes	Crime trends
Evidence-based policy making (EBPM)	Intensive Supervision and Surveillance
Maryland Scientific Method Scale (MSMS)	Programme (ISSP)
Moral panic	Indeterminate sentences of imprisonment
New punitiveness	for public protection (IPPs)
'Nothing works'	Pathfinder programmes
Penal popularism	'What works'
Protective factors	
Randomized controlled trials (RCTs)	
Redeemability hypothesis	
Rehabilitation revolution	
Risk	
Treatability	

(Continued)

A reading of this chapter sets out some critical issues about the legal and criminal justice context, raises some important questions about evaluative research and attitudes towards the rehabilitative and incapacitative objectives of imprisonment, for the stage one knowledge requirement and provides a critical reading of evidence-based practice for stage two core competencies.

Questions addressed

Why does forensic psychology need a political analysis?

Does public sentiment drive sentencing policy?

How can we explain crime trends?

How is the concept of risk defined?

What is risk assessment?

What is new punitiveness?

WHY DOES FORENSIC PSYCHOLOGY NEED A POLITICAL ANALYSIS?

This chapter discusses three interlocking trends that have provided the background to our present criminal justice policies. These are: the politicization of crime, the centrality of risk and the rehabilitation revolution. This introduction devotes some space to explaining why these issues are of importance to forensic psychologists.

As mentioned in Chapter 2, crime and punishment (and rehabilitation) are the 'stuff' of forensic psychology, so a political analysis completes an understanding of the context in which we work. 'Crime involves politics,' says Jock Young (Young, 1994: 117), because 'it is politics which determines the social conditions which cause crime, the degree to which the justice system is egalitarian, and the definitions of what crimes are in the first place and what degree of gravity we allot to one crime against another'. Moreover, Young proposes it is political solutions that solve the problem of crime, thus as the crime rate rose in the 1990s there was a corresponding increase in state intervention and more legislation on the statute books. Law and order became a party political issue. Ryan (2005: 139) notes another key factor, the rise of popularism or 'the public voice', and pinpoints the period of Mrs Thatcher's Conservative government of 1979–90 as the beginning of this trend. As Loader and Sparks (2007: 12) explain, 'crime is no longer managed "off-stage" by experts but has become the subject of political dispute and contest' and policies increasingly come under the influence of 'mass media and "public opinion" and at the mercy of sometimes actively whipped-up popular emotions'. There has been a heightened awareness and increased fear of crime, which Loader and Sparks suggests make it difficult to instil reason and evidence as 'the drivers' of policy. Also of importance is the rise of what has been termed the 'victim' lobby' by Sandra Walklate (2001). She observes the emergence of two significant developments in the late 1960s: the formation of the Bristol Victims Offenders Group, which paved the way for the National Association of Victim Support Schemes, and the arrival of Women's Refuges and Rape Crisis Centres.

Another reason for paying attention to the politics of criminal justice is the genesis of evidence-based policy making (EBPM). In part as a consequence of the value for money regimes, a political initiative was undertaken to justify the expenditure of public money thus inaugurating ideas of 'evidence-based practice' (EPB). Wells (2007) reviews the rise and reasoning behind EBP, which it was argued should enable the making of well-informed and thus better decisions. Research-based evidence became a routine part of evaluation and is now generally woven into the policy making process. Wells is sceptical about the contribution that EBP actually makes and argues that 'ideas, values, political strategies and previous practice are probably of greater significance' (p. 27). Moreover, evidence was deemed to include political knowledge and ministerial judgements such that research-based knowledge is not necessarily given primacy.

This political initiative resonated with the 'nothing works' debate. In brief, this is the label given to a doctrine that interventions with prisoners did not work and which arose from an original critical evaluation by Robert Martinson (1974). Martinson's paper suggested few treatment programmes produced any positive results. Subsequently Martinson revisited his conclusions (Martinson, 1979), and other research was highly critical of Martinson's original methodology (e.g. Thornton, 1987). New methodologies, such as meta-analyses (e.g. Lipsey, 1992), led to a major revision of thinking to create the 'what works' doctrine. McGuire's 1995 book *What Works; Reducing Re-Offending, Guidelines from Research and Practice* is a key text outlining principles for successful interventions.

In 1991 the Home Office held its first 'What Works' conference (Merrington and Stanley, 2000). By 1999 investment in 'what works' dramatically increased through funding provided by the Crime Reduction Programme (CRP). As Raynor notes:

> For community penalties this took the form of several pathfinder projects designed to test various strands of thinking about effective practice. All were externally evaluated and together they constituted the largest programme of research into community penalties ever attempted in Britain, covering as they did offending behaviour programmes, basic skills, community punishment and the resettlement of short term prisoners. (2008: 16)

By 2003/4 some 60,000 offenders were being put through these programmes.

Guidance produced for CRP evaluations was based on quasi-experimental methodologies. Not only were the political pressures to deliver reduced offending considerable (Merrington and Stanley, 2000) but also the evaluations were 'heavily stage managed by the Home Office' (Hollin, 2008: 90). Raynor (2004) points out that the Pathfinder programmes had too short a follow-up time scale (3 years) for full evaluations of properly implemented programmes; were over-dependent on early data from projects; suffered from implementation difficulties; and experienced slow start-up and high rates of attrition. Evaluation results were equivocal and clearly politically disappointing. Raynor (2008) suggests that in part concentration on targets, to the neglect of supportive and motivational offender management, may have contributed to poor performance, whilst Merrington and Stanley (2000) concluded that pressure from Treasury timetables may also have added to the disappointing evaluation findings. Raynor, is of the view that politically the 'blame' was put on research failures, i.e. claims that the evaluation studies were badly carried out or were of the wrong kind.

This led to the adoption of standards for impact studies, heavily influenced by the Maryland Scientific Method Scale (MSMS), whereby studies were ranked in terms of the levels of certainty that could be applied to results. The highest levels of confidence were assigned to randomized controlled trials (RCTs). RCTs are said to be the 'gold' standard of evaluation whereby a tightly controlled experimental design includes individuals randomly assigned to either a control group or a treatment group (Rosenfeld et al., 2011). The MSMS approach to judging research has been sharply criticized, notably by Pawson and Tilley (1998), Farrington et al. (2002) and Hope (2005: 290), who declared at the conclusion of his analysis:

> [D]espite the evidence allure for policy-makers of the experimental paradigm, and the claims made by its protagonists, it may not be the most useful methods of policy evaluation, especially applied to interventions that aim to affect the institutions, norms and social practices of civil society.

Hollin (2008) too is critical of RCTs, not least the practical issue of 'sentence over-ride', i.e. the research requirement to randomly assign offenders to the evaluation or control outcome, ethical issues about withholding treatment and problems of drop-out. In addition, RCTs do not address questions of 'process', in other words *why* an intervention may or may not work. Hough (2010: 19) doubts that such experimental evaluations can ever fully explain the complexity embedded in questions about the effectiveness in working with offenders. His advice is 'not to invest in a huge programme of randomised control trials, but to construct and test middle-level theories about how to change people's behaviour'. By middle level theories he means looking at processes, the quality of relationships and other contextual factors implicated in change.

This discussion raises several important points. Firstly, as Hollin (2008) and Raynor (2008) intimate, is the problem of selectivity in publishing reports. Raynor (p. 82) comes to the conclusion that publication 'is no longer driven by a culture of openness about the results of publicly funded research but instead the culture of information management', whilst Hollin (p. 90) suggests that when evidence does not suit policy the political pressure may often outweigh the integrity of independent research. Secondly, the preferred method employed in evaluation is politically driven rather than necessarily the choice of the evaluator, potentially creating a tension between those researchers working in and for government and independent academics. Thirdly, there has appeared something of a divide in the academic community between those who espouse the value of experimental designs and those who opt for qualitative research methodologies. Shadd Maruna (2013) characterizes this as quantitative experimental designs such as RCTs deriving from the 'what works' doctrine and the more qualitative approaches associated with those interested in desistance. He argues that the former overemphasize evaluation of manual heavy programmes whereas the latter are interested in qualitative explorations of how people change. He and others, such as Raynor (2004) and Brown et al. (2014), argue for mixed methods designs, whilst Hollin (2008) suggests high-quality quasi-experimental designs which minimize threats to the internal validity of the study and offer an alternative to RCTs.

The Pathfinder programmes are not the only evaluations to have received less than clear-cut results. Ellis, Pamment and Lewis (2009) undertook a mixed methods evaluation of the Intensive Supervision and Surveillance Programme (ISSP) introduced by the Youth Justice Board (YJB). ISSPs had been acclaimed politically as a robust community-based intervention. ISSPs were included in the Criminal Justice and Immigration Act of 2008 and are a mixture of 'punishment and positive opportunities' as an alternative to custody (YJB, 2009). Designed to address the underlying causes of offending and to stabilize often chaotic lifestyles, intensive supervision is coupled with electronically monitored curfews. Yet Ellis et al. not only found young people did not see custody as a deterrent but also the ISSP had not reduced offending, provided adequate surveillance to ensure public protection or had a positive impact on offenders' attitudes, improved their life chances or brought structure to their lives. Moreover, the Howard League for Penal Reform undertook their own review of ISSPs with young people who, they found, 'were extremely negative about the content of ISS, the way it is structured and the requirements they are forced to comply with'. Their report concluded ISSPs should be scrapped, although they did find support for the model of advocacy and intensive support provided through ISSP (Howard League for Penal Reform, n.d.). The report collected the views from young people themselves and Box 5.1 contains a poem from one review participant providing a telling and vivid expression of their view of ISSP.

Box 5.1 Anonymous poem from 'Life Outside' by the Howard League for Penal Reform

Fresh out no barz in my eyes

Finally seein those clear blue skies

No more pricks staring me out in that place

I no longer need to set the pace

(Continued)

But I still can't sesh with the man dem

Real talks it still like pen

On road with tag and ISS I swear it's some fucked up shit

It like I'm bein set up to fail

If I breach straight back to pen NO bail

Similarly, evaluation of the programme to assess and treat offenders with danger-ous and severe personality disorders (DSPD) was predominantly negative, with (O'Loughlin, 2014) concluding (p. 179) that the more recent evaluations 'do not give a positive indication of the programme's ability to treat patients and prisoners ... effectively or to progress through the criminal justice system'. Moreover, there was little evidence that supported any differences in treatment outcomes between those in prison-based or special hospital-based units. Yet the Coalition government announced plans in the Green Paper 'Breaking the Cycle' (Ministry of Justice, 2010b) to dismantle the special hospital units in favour of prison-based treatment. O'Loughlin (2014: 186) is of the view that notwithstanding the evidence, finance was a highly significant factor, with secure psychiatric places costing three times as much as a prison placement and as such 'the decision to continue and even expand the prison programme in the face of such unimpressive patient outcomes, significant costs and unfavourable consultation responses is highly questionable'.

The other trend mentioned above in contributing to policy is the public's voice, and never more so than in the area of risk and public safety. It is here that we have an intersection of ideas of 'dangerousness' and 'harm'. Thus Harrison (2010: 423) states 'the existence of and the harm caused by "dangerous offenders" is arguably one of the most persistent moral panics of the late twen-tieth and early twenty-first centuries'. Moral panic (an idea derived from Stan Cohen) is where there is a disproportionate hostile reaction to a person or group defined as potentially threatening societal values and often involves stereotypic media representations, leading to public demand for greater control (Murji, 2001: 175). Paedophiles represent one such stigmatized group, as do other vio-lent offenders. Government interventions in the form of legislation tend to focus on assessment of risk. The Criminal Justice Act 2003 and the Criminal Justice Act 2008 introduced the concept of the indeterminate sentence, i.e. imprisonment for public protection (IPP). Strickland and Garton Grimwood (2013) note that IPPs were designed 'to ensure that dangerous violent and sexual offenders stayed in custody for as long as they presented a risk to society'.

The IPP sentence has been criticized for its harshness, the length of time less serious offenders remained incarcerated after their tariffs had expired, the con-tribution of the rapid increase in IPPs to prison overcrowding and pressure on resources, meaning many IPP prisoners could not undertake the courses necessary

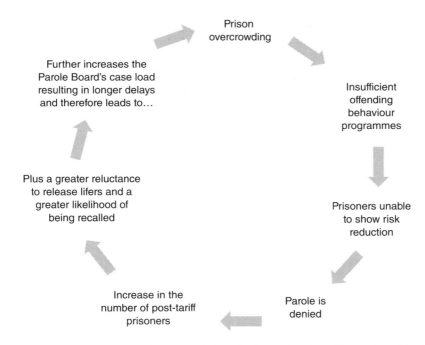

Figure 5.1 Harrison's vicious circle of indeterminate sentencing. (Reproduced by kind permission of Routledge from Harrison, K. (2010) Dangerous offenders, indeterminate sentencing and the rehabilitation revolution. *Journal of Social Welfare and Family Law* 32: 423-33.)

to demonstrate to the Parole Board their reduced risk. Harrison (2010: 431) demonstrates a 'vicious cycle' (see Figure 5.1).

The Coalition government accepted that IPPs were not working and announced their abolition in December 2012, but not retrospectively, on the grounds that the government were not minded to change sentences lawfully imposed by the courts 'simply because a policy decision has now been taken to repeal that sentence' (Lord McNally, House of Lords debate, Hansard, 9 February 2012).

Under the provision of the Legal Aid, Sentencing and Punishment of Offenders Act (LASPO) 2012, a new extended detention sentence (EDS) was introduced if:

- the defendant has been convicted of a specified offence (whether the offence was committed before or after this section came into force);
- the court considers that the defendant presents a substantial risk of causing serious harm through reoffending by committing a further specified offence (the 'significant risk' test is the same as the test for IPP therefore they must meet the dangerousness threshold);

- the court is not required to impose a sentence of imprisonment for life; and
- if at the time the offence was committed the defendant had been convicted of a sexual or violent offence or the current offence merits a determinate sentence of at least four years.

The EDS consists of a custodial term, which should reflect the seriousness of the offending; followed by an extended licence period which is determined by the court on the basis of what the court considers necessary for the purpose of protecting members of the public from serious harm.

DOES PUNITIVE PUBLIC SENTIMENT DRIVE SENTENCING POLICY?

Some commentators put the punitive drift down to politician's response to public sentiment (Frost, 2010; Maruna and King, 2009; Nagin et al., 2006). Maruna and King (2009: 9–10) define this punitiveness in the following terms:

> [h]arsher penalties would involve increasing the quantity of people punished (e.g. the view that too many offenders 'get away' with it), the intensity of punishment (i.e. the feeling that prisons are 'too easy', 'holiday camps') and the length of punitive sanctions (e.g. support for longer sentences, death penalty etc.). The public's overall 'mood' in this regard varies over time and across different jurisdictions (e.g. the general population of some countries is more punitive, overall than others ... and systematic demographic differences in views towards punishment).

Notwithstanding possible temporal and geographic variations, Pratt et al. (2005) argue there has been a rise in punitive attitudes, which they label 'new punitiveness'. They suggest that trends towards mass incarceration and longer sentences together with policies such as the IPPs characteristic of penal policies in the United States but also elsewhere, including the UK, Australia and New Zealand and Europe, have been promoted by notions of the public's opinion (p. xiv). They propose this is in the form of populist appeals by political elites to insecure publics in order to promote a law and order agenda. Frost (2010) and Nagin et al. (2006) declare politicians either 'pander' to the public's punitive sentiments or claim public support for punitive policies with little regard to fairness or effectiveness of the outcome. As we see above, the unintended consequences of the imposition of IPPs created a vicious cycle which was detrimental to the incarcerated offender. Frost questions the evidence to justify an interpretation of punitive public attitudes. She shows, for example, public opinion poll data shifts quite dramatically when people are asked about specific punishments for particular offenders, rather than generalized attitudes, when they are more likely to pursue rehabilitative outcomes. There is also considerable demographic variation, with black people, women and the young being typically less punitive and more likely to support rehabilitative options. There is also a link between punitive public attitudes and political beliefs, with the more conservative holding the stronger punitive attitudes. Nagin et al. (2006) use a technique called 'contingent valuation', whereby the public are asked how much they are prepared to pay for a particular policy, as a more accurate way to estimate favourable or unfavourable attitudes rather than simply asking whether they approve or disapprove of a particular policy. Their results challenge both the media and politicians' claims that the public prefer incarceration to rehabilitation of young offenders, as they found the public are indeed concerned about youth crime and do wish to reduce its incidence but are ready to support rehabilitative efforts rather than imposing punishment and longer sentences.

Another element has been the rise of the 'victims' movement and victims' influence in shaping sentencing and rights to being informed about the release of ex-offenders into their communities (Walklate, 2001). This and policies of making criminal records more widely available is in tension, so Shadd Maruna (2011: 104) argues, with rehabilitation principles, including reputation restoration and re-integration. As he says 'what is the point of "challenging criminal thinking" or providing prisoners with suitable job training if upon their release they will be prohibited from finding legitimate employment because of their criminal records?' This then plays into the 'redeemability hypothesis' which is the belief held by some that people (including offenders) can change. Those supporting this proposition considers whether offenders are either victims themselves who need support or simply people who made bad choices as opposed to those who don't believe in change and that offenders are permanently damaged and/or simply evil. It is this latter group who are the most punitive in attitude, according to Maruna and King (2009). They undertook an analysis of public attitudes and found that belief in redeemability had a strong negative association with punitiveness. Conversely, people who believe that little can be done to modify criminality also support incapacitative sentencing practice.

Research in the UK has indicated a high degree of public support for sex offender registration and community notification of sex offenders living in the area. For example, polls conducted by Mori in 2000 and 2001 showed 76% of the sample agreed that people should know if there is a convicted paedophile in their neighbourhood; and 52% 'strongly supported' and a further 30% 'tended to support' the introduction of the so-called Sarah's Law, i.e. parents of children could ask the police under specified circumstances if a person with regular, unsupervised access to their child has a conviction for a sexual offence against a child.

There is legislation – the Rehabilitation of Offenders Act (1974) amended in section 139 of the Legal Aid, Sentencing and Punishment of Offenders Act (2012) – whose aim is to give those with convictions or cautions under certain circumstance the chance to wipe the slate clean and have these declared 'spent' (Lipscombe and Beard, 2014). A person whose conviction or caution is spent is referred to as a 'rehabilitated' person and treated for all legal purposes as if they had never committed the offence. This, however, does not go as far as Maruna is suggesting. He advocates certification of good character and highlights the legislation is limited in that a custodial sentence of over four years can never be spent. In addition, the rehabilitation period for eligible offences is seven years from completion of sentence for an adult and 42 months for a young person under the age of 18. Moreover, there are a number of jobs, professions and activities called 'excepted positions' for which disclosure of spent convictions may still be required. (We take a more detailed look at the issue of offenders' own victimization in Chapters 8 and 11.)

HOW CAN WE EXPLAIN CRIME TRENDS?

Before discussing crime trends and the politicization of crime, we need to think about what we mean by crime. White and Haines (2004) suggest this is not as straightforward as may appear. Not only are there competing views about what constitutes a crime, acts designated as criminal change over time. In England and Wales the Sex Offences Act of 1967 decriminalized homosexuality between consenting males over the age of 21. Prior to that acts of indecency between men could result in imprisonment (famously a two-year sentence was passed on Oscar Wilde in 1895 for sodomy after his affair with the son of the Marquis of Queensbury came to light, and in some jurisdictions, particularly within Africa and South East Asia, homosexuality remains illegal).

A formal legal definition states that a crime is whatever the state identifies as a crime, i.e. an activity is a crime if it is written into the criminal law and is subject to a state sanction in the form of a specific penalty. White and Haines (2004) give the example of Oscar Schindler, who broke Nazi law in order to help Jews escape the concentration camps. Was he a criminal or a hero? In the same vein one person's terrorist is another person's freedom fighter. This raises social and moral questions and potentially criminalizes those who break what they deem as unjust laws. Often crime is conceived as a social, physical or psychological harm or the consequences of a human rights violation or where a particular group experiences some form of discrimination. As White and Haines (2004: 5) propose, 'crime is not inherent in an activity: it is defined under particular material circumstances and in relation to specific social processes'.

The measurement of crime is not without problems. The idea of measuring crime originated in France and was associated with the development of modern states which wished to compile data on social life both to help plan for but also to keep control over their citizens (Maguire, 2012). The Home Office began to systematically record crime in 1857 for England and Wales, and counted specific offences, together with types and length of sentences. Early use of these statistics was to look at patterns occurring in different parts of the country, assist in the allocation of resources and provide a barometer of the 'moral health' of the nation. Maguire also points out that amongst these early uses of crime data was as a measure of success or failure of government policies.

Approaches to the measurement of crime include the realistic, institutional and critical realist approaches (White and Haines, 2004: 10). The first tries to take into account that not everything is recorded and that a 'dark figure' of unreported or unrecorded crime makes it difficult to uncover the true extent of crime. The institutional approach is the collection of official statistics. In

England and Wales, the Office of National Statistics (ONS) is responsible for the production and publication of crime statistics whilst the Home Office is responsible for the collection and validation of data from police forces. The UK Statistics Authority (2014), in responding to concerns about the accuracy and reliability of recorded crime, removed the national statistics designation, which is the kite mark of reliability, so highlighting the need for caution when analysing these data. Maguire (2010) lists some of the other concerns with the accuracy of officially recorded crime:

- the notifiable offence list determines which categories of crime are included (or excluded) so that additions and removals can artificially raise or lower the overall total;
- Home Office counting rules, which change from time to time, dictate how many individual offences are recorded for a repeat offender over a relatively short time;
- police discretion in what they record or 'no crime' can influence rates (e.g. there has been controversy over the no criming of reports of rape, see Stanko and Williams, 2009: 209);
- the public's propensity to report crime, especially those they do not consider serious, or their degree of faith in the police (see discussion in the Stern Review, 2010: 32).

The critical realist approach recognizes that crime has a social element and is concerned about its distribution, especially against the most vulnerable, and is especially interested in victimization surveys such as the Crime Survey of England and Wales (CSEW), which is the successor to the British Crime Survey (BCS) begun in 1982 and published annually. Whilst the CSEW is held to be a reasonably reliable source of the experience of crime, Mahoney, Davies and Scurlock-Evans (2014) note the survey covers only 'normal' households, excluding those living in halls of residence, nursing accommodation, nursing homes, warden-assisted accommodation and similar multiple-occupancy residences. This introduces a potential bias against the elderly, students, certain occupational groups (e.g., nurses) and individuals with mental health problems and learning difficulties. Also, the survey uses self-identified sexual orientation, which has been questioned as the most accurate method of measuring sexual identity. Maguire (2012: 224) draws attention to other limitations, such as its focus on crime committed by strangers rather than those occurring domestically, which is therefore likely to lead to underreporting of cases of domestic violence. The survey can say relatively little about multiple instances and serial offending.

Maguire (2012: 217) also cautions against a literal reading of the figures without some context. The unitary figure of the annual number of crimes recorded and from which trends are discerned is much vaunted by politicians seeking a headline-grabbing, simplistic measurement to demonstrate the efficacy of their own or the ineffectualness of their opponent's policies. As previously discussed, part of the political focus on law and order in the UK was concerned with the overall rate of crime, which had been steadily rising, reaching

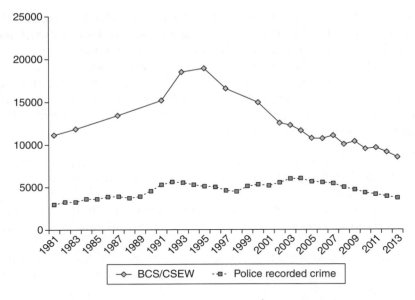

Figure 5.2 Trends in police recorded crime and BCS/CSEW data, 1981–2013

a peak in the late 1990s and thereafter dropped and continues to drop, as Figure 5.2 illustrates. Tseloni et al. (2010) observe that major falls in crime were first noted in the United States, where violent crime, including homicide, fell by 40% during the 1990s.

Calculating from the British Crime Survey (BSC) and its successor, the Crime Survey of England and Wales (CSEW), there was a 49% drop in homicide between 1995 and 2007. The equivalent figure for burglary is 59% and for car theft 65%. Figure 5.2 shows the rise then drop in victimization and rates of police recorded crime.

Forensic psychology has surprisingly little to say about crime trends, or offers reasons for the drop in crime over the last two decades, so it is to the sociologists and criminologists that we must look for explanations. Before trying to explain this reduction, it is important to note international trends. Tseloni et al. (2010) undertook some secondary analysis of European victimization data, and notwithstanding some inter-country consistency problems and statistical adjustments (discussed further in Chapter 8), they found that between 1995 and 2004 the mean international crime reductions were 77% for theft from cars, 60% theft from a person, 26% burglary, 21% assaults and 17% theft of cars. Not only this, but by and large the changes were roughly similar across countries. This then confirmed a general trend in decreasing crime levels reversing the upward trend that had marked much of the twentieth century.

Farrell and colleagues (2010) have undertaken a number of analyses of international crime data. They helpfully review a number of possible explanations, which are summarized in Box 5.2.

Box 5.2   Summary of proposed explanations for the drop in crime (after Farrell et al., 2010)

Abortion rates	Religiosity
Increased numbers of police	Cultural change
Lead-free petrol	Immigration
Increased incarceration rates	Repeat victimization
Policing strategies	Debut crime inhibition
Demographic change	Crime-specific explanations
Gun control	

We can dispose of a number of these explanations. Between 2010 and currently there has been a drop in police numbers in the UK (Independent Commission on Policing, 2013). Thus crime rates and police numbers shadow each other; as one rises so does the other and similarly as crime falls so do police numbers. It is unlikely there is a causal effect, not least because policing strategies at best have a marginal effect on reducing crime. Increases in abortion and decreases in lead exposure have been two particularly controversial explanations. It has been suggested that the legalization of abortion in the United States meant fewer male children being born to particularly at-risk groups. The various Clean Air Acts and the substitution of unleaded petrol undoubtedly reduced lead toxicity in the United States. Knock-on effects of teenagers at risk of delinquency and lessening lead exposure to children (the latter having been linked to increased aggression and impulsivity in childhood, both associated with criminality) has also some partial evidence to support this hypothesis. These may be partial explanations in accounting for reduced crime rates in the United States, but the generalizability of such explanations relies on all industrialized countries liberalizing abortion laws and removing similar amounts of lead at the same time.

If severity of punishment was a deterrent then we would expect crime rates in the United States and the UK to have had sharper drops because of their greater rates of incarceration. This is not the case. The relative strength of national economies and its impact on unemployment rates may be thought a factor. Yet during periods of relative austerity, crime rates still dropped when we might have expected them to rise. Also there appears to be a counterintuitive finding that property-related crime actually decreases during periods of austerity rather than increase as we might predict.

Some of the proposed explanations have equivocal and non-generalizable results; for example, the link between increased gun control and reductions in homicides rates, and reductions in street drug markets and declines in acquisitive crime. Others, such as increased religiosity and cultural change, are either too general or lack any definition of possible mechanisms linking them to reduction in crime to be of much utility.

Farrell and his colleagues (2010) provide a plausible argument that there may be some artefact in the counting of what constitutes a crime. On the one hand some crime may be obsolescent, for example stealing car radios, portable TVs and VCRs, which are likely to have low re-sale value due to higher levels of legitimate ownership and newer models being more socially desirable. On the other hand, new offences may be emerging but not yet adequately captured in data records, such as credit card fraud, internet scams and identity theft. The volume of obsolete and emergent forms of crime is uncalculated and we do not know if, in effect, they cancel each other out.

More promising explanations for the apparent fall in crime include drops in repeat victimization, i.e. the same offender committed fewer crimes and did not return to the same victim. Tseloni et al. (2010) found some support for this with respect to some crime, for example theft from cars, but not for other crime such as assault. Certainly target hardening, whereby car manufacturers for example make it more difficult to break into cars having anti-theft devices such as central locking, immobilisers and GPS tracking is likely to have had some impact in decreasing these thefts. Linked to this is the idea of 'debut' crime. Svensson (2002) suggests participation in certain kinds of offences acts as a precursor to continued and more serious offending. If these early 'debut' crime such as theft of and from cars has been inhibited, might this have a knock-on effect to later offending? In other words, are fewer people progressing into a crime career and/or are offenders starting later? Since we know that a high proportion of crime careers stop, shortened spans might be responsible for reductions in offending.

Farrell et al. (2010: 34) invoke 'the phone' test as a rule of thumb to check the explanatory power of a particular theory. By this they mean the ability of a given explanation to account for discrepancies in the crime trends, as in the theft of mobile phones and other expensive electronic goods such as laptops and SatNavs. It is difficult to see how childhood exposure to lead, or the abortion hypothesis or religiosity, can explain these increases in crime.

In the absence of a convincing psychological theory to account for these trends, the criminologist's 'security hypothesis' offers a clue to changes in behaviour that might account for at least some of the drop (Farrell et al., 2011). This proposes that manufacturers, spurred on by consumer demand, have improved anti-theft devices, particularly for cars. Different security measures work differently to increase the actual or perceived risk to potential offenders to engage in criminal activity. Collateral benefits might accrue from specific security options such as car anti-theft devices. As discussed above, hampering debut crime such as taking and driving cars might inhibit a future criminal career. Farrell et al. (2011) analysed crime and victimization data from the United States, Australia and England and Wales to produce convincing evidence for a relationship between anti-theft measures and crime reduction. They offer an extension to the security hypothesis by suggesting that car theft is a particularly salient crime and inhibiting this may (a) limit opportunities for other crime requiring a stolen car and (b) inhibit the commission of debut crime.

Figures for the number of recorded rapes, however, have not followed this general decreasing trend of crime rates, as Figure 5.3 depicts.

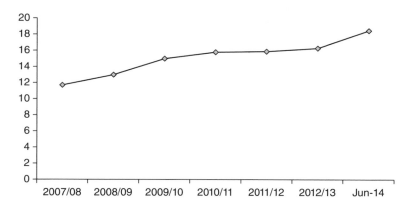

Figure 5.3   Number of police recorded rapes (000s), 2007-2014

In part these increases may be explained by the increased reporting of historic cases following the revelations about the sexual predatory activities of the entertainer and broadcaster Jimmy Savile. The police mounted operation Yewtree as a consequence and data from 27 forces showed an increase of 17% of reports comparing 2011/12 and 2012/13 and an increase of 29% by June 2014. In addition, recording practices may have improved as a consequence of good practice being issued by the Association of Chief Police Officers (ACPO) and additional guidance published by the Home Office in 2010.

HOW IS THE CONCEPT OF RISK DEFINED?

The technical definition of risk focuses narrowly on the probability of the occurrence of an event and the magnitude of a specific consequence (Kasperson et al., 1988). Risk is a much more complex concept than implied by this rather bland definition. There is considerable psychological literature on the public perception of risk (see, e.g., Breakwell, 2007). Breakwell defines risk in terms of the negative consequences, i.e. harm, as a consequence of being exposed to a hazard. Thus risk refers to the extent of harm arising from a hazard. Breakwell notes the two concepts, probability and consequences, are often confusingly used interchangeably. She further articulates the idea that rather as in the concept of crime measurement, the notion of risk assessment is associated with modern society. Scientific and technological development creates hazards and associated risk, i.e. the risk society and the rise of institutional arrangements to protect citizens from adverse consequences and also to apportion responsibility for negligence or unprotected hazards. This in turn has given rise to psychological notions of risk acceptance as a consequence of modern living (for example, most of us drive a car despite 24,160 people being killed on Britain's roads in the year ending March 2014 and 189,880 being injured – Department of Transport, 2014).

Cognitive heuristics – mental shortcuts based on fallacious reasoning – can contribute to biased and erroneous judgements when assessing risk. Table 5.1 provides some examples.

Table 5.1 Definitions of heuristics and biased reasoning

Heuristic	Definition
Base rate fallacy	The ignoring of reliable, broad-based statistical information that is readily available, e.g. ignoring the likelihood that a close family member may be implicated in a child's murder or abduction despite the high incidence of a relative being implicated.
Representative heuristic	Assuming commonality between things that are similar to a prototype and assessing the probability of an event based on the occurrence of the prototype, e.g. erroneously assuming that a suspect who shares characteristics of the stereotypical rapist is necessarily the most likely offender.
Availability heuristic	Evaluating events according to the ease with which they can be imagined, i.e. if a number of instances can readily be recalled it is assumed they are frequent events, e.g. overestimating the number of rapes because the media cover instances in a sensational and memorable way.
Anchoring and adjustment	When making judgements about something they are uncertain about, people are influenced by an initial value suggested by an external source, e.g. the impact of the profile drawn up in the Rachel Nickell murder.
Biases	
Belief persistence	Once an opinion has been formed it is difficult to disconfirm, e.g. the belief that the letters and tapes made by 'Wearside Jack' in the Yorkshire Ripper case were authentic and not a hoax (in fact these were fabricated by John Samuel Humble).
Confirmation bias	This is where more weight is sought to support a view and counter evidence is selectively ignored. e.g. in the 'Wearside Jack' example the investigating officers were led to follow up men with a Wearside accent to the exclusion of other suspects, including Peter Sutcliffe, the Ripper, who actually had a Yorkshire accent.

Source: Almond et al., 2008

Risk too has become a politicized concept. On the one hand the considerable media attention given to the cases involving mentally disordered violent offenders and on the other coverage that widely publicized failures in care leave an impression on the public of both the apparent dangerousness of the mentally ill and the lack of public protection (Doyle, 2011); an example of the availability heuristic. Roycroft, Brown and Innes (2007) argue that certain crimes act as 'signal events' that result from the real or perceived failure of a designated person or the authorities to protect an individual or society at large from some harm. Some crimes have greater capacity to exert influence over the public, and often through media pressure stimulate the authorities in mounting inquiries, such as the re-opening of the inquest into the deaths at the 1989 Hillsborough football stadium disaster.

WHAT IS RISK ASSESSMENT?

Risk assessment and management are key activities for forensic psychologists and involve admission to and discharge from hospital, commitment to and release from prison, child protection, probation orders, anti-social behaviour orders, MAPPA arrangements, charge and bail conditions, notification and registration of lifers and sex offenders (Doyle, 2011: 38). Ward and Beech (2014) explain risk assessment is often misunderstood and that it is about predicting repetition of offending behaviour rather than predicting changes in behaviour, either escalation of seriousness or crossover (i.e. changing the gender or age of a targeted victim). In addition to identifying risk factors that are usually classified as dynamic and static, research identifies protective factors. Dynamic risk factors are aspects of an offender's life that can change, such as having criminal associates or being in an unstable relationship. Static factors are the unchangeable features, such as prior criminal history or early life experiences. Protective factors are features that lower the risk of reoffending and again have been conceptualized as dynamic and static. Thus de Vries Robbé et al. (2015) propose dynamic protective factors include being in stable employment, which may be indicative of propensity towards self-discipline, a work ethic and an ability to manage social relationships. A static protective factor may be having secure attachments in early family life. They suggest that a protective factor may be thought of as the 'healthy' pole of its opposite dysfunctional risk factor, for example the risk factor deviant sexual interest has as its opposite protective pole sexual preference for consenting adults. Sean Hammond (Box 5.3) suggests three key reasons why risk and its measurement became such a salient issue for forensic psychologists.

Box 5.3 Sean Hammond on the rise of interest in risk assessment

Clearly, as psychologists, forensic psychologists are less interested in assessment for diagnosis than for treatment planning. As a substantial caseload will involve potential harm to self or others these treatments lean towards risk mitigation.

(Continued)

In short, I think things kicked off in the 1980s and 1990s and there were probably three main catalysts:

1. The Zito case [the murder of Jonathan Zito by schizophrenic Christopher Clunis in 1992] was a particular catalyst in the UK which corresponded with the high-profile US academic publication of MacArthur Violence Risk Assessment Study (Monahan et al., 2005). A large number of inquiries following the Zito case demonstrated the fact that multi-agency independence was a major problem. Psychologists saw the need to develop assessment portfolios that worked in a multi-agency context (forensic practitioners work in a variety of agencies, unlike other disciplines).
2. A further impetus was the politically motivated move to identify the Dangerous and Severe Personality Disorder (DSPD) criteria. Psychiatrists were very sceptical at first because they could not see how this fitted with their diagnostic medical model. Forensic psychologists, on the other hand, could readily map this onto their trait models of PD, especially Bob Hare's psychopathy construct (Hare, 1998).
3. Add to this a prevailing climate in which clinical judgement was under attack in light of Meehl's statistical arguments brought into forensic practice by Faust et al. (see Dawes, Faust and Meehl, 1989). In fact, this led to some very simplistic and unhelpful deterministic statistical thinking but it did emphasize the need for empirical evidence to support clinical decision making around risk appraisal and management.

I would say these are the three most fundamental forces driving forensic psychology's interest in assessment of PD and risk.

I don't buy into the notion that nothing works. The DSPD services have certainly floundered but probably because these are very damaged individuals and the evaluation approaches were largely unrealistic (normative aggregated methods rather than those with a case-based idiographic orientation). However, as with the rest of psychology, the advance of science is slow and flawed, with some rare gems emerging here and there.

What follows is a more detailed analysis of Hammond's identified catalysts. Coid (1994) describes the Zito case as follows. In 1986, when Christopher Clunis was 23 years old, he was diagnosed with paranoid schizophrenia in Jamaica, where his parents came from. He returned to London and was in and out of various psychiatric hospitals over the following years. He moved constantly and over a five and a half year period he was assessed by or was directly under the care of 30 named psychiatrists. He received 10 episodes of in-patient care and had been remanded into police or prison custody three times. Between June 1988 and 1989 Christopher disappeared without contact with medical and social services. There was little continuity between carers. Christopher had exhibited risky behaviours, such as using a bladed or pointed weapon in response to his delusional ideas and to target his victim's head, especially the eyes. He had stabbed two different patients in 1989, and in 1990 tried to gouge out the eye of a fellow hostel inmate. In 1991 he chased another hostel inmate with a carving knife. In May 1992 he stabbed a resident in the neck in yet another hostel. Two weeks prior to the killing of Jonathan Zito, Christopher was floridly psychotic and potentially homicidal, having threatened with a screw driver a man walking a dog and later chasing two boys, wielding the same weapon. Repeated contacts and telephone calls from victims and their families failed to evoke a response from the police. Not only did the professionals involved minimize the violence or Christopher's assessed propensity to violence in the future they also procrastinated when making decisions about Christopher, possibly because of his threatening and intimidating behaviours. At the time of the attack on Jonathan Zito at Finsbury Park station Christopher was living in a filthy bedsit where a quantity of prescribed medication lay untouched. Christopher, shabbily dressed and acting bizarrely, was ignored by waiting passengers on the station. He came up close to and behind Jonathan Zito and his brother, who were waiting for their train. Without warning, Christopher fatally stabbed Jonathan in the face three times, once in the eye. Christopher was found guilty of manslaughter on the grounds of diminished responsibility and detained in Rampton under section 37/41 of the Mental Health Act 1983.

The subsequent inquiry was extremely critical of Christopher's chaotic care and the Department of Health's Care Programme Approach, which had signally failed, and that there were potentially many other patients in Christopher's predicament. By 1999 more than 35 reports had been undertaken arising from failures of community care since the Clunis inquiry (O'Rourke, 1999). One of the points O'Rourke makes is that the necessary tools were not available to both assess and manage risk.

We have in the previous chapter discussed the invention of the DSPD label. Hammond's second comment in Box 5.3 suggests that concerns about dangerousness are 'mapped' onto issues arising from the psychopathy construct. Psychopathy is a personality disorder that is a chronic disturbance of an individual's relations to self and others and ability to fulfil social obligations (Cooke, 2010). Hare, Cooke and Hart (1999) describe a psychopath as someone who is grandiose, arrogant, callous, superficially charming and highly manipulative, unable to form meaningful emotional bonds with others. Criminal versatility and violence have been associated with diagnoses of psychopathy. It perhaps was not such an additional step to note the risk presented by people on the extreme ends of this personality disorder.

The MacArthur Violence Risk Assessment Study (Monahan et al., 2005), a comprehensive community study, was designed to identify risk factors. The study had two core goals: to do the best possible 'science' on violence risk assessment, and to produce a usable actuarial violence risk assessment 'tool' for clinicians. The Study evolved in six stages and took over a decade to plan, execute and analyse the data. Its novelty was to use the 'classification tree' method rather than the usual linear regression method. A classification tree approach reflects an interactive and contingent model of violence, one that allows many different combinations of risk factors to classify a person at a given level of risk. The particular questions to be asked in any assessment grounded in this approach depend on the answers given to prior questions. Factors that are relevant to the risk assessment of one person may not be relevant to the risk assessment of another person. This contrasts with a regression approach in which a common set of questions is asked of everyone being assessed and every answer is weighted to produce a score that can be used for purposes of categorization. This goes some way to identify risk factors but begs two questions: what means are employed to assess the risk and how best to manage the risk. Hammond's third point is the debate about the relative merits of clinical versus actuarial methods of assessment stimulated by Paul Meehl (see, e.g., Dawes, Faust and Meehl, 1989).

The clinical method is based on the decision maker's knowledge and experience. Its advantage allows the clinician to focus on case-specific influences (Doyle and Dolan, 2002). In the actuarial method, human judgement is eliminated and judgements made on the basis of empirically established relations between the data and the condition or events of interest. Contrasting the two methods, Meehl and his collaborators concluded that actuarial methods were superior because:

- unlike human judges, the same conclusions are drawn from a given data set;
- the mathematical features of actuarial methods ensure that the contributing variables have actual predictive power and relation to the criterion of interest;
- clinicians rarely seek feedback about their judgemental accuracy, which can produce self-fulfilling prophecies;
- past behaviours are selectively recalled and ascribed greater consistency than is warranted;
- clinician's sample of patients is skewed as opposed to the more representative sampling of statistical data;
- clinicians also tend not to observe individuals without significant problems, which further skews and potentially biases their judgement.

Dawes, Faust and Meehl do caution that actuarial methods are not infallible. A specific procedure in one setting may not be as successful when applied to another. Other criticisms made of actuarial methods include the absence of more idiosyncratic features, focus on relatively static risk factors and may exclude factors that logically are important but have not been demonstrated to be so empirically (Doyle and Dolan, 2002). Dawes and colleagues counter the idiosyncrasy criticism by suggesting 'although individuals and events may exhibit unique features, they typically show common features with other persons or events that permit tallying observations or generalizations to achieve predictive power' (1989: 1672).

Second generation actuarial methods consider risk as a continuum, recognizing its continuous and dynamic nature, and the approach has been to establish checklists of a number of predictive factors, each being allotted a score. The total becomes an actuarial probability, graduating the amount of risk attributable to an individual (Doyle and Dolan, 2002). Coid et al. (2011), however, remain cautious about the reliability of structured risk assessments because there is a ceiling effect beyond which instruments are unlikely to improve their accuracy and there is also a degree of 'shrinkage' of results when instruments are applied to populations on which they were not originally standardized. Another problem lies in the use of aggregate scores. Since few studies provide information on the predictive ability of individual items, it is possible that certain items within these instruments do not have predictive ability, and that bi-variate correlations with violence as an outcome are merely the result of a strong correlation with other items, which are truly predictive. They conclude:

> clinicians should be aware of the limitations and be critical when using either an actuarial, structured clinical risk assessment instrument, or a personality disorder assessment instrument, if the intention is to carry out a comprehensive assessment of risk on which to base subsequent risk management or treatment interventions. (2001: 16)

Third generation risk assessment combines clinical judgement and actuarial approaches and here there is a definite shift to incorporate aspects of risk management to include considerations of prevention and treatment and also the conditions under which the risk will increase or decrease (Doyle and Dolan, 2002). The Violence Risk Appraisal Guide (VRAG) and the Historical Clinical Risk Management tool (HCR-20) are examples of these third generation tools (Harris and Rice, 2010).

More recently there has been a critical re-appraisal of the assessment of risk factors (see, e.g., Ward and Beech, 2014). They argue that there has been a neglect of theory (not least because academics researching this area and practitioners applying risk assessments do not appear to communicate). Their proposal is that dynamic risk factors may better be thought of as 'clusters of clinical features or "symptoms" generated by understanding causal mechanisms rather than being causes themselves' (p. 2). They give by way of example the clinical attribute of distorted thinking as being linked to the dynamic risk factor of pro-offending attitudes whilst social difficulties and intimacy problems are linked to the risk factor of intimacy deficits. This constitutes the first step in re-conceptualizing risk factors as a way into identifying causal mechanisms and, as a consequence, lead to more effective interventions.

Evidence-based and theory-driven risk assessment should also inform the management plan for an individual, which, as well as identifying risk, looks at protective factors such as treatment compliance, insight, good relationship with care team and supportive social networks. It was seen in the Clunis case that many of these elements were missing and the lack of an adequate care programme approach was severely criticized.

Another key case, that of Michael Stone, also found shortcomings in the care programme. In October 1998 Michael Stone was convicted of the murder of Lin Russell and her daughter Megan, and the attempted murder of Josie Russell, her other daughter. Prins (2007) summarizes the key facts. Mrs Russell and her two daughters were walking home having attended a swimming gala. They were attacked by a man seen getting out of a car. He took them into the wood, tied them up with torn strips of swimming towels and shoe laces, blindfolded them and hit their heads with a hammer. Lin and Megan died, Josie survived. Their pet dog who was with them was also killed. Mr Stone had received a wide range of services and had frequent contact with mental health professionals. The first GP he was registered with gave him a high standard of care, but this was not his experience with a subsequent GP with whom he registered. His follow-up with forensic community mental health services was inadequate and the care programme approach principles were not applied. His initial requests to be put on a detox programme were ignored, although he did subsequently receive such treatment. Details of his medical history were not made known to the appropriate authorities after his release from prison because they appear to have been lost, although his supervision by probation was conscientious. Michael was diagnosed with a psychopathic personality disorder which was considered to be untreatable and as such he was not detainable under the provisions of the 1983 Mental Health Act.

The Clunis and Stone cases provided the impetus for government to intervene, not least because both were accompanied by vociferous media campaigns. The issue of concern in the Clunis case was his being 'lost' by the system and the risk he presented by his untreated and deteriorating mental condition. Michael Stone had received some high-quality care but here the problem was the treatability status of his personality disorder diagnosis.

As explained above, in response to such cases the government introduced indeterminate sentencing (IPP) through the Criminal Justice Act of 2003 as a way to detain individuals who were deemed dangerous, and the number of individuals held in the period to 2013 is shown in Figure 5.4.

In addition, government sought to reform the 'treatability test' and address their frustration with psychiatrists in their management, or mismanagement, of high-risk offenders with personality disorders (O'Loughlin, 2014). The Mental Health Act of 2007 changed the 'treatability test' into an 'appropriate medical treatment test', the purpose of which was to alleviate or prevent a worsening of symptoms. Under this new test, patients can be detained against their wishes as long as there is a medical treatment available. The MHA 2007 also brought in provisions that emphasized public protection as a goal of

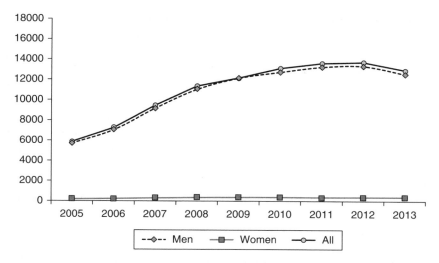

Figure 5.4 Number of indeterminate sentence prisoners in England and Wales, 2005-2013. (Source: MOJ)

criminal justice to manage dangerous offenders. Although not designed especially for DSPD offenders, the majority of those detained beyond tariff by an indeterminate sentence will have been designated DSPD. These two measures form part of a wider political risk management agenda and, as O'Loughlin (2014: 186) states, represent a hybrid of a determinate punitive 'tariff' and an indeterminate sentence which begins after tariff expiry and lasts until the prisoner is deemed safe to release by the Parole Board.

WHAT IS NEW PUNITIVENESS?

As implied above, the 'nothing works' doctrine created disenchantment with the rehabilitation ideals of imprisonment (Nash, 2001). What was the point of programmes if they did not work? However, politically, in the 1990s, during Michael Howard's tenure as Home Secretary, his dictum 'prison works' symbolized a turn towards a more punitive penal climate. The signal in the 1995 Green Paper was its title: 'Strengthening Punishment in the Community'. The community service option available to sentencers became incorporated into a single integrated community sentence (Mair and Burke, 2012: 156).

More contentious was the requirement that the defendant's consent for the option of imposition of a community order should be removed. Mair and Burke suggest this not only had huge symbolic resonance for the Probation Service, as since its inception agreement to participate in a probation order was crucial to the relationship between offender and probation officer, but also resulted in a decrease in community penalties for those having a prior custodial sentence. The election in 1997 of a Labour government did not see a reversal of punitive and populist policies; rather these were continued and to some extent increased, especially with respect to sex offenders (Nash, 2001).

The Home Office's 'what works' project saw in 1998 the roll out of the Effective Practice initiative, largely driven by cognitive behaviour approaches with greater centralized planning and accreditation of the Pathfinder programmes. As outlined in Chapter 4, the 2000 Criminal Justice and Court Services Act turned the Probation Service into a 'fully fledged criminal justice agency', finally moving it away from its social service roots and 'clumsily' changing the names of the three main orders: the probation order became the community rehabilitation order, the community service order became the community punishment order and the combined order, the community punishment and rehabilitation order.

There was also a new exclusion order, whereby an offender could not enter a certain area for 12 months. Fitzgibbon and Lea (2014) observe that since the 1980s respective governments sought to break probationer training links with social work and reduce officers' professional autonomy, and have attempted to turn probation into an offender management and public protection service with a reduced orientation to rehabilitation. They argue that the Coalition's payment by results reforms consolidate the risk management strategy. This migration away from traditional concerns about offender reform and humanitarian programmes towards the 'warehousing' of offenders sorted by their risk levels, according to Feeley and Simon (1992), changed the penal social ethic into one that is rationalized by notions of control and just deserts. More recently, Fitzgibbon and Lea (2014: 29) conclude:

> cost reduction, imposed by competitive tendering and PbR, will steer the security industrial complex firmly in the direction of monitoring and risk management supervised by low cost, increasingly flexible labour force. The more skilled and inevitably labour intensive, traditional forms of rehabilitation through community re-integration will be beyond its capacity.

The Sentencing Council's factsheet indicates that sentencing in England and Wales has undoubtedly got tougher: across the criminal court system, the average sentence length for those sentenced to immediate custody for indictable offences has increased from 15 months in 2001 to 17 months in 2011. In the Crown Court, this has increased from 25 months in 2001 to 26 months in 2011. Conviction rates at the Crown Court have risen – overall 83% of defendants tried in 2011 were convicted. However, the use of fines for indictable offences decreased from 24% in 2001 to 17% in 2011. The use of suspended sentences for indictable offences increased from 0.7% in 2001 to 10% in 2011. The immediate custody rate for indictable offences has increased from 24.9% in 2001 to 25.3% in 2011. Community sentences are the most common disposal for indictable offences, accounting for approximately a third of sentences.

The rates of imprisonment in the UK are amongst the highest in Europe and are increasing, as Figures 5.5 and 5.6 illustrate. Frost (2010: 156) argues that punitive legislation is a response to an increasing punitive public demand.

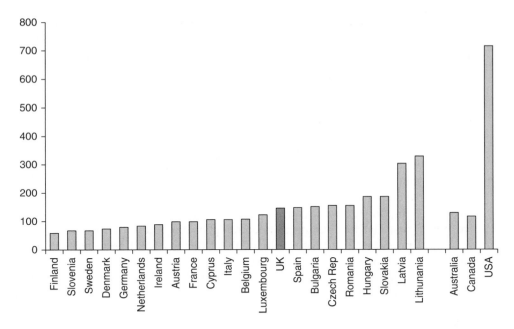

Figure 5.5 Prison population per 100,000 nationals (of national population) (Source: Walmsley, 2014)

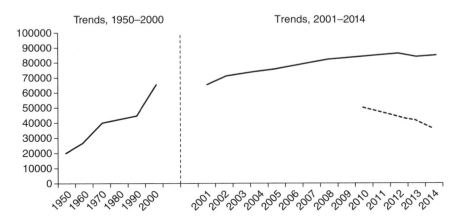

Figure 5.6 Annual prison population rate in England and Wales, 1950-2014, also showing the declining number of prison officers, 2010-2014 (dotted line). (Source: Ministry of Justice)

Against this trend of rises in the prison population, the National Offender Management Service (NOMS) as a whole has had to make savings, £228 million in 2011–12. The savings were delivered by a combination of workforce restructuring;

market testing and privatization of entire establishments and specific services; standardizing costs and services; and reconfiguring the prison estate by closing some smaller, older prisons and increasing the size and number of very large establishments.

Her Majesty's Inspectorate of Prisons produces an annual report and in its latest (Her Majesty's Chief Inspector of Prisons for England and Wales, 2014), the Chief Inspector's assessment is as follows:

- No one should fool themselves that these financial and organizational pressures do not create risks. In prisons, there are fewer staff on the wings supervising prisoners, there are fewer managers supervising staff and less support available to establishments from a diminished centre. Quite apart from the impact of the savings themselves, there is clearly a danger in all forms of custody that managers become 'preoccupied with cost cutting, targets and processes' and lose sight of their fundamental responsibilities for the safety, security and rehabilitation of those they hold.
- Our judgements about the quantity and quality of purposeful activity in which prisoners are engaged plummeted over the year. Put simply, too many prisoners spend too long locked in their cells with nothing constructive to do, and when they are in classes or work, these are often of insufficient quality. Equipping prisoners with the skills, habits and attitudes they need to get and hold down a job is an essential part of the rehabilitation process. Only a few years ago we heard a lot about 'working prisons' and making prisons places of productive activity. More recently there has been a deafening silence on this topic and prisons might be excused if they believe this is no longer a priority.
- A new contract for the provision of training and education began in August 2012 for most prisons in England. We have seen little sign of improvement so far. The range and quality of activity on offer required improvement, there were insufficient opportunities for prisoners to obtain vocational skills or qualifications that employers valued.

Not all criminologists agree with the new punitiveness thesis (see, e.g., Matthews, 2009, 2010, 2014). Matthews is unconvinced by the evidence and what he calls 'conspiratorial theories' that blame increased use of incarceration on popular punitiveness (Matthews, 2009: 349).

Box 5.4   Reflective exercise

The following excerpt is a comment by the journalist Simon Jenkins (www.the-guardian.com/commentisfree/2014/aug/19/chris-grayling-prisons-crisis-inspectors-overcrowded-violent-jails).

No other nation in Europe jails with the same abandon as Britain. As a result, its jails are bursting at the seams, currently with 84,000 prisoners and rising fast. Overcrowding, drug abuse, violence, attacks on warders, and suicide (88 in the past year, up from 52 in 2013) are all increasing. Meanwhile, the prison officer population has been slashed by almost a third in three years. Prisoners are confined to cells for as much as 23 hours a day. Successive inspectors of prisons raise the alarm, to absolutely no effect, the latest concerning the Isis youth prison in Kent, which was called by one inmate a 'gladiator school'.

To all this the Justice Secretary, Chris Grayling, asserts that: 'There are pressures which we're facing but there's not a crisis.' It is 'challenged' but not 'in crisis'. The vocabulary is pure cliché. The only certainty is that the courts are jailing far too many people, and that they and their political masters are hooked on the habit. People should be sent to prison to protect other people, mostly from violence. Yet 70% of male prisoners and 80% of female are non-violent offenders.

All other reasons for so terrible a punishment – the impact of imprisonment, however brief, lasts for life – should be handled by and in the community. It should be through treatment, restorative justice, fines, banning orders.

Do you agree with Simon Jenkins's analysis that politicians are 'hooked' on sending people to jail?

Should the majority of offenders be 'handled by and in the community'?

What have you read in this chapter that helped inform your view?

As a consequence of reading this chapter have you changed your views about imprisonment?

CONCLUSION

Hopefully, this chapter has been persuasive in suggesting that the activities of forensic psychologists do not take place in some value-free environment and that the direction of policy is influenced by political considerations, as indeed is the commissioning of research, and dissemination of results. Political choices are made about what to measure and increasingly how to measure as well as being instrumental in deciding what is to be funded and how much will be spent. Austerity and the imposition of reduced budgets has taken its toll of CJS agencies. In the next chapter on theory we discuss the Good Lives Model and the Risk–Need–Responsivity approach that paints a rather less gloomy picture of what may be possible.

RESOURCES

Many helpful statistics are available from the Ministry of Justice website, such as reports of the CSEW (www.justice.gov.uk/).

The Sentencing Council produces an annual report charting sentencing trends (http://sentencingcouncil.judiciary.gov.uk/).

The account of the past and recent history of the Probation Service by George Mair and Lol Burke (2012) provides an excellent case study of the punitive-rehabilitation debate.

Key journals

British Journal of Criminology

Criminology and Criminal Justice

Critical Social Policy

Psychology Public Policy and Law

6

THEORY

KEY CONCEPTS

This chapter discusses theory, what it is, why it is important and how to evaluate good theory. We look at some general models of offending as well as explanations for specific crimes. The chapter also looks at two of the main theories of rehabilitation.

Knowledge concepts	Practice considerations
Attachment	Age crime curve
Criminal careers	Good Lives Model (GLM)
Criminal differentiation	Models
Criminogenic need	Paradigms
Deduction	Phenomenology
Falsification	Prospective studies
Homology principle	Risk-Need-Responsivity (RNR) model
Induction	Target hardening
Introversion-extraversion	Taxonomies
Knifing off	
Maturity gap	
Moral reasoning	
Neuroticism	
Psychoticism	
Risk factors	
Routine activity theory (RAT)	
Rational choice theory (RCT)	
Violence-breeds-violence hypothesis	

(Continued)

This chapter should give you a grounding in the principles of theory building, the difference between a paradigm, a theory and a model, and introduce you to some of the key conceptual thinking relevant to understanding criminal behaviour and motivation to commit crime.

Questions addressed

What is a theory, a law, a model, a concept and a paradigm?

What is the origin of experimental methods as used by forensic psychologists?

How do we know if a theory is valid?

Why doesn't every teenager become a delinquent?

Why do people commit crime?

Is there a general model to explain why people commit crime?

What specific models and theories explain different kinds of offending?

How are desistance and persistence in offending explained?

What are some of the main theories of rehabilitation?

WHAT IS A THEORY, A LAW, A MODEL, A CONCEPT AND A PARADIGM?

This chapter begins by explaining some terminology and gives some criteria to evaluate 'good' theory. As this is a huge area and we are only devoting one chapter to this topic, what follows is necessarily selective. The present chapter is illustrative of some of the main theories employed by forensic psychologists and is divided into three broad areas:

- abstinence (i.e. why some people never commit crime), persistence (why some people keep committing crime) and desistance from crime (why some people who commit crime, stop);
- why people commit violent, sexual and acquisitive crime; and
- ideas relevant to rehabilitation.

A **theory** is a systematic way of making sense of some phenomenon, enabling us to interpret, reconstruct, explain and predict. Theory gives us a basis upon which to devise research, to generate and test hypotheses and to design interventions to change that phenomenon. In terms of scientific enquiry there are three elements: describing the phenomenon of interest, inferring the underlying causes (rather than merely describing some co-occurring features) and being able to predict aspects of the relationships implicit in the causal mechanisms (Breakwell, 1995).

We can think of an example such as the theory of planned behaviour (Ajzen, 2005). This theory predicts the relationship between attitudes and behaviour as being subject to three main influences: evaluation of the behaviour (attitudes); perception of the social pressures to engage in the behaviour (subjective norms); and perception of the controls governing performance of the behaviour (perceived behavioural control). Underlying these are specific beliefs about the consequences of engaging in behaviours (behavioural beliefs), perceived wishes of important referents (normative beliefs) and those factors that may inhibit or facilitate performance (control beliefs). Norman, Bennett and Lewis (1998) used this framework to explore the influences of these factors on binge drinking in adolescents.

Sometimes a theory draws on two previous ideas, developing a set of hypotheses deriving from this binary combination. Thus Alison and Stein (2001) combined one idea, the ordering of behaviours in a qualitative circle, with a second, incorporating the dimensions of dominance–submission and hostility–cooperation. This combination theory was then used by Porter and Alison (2004) to investigate gang rape and they generated the following hypothesis:

> Within any given case of group rape, offenders' behaviour will co-occur to produce a theme of behaviour that can be described in terms of the circumplex [circular] dimensions. Therefore the null hypothesis states that in any given case of group rape, offenders will all behave in thematically different ways [such] that behaviours will form a random spread of behaviours rather than distinct themes. (2004: 453)

Confirmation of their hypothesis allowed them to describe a structural theory of group rape (see Chapter 7 for more details of this research).

Comprehensive theories, such as described by Ward and Beech (2006) on sexual offending, integrated different factors (biological, ecological and neuropsychological), suggesting genes, social learning and neuropsychological systems interact and together make for a fuller explanation than any one of these domains independently.

Our discussion of the Risk–Need–Responsivity (RNR) model and the Good Lives Model (GLM) later in this chapter provides a worked example of how comprehensive theories are derived.

A theory permits the generation of hypotheses or questions that can then be tested. If theory produces some recurrent and universal findings we may be able to generate **laws** that are conclusions accepted within the scientific community. The laws of thermodynamics in physics are an example. It is doubtful whether the state of knowledge in psychology can generate laws except perhaps in the area of psycho-physics, which have to do with the properties of a stimulus and its perception. As yet we are nowhere near generating scientific laws that will help us with respect to criminal behaviour. Indeed we have no overarching theory that explains criminal behaviour satisfactorily. As Howitt (2002) appositely put it:

> Anyone entering forensic and criminal psychology with a view [that there are natural and largely immutable laws or principles of human behaviour that psychological research should strive to discover] will rapidly be frustrated to find how situationally specific and sometimes, unreplicable findings in the field can be. (2002: 72)

Often a theory will utilize **concepts**, for example 'behavioural consistency', as a way of grouping experiences under a convenient label. This is essentially an abstract idea trying to describe an observed phenomenon but which also has an explanatory quality. Qualitative analysis uses the idea of a grounded concept, meaning that a verbal label is adopted to describe something that collectively has been derived from (or grounded in) interviewees' experiences. Thus Frances Heidensohn used the concept 'transformational scenes' to capture the experiences of the policewomen she interviewed in managing violence in order to be accepted by their male colleagues. Heidensohn (1992: 141–2) explains she used this term because it reminded her of the final stages in an English pantomime in which 'the poor shy heroine is transformed into the beautiful well-dressed princess'. This vividly captures the underlying process these women described they had to go through to demonstrate to sceptical male officers that they could handle the rougher side of policing. However, concepts require thoughtful definition and are often criticized in the research literature for being ambiguous or in need of greater clarification.

Before theories are articulated, **models** may be generated, often in the form of a diagram that is a useful summary representation of concepts and processes and provides some directionality between them. Generally speaking a model does not have the formal status of a theory, although often the two terms are used interchangeably (see Francks, 2002 for detailed explanations of the use of models in scientific enquiry). Farrington's 'simple model of offending' is given later by way of example.

A **paradigm** is usually taken to mean general principles and methods that form the coherent background to science at a particular time. Thomas Kuhn (1922–96) introduced the idea of a 'paradigm shift', when there is a dramatic change in scientific thinking (Kuhn, 1962). This concept is explained by Rom Harré when describing the shift made by some social psychologists in the 1960s and 1970s who moved from the positivist experimental tradition of scientific enquiry *on* 'subjects' to a constructionist approach that negotiated meanings *with* research 'participants' (Harré and Secord, 1972).

WHAT IS THE ORIGIN OF EXPERIMENTAL METHODS AS USED BY FORENSIC PSYCHOLOGISTS?

The work of Wilhelm Wundt (1832–1920) is of particular interest in the development of forensic psychology because it was his experimental laboratory, established in Leipzig in 1879, which was the forerunner of psychology being applied to the law by one of his students, Hugo Münsterberg, often credited as being a founding father of forensic psychology (Brown and Campbell, 2010). Wundt developed scientific rules for investigating observable phenomena. As Chung and Hyland (2012: 52) explain, Wundt was interested in immediate conscious experiences and developed experimental methods in order to:

- analyse the contents of consciousness into their basic elements;
- discover how these elements are connected;
- determine the laws that underlie the connections between elements.

On taking these ideas to America at the turn of the twentieth century, Münsterberg and others, notably James Cattell, conducted numerous experiments to try to understand the limits of memory and recall. The science that Wundt and his students worked with was a form of logic called induction, i.e. the collecting of observations and inducing an explanation. This model of scientific reasoning was famously challenged by Karl Popper (1902–94), who introduced the idea of falsification or the notion that we cannot categorically prove hypotheses to be true, we only accept them if we cannot show them to be false. Falsification is based on deduction. For Popper, science starts by inventing a hypothesis that is a conjecture about some aspect of the world. A working hypothesis has clear theoretical arguments and leads to prediction, that is, it deduces some fact that should occur as predicted by the theory. This is then tested against a number of collected observations (data) to see if the hypothesis is true or false. As Chung and Hyland elaborate, Popper suggested that science proceeds through a series of hypotheses and refutations, i.e. where the prediction arising from the hypothesis is shown to be false, a better hypothesis is constructed and tested again such that the derived explanations or theory are cumulatively refined.

Scientific theory does not simply proceed in a linear cumulative fashion, neither will 'any old' theory do. New conceptual thinking usually starts with consideration of existing theories, and as Bekerian and Levey (2005: 5) put it, 'a central aspect of science consists of competition between theories'. Sometimes there is a complete rejection of the underlying ideas and, as mentioned above, we have a paradigm shift whereby the nature of scientific thinking is changed. The shift in thinking that took place particularly within social psychology which turned its focus to the idea of meaning contributed to the development of an approach called **social constructionism**. Here the scientific enterprise looks at real-world experience and shares the construction of explanations of the phenomenon under investigation with those providing an account of that experience. So rather than the scientist being the 'expert knower' identifying some 'truth', ideas about the world are jointly constructed by scientist and research participants. This recognizes that many phenomena are constructed by society, for example what may constitute bigamy and a crime in one society is an accepted practice of polygamy in another. The methodological implications of these different approaches are discussed in Chapter 7 on research methods. For now we will look at the criteria that have been used to evaluate theories.

HOW DO WE KNOW IF A THEORY IS VALID?

Generally speaking we want to know if a theory gives us a correct description (its phenomenology) and can predict new facts about some phenomenon. Bekerian and Levey (2005) synthesize approaches to theory verification as comprising: disconfirmation and pragmatism. The first derives from the idea of falsification we briefly discussed above. As explained by Bekerian and Levey, simply showing a theory fits the facts is not sufficient, rather there must be 'some logical mechanism in the theory that makes it possible to show it may be false, i.e. a theory must lend itself to being tested to prove it is actually valid'. The standard way of testing theories is by setting up experiments. This can be difficult so a pragmatic position adopts the principle of utility: if the theory is useful, it is valid. This is described by Bekerian and Levey thus:

> The pragmatic approach says that a theory can be regarded as true for practical purposes if it gives an accurate description of the available facts. [This] enables us to isolate theoretical concepts that can be applied to a particular problem, even if parts of the theory are not universally true. We call this the principle of local application. (2005: 6)

Utility is an example of the 'good enough' principle given that we are unlikely to find a complete theoretical formulation that accounts for every circumstance we are interested in.

Ward and Maruna (2007: 41) summarize five different dimensions that they used when reviewing two competing theories of rehabilitation (which will be discussed more fully later in the chapter). Their evaluative dimensions are:

- comprehensiveness – ability of the theory to account for all the existing findings;
- coherence – external consistency with other theories and lack of internal contradictions;
- unifying – brings together aspects of previous and separate theories;
- fertility – degree to which the theory leads to new predictions;
- explanatory depth – ability to describe underlying causal mechanism.

The discussion thus far has provided some definitions and background to theorizing. The remainder of this chapter looks at theories that try to explain:

- Why every teenager doesn't become a delinquent (i.e. what are the protective factors associated with offending?).
- Why people commit crime (i.e. violent, sexual and acquisitive crime).
- What factors are associated with people desisting from reoffending or persisting in the committing of crime (i.e. the age crime curve).
- How desistance from reoffending can be encouraged (i.e. what are the theoretical underpinnings of models of rehabilitation?).

WHY DOESN'T EVERY TEENAGER BECOME A DELINQUENT?

Given the high rates of anti-social behaviour and delinquency in the young, why do some youths commit less crime or abstain completely from offending? Several ideas have been propounded to suggest why this may be so, including the presence of protective factors, situation factors, attitudes towards masculinity, and moral reasoning. Two particular methods have been employed to address this question. The first is to look at young people whose life circumstances would predict a high likelihood of offending yet who abstain from offending (e.g., Hoge et al., 1996; Lösel and Bliesener, 1994) and the second compares an offending with a non-offending sample of adolescents (e.g. Farr et al., 2004; Whittaker et al., 2006).

Lösel and Bliesener (1994) put forward the notion of protective factors that provide resources enabling the young person to deal with stressors, i.e. active coping with problems, having a degree of cognitive competence and experiencing self-efficacy and self-confidence. Other protective factors include being in a stable relationship with at least one parent or other reference person, a supportive educational climate and social support outside the family. Their theoretical formulation derived from Werner and Smith's balance model, which states biological risk factors and stressful life events likely to increase children's vulnerability are kept in check and made manageable by the presence of protective factors. They undertook interviews and administered questionnaires to measure risk load, problem behaviours, personal resources and social resources in a group of adolescent girls and boys having a deprived and stressful background. They were able to classify the adolescents into a non-offending resilient group ($n = 66$) and a deviant group ($n = 80$) in terms of their teachers' assessments. The resilient group tended to have higher levels of intelligence, were more flexible in temperament, had a stronger sense of self-efficacy and achievement motivation, used more active coping strategies (as opposed to avoidant strategies) and had a greater sense of personal autonomy. The resilient group were also more likely to have a supportive reference person in addition to family and have a positive future perspective. The resilient group retained their greater achievement motivation as measured from a two-year follow-up study.

Hoge et al. (1996) looked at protective factors implicated in adjustment and desistance from reoffending in a group of young offenders. They defined protective factors as: positive peer relationships, good school achievement, effective use of leisure time and positive response to authority. They also identified three sets of family related risk factors: relationship problems, lack of discipline and supervision, criminal histories or mental health problems of parents. Outcomes were measured in terms of reoffending rates and compliance with conditions of sentence. They found negative relationships between children and parent, and deficiencies in parenting were associated with higher rates of reoffending and poorer compliance. Similarly the presence of the protective factors was associated with lower rates of reoffending and higher compliance. They suggest that the protective factors acted as a kind of 'buffer' in the presence of risk factors.

Two studies comparing a normative group of adolescent boys with a sex offending group of boys of equivalent age found the ability to empathize was a key attribute that differentiated the two groups. Whittaker et al. (2006) reported that not only were the normative group more knowledgeable about the biology and consequences of sex but that they had greater empathy skills than the offending group. Farr et al. (2004) found that a group of adolescent sex offenders had an impoverished sense of masculinity as well as less ability to empathize than a normative group.

These findings resonate with Moffitt's (1993) hypothesis that there is more likely to be a maturity gap in offending adolescents whereby biological maturity and pubescent bodily changes are out of kilter with age-related social status. Non-delinquent adolescents may not sense this maturity gap. Although Moffitt advances no explanation as to why this may be the case she suggests non-delinquent teenagers may simply lack the opportunity to model anti-social behaviour from delinquent peers because they may not be part of popular delinquent groups. And they may, alternatively, have access to more respectable adult role models.

Another developmental factor, moral reasoning, has been hypothesized to have a role in the onset of offending and by implication resistance to committing crime. Kohlberg's theory (Kohlberg, 1984) has been influential here. He proposed six periods of moral development, which Palmer and Hollin (1998) show differentiate delinquents and non-delinquents. They demonstrate, from a survey of young offenders and non-offenders, that the former tended to operate at the early stages of moral development where the task is to follow rules and avoid punishment, gaining rewards and exercising own self-interest. The latter were more likely to be able to operate at higher levels of moral development by respecting authority and having a set of principles that allow communities to flourish.

Early attachment to parent or carer has also been implicated in later offending (Brown et al., 2014). They reviewed the research literature and concluded (p. 141) a body of accumulated evidence confirms an association between insecure early attachment and subsequent offending and that secure attachment is a valuable psychological resource. Adshead (2002: 89) describes disorganised attachments in childhood, such as that resulting from abuse, can follow through into adulthood. This may result in degrees of disassociation whereby the person has difficulties in monitoring external reality and differentiating between their internal imaginings and the external world. Adshead suggests that not all insecurely attached individuals may become violent but that this in combination with other risk factors is a key precursor.

In summary, the research findings cited above suggest there may be biological, maturational and moral reasoning developmental differences between delinquents and non-delinquents. The presence of compensatory protective factors may act as a buffer for adolescents in high-risk situations of deprivation and poor parental care, and inadequate early childhood bonding with parent or carer is implicated in initial and subsequent offending. The absence of risk factors on the one hand and the presence of buffering protective factors on the other hand are offered as explanations for why adolescents do not offend. The logic of these explanations is that stress associated with low family income and impaired parenting (such as lack of affection and warmth and erratic or harsh discipline) create an environment in which the likelihood of adolescent offending increases. This line of reasoning suggests a question: does it hold therefore that affluence may be associated with 'good' parenting and consequently might we expect less delinquency amongst the wealthy?

Luthar and Latendresse (2005) looked at this conundrum in a study of American school children. They firstly report evidence to indicate elevated rates of depression amongst the wealthy and high pressure jobs may inhibit the formation of support networks. Luthar and Latendresse then asked whether the children of wealthy parents are insulated from their parents' stresses or do they, like others, experience potentially harmful parenting experiences. They looked particularly at parental contact and high parental expectations. They chose participants from sixth grade middle school students (age 11) from two schools, one serving a low income city catchment and the other an affluent community. They assessed psychological adjustment and measured self-reported delinquency as well as obtaining teacher ratings of classroom behaviours.

They report a relationship between parental attachment and psychological adjustment, with low attachment associated with greater vulnerability. It was this vulnerability, also measured by parental contact, which was associated with experimental smoking, drinking and drug taking. They found that of seven parenting dimensions, four were not statistically different between the two groups and that children from poorer families tended to fare worse with respect to parental criticism and after-school supervision, but actually fared better with respect to parental expectations. They concluded socioeconomic extremes did not imply differences in the adequacy of parenting. They found unhappy children who perceived their parents were emotionally distant and overcritical in both groups. They reported no differences between the two groups in self-reported delinquency. These findings suggest that it is not income per se but the quality of attachment and parenting style that seems critical in whether or not the child engages in delinquent behaviours.

WHY DO PEOPLE COMMIT CRIME?

In the previous section, sets of interacting risk factors were implicated as triggers or mechanisms to explain why young people committed crime. Nineteenth century, and now discredited, constitutional theories thought criminality was linked to physical characteristics of the person (summarized in Harrower, 1998: 16–20). Thus particular body types were thought to be associated with criminality, for example broad and muscular types who were said to be aggressive and adventurous were more likely to offend (see also brief discussion in Chapter 9). The work of Hans Eysenck is from this tradition (Hollin, 2007: 89–92; Howitt, 2002: 66–70).

The foundation of Eysenck's theory is that genetic inheritance differentiates people in their ability to learn, or more accurately their conditioning to environmental stimuli (Eysenck, 1987). He defined those who were underaroused, and therefore sought stimulation, as 'extraverts', characterized as thrill-seekers and impulsive. The 'introvert' is overaroused and so avoids stimulation and tends to be reserved and quiet. He defined two further personality dimensions: 'neuroticism' (irritability, anxiety) and 'psychoticism' (preference for solitude, lack of feeling for others and aggressiveness). Both Hollin (2007) and Howitt (2002) observe, notwithstanding the huge number of research papers devoted to testing hypotheses generated by Eysenck's theorizing, there emerged reservations about the theory on the grounds that (a) it could not adequately explain the link between conditioning and socialization and (b) it was based on potentially flawed data. There have also been vociferous arguments about the concept of personality per se. Hollin summarizes the fierce philosophical debate that Eysenck's ideas gave rise to in the following question: is human behaviour determined (by whatever means) or are we active, rational agents shaping and interpreting our own destiny? Those who accept the latter proposition, firmly reject the Eysenckian approach.

Personality still heavily features in explanations of criminality, for example dangerous and severe personality disorder (DSPD), which we have previously discussed (see Chapter 5). Brown et al. (2014) have a chapter devoted to explaining the research literature relating to the measurement and treatability of offenders diagnosed with personality disorders. Whilst certain personality traits may influence whether and how behaviours manifest in a criminal situation, there are certainly other contributory factors.

IS THERE A GENERAL MODEL TO EXPLAIN WHY PEOPLE COMMIT CRIME?

As mentioned above, Farrington (2004) presents what he calls a simple model of criminal behaviour (see Figure 6.1). He makes an important distinction

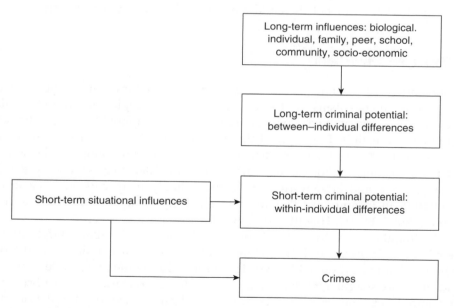

Figure 6.1 Farrington's simple model of crime. (Reproduced with kind permission from Wiley. Farrington, D.P. (2004) Criminological psychology in the twenty-first century, *Criminal Behaviour and Mental Health* 14: 152-66.)

differentiating *inter* (between) and *intra* (within) individual differences. The first is about comparing individuals and the second is looking at change over time of an individual.

Farrington and colleagues carried out a highly influential study called the Cambridge Study in Delinquent Development (Farrington, 2004). This was a prospective longitudinal survey of about 400 London males who were first contacted aged eight and followed though to age 48. Many studies are retrospective in that they look back at past behaviour; in a prospective study a cohort is selected and followed over time to see what happens to them.

The Cambridge study found 41% of the cohort was convicted of criminal offences up to the age of around 50. The risk factors for early onset offending were:

- individual factors (low intelligence, low school attainment, hyperactivity, impulsiveness, risk taking, low empathy, anti-social and aggressive behaviour);
- family factors (poor parental supervision, harsh discipline, physical abuse, cold parental attitudes, low involvement with parents, child neglect, divorce, criminal parents or delinquent siblings);
- socio-economic factors (low family income, large family size, poor housing);
- school factors (attending high delinquency rate school);
- neighbourhood factors (living in deprived, high crime neighbourhood);
- peer factors (delinquent peers, peer rejection, low popularity).

Farrington found risk factors such as periods of unemployment were associated with greater offending for material gain, although not for violent offending or drug misuse. He also reports exposure to peer delinquency predicted differences between boys but not changes for a particular boy over time. His own appraisal of the explanatory power of his model is that the top half of the model adequately describes precursor factors for most types of crime whereas the situational factors of the bottom half are likely to be different for different types of crime.

David Canter has attempted to account for variations between crimes by suggesting a hierarchy of criminal differentiation (Canter, 2000; Canter and Youngs, 2009: 88–101). This model (see Figure 6.2) proposes at the most general level we can distinguish between people who commit crime from those who do not. Thereafter we can specify broad classes of crime (i.e. violent, sexual, property) which will subdivide into types of crime within a class (e.g. within property crime we might have arson or burglary). A further level of differentiation considers the modus operandi in the way a criminal may commit a crime (e.g. a burglar may prefer to break a window to gain entry whilst another looks for an open window). The final, idiosyncratic level, is signature, which is a behaviour uniquely identifying a particular offender (e.g. a murderer may display the victim in a particular pose).

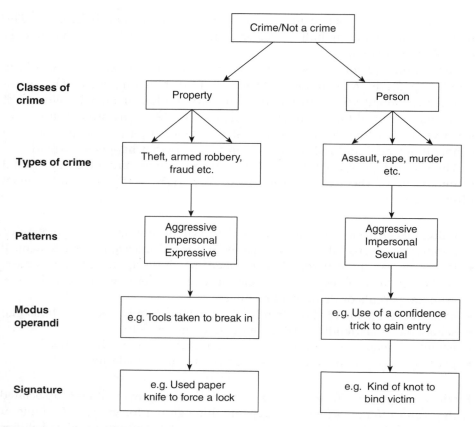

Figure 6.2 A representation of Canter's hierarchy of criminal differentiation

WHAT SPECIFIC MODELS AND THEORIES EXPLAIN DIFFERENT KINDS OF OFFENDING?

SEXUAL OFFENDING

There are a number of approaches in trying to explain sexual offending. Motivational typologies have been developed often through clinically based interviews with convicted sex offenders. Groth, Burgess and Holstrom (1977) identified five types of rapist: anger excitation or sadistic; anger retaliation; power reassurance; power dominance; and opportunistic. Prentky and Knight (1991) provide a more detailed taxonomy in which the opportunist was sub-divided into high and low social competency, the sadistic sub-divided into muted and overt. As well as identifying a different type of anger motivation, they added four new types, those of the non-sadistic low and high competency, and two vindictive sub-types – low and high social competencies. Hazelwood et al. (1995) subdivided rapists into selfish and unselfish.

Typologies have also been constructed to account for female sexual offending. Wijkman et al. (2010) used court reports, and a sample of offenders registered with the Dutch central prosecution service to propose four sub-types: rapists (i.e. penetrative offending with non-familial adolescents), young assaulters (forceful non-penetrative abuse with male family members), psychologically disturbed co-offenders (those with mental health problems and offending with one or more co-perpetrators and no particular preference for victim) and passive mothers (passive acceptance or fascination of male abuse of their own children).

We can see from this typological approach that firstly they tended to be constructed from clinical or criminal populations and thus neither encompasses the many non-pathological rapists, nor do they consider offenders who are never caught. The concepts are used in different ways, and so are not easily comparable. Furthermore typologies tend to assume that an offender remains characterized within one type (although they may display behaviours characteristic of several types) and presumes offenders remain static over time, not allowing for the crossover phenomenon (for example where an offender switches from child to adult victim or from boys to girls, as reported by Cann et al., 2007).

An alternative, a thematic approach, has been attempted. Mention has been made previously of the work of David Canter and colleagues where themes of offence behaviours are identified; for example Canter and Heritage (1990) named intimacy, violence, impersonal, criminality and sexuality as five themes of behaviour that characterize rape behaviours. This approach has been used to predict the type of offender who might have committed a rape defined by a particular theme. This prediction rests on the homology principle (Mokros and Alison, 2002), which proposes there will be a correspondence between behavioural themes and types of offender. They tested but failed to demonstrate this principle that the more similar offenders are the greater the resemblance of their crime behaviours.

Grounded theory has also been used to develop theoretical constructs derived from detailed interviews with offenders to describe different pathways towards offending pioneered by Tony Ward and colleagues (e.g. Ward et al., 1995). They propose different stages in offending against children:

- Background lifestyle factors, such as quality of adult relationships, unresolved childhood experiences.
- Distal planning of contact with a victim, which comprises implicit, explicit or chance planning.
- Nonsexual contact, such as involvement with children's recreational activities.
- Cognitive restructuring, where the offender responds to negative emotions such as feelings of guilt, or positive emotions, such as high levels of sexual arousal.
- Proximal planning, in which the focus is either on self and the offender's own gratification or attempts mutuality whereby the offender tries to provide for both the victim's and their own emotional needs.
- Offence, which could be intense and of short duration, or longer duration, involving less intrusive acts.

- Post offence cognitive restructuring, which may involve feelings of guilt and disgust or enhancing emotional experiences.
- Future resolution about whether to offend again or not.
- Perceptions of lifestyle, which are influenced by the two stages above and which become new background factors.

Ward et al. describe two main pathways: positive affect and negative affect. The former comprises positive emotions, explicit planning, cognitive distortions, deviant sexual arousal, a focus on satisfying mutual needs and long duration offences of relative low intensity. The latter is characterized by negative emotions, implicit planning, alcohol misuse, a focus on satisfying own needs and short duration, high intensity offending.

Polaschek et al. (2001) applied the same approach to rape against adult women. They similarly report phases and pathways comprising:

- Background, including offender's lifestyle, circumstances and mood prior to the offence (positive, angry, depressed).
- Establishment of dominant goals (to experience sexual gratification or redressing harm to self, which is a function of mood preceding the attack).
- Approach, which could be direct or indirect.
- Preparation, which involves evaluation and planning.
- Offending.
- Post offence strategies of dealing with the rape, such as normalizing behaviours or post hoc rationalizations.

The pathways in this study were described as seeking sexual gratification to enhance positive mood; escaping negative emotion through sexual gratification; and redressing harm to self.

Gannon applied the pathways approach to derive a descriptive model of female sexual offending, from the narratives of 22 women sexual offenders (Gannon et al., 2013). Their model proposes a number of behavioural, cognitive, affective and contextual factors that lead up to female sexual offending. These were amalgamated to predict three pathways:

- Explicit-approach – offenders whose motives were mixed (sexual gratification, intimacy, revenge), who chose adults and children as their target victims, who explicitly pre-planned the offence and experienced some form of gratification as a consequence.
- Direct-avoidant – offenders who were coerced into offending by an often abusive male and offended out of fear or a desire for intimacy with the abusive partner.
- Implicit-disorganized – again, offenders had diverse motive for their offending, did not display any explicit planning, were disorganized and impulsive and may have experienced either positive or negative affect as a consequence of the offence.

Box 6.1   Theresa Gannon on theorizing about women sexual offenders

I first realized – with a jolt – not only the limits of my own knowledge, but the limits of forensic psychology more generally when I was asked to develop a treatment plan for a woman who had sexually offended. Naively, I set about searching for comprehensive theories to underpin my work only to realize that there were none available to explain sexual offending in women. In fact, the only theories available were those that had been developed for use with male sexual offenders. Quickly, I learnt that I had to mix and match everything I knew about females and everything I knew about sexual offending to see if I could come up with an assessment and treatment package that was gender-responsive. It wasn't an easy task. And, looking back, the package I developed could have been greatly improved had more information been available about female sexual offending.

Theoretical models are essential for guiding the assessment and treatment planning process. In areas that are well developed, such as male sexual offending, guiding theories can be used to support, guide and scaffold both research and treatment. However, in areas that are new and developing, such as female sexual offending, only minimal information is available. I have learnt from working with and researching female sexual offenders that I can never assume that these women are similar to their male sexual offending counterparts. This is why I became so interested in developing theory to explain female sexual offending using women's own offence narratives. We have to listen to what females themselves say if we want to move further forward in theorizing about female sexual offending.

Proulx (2014b: 33) describes a further set of investigations by Ward and colleagues that incorporated ideas of self-regulation and relapsing of sex offenders, again producing distinctive phases and pathways classified broadly as passive or active avoidance, automatic or explicit approach. These pathways have been evaluated in a sample of child molesters (Bickley and Beech, 2002); a mixture of child molesters and rapists (Keeling et al., 2006); and sexual aggressors with learning disabilities (Lindsay et al., 2008). They collectively found that the approach pathways were the most likely. The 'automatic' offender often has a disorganized lifestyle, unstable relationships and employment, substance abuse and hostile attitudes towards women. The approach offender builds up a history of offences and creates a 'rape script' which is activated when presented with an opportunity. He uses violence to effect the rape. The 'explicit' offender has a lifestyle revolving around sexual deviance, including the use of pornography, and engages in detailed planning of the assault. For this approach offender the assault is a way to fulfil emotional need.

In terms of evaluating the pathways model, there is external consistency with other formulations, for example Pithers' Relapse Prevention Model (RPM) (see Proulx, 2014a for a description and assessment of RPM); it extends the scope of existing formulations; there is a detailed description, it unifies a number of concepts (affect, cognition and behaviour) and it has certainly been fertile in spawning numerous studies. Sample sizes tend to be small and the pathways share similar difficulties to typologies in that to be included in a particular pathway, the offender must have all the relevant characteristics. This makes it difficult to classify offenders who have features from several pathways or an incomplete number of characteristics.

Predictions of sex offending have been made from the presence of risk factors, for example Thornton (2002) identifies four dynamic risk domains: sexual interests, pro-offending attitudes, socio-effective difficulties and self-regulation problems. This approach depends on the accuracy of risk assessment tools, which as Chapter 10 suggests, are not unproblematic.

There are comprehensive theories that integrate different sets of factors (e.g. Beech and Ward, 2004). They suggest that biology (e.g. genetic inheritance and brain development), ecology (e.g. social, cultural and personal circumstances) and neurological factors (e.g. motivational, emotional, perception, memory) interact to create clinical problems such as deviant arousal, offence-related thoughts and fantasies, social and interpersonal difficulties. Sexually abusive behaviour functions to relieve problem behaviours, thereby sustaining the offender's vulnerabilities and possibly resulting in an escalation of the abusive behaviours.

VIOLENT OFFENDING

Blackburn (1993: 210) defines violence as the 'forceful infliction of physical injury', whilst criminal violence is 'the illegitimate use of force and includes criminal homicide, assault, robbery, rape and other sexual assaults'. He conceptualizes aggression as 'the intentional infliction of harm, including psychological discomfort as well as injury' (p. 211). Violence is often thought of in terms of 'malevolent intent', that is having an explicit goal of causing harm to someone who seeks to avoid it.

There were 1.9 million incidents of violence in England and Wales in 2012–13, with just over one in 50 adults victimized, according to the most recently available figures from the Crime Survey for England and Wales (CSEW). According to crime statistics, violent crime has decreased by 13% over the past five years. Some 7.1% of women and 4.4% of men reported an experience of domestic abuse in the last year, which is roughly 1.2 million females and 700,000 males (see Figure 6.3).

The number of homicides recorded by the police increased between 1961 and 2002–03 but has seen a generally downward trend since. The peak includes 172 homicides committed by Harold Shipman, which although they were committed over a long period of time, were recorded by police in 2002–03 as a result of Dame Janet Smith's inquiry. The 551 homicides recorded in 2012–13 were 20 more than in 2011–12, but this is still lower than any other year since 1989, when the total was 521. Figure 6.4 shows the number of homicide offences recorded by the police in England and Wales from 1961 to 2012–13.[1] Two-thirds of homicide victims were male and 45% of the murders of women were committed by a partner or ex-partner, compared to 4% for males.

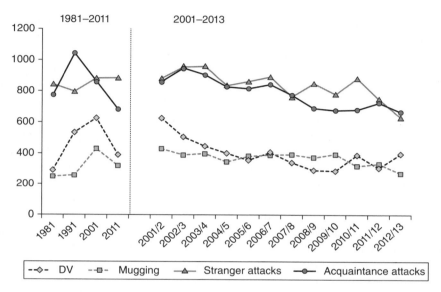

Figure 6.3 Trends in violent offending in England and Wales (000s), 1981–2013. (Source: CSEW)

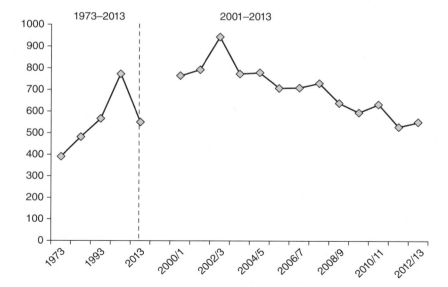

Figure 6.4 Number of homicides recorded by the police in England and Wales, 1973–2013. (Source: Home Office Homicide Index)

Homicide and assault are studied from a variety of theoretical perspectives and there is no single theory that has gained a consensus to explain the perpetration of violence (Rosenfeld, 2008). Theoretical explanations vary in terms of level of analysis and whether they are general or specific.

By and large biological theories for aggression have been subject to considerable criticism because much violent behaviour is instrumental and requires no physiological mechanisms for its cause; in other words, intentional violence is a volitional means to achieve some purpose rather than being an automatic reflex. There are many manifestations of violence which a purely biological theory cannot account for. Social and cultural factors modify aggression; for example, we learn restraint in certain social situations such as the classroom and can use controlled aggression, say, on the sports field. However, chromosomal abnormality (i.e. the XYY syndrome where there is an additional fragment of the male Y chromosome) has been implicated in violent crime although this association is more likely to be as a consequence of or in combination with other factors related to this abnormality, such as lower than average intelligence and above average height, and the social reaction these characteristics create (Harrower, 1998: 18). Deficiencies in serotonin, a neurotransmitter commonly regarded as being responsible for maintaining mood balance has been associated with aggressive behaviour. No simple one-to-one causal relationship has been found between this and level of aggression, leading Krakowski (2003) to suggest serotonergic dysfunction will influence aggression differently, depending on the individual's impulse control, emotional regulation and social abilities.

Howitt (2002) draws attention to Curtis' violence-breeds-violence hypothesis which states that a violent social environment (similar to the factors identified by Farrington) creates violent youngsters and adults. The cycle of abuse (Walker, 1977) describes distinct phases:

- Phase 1 – rising tension, with the man becoming edgy and more prone to react negatively to frustrations and he begins to lash out verbally at his wife/partner for some real or imagined wrongdoing and quickly apologize or become docile again.
- Phase 2 – build in tensions which finally explodes in an acute battering incident; women often forgive the batterer and/or go to elaborate lengths to justify why their men batter them, often accepting blame for the incident.
- Phase 3 – a period of contrite, loving behaviour from the man and he becomes the kind of husband or lover that women have been socialized to expect.

This last phase has been used as an explanation of why some women remain in a violent relationship. Whilst highly plausible that there is some relationship between exposure to a violent environment and subsequent commission of violence there are problems with attempts to flesh out the causal mechanisms: research tends not to involve direct observation (for obvious reasons); studies are retrospective; definitions of what constitutes abuse and violence are problematic.

Theories of learning and social cognition propose that aggression becomes more likely if a person displays or observes aggression that successfully achieves its objective. Bandura (1977) proposed the most comprehensive theory, advocating observational learning is reinforced. This social learning approach to crime proposes that children learn from observing what takes place within families, the environment within which they are growing up and from the media. Behaviour, whether pro- or anti-social, that is seen to achieve rewards is then copied. People are said to develop an expectation about what they can achieve and that in a state of emotional arousal they produce whichever response is strongest in their behavioural repertoire and mute non-aggressive responses (Blackburn, 1993: 22). Howitt (2002), in assessing learning theories, argues that observation is an insufficient mechanism to explain offending, partly because this implies the behaviour is goal-directed and does not help to explain opportunistic crime. Furthermore, social learning theories can neither adequately account for pathological offending nor can it explain the circumstances and situational factors associated with learning.

Anger has been theorized to be an important antecedent to violent offending (Howells, 2004). There are various theories about the role played by anger, and collectively they feature the following:

- triggering events prior to an anger episode;
- cognitive biases in appraising the precipitating event;
- physiological activation of the autonomic nervous system;
- subjective experience of feeling angry;
- poor self-regulation strategies.

Blackburn (1993: 222) contends the conditions that arouse anger are controversial, that there is a moral dimension to anger (i.e. it is a manifestation of people's values and their sense of right(s)) which is not reflected in theorizing. In addition, the actual mechanism of appraisal is unclear.

As Howitt (2002: 108) says, there is no easy way to explain homicide, and whilst it is tempting to suggest murder is an aberration, as most of us do not kill, this ignores a large number of killers who are usually non-aggressive, nor suffer from a mental illness.

The typological approach has been adopted in relation to violent offending, for example by Blackburn (1971) who proposed four types: paranoid–aggressive; depressive; psychopathic; and overcontrolled repressive. Similar criticism can be levelled at this approach as with the sex offender typologies given above, and more comprehensive theories are likely to provide the fullest explanation. Gresswell and Hollin (1994) suggest there are three levels involved in violent behaviours:

- predisposing factors (such as dysfunctional attachment, experience of trauma, fantasy as a coping adaptation);
- maintenance factors (problems in inhibiting aggressive impulse, experience of rewarding aggressive episodes); and
- situational or triggering factors (stressful precipitators such as relationship or financial problems).

Gender differentiation does not often feature in theoretical accounts of violence. Thus Thompson and Ricard (2009) offer a radical feminist perspective to explain women's role in serial killing, using Martha Beck, Myra Hindley and Karla Homolka as case examples. They feature power relations and desire for intimacy in their alternative framework. Gilchrist and Kebbell (2010) also use the idea of differential responses to power to explain male and female motives in domestic violence. Women who lack power may offer violent resistance in the absence of any other resources whilst men who abuse engage in intimate terrorism or coercive control of their partner.

ACQUISITIVE OFFENDING

Central to acquisitive offending is the acquiring of money or goods by illicit means and comprises offences such as fraud, burglary, extortion and robbery (Canter and Youngs, 2009: 256). There has been a downward trend in rates of acquisitive crime, as shown by data from the CSEW (see Figure 6.5).

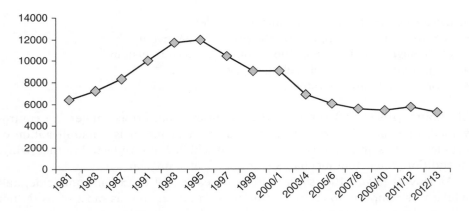

Figure 6.5 Trends in incidence of all acquisitive crime, 1981–2012/13 (number of incidents, 000s). (Source: CSEW)

Again, a typology approach has been adopted. For example, Scarr (1973) considered the relative experience of burglars by classifying them either as professional or amateur. He concludes the motive for domestic burglary is money but that this was driven by different needs to finance a lifestyle, drugs or alcohol dependency or as a way to satisfy a social need such as acquiring status. Butler (1994) undertook a study conducting in-depth interviews with 15 commercial burglars. Here too the need for money was the dominant motive, followed by being unemployed, wanting excitement, the offender being under the influence of alcohol, and for several it was motivated by power and revenge.

Routine activity and rational choice theories (Clarke and Felson, 1993) have been used to account for acquisitive crime. The latter posits offenders seeking advantages through their criminal behaviour by making active rational choices from a number of alternatives. The environment may afford the opportunity for offending, such as an unlocked car door or open ground floor window. The offender makes a rational calculation about the ease of entry, possible gain and likelihood of being caught. Nee and Taylor (1988, 2000) conducted a number of studies looking at burglars' decision making by simulating a residential environment with maps and photographs. They found that target selection was predominantly habit-driven, based on prior learning, and the burglars had amassed considerable expertise in relation to householders, suggesting this was more of a planned activity.

Routine activity theory (Cohen and Felson, 1979) proposes that, as there is a decrease in household and family activities, there is a corresponding increase in activities away from home, which in turn leads to greater criminal opportunities. Offenders may commit crime, or notice opportunities for offending whilst they are engaged in routine activities away from home (such as shopping or socializing). In addition, Cohen and Felson argued it is the absence of 'capable guardians' (p. 589) in spaces outside of the home that acts as a disinhibitor, potentially facilitating crime. For example, an offender walking home by way of a regular route (routine activity) may come across a lone woman possibly the worse for drink (an opportunity to exploit for sex) in a relatively quiet area (where they are unlikely to be seen) and calculates the reward (sex) against the cost (possibility of being caught). Fritzon and Watts (2003: 235), in criticizing this approach, suggest it rather takes the notion of criminal inclination for granted, and use the proliferation of mobile phone thefts (Farrell's phone test idea discussed earlier) as an example, to show the theory does not adequately explain this rise in this crime. In the scenario given above the potential offender does have other choices: he could ignore the woman or he could offer to help her to get home safely. Routine activity and rational choice theories cannot wholly account for his choice to commit a rape. There needs to be some inclusion of motive and prior history to suggest why a particular course of action was chosen as certainly not all men in the situation described commit a rape.

Rational choice theory and routine activity have converged and purport to demonstrate that it is circumstances that shape an individual's acts, which is why this theory has been harnessed in crime prevention initiatives as efforts are made to make it harder for theft to occur by making access more difficult target hardening and surveillance is increased, (e.g. searches at airports) which may be both natural (e.g. removing screening hedges around properties) or more calculated (e.g. CCTV).

Rational choice theory has thus been successfully applied to enhance situational crime prevention but has little to say about who the offenders may be or specific pathologies associated with acquisitive crime (Pease, 2001; Rock, 2012). Rational choice and routine activity theories have been applied with some success in geographic profiling when attempting to determine the likely area where an offender may reside or have some social association with (see Rossmo, 1999).

HOW ARE DESISTANCE AND PERSISTENCE IN OFFENDING EXPLAINED?

A well-established phenomenon in criminal justice is the age crime curve (Moffitt, 1993). This suggests both incidence and prevalence rates of offending appear highest during adolescence, peak around 17 and then drop precipitously in young adulthood. The majority of offenders are teenagers and by their early twenties crime rates drop by 50%, so that by age 25 most offenders desist from offending (Farrington, 1986). Moffitt (1993: 675) declares, 'with slight variations this general relationship between age and crime obtains among males and females, for most types of crime, during recent historical periods and in numerous Western nations'. By way of illustration, incidence data from the Scottish Crime and Justice Survey show this pattern (see Figure 6.6).

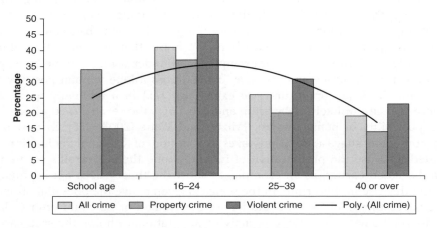

Figure 6.6   Age crime curve (Scottish crime data, 2010/11)

Moffitt theorizes there are two types of offender: adolescent limited and life course persistent. The former offend for only a brief period, usually early to late adolescence. The latter start their offending much earlier and persist into adulthood. Moffitt hypothesizes (p. 679), 'these two groups differ in aetiology, developmental course, prognosis and, importantly, classification of their behaviour'. She suggests the life course persistent offender exhibits anti-social behaviours such as biting and hitting as early as aged four, shoplifting and truancy aged ten, involvement with drugs and stealing cars aged 16, robbery and sexual offences aged 22 and fraud and child abuse aged 30. She suggests neurological deficits may play a role in early anti-social behaviour. Thus verbal deficits may affect receptive listening and reading, problem solving, expressive speech and writing. She further suggests that often, children with neurological problems are not generally born into supportive environments and there is an interaction with criminogenic environments, and she posits that 'the juxtaposition of a vulnerable and difficult infant with an adverse rearing context initiates for the life persistent pattern of anti-social behaviour' (p. 682). These problems can follow the individual and are manifest as erratic work lives and restricted behavioural repertoires. Personal characteristics, such as poor self-control, impulsivity and an inability to delay gratification, increase the risk of sustained offending.

The adolescent limited offender is common compared to the rarer lifelong persistent offender. These limited offenders lack consistency in their anti-social behaviour across situations. Whilst they may be experimenting with drugs or shoplifting with friends, they obey school rules and abandon offending behaviours when more pro-social activity proves more rewarding. Moffitt hypothesizes that a combination of immaturity, teenage self-consciousness and the process of social mimicry provides developmental explanations for short duration delinquency. As development inevitably progresses, Moffitt suggests that the adolescence limited offender experiences a loss of motivation, for example, an arrest record might limit their job and travel opportunities. Other life-changing circumstances such as marriage, moving away from the crime linked neighbourhood or getting a permanent job, may increase the likelihood of desistance. These factors together with an early life in which pro-social behaviours had the opportunity to develop, some basic (or advanced) academic skills and the lesser likelihood of mental health issues, enables these offenders to stop their anti-social behaviours.

Reviews of Moffitt's types have had only equivocal support. Ezell and Cohen (2005) examined patterns of crime and found six different types of persistent offenders, rather than the one Moffitt predicted. Ezell and Cohen concluded they had 'failed to validate the empirical expectations' of Moffitt's approach (p. 259), although their study did support her suggestion that there was a group of people whose offending is confined to their adolescence.

The concept of 'criminal career' has been used to describe the beginning and end or the lifetime of offending (Blumstein et al., 1985). Desistance is normative for most offenders and can occur at any time, although is likely to involve different factors at different ages. Laub and Sampson (2001) employ several concepts to explain desistance: 'turning points', where there are illuminating life-changing experiences; 'knifing off', where the offender is separated from their pro crime environment; and structured role stability, stabilizing of routines and engagement in meaningful activity reflecting some of the points made by Moffitt above. Regular employment and getting married provide opportunities to enact these three processes. They provide social relationships, support and positive emotional attachment as well as introducing social obligations that help routinize and structure life.

Gottfredson and Hirschi (1990) argue criminality is determined by self-control and by early childhood experiences, therefore significant life events such as marriage, child-rearing and employment should make little difference to criminality. Also, they say as criminality remains relatively stable over the life course, the opportunities to commit crimes become less frequent. Thus, reductions in offending reflect changes in opportunity structures. To counter this, Farrall and Bowling (1999) say it is not just getting married or getting a job that matters, it is about what this signifies to the offender and whether such changes represent compelling enough reasons and opportunities to change their life.

WHAT ARE SOME OF THE MAIN THEORIES OF REHABILITATION?

Offender rehabilitation is a central activity of interest to forensic psychology. McGuire (2010) proposes rehabilitation has a broad meaning in that it relates to ideas of resettlement, reintegration and re-entry, and supported transitional processes to allow a discharged offender to once again become a member of society. In its more narrow sense, rehabilitation has come to mean reduction in reoffending rates. In the preceding chapter, we discussed the policy drift into 'new punitiveness', which together with the 'nothing works' doctrine saw a decline in the fortunes of rehabilitation in its broader sense. Nevertheless, there have been some interesting rehabilitation endeavours tagged the 'what works' movement (Ward and Maruna, 2007: 9), giving rise to a further doctrine of 'what helps'.

Two theories of rehabilitation are presented below to provide a comparison of different approaches. They are the Risk–Need–Responsivity (RNR) model and the Good Lives Model (GLM). Both enjoy widespread adoption and there has been a lively debate in the research literature about the relative merits of these two approaches (see, e.g., Andrews et al., 2011; Ward et al., 2012; Wormith et al., 2012). These exchanges provide an illustration of how theories are developed and refined by responding to criticism through peer-reviewed journals.

Ward and Maruna (2007) provide a very clear and accessible account of the origins, aims and preferred therapeutic interventions for both RNR and GLM, which is summarized in Table 6.1. They also evaluate the two theories against the criteria given earlier on in the chapter.

The field of rehabilitation has, until recently, been dominated by the RNR approach (Andrews and Bonta, 2010), with the focus being on assessing and predicting risk, its reduction and management. The overall goal is to target dynamic risk factors of those with greatest likelihood of reoffending in order to reduce harm to the community. Ward and Maruna (2007: 104) conclude that RNR 'represents a significant achievement' and its application by correctional services throughout the world has resulted in reduced recidivism rates and safer communities. Wormith et al. (2011: 114) point to the 'vast accumulation of evidence' in support of RNR, which contributed to the formulation and development of the approach.

Ward and Maruna (2007) suggest, however, that RNR is overly reliant on the efficacy of risk assessment and, as we saw in Chapter 5, this is problematic. Furthermore, Ward and Maruna question the concept of risk itself,

Table 6.1 Comparison of RNR and GLM

	Risk-Need-Responsivity (RNR)	Good Lives Model (GLM)
Example advocates	Don Andrews, James Bonta, Stephen Wormith	Tony Ward, Theresa Gannon, Shadd Maruna
Theoretical origins	Psychology and Criminal Conduct (PCC) General Personality and Social Psychology Perspective (GPSPP) Personal Interpersonal Community Reinforcement (PIC-R)	Positive psychology Humanistic psychology Strain theory Self-regulation
Principle formulation	Crime is caused by distinct patterns of social and psychological factors that increase the probability of offending (e.g. biological, social, cultural, situational)	The human condition pursues 'goods' as a means to a fulfilled life Human beings are more likely to function well if they have access to goods and flourish in communities that provide emotional support and material resources
	The presence of criminogenic need factors (e.g. anti-social cognitions, delinquent associates, anti-social personality impulsivity, poor problem solving) increases risk of offending	Primary goods are, e.g., knowledge, mastery, agency, friendship, community. Secondary goods are the instrumental means to achieving primary goals
	Situational cues (potential rewards gained without any immediate costs, delinquent associates supporting criminal conduct) interact with risk factors to increase likelihood of offending	Offenders have the same need for goods but because of, e.g., lack of skill or external circumstances they seek them through anti-social behaviour, but their underlying motivations are not intrinsically bad Deficits or flaws in a good life plan contribute to offending behaviours
Aims	Primarily to reduce harm inflicted on others or society at large Secondary aim is the offender's welfare	Developing a good life plan through positive holistic treatment promoting reconstruction of the self by approaching the person's psychological and behavioural problems and enhance individual's capacity to live a meaningful and happy life so that they desist from offending by having knowledge, skills, opportunities and resources to live a 'good life'
Assessment	Risk principle: the match between individual's level of risk (criminogenic need) for re-offending and amount of treatment needed to reduce recurrence Assessment of presence and severity of risk and responsivity (e.g. learning style) to match mode of intervention	Offenders participate in recognizing problems. Analysis goes beyond identifying deficits but encourages assessment of what it is that the person is seeking when committing their offence. Joint decision making about appropriate intervention to help the person secure the goods that are important to them in ways that are socially acceptable
Preferred intervention	Target factors empirically associated with highest potential recidivism Treatment directed at changing criminogenic need to reduce likelihood of re-offending Manual-based cognitive behavioural strategies in highly structured environment implemented by those trained in the programme	Shaped to suit the person's circumstances, working transparently with clients (with strong therapeutic alliance) embedded in the client's own good life priorities, e.g. therapeutic communities

Source: Summarized from Ward and Maruna (2007)

saying that there are culturally relevant and social phenomenological factors that create a perception of risk. They also suggest that RNR underplays the role of social disadvantage and economic deprivation, does not consider wider needs of role identity or agency and pays insufficient attention to the relationship between therapist and client. Fortune, Ward and Polascheck (2014: 2) are of the view that RNR's concentration on reducing and managing risk sets its focus too narrowly. They contend this potentially conflates social needs with therapeutic goals and that the outcomes of interventions can be self-defeating and even unethical. In defence of RNR, Wormith, Gendreau and Bonta (2011: 117) point out that motivational factors and social support are critical elements to responsivity and that offender assessment is comprehensive and the approach does consider the offender's strengths. Ward and Maruna (2007) recognize that as yet the evidence base to support the GLM (see Chapter 11) 'is not anywhere near as impressive or compelling as that of RNR. Wormith, Gendreau and Bonta (2011: 114) say research in support of GLM (see Chapter 11) is 'minuscule'. Netto, Carter and Bonell (2014) found no eligible studies of sufficient quality to undertake a systematic review of the GLM and suggested that further evaluation should utilize rigorous methods and measurement. This is an assessment with which Clive Hollin agrees, adding this: 'in the realpolitik of bidding for resources within offenders services aimed at crime reduction, an intervention that promises good lives for offenders is starting a long way behind the competition' (Hollin, 2012: 106).

Consider the extract in Box 6.2 from the play *Equus*. In the play, child psychiatrist Dr Martin Dysart is treating Alan, a troubled youth whose fascination for horses involves extreme cruelty. Dysart recognizes that whilst he can 'cure' the boy of his troubling behaviour, thereby reducing the risk of harm, he may take away something creative and imaginative and return Alan to a dull normality.

Box 6.2 Reflective exercise

Extract from Peter Schafer's play *Equus*[2]

The Normal is the good smile in a child's eyes – alright. It is also the dead stare in a million adults. It both sustains and kills – like a god. It is the Ordinary made beautiful: it is also the Average made lethal. The Normal is the indispensable, murderous God of Health, and I am his priest. My tools are very delicate. My compassion is honest. I have honestly assisted children in this room. I have talked away terrors and relieved many agonies. But also – beyond question – I have cut from the parts of individuality repugnant to this god, in both his aspects. Parts sacred to rarer and more wonderful gods. And at what length ... Sacrifices to Zeus took at the most, surely, sixty seconds each. Sacrifices to the Normal can take as long as sixty months.

What does this extract say to you about the dilemma of reducing an offender's risk and making them more acceptable to normative society?

How do you define what is acceptable, normative conduct?

How tolerant can/should society be of difference?

CONCLUSION

This chapter considers theory in general and then focuses on theories used to explain sexual, violent and acquisitive offending. The latter part of the chapter looks at two theories of rehabilitation, which we revisit in Chapter 11 on treatment and discuss ideas of individuality in more detail. We identified from Ward and Maruna (2007) criteria to evaluate a 'good' theory which suggests that GLM lags behind RNR in terms of its evidence base. We asked you to consider issues of convention, normative behaviour and rehabilitation goals, issues we return to in Chapter 11.

RESOURCES

For further background reading see Davies and Beech's (2012) textbook, which contains a wealth of detailed accounts of different theoretical approaches, and Clive Hollin (2013) has a good introduction to theoretical explanations of different kinds of offending. Ron Blackburn's book *The Psychology of Criminal Conduct* (1993) is something of a classic explaining different theoretical ideas about violence and sexual offending. Howitt (2002) provides a spectrum of theories spanning societal or macro, community, group and individual levels and presents a helpful assessment of their respective pros and cons. Tony Ward and Shadd Maruna's (2007) book on rehabilitation is a very accessible read, outlining the criteria to evaluate good theory and which they apply to RNR and GLM.

Wormith, Grendreau and Bonta (2012) provide a rebuttal to Ward and Maruna's critique of RNR.

David Canter's approach is developed in his book with Donna Youngs (2009) on investigative psychology.

(Continued)

Friedrich Lösel (2003) has an excellent chapter summarizing theoretical approaches to delinquent behaviour in Carson and Bull's *Handbook of Psychology in Legal Contexts*.

Brown, Miller, Northey and O'Neill (2014) have presented a detailed account of working in a prison-based therapeutic community.

The website Goodlivesmodel.com has many references and profiles of those actively researching and delivering the GLM approach.

Key journals

Criminal Justice and Behaviour

International Journal of Forensic Mental Health

Journal of Applied Psychology

Journal of Interpersonal Violence

Personality and Individual Differences

Sexual Abuse: A Journal of Sexual Aggression

Theoretical Criminology

NOTE
1 It is important to note, however, that the figures are based on the year in which offences are recorded by police rather than the year of the incident.
2 Reprinted with the permission of Scribner, a Division of Simon & Schuster, Inc., from EQUUS by Peter Schaffer. Copyright © 1973,1974 by Peter Shaffer; copyright renewed 2001, 2002 by Peter Shaffer. All rights reserved.

7
RESEARCHING

KEY CONCEPTS

This chapter looks at how to do research, discussing the importance of a theoretical or conceptual starting point and describing different methodological approaches using one topic, rape, as an exemplar. The chapter draws attention to the need to comply with appropriate standards in conducting and presenting research.

Material in this chapter covers the research methods component of the BPS stage one knowledge requirements and the research core role of stage two. It provides worked examples of how qualitative and quantitative methods have been done in desk, laboratory and field research. The chapter also provides an appreciation of the emotional load that may be carried when undertaking research on a forensic topic and indicate some ways of coping.

Knowledge concepts	Practice considerations
Abduction	Daubert test
Ontology	Desk studies
Epistemology	Experimental design
Grounded theory	Field research
Meta-theory	Frye test
Reliability	Tarasoff liability
Triangulation	
Validity	

After reading this chapter you should have an appreciation of different approaches to research and the implications of using different methods in terms of the research questions you are asking. This will help with both parts one and two of the core requirements and enable you to undertake critical reading of published research studies.

(Continued)

Questions addressed

Why do we do research?

How do I start thinking about a research project?

Why is it important to choose appropriate methods?

What are epistemology and ontology?

What are the different ways of knowing?

How can I do research on rape?

How can I cope with my feelings when doing a difficult research project?

What are the essential stages when undertaking a piece of research?

WHY DO WE DO RESEARCH?

There are several answers to this question. Breakwell and Rose (2000: 5) suggest that it is to find out what, how and why something happens. The 'something' which is the subject of this book are the topics of interest to forensic psychologists (see Table 1.1). Wrightsman (1999: 125) says there are pragmatic reasons for conducting research, such as it is part of the job, adds to job security and gains recognition from one's peers. But he also says research is the seeking of understanding of some process or elusive phenomenon. We research then to build our practice and to increase our knowledge of causes. But we also research in the interest of just causes, such as the condition of the powerless, or examine differential treatment of the marginalized (see, e.g., the chapter by Tyler and van der Toorn (2013) looking at social justice research). Practice and research are inextricably intertwined: our interventions are enhanced by research and our practice is improved by having a good grasp of research principles.

Part of a programme of study, whether at undergraduate, masters or doctoral level, will require a piece of research to be undertaken. Supervised practice and post-practice also may require critical reading of research, undertaking commissioning of a study for which an appreciation of methodology is clearly important. Research on psychology applied to law has been conducted since the inception of academic forensic psychology in the early part of the twentieth century. Much of that early research effort was concerned with the accuracy of memory recall and veracity of testimony (Brown, 2015, volume 1, p. 7). During the last three decades, research has included aspects of personality, particularly psychopathy and dangerous and severe personality disorder (DSPD), anger, risk assessment and risk management, violent and sexual offending, treatment outcomes and analysis of crime scene data (Davies et al., 2011: 3).

Doing research on a forensic psychology topic is a privilege, in terms of being granted special access to information or data and in being privy to the stories of those occupationally, wilfully or accidentally caught up in some form of legal or illegal activity. To have been involved in the dislocations caused by crime or litigation is certainly stressful, may be life-changing and can be life-threatening or fatal. It is not only the witnesses or victims, offenders or justice professionals who may find the experience intensely disturbing, but researchers too do not remain untouched by what they hear or see. The topics tackled by those undertaking forensic psychology research can involve the extremes of human behaviour: murder, child cruelty, rape and sexual victimization, abuse of self suicide, drug or alcohol misuse.

HOW DO I START THINKING ABOUT A RESEARCH PROJECT?

Some research is done by means of desk studies, whereby mostly resources are made available through IT such as relevant papers from the research literature or already existing databases and some form of secondary analysis is conducted. 'Laboratory' research is a generic term meaning studies that by and large are conducted under controlled conditions and may include analogue studies, (i.e. a simulation such as vignettes or role play) or experimental design. Yet other research will take place in real-world settings and may be conducted by unobtrusive or direct observation, interviews in situ or recruiting respondents from venues where those with relevant experiences may congregate. Thus sometimes research will examine processes in environments contaminated by the messiness of the visceral consequences of crime, or litigation, and involves direct contact with its perpetrators or victims, investigators or prosecutors, assessors or treaters. Other times, research will take place in the relatively protected environment of an organization or institution. Whatever the setting, as well as the obvious need to consider carefully the research question that is being asked and the appropriate methods to be deployed, there are also questions of risk – both to the potential respondent and the researcher themselves as well as the possible emotional load placed on both.

In the investigation or prosecution of a crime or the pursuit of a civil action there are various professionals who are entitled to ask questions and seek explanations. These are the criminal justice professionals, allied practitioners such as social workers supporting victims, and their families, those assessing and/or providing treatment for offenders, members of the public making up juries, or journalists covering cases. They have specific roles and collectively populate the landscape that makes up the domains of interest for the forensic psychologist. In their research role, forensic psychologists often have a helicopter vantage point whereby they have an overview of the entirety of a process that specific participants may have only a partial involvement with or understanding of. Some topics are off limits, such as the activities of the security services or the deliberations that take place in the jury room. Research will need to be more imaginative in researching topics such as jury decision-making (see, for example, e.g. Finch and Munro, 2008; Penrod et al., 2011). Other material may be sub judice in that the information is still subject to court procedures and may not be commented upon. There are also ethical dilemmas about having research participants re-engage some trauma or the researcher hearing information that may be about a previously undisclosed crime or threatens the safety of another. This and more makes research investigations into a forensic psychology topic challenging, difficult, exciting and sometimes frightening. This chapter will offer some reflections on how to prepare for and cope with researching such topics.

What this chapter is not is a detailed treatise on how to do interviews or surveys or how to undertake an experiment or conduct a regression analysis. There are a number of texts on general methods, such as Breakwell et al. (2012), which has an excellent span of data collection and analytic procedures. Robson's book on experimental design is a little dated but still a very accessible account (Robson 1973), and Creswell's (2003) research design book offers useful accounts of qualitative, quantitative and mixed methods. The collections edited by Sheldon et al. (2010) and Rosenfeld and Penrod (2011) are devoted to methods applicable to forensic psychology research, such as grounded theory methods (by Neil Gordon) and idiographic measurement (by Sean Hammond) in the former and meta-analysis (Sporer and Cohn) and legal research techniques (Robbennolt and Davidson) in the latter collection. The plan for the current chapter is firstly to discuss the importance of appropriate choice of methods, epistemological starting points when doing research and the implications this has for the theoretical underpinning of a study and in turn the methodologies associated with theoretical positioning. The differences in approach, the research questions being asked and the methods utilized are illustrated by using rape as a example case study. The final section discusses the emotional load and implications of learning about the distressing material that is the subject of forensic research topics. The chapter finishes with a checklist of considerations when commencing a piece of research.

WHY IS IT IMPORTANT TO CHOOSE APPROPRIATE METHODS?

Application of professional standards and ethical practice in the conduct of research is a given in any area of social science. Knowledge is accumulated through research endeavours and is usually accomplished by means of publication in scientific journals with articles subjected to peer review. Although it is not an infallible process, usually flaws in the research design or interpretation are picked up so that only reliable and valid findings are published. Reliability is the degree to which a measure systematically records the same score over repeated responses whilst validity is the degree to which a scale or psychometric test actually measures what is intended. Suppose you have a weighing machine, its measurement of weight is reliable if you step on twice and the same weight is registered. However, a weighing machine could not, for example, record your height; that is to say, it is valid only for what it is designed for – measuring your weight. These concepts are usually applied to quantitative measurement and are explained in greater detail by Hammond (2000: 181–92). Qualitative methods tend to use other means to demonstrate reliability and validity, such as triangulation, i.e. using different sources of data to demonstrate similar interpretation of findings (see Lyons, 2000 and Moran-Ellis et al., 2006 for more detailed expositions of these criteria).

The BPS and other psychological associations publish ethical guidelines to aid the design and conduct of research and care for potential participants. In the area of forensic psychology, there is another dimension to consider with respect to research. Findings of published research and expert testimony are utilized in courts of law. There are additional considerations imposed by the American courts, which contain useful principles. The criterion for the admissibility of technical evidence known as the Frye test is: 'if scientific, technical or other specialised knowledge will assist the trier of fact to understand evidence or to determine a fact in issue' (Wrightsman and Fulero, 2005: 36). The Daubert test considers whether a particular technique or analysis has been subject to peer review and is accepted by the scientific community. The other consideration, more usually applied to revelations by clients to practitioners but which can be applied to information gained during a research investigation, is the Tarasoff liability (Monahan, 2006), which addresses the limits of confidentiality. This principle arose as a consequence of the murder of Tatiana Tarasoff who was killed by a client who had intimated his intention to his therapist. Arising from this case is the requirement to breach confidentiality if a third party, or indeed the informant themselves, may be at serious risk. In the course of a research investigation, the forensic psychologist may be in receipt of information about a previously undisclosed offence or an ongoing offence. Instructions to research participants such as, 'if you continue to describe your behaviour, I would be duty bound to report this to the appropriate authorities' may discourage a compromising revelation. In any event, discussion with a senior colleague or supervisor should provide a steer on how to handle such eventualities. Thus research designs must be robust and rigorous not least because of the potential of findings to contribute to scholarship as well as being applied to guide policy, practice and elucidate behaviour or motivation in court cases.

A further element to consider is the emotional content of a topic. In her book about researching rape, Campbell (2002) distinguishes between thinking and feeling when approaching research. This chapter develops that idea by looking at attitudes towards conducting research in forensic psychology topic. Taking attitudes to mean cognition (ways of thinking with respect to), behaviours (behaving towards) or affect (feeling about an attitude/object), what follows offers an exposition of theoretical positioning, choice of methods and the emotional toll of undertaking research in forensic psychology.

A useful starting point when considering your research is your motivation for undertaking the piece of work in the first place. The research may be in partial completion of academic studies at undergraduate, masters or doctoral levels. It might be as a result of successfully secured funding from a research council or charitable trust or an in-house evaluation of a programme intervention. Occasionally it may be opportunistic, whereby happenstance creates a sequence of events that can be utilized for research purposes. Whatever the reason, the choice of topic is not accidental but rather draws on the researcher's curiosity about the subject matter, is related to some past experience of the researcher or is more instrumental in fulfilling academic or work obligations. These motives will in turn dictate the time and labour, i.e. resources, that may extend or limit the scope of the research investigation and will certainly have some influence on the type of research question that is being explored and what approach is taken to the new knowledge that is being sought.

Even the most hardened 'objective' experimental researchers bring some assumptions to their topic and the first of these is a value orientation, which comprises moral, epistemological, ethical and prudential values (Ward and Maruna, 2007). Snow et al. (2000) suggest a dichotomy between a value-neutral position and a stance they term 'value advocacy'. The former assumes the researcher has values but keeps these from intervening in the research or intervention through a process of self-awareness and vigilance. Campbell (2002: 14) declares that a strict scientific approach sees the research investigator as a source of contamination in the purity of the research investigation. Thus the researcher should remain outside the design and invisible in accounts of the findings. The advocacy stance is when the researcher declares their position and often writes themselves into the research narrative precisely because their values have a role to play in defining the questions and influencing potential outcomes of the research activity. This approach is entirely in keeping with a political psychology stance. As Fox et al. (2009: 17) declare, psychological research should foster emancipation, and social justice and practitioners should be change agents.

WHAT ARE EPISTEMOLOGY AND ONTOLOGY?

Broader philosophical assumptions, in the sense that there are different ways of learning and knowing, influence approaches to the research task. Thus ontology relates to the claims made about what is knowledge and epistemology is about how the acquiring of the new knowledge is undertaken.

Ontology has to do with the nature of the world we study (Stainton Rogers, 2009: 336). She argues that 'mainstream psychologists' see people as living in a social milieu that is somehow 'out there', separate from us as investigators. This is a world of concrete things that can be objectively evaluated and measured. Thus we may hypothesize that pupils from 'good' neighbourhoods will get higher grades in school compared to children from 'poor' neighbourhoods because the former offer more resources for learning such as libraries and places to play. The assumption is that there is a knowable causal relationship between achievement of school grades and quality of the environment in which a child is growing up. Stainton Rogers explains that critical psychology works from a 'completely different' ontology. Relationships between people and their social world is, by these lights, a product of human effort and gains meaning only from the sense that people themselves make out of it. So from a critical psychology standpoint, research seeks to gain insight into how social rules are made, deployed, re-enforced or broken. Critical psychologists want to know who it is that makes the rules, who is expected to conform and what are the consequences of rule adoption or infringements.

Your ontological position has consequences for epistemology. As Ward and Maruna (2007) put it:

> [t]he basic epistemological assumptions really spell out what constitutes knowledge and how research that informs practice should be undergone. It will include recommendations about research designs, analytic strategies and what kind of evidence is admissible when deciding on best practice. (2007: 36)

For Stainton Rogers, adopting a critical psychological approach sees the corresponding epistemology as focusing on *explication*. She describes this as follows:

> Explication is not about cause and effect but an unfolding – taking little peeks at what is going on as you might do with an origami figure. You would not understand it if you got rid of the folds, because the folds make it work. Explication is about gaining insight and understanding. Complexity in this approach is reduced in part by asking more specific questions – what is going on here, in this situation, to these people? It is also managed by a different logic of inquiry – abduction. (2009: 339)

Abduction is a process by which people make sense of the things that puzzle them, i.e. by examining events or occurrences that stand out, are unexpected or contrary. So when Thomas Kuhn talked about a paradigm shift, discussed in Chapter 6, he was advocating movement from strict hypothesis testing in the experimental tradition to more creative hypothesis generating, which is compatible with a political psychology stance. Political psychology takes a value standpoint in that the research its proponents undertake is about achieving greater social justice and developing strategies and interventions to achieve this goal. Hence the site of research is 'the real world' using qualitative and collaborative methods to negotiate meanings.

Ethical values are also clearly important as these provide the foundational standards both in terms of the ways in which the researcher interacts with their research participants and in terms of what the researcher considers to be of worth when choosing a research topic and what they elect to do with the results. This may relate to how the research is presented to potential participants, for example, it may be that there will be no direct benefit to a particular participant but rather findings may be of help to people in a similar predicament in the future. This links to the idea of prudential values, which Ward and Maruna explain as being benefits that result in an enhancement of well-being. Whether there is a direct benefit (such as gaining positively from the opportunity of explaining an experience to a third party) or indirect (knowledge is gained that might help adjust some programme of intervention), there is an ethical obligation to cause no harm.

Triangulation is an 'epistemological claim' to know more about a phenomenon than findings generated by one method alone (Moran Ellis et al., 2006).

This claim rests on the assumption that if different methods produce similar research findings we can be more confident that accurate means were used to access the phenomenon of interest and so represents a form of convergent validity. If the different research methods employed share some flaw, then the results are likely to compound the error. Moran Ellis and her colleagues suggest the idea of 'integration' as a way to provide a more nuanced and insightful analysis (see, e.g., Brown et al. (2014) on evaluating a prison therapeutic community).

Sorting out values is a good start because this will determine the questions being posed by the researcher, the kinds of theories that will be invoked to provide the conceptual basis for the study and, in turn, will largely dictate the choice of data collecting method and analytic devices to interpret, explain and present results. The often-missing element in researching forensic subject matter is either taking into account or accounting for the emotional load that is associated with distressing experiences. Table 7.1 outlines various pathways that accompany different epistemological approaches.

Table 7.1 Summary of attitudinal domains and components of research

	Attitudinal domains			
Ways of knowing	Cognitions (Thinking about)	Behaviour (Doing)		Affect (Feeling)
Epistemology	Theory	Preferred data collection methods	Preferred data analytic procedure	Coping
Logical positivism	e.g. Formal hypothesis testing models and theories	Experiments Observations Randomized controlled trials Questionnaires	Quantitative statistics	Notionally value free so neutral about affect
Social construction	e.g. Grounded theory whereby concepts are derived from the data	Interviews Focus groups Case studies	Thematic/content analyses Discourse analysis Interpretative phenomenological analysis	Aware and may incorporate researcher's reflections
Advocacy	e.g. Political psychology, in which a value position is often taken and reforms advocated	Interviews Focus groups Questionnaires	Thematic/content analyses Discourse analysis Conversational analysis Interpretative phenomenological analysis	Aware and often incorporates support mechanisms
Meta-theoretical	e.g. Facet theory, which may be used in an exploratory or theory confirming fashion	Mixed methods Secondary analysis of archival material	Multi-variate statistical analyses	Generally ignores

WHAT ARE THE DIFFERENT WAYS OF KNOWING?

The next task for the researcher is to adequately define the phenomenon that is the subject of interest; then map how salient features of the phenomenon relate to each other and move from particular instances to generalizable cases. Finally, the goal of theorizing is to provide a sufficient explanation of the relationships to permit accurate prediction of the phenomenon under scrutiny. (Evaluative criteria for assessing 'good' theory are given in the preceding chapter.) Creswell (2003: 6) discusses four schools of thought about what he calls knowledge claims, i.e. the starting assumptions of a research investigation. These are positivism, constructionism, advocacy and pragmatism. These epistemologies differ in several important respects, not least the purpose of the research enquiry, the degree of control exerted by the researcher, the presence of the researcher in the study and the emphasis on description, explanation and prediction.

Positivism was first used by Auguste Comte (Chung and Hyland, 2012) and defines an approach to human thinking premised on the idea that facts and laws of behaviour were discoverable through systematic observation. Thus 'facts' were thought of as existing in the world awaiting discovery, i.e. as some kind of objective truth whose discovery is essentially benign. Crucial to this view are notions about cause and effect which were thought of as a statistical relationship between independent events. These ideas readily gave rise to the experimental laboratory-based method of investigations because under these conditions variables can be controlled and large numbers of observations undertaken to determine the regularity of the pattern of results. Thus, as Creswell states (2003: 7), causes probably [statistically] determine effects or outcomes. Studies from this tradition often start with a theory and lay out hypotheses, collect data in contrived and controlled (laboratory) settings and seek to refute the null hypothesis through statistical analyses.

A critique of the 'scientific' measurement of human behaviour emerged in the 1970s, most notably by Harré and Secord (1972), who eschewed the implications of the positivist tradition saying it implied too mechanistic and deterministic a model of human behaviour. They influentially argued that, in essence, human beings engage in meaningful behaviour that is interpretable beyond the instrumental. They give the following example (1972: 39) by describing different scenarios in which a person might move their arm: her arm moved rapidly forward and made contact with his face (instrumental description), which can interpreted (explained) differently if this was to caress or slap the other person. If the person was in love or hated the object of her arm movement, we might predict which of the two interpretations accounted for the action. Following from this, is the idea that meanings are constructed and that people engage the world by attempting to make sense of it based on their histories, cultural perspectives and socialization practices. These assumptions then lead to the notion that research participants together with the researcher, jointly construct some understanding of the phenomenon under scrutiny within the research enterprise. Because meanings are subjective they may be varied and multiple and also different depending on the perspective of the person's experience. Enquiries deriving from this starting point often try to reconstruct meanings through talk, hence the use of the interview method. Analytic procedures associated with or arising from the social constructionist position are grounded theory, interpretive phenomenological analysis, conversational analysis and discourse analysis, and seek to explain patterns that occur to account for behaviour (see Howitt, 2011 for a really helpful exposition of qualitative analytic methods). Findings may be presented from the experiential perspective of the relevant participants; for example, McGuickin and Brown (2001) wanted to look at the differences between journalists, police officers and members of the public in how they differentiated between sex offenders, and found differences between these groups.

The third of Creswell's ways of knowing is advocacy. This arose during the 1980s, again as an antidote to the value-free positioning of the positivist tradition (see, e.g., Heron and Reason, 1997; Kemmis and Wilkinson, 1998). What is especially at issue here is to move away from the knowledge claim whereby a notional typical human experience is represented by the often male, white, straight majority and instead reflects the interests and experiences of marginalized groups. Researcher advocates argued that the constructionists do not go far enough in their enquiries in promoting an agenda for change as part of their research endeavours. Thus topics chosen for research often have a political resonance. Feminist perspectives can be catalogued within this epistemology because they often seek to illuminate women's experience from a gendered perspective, arguing this frequently remains hidden in research findings that do not disaggregate gender in reported results. Frances Heidensohn was amongst the early feminist criminologists who examined the experiences of women offenders (Heidensohn, 1985) and women police officers (Heidensohn, 1992) to expose the particularities of a minority largely ignored by mainstream, mostly male criminologists. As discussed in Chapter 6, she used a grounded theory methodology to derive new explanatory concepts that emerge from the data. Thus the phenomena of police women's experience of the occupational culture can be explained by notions such as 'transformational scenes'. Heidensohn's grounded concepts describe and explain qualitatively different experiences of policewomen compared to those of male officers. Sandra Jones in her study of women police (Jones, 1986) ends her account of her research findings on women police officers with an agenda for action to improve the careers, promotion prospects and working lives of women officers in keeping with the advocacy approach.

The position of theory is important in terms of which knowledge claim is being made. As mentioned above, the positivist tradition starts with theory and derives hypotheses which are either confirmed or rebutted and thus accumulated findings lend greater weight to the theoretical stance adopted. Constructionists may start with theory but researchers within this position, and also the advocates, tend to adopt grounded principles whereby theoretical concepts and theory derive from the data. Constructionists and advocates also engage in an iterative process whereby concepts are refined and developed; for example, Brown (2002) writes:

the conceptual tools articulated by Frances [Heidensohn] inspired me to extend the range of my own research enquiries and apply [them] to policing experiences of women within Europe and between Australia and the US. These proved powerful and sustainable conceptualisations that are readily applicable cross culturally ... [these concepts] enabled me to identify a series of temporal stages that seemed to reflect the distinct phases through which jurisdictions responded to the demands of equality of women in policing. (2002: 87)

More recently, Natarajan (2008) applied this temporal framework to women in the Tamil Nadu police service, and found for the most part the model worked in the Indian sub-context. But what Natarajan's studies were dealing with was an intersection of culture and gender (in the form of dowry practices) that meant the Euro-centric model required some adjustment when applied to Asian societies.

The final type of knowledge claim is of pragmatism. Creswell (2003: 1) suggests this arises out of actions, situations and consequences rather than antecedent conditions (as is the case in positivism). Here it is suggested that there is a case to be made for a meta-theoretical framework of which pragmatic psychology is an example. So, unlike the positivist tradition which starts with a theory, and the constructionists who often derive theory from data, this knowledge claim starts with a theoretical framework into which a specific content is built. Thus facet meta-theory, originating from the work of Louis Guttman, is a template within which any content theory can be constructed. Facet meta-theory has four theoretical constructs: definition, specification, rationale and hypothesis (Brown, 2011). Facets are the conceptual specification of the key variables that define the universe of observations and are formally laid out by means of a device called a mapping sentence. From this questionnaire items may be constructed or content analyses undertaken from secondary sources. This represents the definitional model which is then retrieved through analysis of data by means of multivariate statistics. In this way a conceptual structure is defined and then literally retrieved from analysis of empirical observations by means of multidimensional scaling techniques such as Smallest Space Analysis (SSA).

Pragmatic psychology (Fishman and Goodman-Delahunty, 2010), like facet theory, is a knowledge model as well as providing research tools. It focuses on contextualized knowledge in particular situations, being sensitive to the ambiguities of the real world. Fishman and Goodman-Delahunty suggest that one aim of forensic psychology is to apply psychological methods and theory to assist the goals of law, for example, choosing fair juries, assessing the reliability of witness testimony, assessing an offender's dangerousness. In addition, forensic psychology is involved in examining and analysing aspects of the legal system, such as factors that influence decisions to arrest offenders. Another aim is to address the nature and sources of legal power and study factors that promote or diminish compliance or confidence in and satisfaction with criminal justice processes and its agencies. They argue these are diverse goals which forensic psychology has drawn on models of experimental science and the use of sophisticated statistics to test hypotheses. Their point is that the often caveated and limited nature of experimental studies does not suit the requirements of the law in regard to more moral ideological questions or issues having greater subjectivity and intuition, particularly legal concepts such as free will to determine if and when to engage in criminal actions. In looking at individuals, forensic psychologists often immerse themselves in context and qualitative details of individual cases. They argue that a pragmatic psychology framework offers a third way to look at individual cases from which generalizations are inductively inferred by cross-case comparison, and it is particularly appealing because it also adopts an advocacy stance in making practice recommendations.

HOW CAN I DO RESEARCH ON RAPE?

RAPE AS A RESEARCH TOPIC

In this chapter, rape has been chosen to illustrate the different ways researchers have attempted to do research on this issue. Campbell (2002) argues that '"rape" as a topic of scientific inquiry took on the values and norms of the academy itself [i.e. objectivity]. Settings have a profound effect on individuals and the setting of the academic science has had a constraining effect on how rape is defined and studied' (p. 108). As pointed out by Letherby et al. (2008), sexual violence has been conceived as a political phenomenon characterized by power relations within a framework of normative heterosexual behaviours. Sex as violence is an alternative conceptualization. The first formulation is associated with ideas about exploitation and objectification of women and their bodies. The latter places ideas of victimization as central, with rape being seen as deviant criminalized behaviour. Koss and Cleveland (1997) were key advocates in arguing that rape is not a 'problem' caused by the pathological few, rather it is a far more prevalent experience than many have thought or are willing to accept. The research questions posed by these definitions and the research methods employed are somewhat different, as is the nomenclature adopted, for example using the terms 'prostitute' or 'sex worker', 'rape victim' or 'survivor', and the likely research participants.

LABORATORY-BASED EXPERIMENTAL RESEARCH

If the purpose of research is to attempt to predict with a high degree of precision how people will behave under a given set of specific circumstances, then often an experimental paradigm will be invoked that controls the variables of interest.

Gerd Bohner and his colleagues have undertaken a series of research investigations looking at rape myth acceptance. They start with the definitional proposition that rape myths are 'descriptive or prescriptive beliefs about rape (i.e. its causes, context, consequences, perpetrators, victims and their interactions) that serve to deny, downplay or justify sexual violence that men commit against women' (Bohner et al., 2009). Bohner's research group were critical of the various scales used to measure rape myth acceptance because the items were too long and complex, or contained colloquialisms and slang that may date or inhibit cross-cultural reading of the scales. In their studies they use the Acceptance of Modern Myths about Sexual Aggression Scale (AMMSAS) which avoids these problems and has greater reliability in so far as the scores tend to be normally distributed (other scales tending to have skewed distributions by bunching at one or other end of the scale). These considerations are important in experimental designs as it is crucial for those participating in the studies to have a shared understanding of scale meanings and respond in a consistent way. Thus issues of validity and reliability are part of the research design considerations.

Having secured a reliable and valid research measurement, Bohner's group cast their work theoretically within an attribution model and argue that rape myth acceptance is a general schema that guides and organizes an individual's understanding of specific information about rape. An important aspect of their theorizing is that schema-related information goes beyond the information available and infers attributions associated with the rape that were not actually present. Next they undertook a series of experiments to predict the circumstances under which adherence to rape myths influences judgements about guilt or innocence of perpetrators. In one study they addressed the hypothesis that rape myth acceptance would increasingly influence judgements when the available information was mixed or uninformative. Thus Eyssel and Bohner (2008a) conducted an experiment in which students were given pieces of information about a rape case in a sequence of five steps: contradictory information about defendant and victim; summary of expert witness pointing to the defendant's guilt; summary of the expert witness statement pointing to defendant's innocence; extended versions of both expert witness statements. After reading each piece of information, participants were asked to rate the likelihood of the defendant's guilt. Their results confirmed their hypothesis that rape myth acceptance was only influential when the information was contradictory. Other experiments were designed to refine the degree of influence rape myth acceptance exerted. Thus Eyssel and Bohner (2008b) looked at the effect of low or high amounts of case-relevant information. In this study they hypothesized that the effect of participants' rape myth acceptance about a defendant's guilt would increase as the amount of case-irrelevant information increased. Their experimental results showed this to be the case.

Barbara Krahé and her research group at the University of Potsdam also conduct social experimental research looking at aspects of rape. Bieneck and Krahé (2011) examined victim blaming. They use social cognition and schematic processing to generate hypotheses. In this case they tested the proposition that the tendency to blame the victim and exonerate the perpetrator would be more pronounced in sexual assault compared to robbery. They had three specific hypotheses:

- Hypothesis 1: More blame will be attributed to victims of rape than to victims of robbery. Conversely less blame will be attributed to perpetrators of rape than to perpetrators of robbery.
- Hypothesis 2: Information that the victim was drunk at the time of the assault will reduce perpetrator blame and increase victim blame in rape cases but not in robbery cases.
- Hypothesis 3: The closer a prior relationship between perpetrator and victim, the less blame will be attributed to the perpetrator and the more blame will be attributed to the victim, but only for rape case.

They created six vignettes of about 200 words representing stranger, acquaintance and ex-partner perpetrators and two coercive strategies (force and exploitation of the victim's intoxicated state) (Figure 7.1)

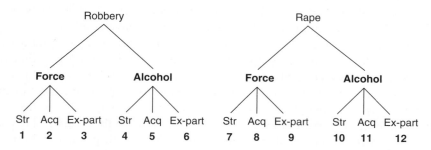

Figure 7.1 Experimental conditions of Bieneck and Krahé (2011). Str = stranger perpetrator; Acq = acquaintance perpetrator; Ex-part = former partner perpetrator

Participants received either rape or robbery scenarios (taking care to eliminate order effects of presentation). Participants were asked to indicate to what extent they blamed the victim, which was answered by responses on a seven-item Likert scale. Cronbach-alpha reliability coefficients were reported to indicate scale reliability and a mixed factorial MANOVA tested the hypotheses. Results are reported in terms of statistical significance and effect size (see Table 7.2).

Table 7.2 Results from Bieneck and Krahé's (2011) study of victim blaming

Crime	Coercion	Relationship	P blame Mean $n = 143$	V blame Mean $n = 143$
Robbery	Force	1 Stranger	6.72	1.68
		2 Acquaintance	6.61	1.79
		3 Ex-partner	6.63	2.15
	Alcohol	4 Stranger	6.49	2.00
		5 Acquaintance	6.27	2.20
		6 Ex-partner	6.38	2.11
Rape	Force	7 Stranger	6.59	1.52
		8 Acquaintance	6.19	2.27
		9 Ex-partner	5.01	3.66
	Alcohol	10 Stranger	5.73	2.92
		11 Acquaintance	5.37	3.56
		12 Ex-partner	4.27	3.47

The higher the score the greater the blame attribution: P blame is the amount of blame attributed to the perpetrator; V blame, the amount attributable to the victim.

By and large the hypotheses were supported. As is often the case in experimental studies, the authors point out limitations to their research design, indicating the differing role that consent plays in rape versus robbery cases and therefore cautioning interpretation of their results. Krahé's approach to research is explained in Box 7.1.

Box 7.1   The experimental approach, by Barbara Krahé

I originally approached the study of sexual assault from the perspective of attribution theory, a social psychological approach trying to understand the way people arrive at causal explanations, including their own behaviours and events that happen to themselves and others around them. Within this field of research, there has been a long-standing interest in the attribution of blame to victims of rape, and I was puzzled to find, in my very first study on the subject, that a woman describing in a short video how she was raped by a stranger was found more to blame for what happened to her when she was introduced as a shop assistant than when she was introduced as a school teacher. How could such a relatively weak manipulation of social status that was in no way relevant to the incident itself produce significant differences in victim blame (and produce corresponding reductions in perpetrator blame in the shop assistant condition)? Today, we know from hundreds of studies that shifting blame from the perpetrators of rape to the victims is a pervasive tendency which plays an important part in the secondary victimization of women who are raped.

I see myself as a social psychologist who approaches the study of sexual aggression on the basis of theoretical models and quantitative methodologies without ever losing sight of the traumatizing impact of sexual assault on the individual victim. In my experimental research on social decision making about rape, I have opted for the use of fictitious rape scenarios because this approach enables researchers to identify the role of stereotypes and rape myths by holding constant or systematically varying the characteristics of the case. I strongly believe that the findings generated by this type of research have the potential to make an impact on policy decisions. They can highlight errors and biases in information processing that work to the disadvantage of victims, and they can also test and evaluate measures designed to reduce and/or dispel these errors and biases. Experimental studies have an important part to play alongside studies looking at real-life cases and/or naturalistic contexts to create a better understanding of the processes involved in blaming the victim and how to address them.

Thus experimental studies carefully control the material they expose to their research participants. Participants are often students in the researchers' institution.

Measures are subjected to careful psychometric scrutiny to ensure their reliability and validity. Experimental manipulations are designed to test formally laid-out hypotheses in line with a prior theoretical formulation. Relatively large numbers complete the research protocol and results are subject to quantitative statistical analyses. Results are often finessing and refining findings and are subject to caveats because of limitations to the degree of control the experiment was able to exert. Conclusions ask for more and better-designed research studies.

DESK STUDY SOCIAL CONSTRUCTIONIST RESEARCH

A very different approach is taken by Irina Anderson and Kathy Doherty (Anderson and Doherty, 2008). They maintain positivist rape perception research by means of experimentation should be dispensed with because (a) cognitive information processing models of human thinking about rape are highly problematic and (b) participation in experiments also is itself a disempowering experience for the research participants who have no way to challenge the assumptions and hypotheses built into the research design. What they seek to do instead is to examine social explanations for rape. They state:

> our focus is on explanations as 'accounts' which are meant to excuse, justify or exonerate the socially sanctionable behaviour of self and others ... where issues such as what happened, why and who is at fault or to blame are discussed and debated. (2008: 2)

They argue from a position that rape is culturally produced and socially legitimated and that reasoning about rape is influenced by gender and heterosexual norms. They find extant examples of 'talk' and present an interpretative analysis. They considered the following examples, which they gleaned from existing sources.

Rape victim cited in Holmstrom and Burgess (1978):

> I keep wondering maybe if I had done something different when I first saw him that it wouldn't have happened – neither he nor I would be in trouble. Maybe it was my fault. See, that's where I get when I think about it. My father always said whatever a man did to a woman, she provoked it.

Anne Robinson, *Daily Mirror* 15 February 1995:

> You may recall that Mr Diggle and the woman in question danced and drank the night away at the Grosvenor House Hotel and returned to a friend's flat, whereupon the lady lawyer undressed in front of Mr Diggle who then made what turned out to be an unwelcome advance. Mr Diggle, given the circumstances, behaved as you would image any half-drunk, virile man would. If any damage has been done to the reputation of the legal profession it is by the stupid, unnamed woman, who apparently continues to earn her living as a lawyer yet clearly possesses not an ounce of common sense.

Judge Bell, *Daily Mirror*, 28 January 1995:

Despite the climate of the times, I regard her invitation to come to her bedroom when she was scantily clad (she was wearing a calf length dressing gown) as opposed to asking you to wait until she was more suitably dressed as an amber light.

They then subjected these to an interpretive analysis, which literally is done at their desks. They suggest the first example is where the victim has internalized her father's view of rape and blames herself. In the second example the journalist Anne Robinson locates the perpetrator as victim and exonerates his behaviour by blaming a feckless, sexually irresponsible woman. In the third extract, the victim is again positioned as the provocateur by sexually arousing her attacker by the clothes she was wearing and implying consent to sex. They conclude that these examples function to minimize the severity of the sex that took place when the woman reported this as rape by re-framing the incident within normative heterosexual behaviour.

So here the concept of rape is being explored by using existing resources, and re-constructing meanings within a cultural and political context. The researchers conclude that beliefs about rape are influenced by gender and heterosexuality norms and that the gender of the victim becomes a crucial issue in terms of the apportionment of blame.

Often where there is relatively little research or theorizing (e.g. gang rape – Porter and Alison, 2004), a speculative model is devised. They start by stating (p. 452) that previous research offers little explanation for variations in gang rape. Porter and Alison suggested a three-dimensional model that incorporated ideas of dominance, submission, cooperation and hostility expressed verbally or physically creating a structural hypothesis termed a 'cylindrex' made up of a qualitative differentiation of behaviour and two modalities of action, i.e. cooperation or hostility and/or dominance or submission. Their hypothesis stated: within any given case of group rape, offenders' behaviour will co-occur to produce a theme of behaviour that can be described in terms of the circumplex dimensions. The null hypothesis was that there would be a random spread of variables rather than distinct themes.

They obtained secondary data from archival sources comprising British and American law reports, the media, published books and journals. They cross-referred media accounts with those from the law reports. In all, they amassed 223 offences and identified 68 variables grouped as: dominance, e.g. gagging, tying up; submission, e.g. letting victim go; cooperation, e.g. getting victim to remove own clothing; and hostility, e.g. use of weapon, verbal threats. They used Guttman-Lingoes Smallest Space Analysis (SSA) to reproduce their conceptual model from an analysis of the observations obtained from their constructed archival database. SSA as a non-metric technique ranks correlations between items and represents them visually as linear distances in a statistically derived space. Principles from facet theory allow the multidimensional space to be interpreted. The principle of contiguity says that aspects of a facet, for example those elements comprising hostility, being functionally related will be correspondingly co-located in the SSA. The representation of the SSA in Figure 7.2 shows that the four facets as predicted are indeed retrievable from the empirical observations.

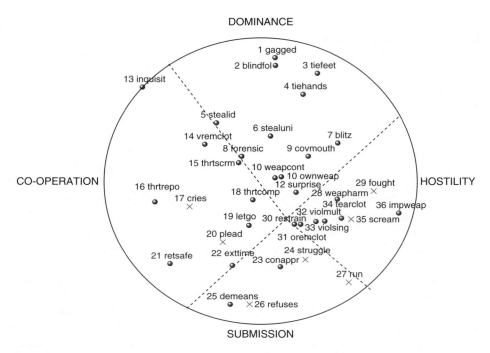

Figure 7.2 Vector 1 x vector 2 of the three-dimensional SSA plot (front view). (Reproduced with permission of Wiley from an original kindly supplied by Louise Porter; Porter, L. and Alison, L. (2004) Behavioural coherence in violent group activity; an interpersonal mode of sexually violent gang behaviours. *Aggressive Behaviour*, 30: 449–68.)

It is this correspondence between the conceptualization and the empirical observations that contributes to theoretical confirmation. Porter and Alison note that only seven of the input variables were not in their hypothesized region, although they were very near. A further partitioning of the SSA illustrated a division by way of the facet verbal and physical modality of behaviours, thereby confirming the postulated cylindrical structure to gang rapes, i.e. the qualitative distinctions between hostility, cooperation, dominance and submission can be reproduced to describe both verbal and physical behaviours. They conclude by saying (2004: 466–7) that their findings support the idea of structural coherence of gang rape behaviours and that these four interpersonal styles could prove helpful in predicting characteristics of offenders exhibiting such styles and provide insights into the likely different experiences of victims of a given style, itself having implications for recovery interventions.

Box 7.2 Comment from Laurence Alison

Our work on gang rape seems like a very long time ago and emerged as a consequence of Louise Porter's PhD studies – which I had the great privilege of supervising. My approach has always come out of a desire to make sense of complexity and often extreme forms of behaviour or extreme and difficult decisions. In this case it was a form of sexual violence that had, hitherto, been poorly understood. As a forensic psychologist you can't ever lose sight of the fact that, ultimately, you do remain remote from the reality (at least whilst conducting the research) and you only ever really have it hit you when you are in court and you see the people that it has affected.

In the case of these studies with Louise, I drew on this work as one of the components that assisted me in a highly controversial case overseas. A young man was convicted of rape and murder. He had spent many years in prison for this and over a decade later further evidence came to light to suggest another offender. The question was whether the newly identified (through DNA evidence) male had worked with the young man originally convicted and thus the young man should indeed still remain in prison (i.e. was this a group rape/murder?).

Our research on gang rape went some way to assist me in suggesting that this was rather unlikely and that the man that recently came into the frame had worked alone. It's always been important to me to approach research impartially and, to be honest, somewhat coldly – without an agenda, axe to grind or without allowing emotion to cloud thinking. The reason that this is so key is because you can't ever tell how the work may eventually play out. In this case I'd have struggled to predict that our work would be useful to this important defence case. The work has to be objective, impartial and without political agenda, personal viewpoint or a preferred vision of the world subtly or overtly communicated in the work. You can't indicate a preference for a 'side' to work on (defence/prosecution). I've found sitting with victims deeply distressing and I've also sat and talked with individuals falsely convicted.

There are few happy stories on either side. As such the work must stand separate from oneself. In that way, and however upsetting a case may be, when you meet the victims, the offenders or the falsely accused who are now directly going to be influenced by your work you know you've done the best you can by driving for an evidence-based approach to your thinking and that, quite rightly, any effect you have is a function of the science, of the evidence and not of your own world view or personal preference.

Alison and colleagues have also utilized pragmatic approaches to forensic psychology, notably in the area of offender profiling, or behavioural investigative advice to give this activity its newer name (Alison et al., 2004;

Alison et al., 2010). They argue (Alison et al., 2010) that pragmatic psychology offers a bridge (Fishman's third way) between the practitioner and profiler. Whilst their papers do not directly address rape, clearly rape and sexual violence is a key arena for behavioural investigative advice. As outlined above, Alison rehearses the case for pragmatic psychology in that it is a method for the collection of detailed case studies and permits the analysis of this material to present broad trends. More particularly, Alison and colleagues hold that this offers an opportunity for academics and practitioners to work together in creating an archive of cases given that the behavioural investigative advisers (BIAs) are interested in individual cases and the academics in patterns and trends. Thus there is an incentive to develop protocols for data derived from cases that adhere to the rigorous demands required of research enquiry.

FIELD-BASED ADVOCACY RESEARCH

Jan Jordan undertook a series of studies in New Zealand about rape, in part motivated by the public criticism of police generally and of its handling of rape cases in particular (Jordan, 2001, 2004, 2008a). In the last of these papers she uses the conceptual device of 'the perfect victim' to evaluate police response to women rape complainants, using qualitative, in-depth interviews. A crucial point of this research was to consider the lessons learnt and provide recommendations to improve police practice. Jordan (2008a: 703) explains how this research came about:

> In the late 1990s 'I ... got lucky'. One of the most prominent serial rapists in New Zealand's history, Malcolm Rewa, was tried on 45 counts involving 27 different women ... The victims were mostly well-educated, professional women, whom he typically attacked while they were in their own homes, asleep, with no other adults present in the house. Most of these women had usually little previous contact with the police and they clearly fitted the stereotype of the 'perfect' victim ... As a result of previous rape research I had been involved with a senior police investigator approached me after the trial at a time when he felt some of these women might be willing to be interviewed.

After securing permission from one of the complainants, the investigating officer gave her contact details to Jordan, who arranged to meet her and four other victims. As she describes:

> ... the gathering provided an opportunity for them [the complainants] to exchange thoughts and feelings, compare processes, and validate each other's experiences. As the afternoon progressed, my role and purpose faded to the extent that at times I almost felt surplus to requirements. This was important, however, in signalling to the women more powerfully than any verbal promise on my part that it was their perceptions and accounts that were of central importance. (2008a: 703)

Jordan interviewed 14 of the 23 women in the court case, using in-depth qualitative interviews with questions jointly conceived between the researcher and researched. This was because 'it seemed particularly important to use research methods that would reduce the power differential between the researcher and the researched, given these women had experienced the extreme loss of control that is rape' (2008a: 704). In the event, the interviews were more free flowing and Jordan epistemologically 'accepted the women's accounts of their experience as constituting legitimate sources of knowledge in their own right' (p. 704).

As a consequence of her research and its findings, Jordan held that the results presented clear implications for the organization and conduct of police investigations, and also the importance of heeding the impact of such research on the researcher herself. The raped women reiterated how important being believed was, and that having a sense of safety and privacy and the validation of their accounts was paramount. Jordan then advocated:

1. The need for police interacting with rape victims to understand the nature of rape and its impact on victims and being exposed to challenges to dominant rape myths.
2. Police organizations to consciously and reflexively address why it is so difficult to change police officer attitudes.
3. Resources and prioritizing rape was commensurate with its being the second most serious offence on the statute books in New Zealand.
4. Dedicated specialist police units to ensure consistency and continuity of contact.
5. The need to establish positive relationships with complainants, balancing their need for safety and protection against restoring a degree of control to the complainant.

This is how Jordan reflects on her motivation to undertake the research in the way that she did.

Box 7.3   The advocacy approach, by Jan Jordan

How do I know what I know, and why do I believe what I believe? Growing up female did not make me a feminist, since the world I was raised in assumed gender inequality was the norm and girls definitely could not do any thing. What my upbringing gave me was a passion for justice, so that as a teenager I began visiting inmates in a maximum security prison and campaigning against apartheid and French nuclear testing. Recognizing gender injustices came later, while trying to make sense of my own experiences of victimization and the realities of my mother's, and other women's, lives. Studying sociology and criminology,

(Continued)

and focusing on how women experienced and survived male systems, produced a passion for two things – knowledge and activism. How could I know of the pain of others without doing something to change it? Since then my career as an academic has enabled me to research, write and acquire knowledge while trying to disseminate it in ways and contexts that hopefully will make a difference. What inspires me is a vision of a world in which women and girls live safe from the pain and fear of violence, secure in the value, worth and beauty of their female identities.

HOW CAN I COPE WITH MY FEELINGS WHEN DOING A DIFFICULT RESEARCH PROJECT?

As mentioned above, Jordan (2008a) notes that the literature has relatively little acknowledgement of the impact that conducting research into rape has on the research investigator(s). She explains hearing women's rape stories can make for arduous listening. There is the potential for researchers to be reminded of their own previous victimization and provoke fear about future possible victimization. This is what she wrote in her research diary:

> I've been back in Wellington several days now and can't get these women's stories out of my head ... hearing so much talk of the fear this man generated and the way it oozed throughout these women's lives got to me. The same fear oozed into me after a while so that I was paralysed about going into dark rooms.

Jordan is not the only researcher to document such concerns and advocate a role for the researcher to change the way things are. A number of researchers tackling the topic of sexual violence have commented on the personal impact such an undertaking has had on them. Betsy Stanko (1997) writes that emotion and pain are never far from you when you are teaching or researching sexual violence. She records weeping, being overwhelmed with anger, being tired, fearful and at times frustrated. Indeed she commented (p. 75), 'to me burnout is reached when I wake up wishing I had become a botanist or better a tap dancer'. Kelly (1988) describes experiencing flashbacks and acute feelings of fear about her personal safety and being overwhelmed by anger and sorrow at the stories she heard from her research participants. Cooke and Woodhams (2009) document similar reactions when describing their study examining rapes through a database. Thus their exposure was by means of secondary data rather than direct contact. Nevertheless, they found themselves surprised at how the impact of the rapes they were analysing affected them. Both had flashbacks, with some outside event triggering a memory of a disturbing image in the material they had been reading. They decided to keep diaries and record their feelings, often conflictual, illustrated by the following extract reported in their conference paper:

I felt quite detached from the data today – focusing on the task of putting the person's narrative into a depersonalised list of behaviours. I some-times wonder if I am doing the victims a disservice in reducing their experience into a list. I think the depersonalising of an account is a neces-sary step if you are to engage with the data without what? ... damaging yourself isn't the right term. I think perhaps it is fear of what might hap-pen if I were to engage with the emotion in the account rather than just 'sanitised' behaviours.

Jo Moran-Ellis (1996) undertook research utilizing a series of focus groups look-ing at experiences of child sex abuse and she also recounts the impact this had on her. She writes that of the accounts she heard 'some caused me distress or provoked the need for support, others caused me anger ... [p. 178] ... I could barely contemplate the pain they [the children] had felt, these unknown chil-dren all from the ages from babyhood to adolescence [p. 181] ... researching sex abuse also changed my life to some degree because it changed me, and that was not something I had anticipated happening [p. 184]'.

Stanko (1997) eschews the idea that social scientists remain detached, but rather those whose work and research brings them into contact with sexual violence should acknowledge the toll its impact has not only on those who have been raped but also on the researchers (and teachers) who have direct contact with primary participants. This is a point reiterated by Jo Moran-Ellis (1996), who argues that a spurious objectivity can immunize the researcher by objectifying the horrors of sexual abuse. She argues emotional reactions to research should give rise to reflections about the anodyne manner in which accounts of sexual violence research are reported in the literature and by uti-lizing reflection, the outcome of research can contribute to ending children's oppression.

Rebecca Campbell (2002) also writes about the sense of responsibility felt by her, the researcher, who was often going to be the first person a victim/survivor had told their story to: 'I was being given something very fragile ... it was a sobering responsibility. We both knew that what was coming was going to be hard on both of us' (p. 6). She developed the idea that acknowledging feelings about rape made her and her research team think differently and provided new academic insights. The first was a contribution to understanding the concept of compassion fatigue or vicarious traumatization, i.e. 'the transformation in the inner experience of the treatment of provider that comes about as a result of empathetic engagements with the client's trauma material' (Pearlman and Saakvitne, 1995: 1). Campbell's (2002) position is that she and her team of researchers had similar emotional reactions, arguably parallel to rather than iden-tical with and less intense and of shorter duration than those of the rape survivors they were interviewing. She argues this insight suggested an under-conceptualiz-ing of rape trauma, and the experience of herself and her team led them to suggest extending the research into the families and friends of rape victims, who are part of the wider collateral damage caused and a group not traditionally the focus of research activity. The second major insight was in capturing the lived experience of their research participants. Campbell (p. 107) notes the disconnect between the experiences of the interviewed rape survivors and the academic texts, which were distant and devoid of emotion. This she argues represents a failure to accurately record an important dimension of what it is to be raped.

Betsy Stanko and Rebecca Campbell provide some reflections on their experiences as researchers of sexual violence in Boxes 7.4 and 7.5.

Box 7.4 Emotional impact revisited, by Betsy Stanko

Over a decade ago, I wrote about my reflections on the emotionality of doing research on sexual violence (Stanko, 1997). I confessed that I felt 'anger, frustration, fear, and pain during my own research experiences' (1997: 75). And now I've been asked: do I still feel the same way?

Yes, but not as much. In the past five years, I have kept sexual violence part of the frame in my current work, as I have been monitoring 'who' reports rape to the Metropolitan Police. Through an exploration of every allegation recorded during the months of April and May, I have examined the key features of rape complainants. I know that the police in London are contacted by victims who are largely either under 18, have consumed alcohol and/or drugs prior to the rape, been attacked by partners/former partners or have mental health problems in nearly nine out of every 10 contacts. In short, victims who allege rape in London are specially vulnerable, often targeted by their assailants because they are vulnerable.

This work brought me face to face with the emotionality and frustration of trying (and continually trying) to explain why such vulnerability makes such a difference to the way a police officer manages an investigation and the fragility of a victim's commitment to the criminal justice system in light of that vulnerability. Am I still angry, sometimes. And sometimes that frustration spills into my day-to-day work environment. But in the past three years it is better. I simply channel my energy to assist in any way I can to make victims' experiences of policing better.

Perhaps I am just getting older, but I have decided that it is better for me to be working on the inside to transform how police treat victims who contact them. And to do this, I have to find a way of controlling my anger about violence against women. But do I ever feel like I should have been that tap dancer I mentioned those years ago? Absolutely.

This suggests that the feelings associated with researching rape can be attenuated, in this case rather as Jo Moran-Ellis proposed, by some active intervention that tries to address the problem. Becki Campbell's reflections also show that by actively engaging the problem of emotion, in this case supporting researchers, that too may help vitiate the pain.

Box 7.5   Emotional impact revisited, by Rebecca Campbell

It's been 10 years since *Emotionally Involved* was published. The first year was pretty quiet – friends and close colleagues sent notes of congratulations for finishing what felt like a forever-task of getting the messy feelings of researching rape into coherent order on paper. In the second year, I started receiving short, almost tentative emails from people I'd never met – quick notes of 'hey, thank you, I thought I was losing my mind, good to know I'm not alone'. I wrote back eagerly, hoping to open more dialogue about the emotionality of this work. Bit by bit, this topic started becoming less stigmatized in our field. The third year was the real turning point: I started receiving a steady stream of emails from graduate students and early career researchers *proactively* seeking advice and guidance on preparing for this kind of research. I was so thrilled that emotional preparation was getting consideration right along with theoretical and methodological planning. I'm often asked: Can it be prevented? Is it possible to do this work without feeling pain? I often respond: Why would you want to – even if it were possible, which I don't think it is. I don't like hurting and I don't want others to hurt, but cutting ourselves off from the pain of researching violence against women isn't going to improve our scholarship or create social change. We need to take care of ourselves and attune to the emotional needs of our research participants because it's simply necessary, but also because it brings us closer to the problem itself. I still feel that closeness many years later and it remains my primary source of inspiration to keep at it, even when I'm tired, even when I'm hurting.

What then can researchers into rape do both to cope with the emotional load and use the insights gained to further scholarship in this area? One approach is to adapt the clinical supervision model. Milne (2007) notes that supervision is an increasingly recognized part of both clinical practice and research and his definition suggests this forms a relationship that manages, supports, develops and evaluates the work of colleagues. The main method employed is corrective feedback on performance and so differs from coaching and mentoring. Barnett et al. (2007) note the importance of creating a safe environment in which emotional insecurities may be discussed and where experimentation to develop new strategies is encouraged. Stanko (1997: 87) offers some suggestions:

- as a researcher share your personal emotional reactions by finding a sympathetic person or making links with grass roots organizations
- as a supervisor anticipate the needs for providing emotional support to fellow researchers, especially students;
- as a principal investigator be prepared, if emotional dimensions are acknowledged in research write ups, to be baited and have your scientific credentials undermined.

Moran-Ellis (1996) advocates ensuring that issues of support are clearly dealt with when preparing an ethical proposal and no proposal should be approved without utilizing such support and reflection.

Another approach is proposed by Campbell (2002), who developed a methodology for researching the researcher as part of the project. So as well as taking care in planning the approach to potential respondents and training the interviewers, weekly meetings were held to discuss cases and share emotional experiences separate from functional meetings that discussed the business of conducting the research. As the supervisor, Campbell kept detailed field notes, which became her medium to document activities of the project and reflect on her experiences. Thus her field notes became one source of data collection. She also conducted individual exit interviews with research staff on completion of the project. These served the dual purpose of achieving some closure for the researcher and provided an additional source of data about the research process. She emphasizes as a supervisor the importance of being transparent in terms of the purpose of these interviews and also to engage with staff to construct thematic categories under which to reflect their collective experience.

Cooke and Woodhams (2009) opt for an auto-ethnographic approach as their means for examining vicarious traumatization as a consequence of researching rape. This then is the individual research responsibility and provides both an account of the research process and acts as a therapeutic device to offset the emotional impact of the content of the material the researcher is exposed to.

At this point we ask you to consider some questions in the reflective exercise in Box 7.6.

Box 7.6   Reflective exercise

A good friend and fellow student has in the past been stalked by an ex-boyfriend. She does not want to tell her research supervisor about this experience. She still gets mild panic attacks when she thinks about what happened and reasons it might help her if she could understand how other people felt under similar circumstances. She asks you in confidence whether you consider it is a good idea that she undertakes her MSc dissertation on the topic of stalking.

What advice would you give?

What other information would you ask for to help you form a view about what to advise?

How would it make you feel being put in this position?

People may be drawn to a research topic because of some personal experience. This may give them additional insight and be of value when approaching potential research participants. The downside is that their experience may mean they over-identify with their respondents; it may also re-activate unprocessed psychological material from their own experiences. They may lose their sense of balance by approaching the topic from an emotional and victim-centred perspective. In the hypothetical scenario above, it would be a problem for a student to withhold a highly relevant piece of personal history when tackling an emotive topic such as stalking. If research supervisors are to make a risk assessment about research with potentially vulnerable participants, they will need to be fully apprised of any vulnerability in the research investigator for them to carry out their duty of care properly. Moreover, there is a hint in the scenario that the student may still be traumatized, which could be exacerbated by further exposure to other victims' trauma. Research suggests that prior trauma is a good predictor of experiencing vicarious victimization. Do any of these considerations make you re-think the advice you might give in the above scenario?

WHAT ARE THE ESSENTIAL STAGES WHEN UNDERTAKING A PIECE OF RESEARCH?

CHECKLIST

A useful seven-step guide to approaching research is offered by Davies et al. (2011: 7–14). Their framework has been adapted and extended and presented below.

- Identify the research topic and refining your research question, which will involve

  o reviewing the literature to check how the research in question has been tackled before
  o clarifying what is known, any contrary findings and the limits of knowledge
  o assessing viability and utility of the research as proposed
  o determining the limitations, such as conclusions that may be drawn without an appropriate comparison group
  o preparing an ethics approval application (this may include recognition of any risk factors and the means to address any possible adverse consequences)

- Confirm the approach to be taken in data collection, analysis and sampling

  o select a method consistent with the epistemological stance taken
  o check viability of potential respondents (how accessible, whether a comparison group is required, how representative of the general, or forensic, population), whether especially vulnerable; are secondary sources available if difficulties are encountered in recruiting an actual sample – some quantitative research may require a power calculation to determine the number of research participants (these may be required in the ethics submission and can be done using computer programs, e.g. G*POWER)
  o decide what form of data is required: words, physiological or psychometric measurements, numbers (such as response scales)

- o if using published psychometric scales ensure permissions obtained if there are copyright restrictions
- o it is often helpful to pilot the research instrument to ensure the researcher is confident in its use and that it makes sense to potential participants

- Writing the proposal

  - o prepare an outline of the research context (i.e. reference to the appropriate literature), purpose, questions and/or hypotheses
  - o detail sample – size, source (inclusion/exclusion criteria and a power calculation if appropriate)
  - o provide informed consent protocol and information sheet that will be given to potential respondents
  - o give an account of analytic method(s) to be used
  - o anticipate resources – any costs incurred, amount of time needed by researcher, how long the data gathering will take the research participants, will there be any form of remuneration to respondents, involvement of supervision (it is often helpful to include a timetable to indicate periods allocated to preparation, review, data collection, analysis, presentation of data in tabular or graphical formats, writing, receiving feedback and final presentation)
  - o intimate intentions for dissemination and any practice potential for the findings
  - o it may also be useful to keep a research diary and jot down ideas, references as they build up, any difficulties and how overcome, reflections, appointments

- Scientific and ethical review

  - o this may be by research supervisor, an ethics committee and/or a formal independent referring process with a view to identifying any potential flaws or weaknesses
  - o an ethics application may require submission of the research proposal as well as completion of any particular forms required by the ethics committee
  - o permissions can take a while so prepare and submit in good time and be prepared to make any adjustments required by the ethics committee
  - o note that an ethical permission is not the same thing as permission to access a particular research population (you may need both)

- Data collection

  - o keep to timetable
  - o have a contingency plan if a source of potential research participants proves unavailable or dropout rates compromise the required numbers
  - o ensure raw data are kept secure and you comply with any ethical requirements in disposing of these records

- Analysis

  - allow sufficient time, especially processing qualitative data (as a rule of thumb it takes about three hours to transcribe one hour of tape)
  - ensure researcher has appropriate knowledge (or seeks advice) on the application of particular statistical procedures or qualitative method

- Writing and dissemination

  - write appropriately to suit the product, i.e. feedback to participants, as a thesis (where there are likely to be institutional guidelines), report to management, report to a funding body, journal submission (where there are guidance to authors for the specific journal's style)
  - keep to the guidance especially the word length
  - add any additional material (e.g., ethics permissions, interview protocol, questionnaire, information to respondents, informed consent protocol) as appendices
  - keep a secure copy of the manuscript in a different medium, e.g. memory stick if working on a laptop
  - make sure you date the copy you are working on to maintain 'version control'
  - if you have a supervisor make sure they obtain drafts for comment in good time in order for you to respond to feedback
  - spell check your draft and/or get someone else to proof read, as typographical mistakes, grammatical errors or unclear sentences are difficult for you to spot when you are over-familiar with your own script.

CONCLUSION

The benefits of conducting a well-crafted research study are not only the knowledge gained, but also your experience of the process. Do you feel passionate about the research you undertook or was this more an instrument, as Wightsman (1999) suggested at the opening of this chapter? Did you enjoy doing the research and was it fun, as Wendy Stainton Rogers (2009) thinks it should be? Are you committed to research having a social and/or political purpose or do you feel more comfortable adopting a neutral, detached observer standpoint? Should research challenge the status quo as political psychologist advocate, or does it, as Michele Fine argues, retreat from the uncomfortable questions (Fine, 2012: 416)? These are awkward and difficult questions with no easy answers, but ones we entreat you to consider when conducting research yourself, reading published research as well as commissioning research for others to conduct.

RESOURCES

The edited collections by Sheldon, Davies and Howells (2010) and by Rosenfeld and Penrose (2011) provide helpful review chapters of research techniques applied to forensic psychology. The edited collections by Breakwell et al. (4th edition, 2012) are good all-purpose guides to conducting research.

Helen Gavin has a useful chapter on conducting research in her book *Criminological and Forensic Psychology* (2014: 21–49).

Canter and Alison (2003) have a helpful review paper on secondary sources for forensic topics.

Daniel Fishman and Jane Goodman-Delahunty describe the potential of case studies consistent with a pragmatic psychology (Fishman and Goodman-Delahunty, 2010).

Wendy Stainton Rogers (2009) has a lively account of the methodological implications arising from a political psychology position.

Key journals

Criminology and Criminal Justice

Howard Journal of Criminal Justice

Journal of Contemporary Criminal Justice

Legal and Criminological Psychology

Professional Psychology Research and Practice

Psychology, Crime and Law

8
VICTIMS

KEY CONCEPTS

This chapter will focus on victims. It will consider the difficulties in defining and measuring victimization, examine fear of crime and risk of victimization. It will highlight the impact of victimization, to the victims themselves and to wider society, and how this can be inflated by the criminal justice system. The introduction of policies and services for victims is also discussed. A key theme of the chapter is to advocate how understanding of victims is essential knowledge for the variety of roles utilizing psychology in a forensic setting. This will be explored first in relation to attempting to identify and bring offenders to justice; second in attempts to assess and treat offenders; and finally in recognition that the division between 'offender' and 'victim' is likely to be false, with many offenders often also being victims themselves.

Knowledge concepts	Practice considerations
Definition	Assessment
Deserving victim	Crime analyses
Fear of crime	Expert evidence
Impact of victimization	Eyewitness testimony
Prevalence	False 'offender'/'victim' dichotomy
Risk of victimization	Interviewing witnesses
Secondary victimization	Offence linkage
Social construct	Offender profiling
	Restorative justice
	Treatment

This chapter provides a basic understanding of the main issues related to studying victims and highlights the importance of consideration of victimology

(Continued)

in many forensic settings. The material covers stage one aspects of knowledge of forensic settings, assessment and formulation, interventions and research methods; together with how recent polices have influenced different settings for stage two.

Questions addressed

Who are the victims?

How many victims are there?

Are those who fear crime the most at risk?

What is the impact of being a victim?

Do victim services and policies assist?

How is victimology important to the work of forensic psychologists?

How is victimology important pre-trial?

How is victimology important post-trial?

Is offender/victim an artificial divide?

INTRODUCTION

The role of forensic psychology in relation to victims is not clear-cut. The focus on much of our work is predominantly offender-led – helping to identify them, ensuring they have a fair trial, assessing, managing, treating and assisting their path to desistance. Yet at the heart of most offending, are the victims. Victims may well have been traumatized as a consequence of being involuntarily involved in a crime. Even as an undergraduate student wishing to eventually work in the field, one of us (T.C.) envisaged at the time this was most likely to be with offenders in a prison. She felt it necessary to get an insight to this vital link with victims in the criminal justice system. Her considerations are outlined in Box 8.1.

Box 8.1 Terri Cole's considerations in volunteering for Victim Support

I was reading Psychology and Criminal Justice as an undergraduate at the University of Plymouth. Unlike many of my peers who did not know what they wanted to do with their degrees once we finished – despite the low wages and potential stress – I always knew I wanted to work in the field of forensic psychology. I knew the competition would be tough, I knew jobs were few and far between, I knew experience was valued and I had chosen a university where a gap year working in this field was possible. So my first (somewhat selfish) consideration was that I wanted to learn as much as possible and get as much experience as I could so I could get a job when I graduated. Yet if I was going to work with offenders, talking to them about their offending and hearing how they felt they had come upon this path, how would I know they were telling the truth? Would I empathize with them? If not how could I effectively help them? So my second (rather more altruistic) consideration was how could I listen to offenders' life courses and empathize with or at least understand their narratives without experiencing what it had been like on the 'other' side, without hearing the tales, and first attempting to help the victims whose lives they had affected? Were they not as, if not more, deserving of my efforts? Would this insight allow me to have a more realistic and objective stance when listening to offenders' version of events?

So I became a Victim Support volunteer. I listened, I made tea, I helped clear up, I assisted filling in claim forms, I was there. A lay 'nice person' in society to counteract the menace they had encountered – detached from the chaos that was going on in the victims' lives, with time to support and listen to them. From my perspective it was easy, it was a good thing to do, and I loved doing it. So prompted by both selfish and altruistic ends, I personally got a lot out of it, professionally it enhanced my insight and taught me 'real' people were involved at sometimes considerable cost – one of my burglary victims entered and never came out of hospital after the incident; another took months to return home. Most importantly, I felt I actually made a difference.

Victimology is defined as the study of the victims of crime and the effects of their experience. It considers the extent, nature and causes of criminal victimization and the consequences for those involved (Spalek, 2006). This chapter highlights the experiences of those directly involved in crime as victims and also looks at the more pervasive fear of crime phenomenon. We also look again at the experiences of eyewitnesses (mentioned previously in Chapter 3) and touch on offender profiling and behavioural analysis of the crime (which is dealt with in greater depth in the next chapter).

WHO ARE THE VICTIMS?

Clearly a single chapter cannot cover the scope of research, policy and practice related to victims and victimology and there are many books and journals dedicated specifically to this topic (see, e.g., Goodey, 2005; Walklate, 2007). Suffice to say there are debates surrounding the scope, definition and even the use of the 'label' victim; the extent victims themselves, the state or society should be held responsible or 'blamed', or whether there are truly 'deserving' victims; the differences in the types of victim (crime types, demographic features of the victim); and the type of harm caused, both directly to the victim and indirectly (for example via societal fear of crime).

The rise of awareness and dedication of both research and policy resources in recognizing the needs of victims has been charted by Goodey (2005) and Walklate (2001) as follows:

- increase in crime rates in the latter part of the twentieth century;
- politicization of victim issues;
- increased attention as a corollary of injustices highlighted by the civil rights and second wave feminist movements;
- inauguration of crime/victim surveys;
- recognition of fear of crime as a phenomenon;
- increased spotlight on the plight of victims by the media;
- establishment of Victim Support and issuing of Victims' Charters.

As noted in Chapter 5 in relation to measurement of crime, defining what constitutes being a victim, and ascertaining the prevalence and incidence of victimization, are in themselves problematic. As Goodey (2005: 255) says, many victims do not engage with the criminal justice system because they consider the matter too trivial, they have no insurance cover that requires a police crime report or they anticipate a hostile reception to their report. Spalek (2006) outlines how in some cases individuals may not realize they are victims (e.g. a child being sexually abused); not wish to be labelled as such (e.g. a rape 'survivor' who believes the label of 'victim' continues her disempowerment); may only realize later (a woman thinking she is getting a legitimate job only to find herself trafficked to work in the sex industry); be made to feel foolish (e.g. a victim of fraud); or may not be individually recognized (e.g. disaster victims, victims of terrorist attacks or of abuses of power). In addition, crimes that are reported may not be recorded. A recent inspection by Her Majesty's Inspectorate of Constabulary (2014: 18) concluded:

> Victims of crime are being let down. The police are failing to record a large proportion of the crimes reported to them. Over 800,000 crimes reported to the police have gone unrecorded each year. This represents an under-recording of 19 percent. The problem is greatest for victims of violence against the person and sexual offences, where the under-recording rates are 33 percent and 26 percent respectively. This failure to record such a significant proportion of reported crime is wholly unacceptable.

One of the most comprehensive definitions of victims is that given by the United Nations in their 1985 Declaration of Basic Principles of Justice for Victims of Crime and Abuse of Power and includes the following:

'Victims' means persons, who individually or collectively, have suffered harm, including physical or mental injury, emotional suffering, economic loss or sustained impairment of their fundamental rights, through acts or omissions that are in violation of criminal laws operative within Member States. (Goodey, 2005: 10)

The Declaration indicates that this definition holds even if the perpetrator is not identified, prosecuted or convicted and is independent of the familial relationship between perpetrator and victim. Moreover those collaterally affected, such as the victim's family or dependants, are included within the definition.

Debates over who are the victims are intrinsically linked to considerations regarding who are the offenders. Crime is a social construct. It changes over time – homosexuality was illegal in England and Wales until 1967; between countries – as mentioned in Chapter 6 what is considered bigamy in one country is polygamy in another; and whilst some acts may not be seen as legally criminal, some may deem them morally so. Some instances, such as being shouted at, intimidated or bullied in the street or having persistently noisy neighbours, may not develop to levels that constitute criminality, but they may be defined as nuisance behaviour and cause us to feel victimized. Are those who break such rules offenders? Or are they victims of such rules (e.g. consenting adult homosexuals in the 1950s)? Legislation together with societal beliefs and attitudes regarding who are the offenders and victims are therefore constructed and situated within a specific time and place, and are amenable to change. Such definitions and positioning, however, greatly impact upon treatment of such individuals within the criminal justice system. An interesting example in such debates is in relation to treatment of individuals involved in the sex industry. Whereas traditionally, sex workers themselves were predominantly arrested and prosecuted as offenders, more recently there has been greater recognition that many of these individuals are extremely vulnerable. As such there has been a movement away from prosecuting them, and instead prosecuting the users who solicit their services. The Crown Prosecution Service website (2014) outlines that the CPS recognizes 'prostitution as a victim-centred crime, and that those who are abused and exploited require holistic help and support to exit prostitution ... At the same time, those who abuse and exploit those involved in prostitution should be rigorously investigated and prosecuted ... such as kerb crawlers'.

The Netherlands offers an interesting example of how changing attitudes can influence identification of prostitutes as free agents selling sex as a commodity or as exploited victims. Huisman and Nelen (2014: 624) explain how there has been a reframing of prostitutes as victims in the last few years from a normalizing position that legalized prostitution. There has been a greater emphasis on the dark side of prostitution, exacerbated by worries about immigration and illegal sex trafficking.

However, we need to be measured in our approaches if those who engage in seeking sexual services such as kerb crawling behaviour are to learn about why they do so. Swinging the punitive pendulum back towards the offender may seem equally repressive and retrograde.

Box 8.2   A diversion scheme for kerb crawlers, by Yvonne Shell

Over a decade ago, myself and a senior probation colleague were approached by Hampshire Police to design and deliver a one-day court diversion programme for men who had received a caution for what was then known as the offence of kerb crawling, now known as soliciting. The group this targeted was first time offenders, with no history of previous sexual or violent offences who had been caught and cautioned for the offence of trying to pay for a sexual act from a street sex worker. Neither my colleague nor myself had any previous experience of this work, having both worked previously with high-risk offenders. However, we both had significant experience of working with sex offenders and the nature of this offending came under the Sex Offences Act.

We went on to develop a one-day programme, encompassing elements of psycho education, cognitive behavioural therapy and relapse prevention. To date this programme has run in over a dozen police services. It has been independently evaluated on a couple of occasions, most recently by Hamilton in 2010. We learnt quickly when we started to run the course. This learning included that we needed to weight the emphasis not on the hardships endured by the women, but on the considerable risks and threats to the course attendees' lives that their engagement in this behaviour presented.

Other such programmes have indeed included street sex workers talking about their often-harrowing accounts of their daily lives. Our learning was that the men who attended the course were not able to tolerate any increased level of blaming and shaming with regard to this behaviour and to confront them with a knowledge that they already knew to a degree served only to increase resistance and defensiveness as they sought to maintain a sense of themselves as a basically decent person. And so, the approach of the course developed into one that is echoed in other chapters in this book, particularly Chapter 11 on treatment. We understood that the day could be a day of meaningful reflection on the part of attendees, that they could use this time to consider with non-judgemental support from facilitators the risks they had been taking with regard to themselves, their loved ones and their wider lives.

I can honestly say that my personal journey on this has been one of profound respect for the majority of those course attendees, as they shared in a group their vulnerabilities around relationships, loneliness, physical and mental health concerns. This course is not an easy option for those that attend. It is effortful, at times upsetting but ultimately, in feedback at the end of the day, men say it has been a positive experience, one in which they leave feeling heard and understood and with the framework, often including signposting to wider services, to move beyond this episode in their lives.

Finally, it is perhaps important just to note that the course is self-funding and that to attend the men pay a fee less than they would if they went to court. This money is used to pay for the course in terms of minimal course running fees. The remainder of the money generated is returned to the local police authority in which the course runs and the police decide how this money is used in the local community in which this offending has occurred. Communities see visible reparation and to date money has gone to support women's refuges, mental health charities and youth clubs.

Such debates are also interwoven with notions surrounding 'undeserving' versus 'ideal' victims and whether any blame, or how much responsibility, should be levelled at them rather than the offender. This is particularly pertinent in cases where the victim may be deemed to have precipitated the incident in some way. Do some victims 'deserve' greater justice or support than others? If an offender is beaten by a violent gang he is a member of, a car broken into as a laptop was left in clear view on the back seat, or a woman is attacked when she willingly goes back to her date's flat after a night out with him – are these victims any less deserving of justice? Conversely if the home of a sober, safety conscious, monogamous, married woman is broken into and she is beaten and raped despite putting up a great deal of physical resistance – as an 'ideal' victim, is she any *more* deserving of justice? Spalek (2006: 35) comments on the thin line between blame and responsibility and notes some emphasize the 'duty' of citizens to avoid victimization. Many victims also blame themselves for their actions (Barnes, 2013). Indeed some measures, such as payout from criminal injuries compensation (see below), may also factor in a measure of 'deserving' by, for example, only making payments to non-criminal (even if their previous criminality may be unrelated to the current event) and completely 'blameless' victims whose behaviour did not contribute to the incident and who have cooperated with the police.

HOW MANY VICTIMS ARE THERE?

As highlighted in Chapter 5, in England and Wales official statistics regarding the number and types of crime are recorded by the police and collated by the Home Office and the Office of National Statistics. The latest figures show that 3.7 million offences were recorded by the police for the year ending March 2014 (Office of National Statistics, 2014). As mentioned above, not all crime gets reported to police. It is widely recognized that the police are informed of only a minority of sexual assaults (e.g. HMIC, 2014; Kelly, 2002; Walby and Allen, 2004). Myhill and Allen (2002) indicate the police are aware of only 20% of rape offences which is illustrative of the potential 'dark figure', of crime concept introduced in Chapter 5. Non-reporting, and non-recording of crime can affect assessment of how many 'victims' there are, and will impact upon how they are defined and treated within the criminal justice system.

In an attempt to elicit a more accurate picture, including non-reported and non-recorded crimes, crime victim surveys have been conducted in different countries for a number of years, asking samples of people about their criminal victimization. For example, the 2001 British Crime Survey on average 'counted' crimes as four times higher than those reported to the police (Kershaw et al., 2001). More recently, the Crime Survey for England and Wales (formerly the British Crime Survey) highlighted there were an estimated 7.3 million incidents of crime against households and resident adults (aged 16 and over) in England and Wales for the year ending March 2014 (Office of National Statistics, 2014). Other countries, including the United States, Australia, Canada, Finland, France, Germany, Netherlands, Sweden and New Zealand, have similar surveys but their methodologies, periods studied and response rates differ, making comparisons problematic. Attempts at standardization and cross-comparison have been made, for example by translation of questions into different languages, but differences in sampling, interview lengths, political considerations and cost mean that direct comparison remains difficult (Mayhew, 2000; Office of National Statistics, 2014).

Thus it is difficult to calculate accurate rates of victimization with any precision. Furthermore, studying incidence and prevalence misses consideration of the indirect effects of wider society – for example fear of crime.

ARE THOSE WHO FEAR CRIME THE MOST AT RISK?

Although fear of crime has not attracted as much attention as the analysis of crime trends (Gray et al., 2011), what is clear is that fear of being harmed in some way by crime is as, if not more, prevalent in the population than experience of an actual crime, and has been recognized as a phenomenon since the 1990s (Hale, 1996). Fear of crime is compounded by media effects and may lead to a heuristic bias in estimating the volume of crime (e.g. the availability heuristic, which is a tendency to inflate frequency of occurrence if reported in a particularly vivid and memorable way, such as child abduction or stranger homicide – see Table 5.1 for more examples of such biases). It has been argued such fear has increased demand for and consumption of security goods such as CCTV, alarms and insurance (Green, 2007).

Farrall and Jennings (2012) highlight how fear of crime may change over time, for example law and order was highlighted as the most urgent problem facing the UK in 1980, but by 2007 this was overtaken by the financial crisis. Trend data from Ipsos–MORI in Figure 8.1 shows the decline in concern about crime and an increase in concerns about the economy and race/immigration issues.

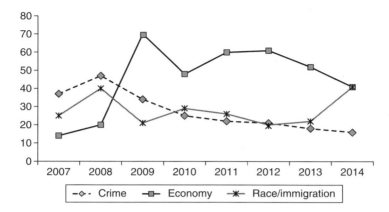

Figure 8.1 Trend data on issues the public felt were the most important facing Britain, 2007–2014. (Source: Ipsos-MORI Trend issues www.ipsos-mori. com/researchpublications/researcharchive/2905/Issues-Index-2012-onwards. aspx?view=wide)

Concern about crime appears to vary according to age, sex, mental health, physical functioning, area lived in, socio-economic status, quality of life and race (Modood, 1998; Stafford et al., 2007). It also seems to differ in relation to perceived likelihood of being victimized, the perceived seriousness of an offence and individual vulnerability (Warr, 1987). For example, LaGrange and Ferraro (1989) found that women and older people tend to be more fearful, and around one in five of those with a household income of less than £10,000, living in areas with high levels of physical disorder, or living in multicultural areas are likely to worry about burglary or violent crime.

However, fear of crime does not necessarily track objective rates of actual victimization; for example, young, low-income males tend to be the least fearful yet actually are at greater risk of victimization than other groups (Lea and Young, 1984; Wolhuter et al., 2009). Conversely, although women generally and the elderly may fear crime the most (Hale, 1996), they are actually the lowest risk groups of physical attack (Wolhuter et al., 2009). One study found 16–29-year-olds were subject to violence at a rate 17 times higher than those aged 60 years or over (Chivite-Matthews and Maggs, 2002). Wolhuter et al. (2009) argue crime may affect some victims more because they feel vulnerable and less able to protect themselves. Hidden violence occurring in private may account for some of the enhanced fear in women and older people.

Analyses combining *how* worried a person is with the frequency of being worried distinguishes three responses – the unworried, the worried (i.e. those who could recall a recent incident and stated they were worried) and the anxious (i.e. those who could not recall a recent incident yet were still worried) (Farrall et al., 2009). They also distinguish functional worrying, such as taking appropriate measures to alleviate harm, and dysfunctional worrying, where disproportionate precautions are taken. In one study (Gray et al., 2011), 21% of their sample were categorized as worried (with about three-quarters described as dysfunctionally worried) and 14% were classed as anxious (of which 73% were classed as being dysfunctionally anxious). Of interest was that women were twice as likely to be worried compared to men, and a perception that if your neighbourhood is disordered and being a prior victim was also associated with worrying. Prior victimization and poor health were associated with being dsyfunctionally worried. Fear of crime can therefore have a significant impact on the lifestyles and quality of life of some individuals, with some restricting their activities, such as avoiding certain areas, because of it (Bowling and Phillips, 2002; Phillips and Sampson, 1998).

WHAT IS THE IMPACT OF BEING A VICTIM?

Although fear of crime can impact lifestyle, becoming a victim of an actual crime can have severe effects upon both the victim themselves and cause collateral damage to family, friends and relatives (Eschholz et al., 2008). The consequences of victimization have been an active topic of research since the 1970s. The notion of secondary victimization has also been widely discussed – when the actual investigative process and prosecution system itself causes additional distress to the victim.

DIRECT VICTIMS

There are potentially many effects on those who have been directly victimized, including physical (injury), emotional (fear), behavioural (avoidance) and financial (loss of earnings), and these can be immediate, but can also be long-lasting depending on the nature and severity of the event, the characteristics of the victim and the support available to them (Spalek, 2006). One particularly impactive study details the narratives of women who had survived attacks from a serial sex offender, Malcolm Rewa, in New Zealand (Jordan, 2008b). The following comments exemplify the psychological impact direct victimization can have:

> ... you just can't describe it. It goes through your mind that you are not going to see your family again. (Kathleen, p. 10)

> ... even though the sexual side of it was revolting, it was that fright, when he burst into the room and kept beating me – that has been worse to get over than the sexual bit. (Suzanne, p. 11)

> ... there was no violence in it, which was actually something I found really difficult to cope with afterwards. (Karen, p. 18)

The impact of a 'one-off' criminal event can be enduring. Indermaur (1995) found victims of violent property crime experienced lengthy periods of disturbance. Consequences can be pervasive, such as beliefs that the world is not 'just' or they have lost control over their lives (e.g. Kelly, 1988).

However, victimization can also be continual, as in repeated cases of domestic, sexual or racial abuse, and some people live in conditions of a continual threat of violence and fear it may happen again (Bowling and Phillips, 2002; Dobash and Dobash, 1979; Radford, 1992). This has been conceptualized as 'spirit injury' (Davis, 1997; Williams 1997).

The effects of victimization can also be catastrophic, as the case of Frances Andrade highlights, summarized in Box 8.3.

Box 8.3   The case of Frances Andrade

Frances was sexually abused by her music teacher, Michael Brewer, whilst she was a teenager. She eventually told a friend in 2001, who contacted the police. The police investigated and Frances became increasingly withdrawn and depressed. As her abuser's trial approached she deteriorated further and she took repeated overdoses. The judge in the trial ordered the jury to return a number of not guilty verdicts due to points of law that had not been explained to Frances, and it was the day after this that she committed suicide, on 24 January 2013. She was 48 years of age. She did not live to see her abuser jailed for six years. The Coroner said mental health professionals failed to appreciate the risk she posed to herself, and that it was clear she found giving evidence extremely traumatic, that she had sunk into 'incredible despair' and felt the defence barrister seemed to be attacking her personally.

The Guardian, 24 July 2014 (www.theguardian.com/society/2014/jul/25/frances-andrade-failed-by-mental-health-services-coroner)

Some groups of victims, such as the elderly and those living alone, may be more vulnerable to different types of victimization, such as distraction burglary (Budd, 1999), and the impact it may have upon them can vary depending on variables such as age or physical connection to an area. For example an able, elderly person living in a poorer area may be more likely to be a target for burglary or robbery whilst out shopping; however a frail, housebound elderly person living in sheltered accommodation may be more at risk of abuse or theft by their carers. Both types of offence may have severe effects on the victim in relation to the physical impact, their future socialization (going out, or trusting others). Conversely, a young male involved in a street brawl may incur minor injuries, may not report the matter, nor think much else of it. However it is important to remember that different individuals have different reaction thresholds and generalizing from stereotypic reactions may not be appropriate. The elderly lady may be resilient and cope whereas a young man may be severely traumatized. One study found, for example, the effects on adults of less serious crimes can be pervasive and persistent (Norris and Kaniasty, 1994) and another found male victims of assault often had phobias, sleep disturbance, hyper-vigilance and a reduction in self-confidence (Stanko and Hobdell, 1993).

INDIRECT VICTIMS

In addition to 'direct' victims there are also others – friends, family, co-habitees and relatives – who also may be affected by the offence (Rock, 1998). They may be attempting to support the victim without a full understanding of what they themselves are suffering. They too may become more fearful of crime, experience feelings of powerlessness or self-blame, have 'survivor guilt' at being left alive (for example as a survivor of a school shooting or terrorist incident) or having to deal with the permanent loss of family and/or friends. One mother captures the moment she was told her son had been murdered: 'I didn't hear what he said ... I was in shock ... I could hear him calling me ... I could hear myself screaming ... I thought wow – my world is going to come to an end' (Thompson, 2007: 109).

It has been estimated that 16 million US adults have lost a relative or close friend to homicide. Symptoms of post-traumatic stress disorder, depression and anxiety in these individuals are common (Amick-McMullan et al., 1991). Suicide, avoidant behaviour (i.e. avoiding situations associated with the trauma) and drug and alcohol misuse are also found amongst those collaterally affected by crime. In addition, individuals who have lost someone to murder may have had their assumptions regarding the world as being a safe place shattered. They may blame themselves for not protecting their loved one, and may exhibit greater concern regarding their own or their family's safety in the future (Rinear, 1988). The effects of indirect victimization on children can also be significant, with many emotional and cognitive problems being reported over the life span (Turner et al., 2006).

SECONDARY VICTIMIZATION BY THE CRIMINAL JUSTICE SYSTEM

This occurs when a victim feels they are victimized again by the very processes of the criminal justice system (Pointing and Maguire, 1988). Secondary victimization is a relatively common phenomenon, especially in cases of sexual violence, and may dissuade victims from proceeding (Ellison, 2002). Having reported a sexual offence, many withdraw from the process for fear of the way the criminal justice system will treat them (Feist et al., 2007). Ullman and Townsend (2010) found 72% of rape victims had a negative experience of the criminal justice system. This can impact both the victims themselves, and those around them. The death of any loved one is stressful, but as outlined by Thompson (2007) in murder cases this can be exacerbated, as the death is often sudden, there may be additional stigma attached (others may blame the victim's lifestyle for the attack) and they may have additional difficulties in having to navigate the criminal justice system. The offender may not be caught; injured parties may not feel justice has been done; the trial may bring the pain and loss back; and this may be continual with appeals and the potential eventual release of the perpetrator (Bucholz, 2002; Ogelsby, 1997; Schlosser, 1997). Research has found those suffering the most psychological distress were the least satisfied with the criminal justice system (Amick-McMullan et al., 1989).

In relation to victims of sexual and domestic violence, Herman (2005: 581) commented 'the single greatest shock was the discovery of just how little they mattered'. The victim may undergo physical examinations, their property may be sealed or taken as evidence, and giving statements can be a lengthy exercise. For example, one victim in Jordan's (2008b) study of rape victims stated that being asked 'to go into the itty bitty, nitty gritty details is really quite difficult' (Kathleen quoted in Jordan, 2008b: 41). Sexual offence victims may be embarrassed, describing the offence to others – another of Jordan's respondents reported her attacker used this as a method of control, stating 'if you go to the police you will be embarrassed' (Connie quoted in Jordan, 2008b: 10). Victims may also not be allowed to shower until after a physical examination by a police doctor, may have to see male professionals and may have to be referred to sexual health clinics in relation to pregnancy or sexually transmitted diseases, which can all add to and extend the length of their trauma (Jordan, 2008b).

Although considerable advances have been made, societal beliefs exemplified in rape myth studies (see the work of Bohner and colleagues discussed in Chapter 7) can impact or be reflected in the attitude of some officers within the criminal justice system. There are major inconsistencies in how victims are treated internationally (Gilmore and Pittman, 1993; Gregory and Lees, 1999; Herman, 2005; Jordan, 2001), despite the fact that this can be critical to a victim's recovery (Gilmore and Pittman, 1993). As highlighted by an FBI officer, 'investigators often judge the victim reaction to what they'd do without taking into account the victim's personality, the circumstances surrounding the assault, and the fear factor involved' (Hazelwood and Burgess, 1999: 143). Many features, such as the relationship to the victim or the amount of physical injuries sustained, can account for 'judgements' made by criminal justice system personnel (Gregory and Lees, 1999). Furthermore, in an adversarial system victims may have to be questioned by both the prosecution and defence at court, which can be arduous when attempts are frequently made to diminish their credibility. Victims may be upset by having to recount harrowing details, often some considerable time after the offence has occurred. They also feel a level of responsibility in needing to get it right, and many are simply terrified of taking the stand (Jordan, 2008b) and feel that it is they themselves who are being accused (Winkel and Koppelaar, 1991). This is often experienced as re-victimization (Jordan, 2008b). Although some have found that most witnesses give evidence with little difficulty, victims were generally more negatively affected by giving evidence in court (Spalek, 2006). Van de Zandt (1998) has labelled these experiences as 'state-sanctioned victimization' whilst Herman (2005: 574) commented 'if one set out intentionally to design a system for provoking symptoms of traumatic stress, it might look very much like a court of law'.

VICARIOUS VICTIMIZATION

Observing the stress and suffering of someone who has been damaged by the impacts of crime can sometimes induce a set of mimicked symptoms, variously called compassion fatigue, or vicarious or secondary victimization (Pearson et al., 2010: 288). It is not unusual for police officers and mental health professionals to experience symptoms akin to post-traumatic stress disorder, including substance abuse, depression, somatic complaints and sleep disturbance. Levin and Greisberg (2003) describe risk factors as follows:

- identification with the dead and the survivors;
- working with child survivors;
- low levels of social support;
- lengthy exposure;
- prior history of trauma;
- prior treatment for a psychological disorder;
- limited experience; and
- lack of supervision.

Campbell (1994) suggests there may be a continuum between victims themselves, who experience some crime-related trauma, professionals such as police officers who have first-hand exposure to the results of the trauma, and therapists who have secondary exposure by virtue of hearing accounts of the trauma.

Brown and Anderson (2000) employed Figley's (1995) compassion fatigue questionnaire, which was completed by 27 male officers and 30 female officers. They found that 44% of officers fell into the extremely high risk group and only 2% into the extremely low risk group. Prior traumatic experiences were the most important feature predicting high compassion fatigue scores. Brown et al. (1999) reported a vicarious stress factor associated with the investigation of sexual crime and that women officers were more likely to indicate adverse symptoms than men. Women working in rural areas, where there is likely to be less support and where the officer felt isolated with no peer support, suffered most. Interestingly, threats to belief in a just world impacted men more than women.

Campbell (1994) identifies a series of reactions of therapists working with victims of trauma:

- mirroring of client's emotions of terror, rage and despair;
- emotionally overwhelmed;
- revival of own past traumatic experiences;
- intrusion of client's imagery into own thoughts;
- challenges own sense of vulnerability;
- loss of belief in efficacy of intervention;
- adoption of role as rescuer;
- over-identification with client's sense of anger or grief;
- voyeuristic interest;

- bystander or survivor guilt;
- adopting client's sense of bewilderment, disassociation or feelings of manipulation.

Monitoring and supervision is important to avoid the potential of damaging effects in both professionals as well as collateral victims.

DO VICTIM SERVICES AND POLICIES ASSIST?

An increased understanding of the impact of becoming a victim and attempting to address victim issues has led to the emergence of a number of services and policies being provided in the latter half of the twentieth century. Support for victims in the form of counselling, compensation, reparation and mediation has been developed.

For example, Newburn (2003) highlights how criminal injuries (financial) compensation being paid to victims was introduced from the 1960s in New Zealand, Australia, Canada and many European countries. The late 1970s and 1980s saw the introduction of counselling and charity-run support services such as Victim Support, Rape Crisis Centres, sheltered homes and Childline. The 1980s also saw a rise in victim-led calls for justice, such as to the police to keep victims informed of the progress of the investigation and the introduction of mediation initiatives (Walklate, 2001). In 1990, the Victim's Charter was introduced outlining standards of services victims should expect to receive, in 1991 the Criminal Justice Act meant compensation would be paid out to victims before fine fees were collected, and in 1995 reports could be presented to courts taking victim views into account. In 1997 Victim Support was expanded to include support to victims and witnesses giving evidence in court.

In 1999 special measures were introduced to help vulnerable and intimidated witnesses give their best evidence and relieve some of the stress in court (Bull, 2010). Provisions included screens being put up in the courtroom to prevent the witness from seeing the defendant, witnesses giving evidence via a live video link rather than being in the courtroom, removal of barristers and judges' wigs and gowns, and clearing the public gallery. Intermediaries were also brought in to assist witnesses with communication difficulties. Victim personal statements (victim impact statements) were introduced in order to provide victims with the opportunity to comment on how the crime has affected them. Initiatives such as the victim contact scheme also mean victims should be better informed when offenders are released.

However, critics suggest that many services are falling short of expectation and we have a needs- rather than rights-based approach with victim policy in Europe, focusing on the provision of services rather than the US model which is more focused on the rights of victims (Hall, 2009). In addition, whilst such policies are purportedly aimed at assisting victims, some have argued this has been grounded in wider political concerns. For example, it has been suggested that victims are used by governments to highlight that crime is inevitable (so governments should not be expected to solve all crime) and for a justification of punitive policies – they provide an achievable popular goal (Garland, 2001).

Whilst initiatives such as personal statements can be seen as a positive step in giving victims a further voice and providing courts with a deeper understanding of the sometimes devastating impact a crime has had upon them, there is great variation in how such statements are written, awareness of their existence and purpose is limited, and their impact on sentencing has been relatively minimal (Graham et al., 2004; Hoyle et al., 1999). Similarly, support from agencies such as Victim Support appears to lead to better recovery and make a difference to those who receive it (Corbett and Maguire, 1988). However, voluntary services are struggling, with limited finances and focus upon 'ideal' and 'majority' victims, with many victims (e.g. male victims of domestic violence) and crimes (e.g. so-called victimless crimes such as large-scale fraud) still remaining outside the remit of some victim services. For example, until relatively recently the majority of research on youth crime focused on their offending, rather than their victimization experiences (though see now Pain and Gill, 2001). Moreover, there seems to be a lack of response to specific victim groups despite knowledge that individuals differ in the type of support they require, which may be on the basis of cultural, religious or other personal grounds (e.g. Choudry, 1996).

Hence despite such initiatives, the experience of many victims involved in the criminal justice system still tends to be somewhat negative. It seems that whilst policies do exist, in practice cultural barriers and processes undertaken by lawyers and court staff have not yet caught up with the good intentions (Hall, 2009). Spalek (2006) outlines that a truly victim-centred trial would:

- be set up to respond to the needs of the victim (procedures, personnel etc.) especially keeping to time schedules;
- understand and accommodate a full, uninterrupted victim narrative and construction of incidents from a victim perspective rather than merely allowing for presentation of 'bits' of their story when giving evidence when questioned by lawyers; and
- involve a culture that is both receptive and understanding to the victim (and ideally this should expand to the criminal justice system as a whole) with a less confrontational tone in cross examination.

In recognition that the criminal justice system can exacerbate problems and may not address the roots of the offence (Clear and Rose, 1998), restorative justice has been advocated in many cultures as a method of bringing 'harmed parties together in the presence of the offender' (Eschholz et al., 2008: 179). Restorative justice can involve a range of methods (e.g. meetings can be with only the offender and victim, or can include family, friends, witnesses, community members); a variety of mediators (e.g. police, court personnel, trained individuals, volunteers); and can be undertaken at any time during the criminal justice process (from pre-charge to post-release and virtually anywhere in between). It involves relevant parties sharing their experience and understanding the role of the other parties (Eschholz et al., 2008). It has been argued that the criminal justice system 'steals' the role of the victim and restorative justice permits them a forum in which they can tell their story, express their pain and ask questions (Eschholz et al., 2008; Tutu, 1999). McCold (2003) outlines there is little public opposition to restorative justice, and consistent benefits to victims have been shown, including providing an understanding of the offender, a lesser desire for revenge and a reduction in anger and fear (Hall, 2010). Offenders too seem more satisfied with the outcome of restorative justice compared to traditional methods of disposal, and studies have shown recidivism rates may be reduced, particularly by more recent restorative justice methods (Bonta et al., 2006; Latimer et al., 2005). Hall (2010) highlights, however, that it is important such methods do not sit alone, but incorporate other means of addressing offenders' problems.

HOW IS VICTIMOLOGY IMPORTANT TO THE WORK OF FORENSIC PSYCHOLOGISTS?

To summarize thus far, we have seen measuring the incidence of victimization is problematic, fear of crime and its impact can be severe, and although there are increasing policies and services for victims, these are still somewhat restricted in practice. The very experience of victimization can be further exacerbated by the criminal justice system itself. Yet what does this have to do with most forensic psychologists' roles? The next section of this chapter will consider why knowledge and an understanding of victimology is of importance in our work. This may be at a strategic level, influencing policy and practice, or at a more individual level, in relation to specific cases. We will segregate this in relation to the work of forensic psychologists pre-trial and post-conviction. Their work during trial is considered in Chapter 3.

HOW IS VICTIMOLOGY IMPORTANT PRE-TRIAL?

COLLECTING THE DATA

After an offence has occurred a vast amount of material is available to the investigator from a number of sources, including from the crime scene itself (e.g. forensic evidence may have been left), passive data sources (e.g. CCTV) and predominantly from witnesses and victims. Appropriate collection, retention and presentation of these 'data' brings offenders to justice and some of these processes have been assisted by forensic psychologists.

One area in which psychology has provided significant input is in relation to data collection from victims and witnesses during the interview process. Historically psychologists have studied cognition and memory, and accurate and detailed recall of information can be vital in attempting to identify, trace and locate an offender. The cognitive interview (Fisher and Geiselman, 1992) has been developed and used as a method by which to interview cooperative witnesses (which includes cooperative victims) in order to obtain the most reliable evidence. It involves the use of techniques such as mental reinstatement of events, reporting every detail, describing the event in different orders or from different perspectives and enhancing communication between the interviewer and interviewee, such as tailoring the language to suit them (Milne and Bull, 1999). (See Chapter 13 for further discussion of this.)

ANALYSING THE OFFENCE

Consideration of why a person became victimized or property was attacked at a specific time at a particular location is key to efforts in analysing the offence behaviour. For example, crime analysts may be asked to analyse patterns of offences in order to assist in targeting detection or prevention. Street patrols or letter drops/posters may be localized and target-hardening measures, such as better lighting or greater security, can be deployed. The key to this is consideration of the victim – their 'occupation', where they live, when they are in residence and lifestyle.

Which victims or properties are targeted may also give clues as the type and motivation of an offender responsible for a crime. For example, research has indicated a burglar in need of cash may select a property because she/he knows the area but does not live too close within it, the property has low security measures (e.g. is unoccupied, has no dog, alarm, or security cameras), is not overlooked, is accessible yet has good means of escape (see for examples Nee, 2004). However the choice may be relative, the property may not be 'ideal' but may be the best available at the time. Other more professional burglars who wish to steal expensive jewellery or art may target specific locations accepting the inevitability that limited knowledge of the area and security measures will need to be overcome.

The choices the offender makes in relation to victim selection in interpersonal crimes can also potentially assist in offence linkage (i.e. determinating whether one offender is responsible for more than one offence). When considering linkage, in the absence of forensic evidence, analysts – for example in the case of sex crimes – would consider features such as whether victims were all attacked or followed from the same area, were of the same sex or ethnicity, were a similar age, went to same school, shopped at same shop, employed the same window cleaner etc.

Victim selection can also indicate the type of person responsible, for example in homicide offences. A behavioural investigative adviser asked to produce an offender profile (providing background information regarding the likely type of person responsible for the offence) for a murder, would attempt to ascertain as much as possible about the lifestyle of the victim. For example, a 20-year-old male who is known to police for violence and drug dealing found shot in his own home is likely to have been killed by a violent criminal known to the victim. A murderer responsible for the death of a 14-year-old girl who has been found in a forest, strangled and sexually assaulted is more likely to be a stranger to the victim.

Consideration of the potential options available to offenders and the specific decisions taken by them – where to attack, how to attack and *who* to attack – are therefore central in behavioural analyses. It is, however, unwise to make unfounded assumptions about certain decisions the offender may or may not have made in relation to victim selection.

A rapist may target an attractive victim whom he has seen before, been following and stood waiting for because he knows her route. However, she may be chosen at random as an available female who has crossed his path at a time co-incidentally when no one else was around. Similarly, in murder whilst the many potential motivations in victim selection can be considered if it assists the police in trying to locate potential suspects, the actual motive of the offender may be a complex interaction of factors, or may never be known. For example, a killer may target a prostitute because:

- street workers are relatively easily available and may not quickly be identified as missing;
- she did something to annoy the offender – laughed at them, belittled them, would not do as asked, reneged on the 'deal', or asked for too much money;
- alternatively the offender may have a vendetta against prostitutes, may be displacing anger from someone/something else, was told or paid by someone else to do it or is mentally ill and has delusional/paranoid thoughts; or
- the choice of a prostitute may have been a coincidence (the victim was 'off duty' at the time – merely in the wrong place at the wrong time).

Yet consideration of victimology is more than just related to demographic details such as gender, age, occupation and location. Sometimes the nuances of human behaviour are taken into account alongside how victims are known to have behaved in the past. Someone found murdered in their own home with no signs of forced entry who is genuinely (and known to be) extremely security conscious, never answering the door to strangers, seems more likely to have been killed by someone known to them. Someone known to have successfully put up a fight during a previous robbery attempt is less likely to fully comply with any future offender's demands. However, someone stabbed during a previous robbery attempt may be more inclined to hand their money over next time. This introduces the notion of behavioural consistency and change. This will be explored further in Chapter 9, however it should be highlighted that both victim and offender behaviour may be consistent but also can change as individuals learn and develop. This is especially important when considering offence linkage – the same offender faced with a compliant rape victim may not display any level of violence, however if in a future attack a victim does not comply, he may subject her to further verbal or additional physical attack. Some victims themselves recognized this and adapted their behaviour accordingly during an attack – 'the more you fought, the bigger hiding you got' (Suzanne quoted in

Jordan, 2008b: 9); and 'what he wants he will get, talking to him is a waste of time' (Raquel quoted in Jordan, 2008b: 21). Although some offences may on the face of it appear different, when victims' behaviour is taken into account, the change in offender behaviour can be more easily understood.

HOW IS VICTIMOLOGY IMPORTANT POST-TRIAL?

ASSESSING AND TREATING THE OFFENDER

In respect to assessing and appropriately treating the offender post-trial, we argue consideration of the role of the victim should also be a factor, certainly by a forensic psychologist, if not by the offenders themselves. For example, in relation to a sexual offender, this can include consideration of the initial motivation – to gain sex, to vent anger, violence, power, domination or exert control. An offender may deny he knew his victim was underage due to her being in a nightclub, and the way she looked or was dressed at the time.

Consideration of why offenders did what they did and why a particular victim was chosen may be key in making an accurate assessment in relation to the risk posed and treatment needs. An offender denying he knew the victim was only 14 years old – hence purportedly believing it was consensual sex – poses a different type of risk to different individuals than if the victim was an adult woman.

The role of the victim is outlined in restorative justice methods, and deficits in victim empathy are addressed in some structured group work with certain types of offender (e.g. in sex offender treatment – see, for example, Stockton and Crighton, 2003). However, recent changes to such intervention programmes have significantly reduced the 'victim empathy' component. The rationale for this is the lack of or weak evidence to indicate that focusing on victim empathy results in reduced offending rates (Jollife and Farrington, 2004; McGrath et al., 2010). The focus increasingly is upon protective factors and ascertaining the underlying reason for why empathy was blocked at the time of the offence and addressing these issues directly (Barnett, 2014). This could be due to underlying beliefs regarding women or due to sexual preoccupations, and may require a different emphasis in treatment.

In other programmes retrospective consideration of the victim seems to be even less evident, choosing to focus on the offender behaviour, rather than highlighting the impact on the victim (e.g. with violent offenders). For example, as Jennings (2003: 97) highlights, 'a major problem with a "typical" anger-management programme was an absence of an emphasis on the experience of victims of violence and any debate about the immorality of temper loss and violent acts'. Domestically violent offenders may reduce their physical violence towards their partner, but may increase emotional abuse – i.e. in controlling their physical aggression they may merely utilize other methods of hurting their victim.

IS OFFENDER/VICTIM AN ARTIFICIAL DIVIDE?

It is widely recognized that the dichotomy between offender and victim is naive, and that distinguishing between 'offender' and 'victim' is not clear-cut (Walklate, 1989). In a review of the literature, Jennings et al. (2012) identified 37 studies from 1958 to 2011 which assessed the overlap between victimization and offending. Of these, despite the use of a diverse number of methods, time spans and cultures, 31 found considerable support for an overlap, demonstrating many offenders are victims and vice versa. Offenders and victims share similar characteristics (Fattah, 1989). A large number of victims have, or go on to obtain, subsequent criminal convictions (Dignan, 2005; McGrath et al., 2011) and offenders are themselves also victims of both reported and unreported crimes (Barnes, 2013). These could be directly related to the incident for which they are convicted, for example serious acts of violence committed by women upon men may come after they have suffered years of abuse themselves (Pakes and Pakes, 2009). Children who kill their parents often have intolerable home lives and act violently to save themselves from future abuse (Lyall, 2014). Conversely, the victimization may be totally unrelated – for example an offender's house may have been burgled – or partially related, for example an offender may have been assaulted whilst incarcerated, or sexually abused as a child which affected their own subsequent offending patterns. For example, Felson and Lane (2009) found that inmates sexually abused as children were eight times more likely to commit a sexual offence against a child.

There are several theoretical reasons as to why offending and victimology may co-occur. These include routine activity theory (Cohen and Felson, 1979), which posits an interpersonal offence can only occur when a suitable target (in the absence of a capable guardian) comes into proximity of a motivated offender – i.e. the dynamics of the situation in which individuals come into contact with one another could increase the likelihood of both becoming an offender or a victim. Gottfredson and Hirschi's (1990) general theory of crime also accounts for an overlap between offending and victimology, identifying how a lack of adequate parenting and socialization (e.g. not recognizing or dealing appropriately with deviant behaviour) can lead to low social control, which in turn could result in delinquency and criminal activity. As such a 'victim' of poor parenting may become an offender. Similarly, the 'Cycle of Abuse' (see Glasser et al., 2001) witnessed when victims of child sexual abuse become sexual perpetrators themselves has been explained by social learning theories, which identify that individuals learn and model criminal behaviours through interaction, observation, justification and 'normalizing' of attitudes and actions from socialization with family and peers (e.g. Bandura, 1977; Felson and Lane, 2009). If children exposed to family violence perceive it as being successful in solving problems, then replication is even more likely to occur (Akers, 2009). However if social learning does occur, whilst the majority of sexual assault victims are female, the majority of such offenders are male. Some have argued males may suffer more from the trauma, view themselves as capable of preventing an attack, or tend to internalize victimization without seeking help (McGrath et al., 2011). The offender/victim overlap, and related issues are exemplified by Setanta O'Kelly (see Box 11.2 in Chapter 11).

Discussion in the criminological literature has also considered wider societal victimization of offenders. Subcultural theories emphasize how society, culture and the environment create opportunities where both offending and victimization are possible. By means of example, Anderson (1999) highlights how if within a neighbourhood respect or 'street cred' is gleaned by exertion of physical superiority, this leaves an 'offender' vulnerable to subsequent victimization at the hands of another also wishing to glean such status. It is widely recognized that there are a number of 'criminogenic factors' which are common to many offenders and research suggests some of these factors are shared by victims; as such, it is unclear if it is these, or a delinquent lifestyle that makes some individuals prone to both offending and victimization (Jennings et al., 2012).

Andrews and Bonta (1994) highlight risk factors such as poor education, low employment, a lack of support from partners/family, problems with substance abuse, peers who are criminal, and generally living in environments with poor community functioning (i.e. having financial or accommodation problems). Hence it could be argued that offenders may be 'victims' of the class, society and environment in which they were raised. Offending behaviour programmes focus upon more personal/emotional factors such as dysfunctional thinking patterns around aggression, impulsivity, problem solving or anti-social attitudes towards certain groups, such as anti-authority, sexism or racism (Towl, 2003). However, the wider 'macro' elements and difficulties encountered by offenders in the communities in which they will return are more difficult to address. Whilst schemes assist in increasing their education and employment opportunities inside prison, these may be of less relevance in the outside world where competition for jobs is great and their criminal record may stand against them. Understanding the life course of the offender is central in understanding in any assessment, and this may include their victimization. These wider issues are beginning to be considered, particularly in relation to the 'Good Lives Model', which will be further explored in Chapter 11.

Box 8.4 Reflective exercise

1. A 16-year-old boy lives with his mother and younger sister. He has never known his father. He meets a girl his age, they start going out, and want to commence a sexual relationship. He has a part-time job, but most of this money goes towards feeding his family. He is caught stealing a packet of condoms from a shop that has a policy of prosecuting all shoplifters.

Is he an offender or victim? How would the situation have been different if someone had informed him he could get free condoms from his local Family Planning Clinic?

2 . Imagine you have been burgled, sentimental (but relatively worthless) jewel-lery, cash and electrical items have been stolen and the offender took an expensive knife out of the kitchen drawer and left it on the surface. Rank in order of preference – what do you need?

a) Emotional support – you are very upset regarding the loss of the jewellery.
b) The offender to be punished.
c) Financial support or a swift insurance payout.
d) Practical support such as advice regarding increased security – you are scared the offender may return.
e) Information – when will you get back the knife the police have recovered for forensic evidence?

How would the current system of criminal justice assist you? Is this sufficient?

3. Should we put the victim at the centre of the criminal justice system? Is it fair for someone to receive a greater/lesser sentence dependent upon the impact of the crime on the victim/s?

CONCLUSION

In this chapter we outlined some of the difficulties involved in defining and measuring victimization. We discussed fear of crime, indirect and second-ary victimization as well as the potentially severe impact on the victims themselves. We briefly considered policies and services for victims, high-lighting that the focus may not always be victim-led. A key theme of the chapter was that understanding victims is essential in many forensic psychology roles, be that pre- or post-trial. We drew attention to the fact that victims can become offenders and many offenders are themselves vic-tims, making the 'divide' between them ambiguous and necessitating we understand both.

RESOURCES

Sandra Walklate's (2013) *Victimology: The Victim and the Criminal Justice Process*, first published in 1989, is a good introduction to the study of crime victims and the way they are treated. Her *Handbook of Victims and Victimology* (2007) is an edited collection of work by key researchers in the field outlining theoretical perspectives and policies focused on victim issues. Jo Goodey's (2005) *Victims and Victimology* provides a comprehensive overview. Basia Spalek (2006), in the book *Crime Victims: Theory, Policy and Practice*, provides

(Continued)

an accessible account of the theory and practice in relation to crime victimization and criminal justice policy.

In the book *Victims of Crime – Policy and Practice in Criminal Justice*, Hall (2009) outlines what is meant by a victim-centred criminal justice system and what this has meant in practice.

Serial Survivors by Jan Jordan (2008b) provides a harrowing yet insightful account, detailing women's narratives of their experiences surviving rape at the hands of Malcolm Rewa.

Liz Kelly's (1988) *Surviving Sexual Violence* presents a detailed account of the prevalence of sexual violence in the lives of 60 women from a feminist perspective.

Key journals

British Journal of Criminology

International Review of Victimology

Journal of Law and Society

Violence and Victims

9
PROFILING OFFENDERS

KEY CONCEPTS

This chapter will look at offenders through the lens of behavioural investigative advisers (BIAs), who assist the police in identifying and bringing offenders to justice. The origins, and development of the profession from offender profiling to behavioural investigative advice are outlined. The chapter also describes the theories used and the assumptions and principles that underpin such work as well as reviewing the evidence surrounding the evaluation of such advice. A checklist for writing a BIA report is provided, which can be adapted to fit other forms of report writing. Finally, the chapter will offer commentary on what has been learnt and the emotional impact of working in this field.

Knowledge concepts	Practice considerations
Burnout	Arrest strategy
Evaluation	Crime scene assessment
Definition	Forensic interference
Origins	Interview strategy
Principles	Investigative suggestions
Proponents	Media appeals
Techniques	Offence linkage
Theories	Offender profiling
	Report writing
	Risk assessment
	Search

This chapter provides a basic understanding of the main issues related to the provision of behavioural investigative advice, particularly the behaviour of

(Continued)

offenders. The material covers stage one aspects of knowledge of forensic settings, assessment and formulation, interventions, research methods, advice and consultancy. In addition it considers communicating psychological knowledge and advice, and staff training and development, appropriate for stage two.

Questions addressed

How did offender profiling begin?

What are the underlying theories?

How has the profession advanced?

What services do BIAs provide?

What techniques are involved in the provision of behavioural investigative advice?

How good is the product BIAs provide?

How good is the process by which they get there?

What are the essential elements to include in a report?

What have we learnt?

How can we cope with our feelings when working as a BIA?

INTRODUCTION

The role of the forensic psychologist in relation to offenders is dealt with in Chapter 3 (assessing competency to stand trial and the role of expert witnesses), Chapter 6 (looking for causes – who offends and why), Chapter 10 (assesment), Chapter 11 (treatment and rehabilitation). This chapter looks at the behaviour of offenders and the role of a behavioural investigative adviser.

For the purposes of this chapter, offenders are defined as those responsible for committing a criminal offence. Offences can be committed against persons known to the offender or strangers, may be against individuals or the state, and encompass anything that involves breaking the law. Common to other areas of forensic psychology, there are debates surrounding definitions:

- who are offenders (e.g. should governments or corporations be included and under what circumstances?);
- the extent of blame attributed and to whom (to offenders themselves, their upbringing, the state or society for 'creating' the circumstances which may precipitate offending);
- similarities and differences in types of offender (demographic features, the extent to which they are specialists in one type of crime and which type, or generalists undertaking many); and
- the ways to minimize their causing future harm (to either themselves or others).

This chapter will focus on the beginning of the criminal justice process, considering our role in assisting the police with their investigations.

HOW DID OFFENDER PROFILING BEGIN?

Initially, psychologists' roles assisting the police focused on areas such as recruitment and selection of police officers, and occupational stress (Brown, 2000; Howitt, 2009). Yet, as outlined by Canter and Youngs (2009), investigators have always drawn upon the science of the day to help solve crimes, and as such, with the growth of forensic psychology, the role of the psychologist has been expanded to directly assist the police in the investigative process. With an increasing demand for accountability in the Police Service, the merits of social scientific endeavour have been realized, and the role of the 'police' psychologist has expanded, as outlined by Brown:

> The practical content of the work undertaken ranges from organizing and managing staff, training, health and welfare to providing operational support such as offender profiling and witness interviewing. (2000: 71)

Medieval methods of dunking to identify witches might be thought of as early attempts at profiling – the prediction from this process was that if the woman sank she was innocent and if she floated she was found guilty of witchcraft. Nineteenth-century classifications of criminals were based upon their physical features, i.e. constitutional theories. Lombroso (1911) thought criminals could be predicted from their features, such as ear size, a sloping forehead and long arms. These are now largely discredited explanations (Blackburn, 1993), but understanding criminal behaviours and propensities was recognized as important, as was the awareness that offenders can differ and police investigative practices could be enhanced by use of the scientific method (Canter and Youngs, 2009). One manifestation of a more scientific approach was the creation of 'pen pictures' of individuals who may have committed crimes. The more famous ones include:

- Dr Bond's 1888 description of Jack the Ripper – for example that he may be middle-aged, a loner and mentally unstable (see Alison et al., 2007);
- Dr Langer's 1943 profile of Adolf Hitler – considering his difficulty establishing close relationships and sadistic tendencies (Langer, 1972); and
- Dr Brussel's 1956 account of New York serial bomber George Metesky as being a disgruntled former employee of a targeted company, middle-aged, unmarried, wearing a fully buttoned double-breasted suit (Brussel, 1968).

More recently, formally recognized 'offender profiling' advice has been provided to predict the likely socio-demographic characteristics of an offender, based on the information available at the crime scene (Alison et al., 2007). Although psychologists and psychiatrists had been asked for opinions regarding likely perpetrators for a number of years, formal use within the Police Service originated in the Behavioural Science Unit of the Federal Bureau of Investigation (FBI) (see for example Burgess et al., 1986; Ressler et al., 1988).

WHAT ARE THE UNDERLYING THEORIES?

THE FBI APPROACH

FBI training courses began teaching behavioural techniques in 1972, and although the focus was upon serial crimes, there was an increasing recognition of the importance of studying offence behaviour and systematically collecting and recording data regarding offences and offenders (e.g. via the Violent Crime Apprehension Program – VICAP – database). Such detailed behavioural analyses and profiling the likely background of the offender could provide investigative suggestions, develop new lines of enquiry, narrow down searches for suspects and offer assistance in relation to offence linkage.

The FBI approach recognized the need for research to classify offence scenes into types in order to infer the most likely offender associated with a particular crime scene. Following interviews with 36 sexual murderers, crime scenes were categorized as either organized or disorganized. Furthermore, dis/organized scenes were said then to be able to predict a dis/organized offender (Ressler et al., 1988). An organized offender plans the offence, targets victims and acts in a controlled manner at the crime scene, with everything ordered, suggesting she/he may be intelligent and controlled. A disorganized offence, however, is unplanned and spontaneous, which may be due to the offender's likely young age, drugs and/or alcohol misuse, mental deficiency, other stressors or merely a lack of criminal sophistication. Features apparent at crime scenes and characteristics of likely offenders are summarized in Table 9.1.

Table 9.1 Organized/disorganized dichotomy

	Organized	Disorganized
Crime scene	Planned	Spontaneous
	Targeted stranger	Victim may be known
	Personalizes victim	Depersonalizes victim – face may be covered/body rolled over
	Controlled conversation	Minimal conversation
	Initial contact via initiating conversation or impersonating another (e.g. police officer)	Sudden violence/blitz attack
	Controlled scene	Chaotic, random, sloppy scene
	Restraints used	No restraints
	Victim or body moved to a separate location	Crime scene is often also the death scene, but within this scene the victim may be moved to a position of personal/sexual significance

	Organized	Disorganized
	Body concealed	No or minimal concealment
	Weapon taken to scene	Uses weapon from scene
	Weapon removed from scene	Weapon left at scene
	Little or no evidence	evidence present
	Aggressive acts prior to death	Overkill or excessive mutilation
	Sex prior to death	Sex post mortem, when unconscious or dying and often involves foreign object insertion
	Scene may be staged to look like something else (e.g. robbery, kidnap) and mislead the police	No attempt to deter detection or mislead police but there may be secondary criminality (e.g. theft)
	Cause of death often asphyxia	Cause of death asphyxia, strangulation, blunt force or use of pointed sharp instrument
Offender	High intelligence	Below-average intelligence
	Socially adequate	Socially inadequate, will be considered 'odd' by others
	Lives with partner	Lives alone or with parents
	Sexually competent	Partner much younger or older
	High birth order	Low birth order
	Harsh discipline in childhood	Harsh/inconsistent discipline in childhood
	Controlled	Anxious during crime
	Masculine image	Nocturnal
	Returns to crime scene	Returns to crime scene
	Charming	Significant behavioural change post offence, may change eating habits, drink more alcohol, increased nervousness
	May interject self into investigation post offence	Possible inappropriate interest in crime post offence, e.g. frequently talking about it
	Geographically and occupationally mobile	May change residence or job post offence
		Lives/works near crime scene
		Poor personal hygiene, dishevelled
		Unskilled worker, inconsistent or poor work performance

Source: Adapted from Douglas et al., 2006, and Holmes and Holmes, 1996

The advice provided by the FBI has been refined and developed over the years, for example there are now five classifications of sexual homicide (organized, disorganized, mixed, sadistic and elder). Their profiling methods together with case studies are detailed in the Crime Classification Manual (Douglas et al., 2006). However, their work is still based predominantly upon their detective experience and case studies (e.g. Burgess et al., 1986; Douglas et al., 2006; Ressler et al., 1988).

Whilst this contribution has been recognized for its practical application and multidisciplinary research collaboration (Dowden et al., 2007), the FBI approach and use of typologies has received much criticism. For example, the organized–disorganized dichotomy is based on a limited, non-random sample of convicted offenders, which (a) is reliant upon truthful self-reporting and (b) does not tell us about those offenders who were not apprehended. As discussed with respect to typologies, individuals rarely fall neatly within distinct mutually exclusive type (as evidenced by the FBI themselves by addition of a subsequent 'mixed' category). Scene interpretation may be subjective because it fails to take into account progression over time. The practical utility of some of the traits identified has been questioned (e.g. Canter et al., 2004; Dowden et al., 2007; Poythress et al., 1993). Moreover, attempts at testing such classifications have not been successful (Canter and Wentink, 2004) and statistical evidence to support the organized–disorganized dichotomy is lacking. One replication by Canter et al. (2004: 313) indicated the typologies do 'not garner even the weakest support from the data examined here'.

THE UK PERSPECTIVE

In the UK, whilst some detectives became profilers, they are not a homogeneous group (Bekerian and Jackson, 1997; Gudjonsson and Copson, 1997). Initially, in the early 1980s requests came from the police to individual psychologists for assistance on a case-by-case basis (e.g. Britton, 1997; Canter, 1994). The majority of profilers had backgrounds in research, clinical psychology or had access to relevant statistical databases working for the police, in universities or psychiatric hospitals (Smith et al., 1998). They applied theories and methods from their areas of expertise and used these to assist in criminal investigations. So, for example, a clinician working in a forensic hospital may use their knowledge from case studies of previous patients to conduct a predictive diagnostic evaluation (Wilson et al., 1997) to inform judgements regarding the type of person who may have committed the crime in question (see Badcock, 1997). Academics may utilize current or conduct new research to develop theories and test hypotheses regarding offenders, and apply these to cases (see Boon, 1997; Davies, 1997). Canter (1994) drew on principles and concepts from social and environmental psychology when constructing his profile of John Francis Duffy, who turned out to be the 'railway' rapist.

Throughout the 1990s this somewhat ad hoc provision of advice to investigations continued when a central unit, then called the National Crime Faculty (NCF), was set up to ensure investigations received appropriate specialist advice, including offender profiling. It was recognized there was limited governance of profilers or quality assurance over the advice being given. A system was introduced whereby consultants were selected who were deemed to have the relevant qualification and experience, and these were placed on a list accredited by the Association of Chief Police Officers' (ACPO) Sub-Committee for Behavioural Science. By the turn of this century, full-time offender profilers had been recruited centrally and a change in title from 'offender profiler' to 'behavioural investigative adviser' (BIA), was made (West, 2001), reflecting an increase in the types of services provided to investigators beyond mere 'profiling' of the offender. Box 9.1 highlights these developments from the perspective of an investigator turned BIA who was present throughout these changes.

Box 9.1 Paul Lobb's reflection on becoming a behavioural investigative adviser

After a fairly traditional police career path, firstly from uniform patrol and response duties, to eventual specialization in the CID, with a brief foray into community-based policing and youth justice work, in 1990 I enrolled on a degree course in Social and Organisational Studies (Criminal Justice) at the University of Plymouth and graduated with a BA (Hons) degree in 1996. Meanwhile, I had returned to CID as Detective Sergeant in 1992, and was responsible for numerous investigations into rape and serious sexual offences which led to a realization that, although I knew a great deal about what offenders did in the course of their offending, I knew less about how they migrated into offending or the life choices (or lack of) they made along the way.

In 1997 I enrolled on a masters degree course in Forensic and Legal Psychology with the University of Leicester. I was also fortunate at that time in attending a course on the Management and Investigation of Serious Crime and being accepted for a post as detective sergeant with the newly established National Crime Faculty based at Bramshill, where I was responsible for assisting and advising SIOs around the UK who were investigating difficult-to-solve crimes such as stranger rape and murder. As a result I also worked alongside 'offender profilers' who were all ACPO approved psychologists, but who also had full-time day jobs in universities and special hospitals. This sparked an interest in the more detailed aspects of understanding offenders, so for my masters I was granted approved access to a confidential dataset on sexual homicide and conducted a comparative study of the criminal careers of sexual homicide offenders for my dissertation, completed in 1999.

Although I briefly returned to my home force in 2000, I applied for a second attachment to the NCF in 2001 and in 2002 was accepted for training as a BIA. There had been a sea change around the same period, where the previous system of offender profilers was to be supplemented by full-time staff employed by the NCF. This was in recognition that profiling needed to extend beyond a list of potential offender characteristics and evolve into more holistic support grounded in behavioural science, to develop a tailor-made, or bespoke, service that focused upon the individual needs of each investigation.

Whilst in a police environment the provision of behavioural investigative advice continues, there has been recognition that simultaneous scientific study is also required. This has been undertaken either by researchers using and developing theory, building and applying methods and models relevant to the provision of behavioural investigative advice, or by academics and BIA practitioners undertaking joint research (e.g. Alison, Smith, Eastman et al., 2003; Cole and Brown, 2013; Ressler et al., 1988).

One advocate of the need for development of rigorous, scientific research, based upon empirical evidence, is David Canter. He introduced the study of 'investigative psychology' as a means of providing 'a framework for the integration of many aspects of psychology into all areas of ... investigations' (Canter and Youngs, 2009: 5). Investigative psychology considers 'what all those involved in crime and its investigation do, feel and think' (Canter and Youngs, 2009: 3). It involves the systematic study of investigative information (how information is retrieved, organized, evaluated and utilized), police actions and decision making, and inferences that can be made in relation to criminal activity. Canter (2000; Canter and Youngs, 2009) highlights significant scientific questions in relation to:

- Salience – what facets of an offence are the most behaviourally important and psychologically revealing (e.g. are less frequent actions or behavioural themes of more significance)?
- Consistency – how consistent are offenders? This can involve consistency between different offences (e.g. how consistent are serial offenders?) Yet would also consider consistency between their offence actions and behaviour in other areas of their lives (e.g. if they commit a particularly violent crime are they likely to be violent in their day-to-day interactions?)
- Change – how and why offenders develop and change over time (e.g. due to potential learning, maturation or situational factors)?
- Differentiation – in what ways do offenders differ from one another (e.g. do they have, or assign victims to, different roles)?
- Inference – is it possible – and if so how – to show associations between different themes of actions within crimes and the characteristics of offenders?

Canter cast the inferences that can be made in relation to how actions in a crime can lead to identifying the likely characteristics of an offender as the 'A $\rightarrow$ C equation'. Some regard this as somewhat simplistic. Wilson et al. (1997) suggest Canter's work does not offer anything new and utilizes the same factors as the FBI model but putting them into psychological theory. Canter and others have attempted to explore more complex relationships and facilitate the production of theory. This has been demonstrated in relation to arson, where it has been shown that with knowledge of the target of the arson, inferences can be made regarding the likely characteristics of the offender (Fritzon et al., 2001). Thus an 'expressive' arson where the behaviour is purposive, such as attacks on buildings of significance to the offender, is suggestive of an individual who repeatedly goes missing from work or school to set fires and makes fire alarm phone calls.

In summary, theory underlying behavioural investigative advice is developing, and the provision of such advice has grown. Whilst proponents may work for specific organizations or undertake a primary role as 'either' an academic or practitioner (see Table 9.2), in reality there is much cross-over. Consultants assist law enforcement, practitioners to conduct research and all work together to develop the profession further.

Table 9.2 A sample of proponents developing the provision of behavioural investigative advice

Practitioners working in:		Academics working in:
Clinical setting	Law enforcement	University
Badcock	BIAs, e.g. Cole, Lobb, Gregory, Rainbow	Alison
Britton	Davies (forensic scientist)	Boon
Dietz	FBI agents, e.g. Douglas, Hazelwood, Ressler	Canter
West	Heritage (police officer)	Jackson, Kocsis, Woodhams

Source: Adapted from Wilson et al., 1997: 2

HOW HAS THE PROFESSION ADVANCED?

Academic guidance regarding the professional responsibilities of BIAs and recommendations regarding the format in which reports should be presented have been suggested (Alison, Smith, Eastman et al., 2003; Alison et al., 2005, 2007; Almond et al., 2007) and where feasible incorporated in practice. This has included considerations being given to the wording or the structure of statistical reporting. For example, Villejoubert et al. (2008) found that the use of the word 'suggests' was ambiguous and could be interpreted as denoting very low *or* very high probability of occurrence, whereas 'likely' or 'very likely' were far less ambiguous. In addition, suspects with characteristics reported as having a low probability of occurrence may still be (erroneously) prioritized, presumably due to the mere presence of being mentioned (Villejoubert et al., 2008).

In addition, in relation to report writing and presentation to investigations, there is an increasing awareness of the target audience. Although many detectives now have graduate and postgraduate degrees, and are obliged to write a formal policy log justifying their decision making, they may not have detailed statistical knowledge. Good practice dictates that clear evaluation of the relevant research is given, providing a balanced, evidence-based, transparent argument to justify any conclusions made. Presenting descriptive statistics and explaining the application of these for their enquiry is appropriate although detailed explanation of the intricacies of a logistic regression may serve to confuse and distract rather than help illuminate an investigation.

Over the last several years, there has been an increased formality and procedural changes – for example, BIAs now have to conform to specific working practices; a strategic board (consisting of both academic and investigative practitioners) regularly quality assess the content of reports, and strategic reviews of BIA training, practices and procedures continue to enhance service provision and the development of the discipline (see Rainbow, 2008). How such developments have been implemented in practice is explained in Box 9.2.

Box 9.2 Paul Lobb on the development of behavioural investigative advice

BIA training involved exposure to various crime types and the development of specific skills in the identification of relevant empirical data to write clear unambiguous reports for investigators. The training was fairly lengthy, but was also a reciprocal process, which I feel assisted not only my own development, but also that of my colleagues, in that I was able to pass on my knowledge of policing and investigation to the other BIAs, who were mostly from academic and analytical backgrounds.

Behavioural investigative advice now requires appropriately qualified people, but is also hugely dependent upon reliable and relevant data to support inferences with empirical evidence, whereas some of the offender profile reports pre 2001 tended to be more opinion-based and inferences often lacked empirical support, chiefly due to a dearth of such evidential-based studies at that time. Another change is the more applied nature of the role, as it is now very much an integrated part of the investigative process, requiring a greater understanding of offenders and crime scene behaviour, as well as the full range of investigative options available. I often feel that while the senior investigating officer (SIO) has the task of managing the investigative process, my role as a BIA is to support the SIO in the decision-making process by managing and prioritizing information gleaned from a crime scene – to create order from what can often be a chaotic jumble of seemingly unrelated aspects.

As such, an important attribute for the BIA is attention to detail, as sometimes the smallest snippet of information can substantially alter conclusions and move investigative focus for the SIO. While I enjoy the challenge of the role and derive satisfaction from accurate assessment of the crime scene and offender behaviour, it comes with great responsibility, in that incomplete or potentially erroneous judgements can be detrimental to an investigation and have serious consequences.

The role also has a national remit, involving extensive travel and time spent away from home, which is a negative aspect, but there is some recognition that although behavioural investigative advice may play only a small part in the overall investigative process, it is in fact a useful aide for the SIO and can make a valuable contribution to the progress and proper management of any investigation.

When I started my police career, I never dreamed it would eventually lead me into what turned out to be the challenging role of BIA, but it has proved to be one of the most rewarding and satisfying areas of policing that I have experienced.

Currently in the UK, although consultants are still utilized if specific areas of expertise (e.g. regarding a specialist expertise, crime type or behaviour) are required, there is no longer a list of externally accredited BIAs and the majority of advice to serious crime investigations is now delivered by the full-time BIAs and consultant forensic clinical psychologists (FCPs).

Worldwide, similar systems prevail using police officers and/or civilian psychologists, in combination with either in-house or external clinical consultants (e.g. Germany, the Netherlands, South Africa, Australia, Canada). Both the research literature and practical use of behavioural investigative advice has increased over the past 30 years in Britain (Ainsworth, 2001; Dowden et al., 2007; Snook et al., 2007) and across the world (Homant and Kennedy, 1998). Although somewhat ad hoc, internationally BIAs regularly consult each other, work together and attempt to enhance the profession as required.

WHAT SERVICES DO BIAS PROVIDE?

Behavioural investigative advice involves assisting investigators' decision making by drawing inferences about an offender or an offence from behavioural examination of the actions within a crime (ACPO, 2006). BIAs predominantly work on cases of stranger murder or sexual offences rather than property or drug-related crimes (Wilson et al., 1997), unpicking associated offence features such as theft, sexual behaviour, violence, speech, control and weapon use. BIAs focus upon assisting the police, usually in relation to undetected cases – i.e. before the identity of the offender is known. As outlined above, the change in title from offender profiler to BIA was prompted by recognition of the services regularly supplied which are beyond the sole provision of an offender profiler. Although the list is not exhaustive, the predominant services currently provided by UK behavioural advisers (and similar to services offered elsewhere in the world) are summarized below. It should be noted that although individual reports are written by the BIA, these services are often delivered as part of a multidisciplinary team in conjunction with other specialists (e.g. geographic profilers, analysts, experienced detectives, interview, search, or forensic advisers):

- Offender profiling – making investigatively useful predictions regarding the type of person most likely to have committed the offence. For example, predictions regarding the likely relationship between the offender and victim; the offender's probable age, ethnicity or previous convictions. This can be extended, for example into:
  - o generation of potential pools or individual persons of interest to the investigation; or
  - o prioritization of persons by constructing a scoring matrix. For example, on the basis of the offender's likely age or area, BIAs can assist in prioritization of individuals likely to be the offender, or related to the offender (see Gregory and Rainbow, 2011; Rainbow and Gregory, 2011).

- Crime scene assessment – looking at minute detail regarding traces of the offender, victim and location, in an attempt to generate and discuss hypotheses about what is likely to have happened at the crime scene. This encourages investigators to keep an open mind, tests the reasonableness of interpretations; highlights knowledge gaps; and anticipates potential court arguments (ACPO, 2005, 2006; Ault and Reese, 1980).
- Offence linkage – in the absence of more substantial linkage factors (such as forensic evidence), BIAs consider the similarities and differences between offences, and the potential reasons for these, in order to give an opinion regarding the likelihood of two or more offences being linked (i.e. having been committed by the same offender(s)) based on their behavioural similarity.
- Search advice – provide advice in relation to where to search for items or a person on the basis of likely behaviour and with an appreciation of relevant research.
- Investigative suggestions – additional actions the investigation could undertake which may be of assistance to the enquiry on the basis of behavioural interpretation.

Due to their experience assessing and treating individuals, consultant forensic clinical psychologists (FCPs) provide additional advice to investigations, usually in relation to known individuals. They provide services predominantly in relation to the following:

- Interview – using what is known regarding both the offence and suspect (or witness) to assist in the development of an interview strategy in order to enhance the interaction and optimize information retrieval.
- Risk assessment – assist in highlighting the likelihood and outlining the circumstances which may lead to an individual reoffending.
- Media – utilize what is known about the offence in order to maximize media appeals to potential witnesses or suspects.

- Arrest – using what is known regarding both the offence and interviewee, to assist in development of an arrest strategy in order to maximize the safety of all involved and optimize evidence retrieval.

In addition to the specific services outlined above, the multifaceted nature of the potential contribution of BIAs can be of use in the following:

- Casting a 'critical eye' over the investigation (West, 2001) or bringing a new perspective (Kocsis et al., 2000) particularly where there are few leads (Wilson et al., 1997).
- Bringing new skills (Kocsis et al., 2000), for instance highlighting the scientific importance of methodological considerations such as:

  o falsification and testing the null hypothesis as opposed to focusing upon looking for information to 'prove' hypotheses; whilst a great deal of material may be required to 'prove' hypothesis at levels satisfactory for court, potentially only one piece of evidence may 'disprove', or at least lower the priority of hypotheses;
  o highlighting the differences between correlation and inferred causation.

- Confirming thoughts previously held by the investigation team (Copson, 1995), sometimes being used 'as an insurance policy' (Alison et al., 2004: 81) to demonstrate all avenues have been pursued.
- Providing probabilistic rationale and justification for investigative decision making (Jackson et al., 1997), such as regarding prioritization of resources, persons or lines of enquiry (Wilson and Soothill, 1996).
- Bringing an understanding of behaviour, for example via:

  o consideration of the frequency and likely co-occurrence of behaviours. This can be in terms of themes (for example Canter, 2000; Canter and Heritage, 1990) or typologies (see Holmes and Holmes, 1996; Kocsis et al., 1998); and
  o enhancing understanding of specific psychological issues, such as paraphilias or aggression (Badcock, 1997; Wilson et al., 1997).

All of this potential assistance needs to be worked up and interpreted as a whole and also must consider the utility principle, i.e. is the advice of practical use to the police? Cole and Brown (2011) asked SIOs what information they wanted from BIAs, when they wanted it and in what format. The results showed SIOs want information such as an offender's likely age and criminal history, and they wanted it evidence-based – supported by research, statistical information or experience. They wanted to receive the advice in writing, but ideally also wanted findings presented verbally (as is routinely undertaken in other countries such as Germany). However there were other areas in which they thought BIAs or FCPs could assist, such as with house-to-house questionnaires (when occupants in the vicinity of a crime are asked about what they saw or heard or their awareness of any material information such as rows taking place in neighbouring houses), prioritization of messages into the incident room and assistance with team morale and welfare on protracted enquiries. The SIOs also wanted the assistance throughout the course of the enquiry, but when they were ready for it. They recognized at the very early stages of an investigation some of the data required by the BIA may not be known, and the investigation team may be too busy following up initial enquiries. How BIAs can be of use to SIOs is exemplified in Box 9.3.

Box 9.3   Detective Superintendent Paul Williamson explains his role as an SIO and how BIAs can be of use

The senior investigating officer (SIO) plays a pivotal role within all major crime investigations and it is not a role for the faint-hearted. The SIO role is extremely complex and requires a combination of management skill, investigative ability and relevant knowledge across the entire investigative process, from initial crime scene assessment through to post-charge case management and trial.

The role is important because some of the major criticisms of the police have come about as a result of major crime investigations. From the Yorkshire Ripper in the 1970s and 1980s, the murder of Stephen Lawrence in the 1990s and following the shooting of Jean Charles de Menezes in 2005 it has been 'absolutely essential that such crimes are investigated with the utmost vigour and efficiency' (Stevens, 2005: 321). For these reasons, leading a major crime investigation places extremely high personal and professional demands on the SIO. As a consequence, the 'Professionalising Investigation Programme' (PIP) introduced in 2004 represented a joint Home Office and Association of Chief Police Officers (ACPO) initiative aimed at embedding a structured method of ensuring those charged with managing highly complex investigations have the necessary training and 'on the job' investigative experience to fulfil their professional responsibilities and, all importantly, retain public confidence.

I have spent over 10 years as an SIO investigating numerous major crimes, including criminal enterprise homicides, hate-related homicides, multi-handed homicides involving joint enterprise, gangland kidnaps and other serious crimes. In many cases there is nothing complex about the act itself. Complexities arise from the lack of key solvability factors that direct and credible eye witnesses, forensic material, analysis of communications data or CCTV can provide. The SIO must then put together facts like jigsaw pieces to create a picture, no one piece being determinative, each having a degree of persuasiveness, but all being weighed against countervailing or absent pieces of the jigsaw.

Against the background of a complex, hard to solve case with low solvability factors and where the identity of the offender is not immediately apparent, the SIO must draw upon a compendium of investigative tactics and specialists to help and provide justice for victims and their families. One such tool is the behavioural investigative adviser, who has the potential to add value to the SIO decision making process through an enhanced understanding of the offence and offender. My positive personal experiences of utilizing BIA investigative support include a rare 'whodunnit' homicide by arson. I faced the problem of an unknown offender, a scene destroyed by fire, numerous potential motives (due to the victim's lifestyle) and no direct evidence. The BIA conducted a crime scene assessment and contributed to the immediate generation of hypotheses. The BIA then conducted predictive profiling and produced a prioritization matrix where each facet of a potential suspect was numerically scored. This tactic proved highly successful in focusing my main lines of enquiry and prioritizing a large number of potential suspects to a manageable level in conjunction with geographic profiling. Ultimately, the tactic made a significant contribution to providing the necessary focus that led to the identification and conviction of the offender. The case later received the National Investigators Award for 'Outstanding Leadership in an Investigation 2014'.

In summary, the role of SIO is challenging, highly accountable yet rewarding. Reflecting developments in SIO accreditation, BIA has also undergone significant professional development over recent years. It is another tool for even the most experienced SIO to draw upon in difficult to solve cases requiring additional perspective and support to decision making. The challenge for the future will be how to incorporate behavioural investigation into the rapidly evolving world of cyber and other types of crime.

The potential usefulness to an investigation needs also to be weighed against the reliability of what is being suggested. For example, predictions of global traits are unlikely to be of great use (Alison et al., 2002). Described as the 'bandwidth-fidelity' trade-off or abstraction issue, Alison et al. (2002) suggest that whilst prediction of a specific behaviour such as punctuality may be helpful, this is only predictive of a small range of behaviours. The prediction that the offender is likely to be a male aged between 10 and 90 years is most probably accurate, but is of little practical utility. Predicting the offender is likely to be aged between 20 and 25 years would be far more useful, but the margin for error wider. To be of practical assistance a balance must be sought, prediction of specific traits is required if the advice is to be of assistance to investigations, yet this cannot be at the expense of the reliability of the claims.

WHAT TECHNIQUES ARE INVOLVED IN THE PROVISION OF BEHAVIOURAL INVESTIGATIVE ADVICE?

Over the years there have been a number of papers published by practitioners explaining 'how' BIAs go about conducting their work (e.g. Copson et al., 1997; Hazelwood et al., 1995; Rainbow and Gregory, 2011; Ressler et al., 1985; West, 2001). All advocate initial data collection, which ideally includes attendance at the crime scene/s, obtaining photographs, maps, interviews and statements, a briefing from the investigation team, and the negotiation and setting of terms of reference outlining what the investigator wants (or thinks they want) and what the BIA believes they can most usefully provide. The BIA then takes away the data, analyses them, makes inferences in line with the terms of reference and summarizes the findings, including any appropriate justification and rationale, in a written report.

There is limited work available that addresses the actual *process* of interpretative analysis. This is due to a combination of factors; firstly, most individuals providing advice are employed to do just that, and are given limited time to contribute to the academic literature. Secondly, there are individual differences in this process based upon the background, experience and methodology of a particular BIA/FCP, and upon the specific requirements of the investigation. Finally, there is an ethical dilemma: if details are disclosed about how interpretations are conducted, there is the potential dilemma of encouraging 'forensic interference' with a crime scene. What follows therefore is an informed, yet conscious generalization of how such work is conducted, which in practice in the UK currently involves an eclectic mix and application of one's own, and others' experience.

CONSIDERATION OF RELEVANT RESEARCH AND THEORY

In attempting to consider the crime scene and make inferences about the offender or the offence, consideration is given to the academic literature, theoretical concepts or empirical findings, which may be of assistance. Literature searches on specific topics are undertaken as required, which may be general – for example, what does the research say about individuals who indecently expose themselves; or more specific – for example, if a rapist steals from a victim does this mean they are more likely to have a previous conviction for theft?

There are several difficulties in utilizing research. There is an insufficiency of reliable, relevant, applicable published research that is of practical use to BIAs and investigators. Of the research that is available, much relies on police data, which can be difficult to gain access to and has inherent reliability and validity difficulties (Ainsworth, 2001; Farrington and Lambert, 1997; Horvath and Brown, 2006). For example, such data:

- are initially collected as evidence to be presented in court, rather than for research purposes;
- do not include unreported or unrecorded crimes;
- are usually limited in both quantity and quality (for example, the data may rely upon witnesses' memory or offender accounts);
- often have omissions (missing or incomplete entries) or inaccuracies;
- are often extracted from secondary sources (for example via statements); and
- in some offences, for example a murder occurring without any witnesses, observation and interpretation predominantly consist of the consequences of actions – for example, the victim was stabbed and died at that location; rather than any context regarding how, why or precisely when this occurred.

There may also be other methodological problems, such as a lack of theoretical base, small, skewed or culturally different samples (see, e.g., Aitken et al., 1995; Bukhanovsky et al., 1999; Dowden et al., 2007; Hakkanen and Laajasalo, 2006; Wherton, 2004). Additionally, with no control groups usually available, experimentation cannot assist in confirming or refuting hypotheses and much of the work is correlational or exploratory.

As such, although utilization of relevant research is advocated, its use can be problematic and needs to be applied with appropriate caveats.

COMPARISON OF RELEVANT DATASETS

Practitioner BIAs and researchers may also gain access to relevant databases from which they are able to provide statistical regularities from previous offences regarding the frequency of offence behaviours or background characteristics of offenders. In the UK there are several nationally collated datasets holding offence and offender details.

The statistical analyses undertaken often consist of the provision of base rates. In relation to offence linkage the question to be addressed is how common or rare certain features are. Unusual features, particularly if co-occurring in different crimes, may indicate the offences are linked to one another. For example, rape offences are unlikely to be linked on the basis of removal or moving of clothing (prevalent in the majority of rapes); however, if a knife was used, the victim was bound and tied with a particular knot, or certain phrases were repeatedly used (each individual action being relatively rare in rape offences) in several offences, it is likely to have been committed by the same offender. As such, whilst similarities and differences are analysed when looking at offence linkage, the relative distinctiveness of behaviours when compared to other offences also needs to be considered (see Woodhams, 2012; Woodhams et al., 2007).

Similarly, if tasked with profiling the offender responsible for a murder of a prostitute who was found stabbed, strangled and sexually abused in the street, knowledge of the backgrounds of all other previous offenders who had committed such offences (e.g. they may have previously been a client, and most likely will be male) may be of benefit. Some researchers have attempted such comparisons between offence features and offender characteristics, for example Marogna (2005) explored the offending history of 117 stranger homicide offenders. Base rate statistics report 70% had a previous conviction of some kind, and nearly 57% were for theft-related offences. Her findings also indicated that if the offence involved stabbing the victim, the offender was twice as likely to have a previous conviction for a violent offence. Similarly, Francis et al. (2004) looked at 2,145 solved cases of adult homicides from the period 1995–2000. They found 78% of convicted offenders were white. Frequencies also identified, for example, if the victim was aged 30–39 years, 92% of previous offenders were found to be aged 18–49 years, with most being aged 30–39 years at the time of the murder.

Some researchers have used more complex statistics to make inferences regarding the offender on the basis of offence information (see Aitken et al., 1995; Davies et al., 1998; Grubin et al., 1997; Hakkanen and Laajasalo, 2006; Salfati, 2000; Santtila et al., 2004). For example, Francis et al. (2004) used a multinomial logistic model to determine which victim and offence characteristics were important in predicting offender characteristics. However, choice of some of their variables was questionable – for example it is arguable whether investigations would know prior to capture that the offender was 'of imbalanced mind' (p. 34) or the offence involved a 'rage or quarrel' (p. 33). Overall, they found their more complex statistical model was more accurate at prediction than simply utilizing database frequencies, however, they highlighted the frequency approach may be of use when the number of similar cases is small, and may out-perform the statistical model for some groups of homicide. Cole and Brown (2012) subsequently found that prediction of offender characteristics based upon descriptive statistics (base rates) can be as useful as more complex statistical predictions (configural frequency analyses and logistic regression).

Justification of rationale and prioritization by use of statistics may be appealing to investigators who are increasingly held accountable for their decision making. Additionally, investigators are becoming more familiar with statistical reporting, from consideration of forensic evidence. However, estimates may mistakenly be perceived as 'actual', and as such careful caveats should be articulated by the BIA as there is no guarantee a particular offender fits within suggested parameters. There are further difficulties in utilizing such statistics; for example, the user has to reduce qualitative detail of the offence to quantitatively coded variables, the choice of variables may be subjective, the databases from which information is gleaned are limited in crime type and number, are based upon information derived from the convicted, and are reliant on compliance with data entry protocols.

In summary, if extracted from relevant datasets, and reported with appropriate caveats, research findings and bespoke searches based upon statistical analyses of previous cases can be used in the provision of behavioural investigative advice. Indeed, the provision of simple descriptive statistics on an individual case-by-case basis is one of the methods currently utilized by BIAs (Cole and Brown, 2012). As discussed in Chapter 5, there are also potential biases in reasoning and decision making (see Table 5.1 for a summary of these). As searches become more specific, the number of similar cases with which to compare decreases. Sometimes therefore more individualistic examination is required.

APPLICATION OF EXPERIENCE

Throughout analyses, BIAs utilize both their own, and others' experiences to inform their decision making. In some instances there is no available research or statistical database to provide an evidence base and offences may be highly unusual and idiosyncratic, with very few or no previously similar cases with which to compare. This is when the accumulated experience of the BIAs is called upon, applying their knowledge from other cases seen by themselves or colleagues. For FCPs, their prior clinical experience of working with patients may provide informed insights. In addition, it is now common practice that all BIA reports are peer reviewed before submission to the investigation team, and case conferences regarding difficult, complex or unusual cases often occur. As such, application of experience still remains an important technique utilized by BIAs and FCPs.

Recently, attempts have been made to deconstruct the expertise built up from experience of previous cases. Using the technique of Applied Cognitive Task Analysis, Knabe-Nicol and colleagues (Knabe-Nicol and Alison, 2011; Knabe-Nicol et al., 2011) conducted in-depth interviews and observations of BIAs from the UK, their equivalent (Operative Fall Analytiker) in Bavaria Germany, and geographic profilers from the UK in order to explore the nature of such expertise. They found evidence of behaviours such as selective focusing on salient information; identification of anomalies; grouping behaviours into themes or chunks; attention to detail together with holistic analysis of the case; and having an awareness of common mistakes or distractions. They argue specialized skills, knowledge and decision making demonstrate many of the hallmarks of expertise. This is distinct from novices who may miss information or pay too much attention to certain features. Knabe-Nicol et al. (2011: 78) summarize their view: 'These professionals have indeed developed an expertise in their discipline.'

Kocsis et al. (2000) compared proficiency in profiling by police officers, psychologists, undergraduates and self-declared psychics to find the psychologist as having superior profiling skills to the other groups, suggesting psychological knowledge does indeed provide profiling expertise. The psychics simply relied on stereotyping. Although this type of analysis may be based on unrepresentative and small samples, nevertheless the findings do indicate the presence and application of psychological knowledge does contribute to developing profiling skills.

The utilization of these methods in combination, in order to present a transparent evidence base when reporting to investigators, is commented upon in Box 9.4.

Box 9.4   BIA Head of Profession Lee Rainbow's reflections on contemporary behavioural investigative advice

The contemporary role of behavioural investigative advisers (the new generation of 'offender profilers') is far removed from popular media accounts and indeed the recent proliferation of uninformed commentaries within the academic literature. Behavioural investigative advice has the potential to contribute to many aspects of the investigative process and may take many forms throughout the life of the enquiry. Whilst all of the products and services available offer tactical or strategic solutions in their own right, all are underpinned by a broader philosophy of adding value to the decision making of the SIO, through an enhanced understanding of the offence and offender from a perspective different from that routinely employed within major crime investigation teams. Such differences in perspective can be broadly characterized as evidence (SIO) versus understanding (BIA), although both are directed at supporting the single goal of case resolution. It is this additional perspective and associated expertise that should be recognized as the critical success factor of behavioural investigative advice.

The role of the BIA has undergone a significant evolution in recent times. Contemporary BIAs are no longer isolated experts restricted to generating inferences about offenders in an investigative void. Rather, they have become a professional group of individuals with a vast experience of serious crime and how best to integrate their behavioural advice into the modern day major investigation. Today's BIAs undergo a two-year training programme, focused on seven competencies required to offer behavioural investigative advice effectively: (1) inter-personal and verbal communication skills; (2) personal integrity; (3) writing skills; (4) critical thinking skills; (5) managing the work; (6) familiarity with the techniques of behavioural science as applied to criminal investigations; and (7) knowledge of the investigative and legal process.

When I joined national policing as the first-ever full-time 'offender profiler', my excitement at the new role was completely uninformed by any knowledge of the task and challenges that lay ahead. Against the backdrop of much excitement about the potential for psychologists and behavioural experts to generate 'profiles' of offenders from the latent behavioural traces left at a crime scene (fuelled by media portrayals of FBI practice), loomed the very public failings of such contributions to the Rachel Nickell murder investigation. As such, my career has been focused as much on the continued professionalization of this discipline as in the provision of products and services to inform individual investigations. Contemporary BIAs are no longer isolated experts restricted to generating inferences about offenders in an investigative void. Rather they have become a professional group of individuals with a vast experience of serious crime and how best to integrate their behavioural advice into the modern day major investigation. When training new BIAs, the central mantra is one of evidence, evidence, evidence. BIAs are drilled in the 'scientific' approach, such that all advice should be grounded in empirical research and testable theory. Without such supporting rationale the advice becomes little more than amateur sleuthing, and echoes previous failings where such rationale was substituted with implicit requirements of absolute trust in individual opinion.

I am often asked what skills are required to become a BIA. In my view, a sound understanding of behavioural science, investigative and legal processes are clearly key, but these must be complemented by excellent critical thinking skills, effective inter-personal and writing skills and high personal resilience. The job is hugely demanding, both intellectually and emotionally, and whilst tremendously rewarding, does not come without cost to a healthy work–life balance.

HOW GOOD IS THE PRODUCT BIAS PROVIDE?

In a similar vein to other areas of forensic practice, deliberation of 'what works' has been evaluated in relation to behavioural investigative advice although these tend to consider the offender profile, which as outlined above is only one component of advice. Similarly, many of the studies are now somewhat dated and current practices have significantly changed. Nevertheless, salient findings will be summarized below, which predominantly fall into two categories – evaluation of the accuracy of profiles and user satisfaction surveys.

ACCURACY

A profiler who gets it wrong may be responsible for many hours of wasted police time ... it is essential that anything that is done in the name of profiling is subject to scrutiny and testing. (Ainsworth, 2001: 153)

The importance of accuracy is obvious, however evidence is somewhat varied. Successes have been articulated by some profilers themselves (e.g. Britton, 1997; Douglas and Oleshaker, 1995), with some profiles being cited as extremely accurate (e.g. the Mad Bomber of New York), whilst others (e.g. the Boston Strangler) were more wide of the mark (Holmes and Holmes, 1996). Due primarily to the confidential nature of the work, only limited (and mainly successful) evaluative case studies have been published; for example, Canter was correct on 13 of his 17 suggestions to the police regarding John Duffy (Smith, 1993). Although even in this instance, some of these 'hits' are attributable to eyewitness testimony of surviving victims, physical forensic evidence and the rather obvious prediction that the offender was male.

Formally assessing the accuracy has proved problematic for a variety of reasons (Gudjonsson and Copson, 1997). First, research can only be undertaken once the perpetrator is apprehended (Grubin, 1995; Homant and Kennedy, 1998; Smith et al., 1998). Also, as there are many potential variables of interest it is difficult to assess whether the suspect was captured due to suggestions of the BIA, or due to other aspects of the investigation. In addition, there are no control groups (of similar offences where a profile was *not* used) from which to empirically compare success rates, and even if someone is caught, there are likely to be many unknowable and therefore un-testable features (Gudjonsson and Copson, 1997).

Fundamentally, there are initial considerations in relation to what is meant by accuracy. There is the threshold problem. Ainsworth (2001) asks whether 80% of correct profile features is enough to be considered accurate? Also, as we have seen, BIAs do not talk in terms of certainty but probability, and as such nothing is truly 'inaccurate' if presented appropriately. If evidence-based, then just because one case is 'wrong' (i.e. is an outlier), the same inferences may be made in the future, as in the majority of cases they would have been right. Importantly, as outlined above, the inclusion of accurate information in BIA reports does not necessarily mean that it is useful. So whilst accurate assessments of the offender's personality may have been outlined, these are not necessarily of *use* to the investigation in a proactive search for the perpetrator (Ainsworth, 2001; Kocsis, 2006).

Despite such difficulties, evaluations have been attempted. Pinizzotto and Finkel (1990) found profilers wrote richer and more accurate sexual profiles when compared to detectives, but the former were far less successful in relation to profiling in murder cases. In addition, the FBI gave 64 murder scenes to six profilers and found 80% congruence in their findings. However, with the same training provided to all participants, and with only dichotomous categorization (into organized or disorganized) required, it is questionable if such levels of inter-rater reliability are sufficient (Oleson, 1996).

Snook et al. (2007) undertook a meta-analysis of four criminal profiling articles to assess the predictive validity of profiling advice. Overall, they found the self-labelled profilers (66.5% success rate) outperformed comparison groups (33.5% success rate) in relation to predicting overall offender characteristics. Their conclusions that such advice is therefore 'as likely to be hazardous as it is to be helpful' (2007: 447) and 'profiling appears at this juncture to be an extraneous and redundant technique' (p. 448) appear somewhat overstated, yet they rightly highlight the need for further research in this field.

In the UK, Copson and Holloway (unpublished, cited in Gudjonsson and Copson, 1997) examined 111 profiles testing the goodness of fit between the points provided by the profiler, against the known facts concerning the offence and/or the offender which could be verified through police records. They found many of these features were accurate, although there were large individual differences between the accuracy rates of different profilers. However they conclude: 'If success in profiling were synonymous with accurate prediction, then profilers could claim much success' (Gudjonsson and Copson, 1997: 73).

USER SATISFACTION SURVEYS

Pinizzotto (1984) found 77% reports produced in the United States were described as being successful in focusing the investigation, and in the Netherlands advice was rated 'highly' (Jackson et al., 1997). Haines (2006) surveyed 51 Canadian police officers and found 94% agreed profiling was a viable investigative tool. In the UK a small sample of detectives stated their support for profiling as part of research by Adhami and Browne (1996). In the largest published study of its kind in the UK to date, Copson (1995) surveyed detectives enquiring about the usefulness of 184 offender profiles. Whilst the majority found the profiles operationally useful (82.6%), this view was not dependent on either assistance in solving the case (14.1%), nor even in adding anything new to the investigation (53.8%). It was found that the profiles rarely led directly to the identification of the offender (2.7%) but instead the reports furthered their understanding of the case or offender (60.9%) and/or reassured their own judgement regarding the case (51.6%). Nearly all stated they would probably or definitely use a profiler again (92.4%).

In general findings from satisfaction surveys indicate respondents have stated the reports may be of assistance in focusing the investigation, prioritizing suspects, saving time, generating new ideas, furthering their understanding of the offender and in ensuring a complete investigation has been conducted (Britton, 1992; Copson, 1995; Douglas unpublished, cited in Pinizzotto, 1984; Haines, 2006; Jackson et al., 1997; Wilson and Soothill, 1996).

Whilst the findings of such surveys are of interest, the results should be interpreted with caution. Firstly, it is problematic to determine to what degree the profile has assisted the investigation (Douglas unpublished, cited in Pinizzotto, 1984). Secondly, satisfaction surveys are reliant upon the individual views of a usually small number of investigators who may have their own biases which could lead them to over/under-exaggerate the contribution of the BIA's predictions (Copson, 1995). Indeed, studies have indicated that the Barnum Effect may be evident in interpretation of profiles (Alison, Smith and Morgan, 2003). This involves people accepting vague and general personality descriptions as being specific to them. In this context investigators could selectively and erroneously fit ambiguous information from a profile (which may 'fit' many individuals) to a suspect (Alison, Smith and Morgan, 2003). Similarly, research has shown the more a police officer believes in profiling, the more likely he or she is to perceive the profile as being accurate, irrespective of content (Kocsis and Heller, 2004). Also, perceptions regarding accuracy may be related to the perceived identity of the BIA (Kocsis and Hayes, 2004). Research has additionally shown that individuals may also be influenced dependent upon whether the advice supports or challenges their own beliefs (Marshall and Alison, 2007).

HOW GOOD IS THE PROCESS BY WHICH THEY GET THERE?

Due to difficulties in objectively assessing the accuracy of the product, attention has turned to assessing the processes involved in the provision of behavioural investigative advice. Consideration of the assumptions underpinning the provision of such advice, and evaluation of the process by which decisions are made and the rationale provided to support them, have been the subject of more recent evaluative endeavours.

UNDERLYING ASSUMPTIONS

There has been considerable criticism levelled at the provision of behavioural investigative advice both academically (e.g. Chifflet, 2014; Devery, 2010; Gekoski and Gray, 2011) and in high-profile cases such as the murder of Rachel Nickell (see Alison and Eyre, 2009). Some have stated it 'is still very much a discipline that is yet to be proved' (Muller, 2000: 260). Advice relies upon several considerations with mixed findings, for example:

- Alison (2005) highlights there is considerable reliance on 'naïve trait' theory, attributing behaviours to the underlying personality of the offender which may be nomothetic (general); deterministic (assume all offenders are the same); non-situationist (assume behaviour is likely to remain stable between situations); and tautological (self-fulfilling – with traits such as violence being both inferred from and explained by behaviour – a violent offence may indicate a violent offender, but the very fact that the offender has committed an offence in this way, makes them such).
- Behavioural consistency is key to both linkage (offenders behave consistently in different offences) and profiling (offenders are consistent in their everyday and criminal interactions – e.g. someone committing a violent offence is likely to have been violent on other occasions). There is some evidence of consistency in serial offending (Bennell and Jones, 2005; Clarke, 1999; Fox and Farrington, 2014; Grubin et al., 1997; Salfati et al., 2014; Santtila et al., 2005, 2008). However, the findings are mixed (e.g. Trojan and Salfati, 2011) and reference the need to consider the role of situational factors (Butterworth, 1997; Salfati and Bateman, 2005); the role of learning and development; and factors such as crime type, jurisdiction and which behaviours are included can all influence consistency (Bennell et al., 2014).
- The homology principle is the notion that offenders with similar backgrounds will commit similar offences. Although there has been some success at finding correspondence between certain crime scene behaviours and offender characteristics (Davies et al., 1998; Tonkin et al., 2009), other studies have not found such links, highlighting the importance of the context and situation in offender behaviour (Doan and Snook, 2008; Mokros and Alison, 2002). Recent debate continues in relation to the importance of homology and accuracy (Kocsis and Palermo, 2015).

As such, in relation to several fundamental underlying principles, further research is required.

EVALUATION OF BIA RATIONALE

Some of the above difficulties can be overcome by examining the evidential basis given by BIAs in their decision making. If appropriate caveats are supplied, and investigators can see on what basis inferences are made, then arguably it is up to them to decide whether and how much weight to attribute to such advice in the same way as they should for advice received from anyone involved in the investigation. However, Copson and Holloway (unpublished, cited in Gudjonsson and Copson, 1997) found the reasoning behind the different elements of advice offered was provided on only 16% of occasions. Moreover, the mere presence of justifications for inferences does not mean they are necessarily adequate. For example, a statement that the offence was sexually motivated because the victim was stabbed in the neck provides justification, though the validity of this inference may be questioned (Smith et al., 1998).

Snook et al. (2007) reviewed 130 published profiling articles. Whilst noting caution be taken given the wide confidence intervals (limiting the conclusions), of concern is that common sense (e.g. things that 'everybody knows', based on authority or anecdote) were used more than empirical (quantitative, based on evidence from literature, case histories or studies) arguments, 58% of the time. The use of common sense arguments was more frequent in clinical articles, those published before 1990, those published by law enforcement agencies (rather than academics), and those originating from the United States. Of interest is that such arguments were also more frequent in those articles expressing a positive opinion of, and in support of, profiling.

Assessment of profilers' articulated reasoning process within their written reports has been undertaken in a series of papers by Alison and colleagues (Alison et al., 2003; Alison et al., 2005, 2007). They tested the strength of an argument's component parts by examining the claim or opinion proffered by the BIA (e.g. *the murderer is under 30 years*), and looking for justification, by examining the underlying grounds for the claim (e.g. *because this is a murder of a 23-year-old female*), the specific warrant for the claim (e.g. *the majority of murderers of females under 25 years are under 30 years old*) and the rationale to give the claim credence (e.g. *research by XXX, or data from XXX database*). Where possible some form of modality or the strength of the claim (e.g. *there is an 87% chance that ...*), with relevant rebuttals to explain the conditions when this may not be true (e.g. *unless other indications ...*) should also be articulated. If any of the elements are missing, the claim is weakened.

Assessment using this method suggests significant improvements in relation to the presentation of more transparent, coherent and evidence-based reports in recent years. Alison et al. (2003) analysed 21 profile reports – 13 profiles from the UK, five from the United States and three from other European countries – primarily from the period 1997–2001. The research found that much of the information contained in the profiles was already known to the investigation, and out of nearly 4,000 claims made, 80% were unsubstantiated, containing no grounds, warrant, or rationale. In addition, 20% of the claims were ambiguous (providing vague information – such as 'the offender will have poor heterosocial skills'), 80% could not be falsified (or proven to be false – such as 'the offender will have a pornography collection') and nearly 50% were unverifiable (cannot be verified post conviction – for example included comments such as 'at the time of the offence the offender was feeling no remorse', 2003: 181). This has obvious implications, with a number of potential suspects easily being able to 'fit' the profile. However, a comparison sample of 47 reports, written in 2005, found that out of 805 claims made, now only 4% contained no grounds, although only 34% had formal support or rationales. In addition, now an increased 70% of the claims were verifiable, although still only 43% were falsifiable post conviction. Nevertheless the analysis indicated a

> very large positive difference between the contemporary behavioural investigative advice sample and previous ... advice in terms of the substantiveness of their arguments. Contemporary ... behavioural investigative advice has clearer boundaries around the claims made and presents material in a more coherent and evidence-based format. (Almond et al., 2007: 1)

Therefore, contemporary BIA reports appear to be far more evidence-based, transparently articulating the reasoning behind decisions made and inferences suggested.

WHAT ARE THE ESSENTIAL ELEMENTS TO INCLUDE IN A REPORT?

In this section we identify elements that should be included in a BIA report. The guidance outlined by Alison, Goodwill and Alison (2005: 242), and more recent work by Cole and Gudjonsson (2013), has been adapted and is presented in the form of a checklist below. It is intended, however, as a multi-purpose checklist that can be utilized, considered, added to and developed in line with the purpose of any kind of forensic psychology report you are being asked to write. However, for advice regarding suggested content of reports for court, please see Box 12.3.

CHECKLIST

A report should include:

- Contact details of author
- Statement of competence (background, qualification, training, experience, expertise) of author
- Date written
- Version number – versions may be revised if, for example, reports are amended after significant changes from peer review or new information is received
- Time scales – as agreed with person commissioning the report – for example, report commissioned [date] and report submitted [date]

- Terms of reference – purpose of report as agreed with person commissioning the report – for example, this report is to provide an opinion as to whether or not the incidents involving [offence] and [offence] are likely to have been committed by the same offender
- Materials used – for example, list of statements (together with details of any materials requested but not forthcoming) used; dates of briefings
- Summary of case – to ensure author's understanding is correct and highlight salient variables (which if changed may impact findings)
- Usage – how report can be used – for example, as intelligence to assist the investigation, but not as evidence in a court of law; should not be disseminated further without prior agreement of author
- Method – methodology utilized should be explained
- Caveats – detailing limitations, for example, advice may change on the basis of new information; statistical recommendations reflect probability not fact; report is only to be used for this particular case
- Inferences and suggestions should be sourced and clearly referenced where appropriate – for example, based on research by [xx]; based on findings from [xx] number of cases from [xx] database
- Investigative suggestions should be included where appropriate
- A summary of the report is included (although it is recommended that the report be read in its entirety)
  In addition, the report:
- should ensure the terms of reference have been met (it is valid);
- is written with clarity for the appropriate audience – for example, if for a police officer it does not contain unexplained psychological jargon;
- is objective – for example, it should outline alternative hypotheses or any significant research findings that conflict with the recommendations reported.

WHAT HAVE WE LEARNT?

As can be seen, the discipline has rapidly developed and has enjoyed a great deal of interest in recent years. Summarizing what we have learnt from research, database comparison and experience is difficult, however there are several consistent themes:

- Offenders can learn. In the same way that we may learn to take a short cut if there is always a queue of traffic on the route to work, offenders can learn and may develop and change throughout their offending career. If they are convicted due to leaving fingerprints at a crime scene, they are more likely to wear gloves on the next occasion.
- Stranger sexual offenders appear to be generalists with many having previous convictions of some kind often unrelated to their subsequent sexual offending. The debates surrounding whether or not offenders are generalists committing many different crimes or specialists focusing upon a specific crime type is beyond the scope of this chapter. However, stranger rapists are

more likely to have a previous conviction for a theft or burglary offence than for a sexual offence (Davies et al., 1998). For many offenders crime is not confined to one particular sphere and may be reflective of a criminal lifestyle or one in which non-conformity to societal rules in general is the norm.

- Although many stranger sexual offenders may spend some considerable time searching for victims, offenders may attack the 'best available' victim at the time. Although offenders may have a preference for a specific type of victim, they are unlikely to target solely on the basis of age or hair colour but merely due to the fact that someone is present in the right place at the right time for them.
- Not many offenders are as clever as Sherlock Holmes' nemesis Professor Moriarty. Although we may have a media image of a highly intelligent serial killer pitting their wits against the police, thankfully, at least in the UK, most offenders responsible for murder are apprehended swiftly.
- Things do not always go to plan for the offender. Victims do not comply, bodies are heavy, witnesses interrupt the offence and hence offenders may have to improvise.
- Usually, once caught, there are risk factors and precursor incidents that potentially could have raised alarm bells about the individual responsible for the offence. The difficulty is in identifying these individuals (as they may not have come to the attention of the police) and prioritizing relevant individuals (as many may have relevant risk factors yet not go on to offend).

HOW CAN WE COPE WITH OUR FEELINGS WHEN WORKING AS A BIA?

I see the most grisly and horrifying aspects of the homicide and daily face the devastating and demoralizing truth about what one human being can do to another. (Keppel, 1998: xx)

In the commentaries by BIAs in Boxes 9.2 and 9.4 mention is made of the 'great responsibility' held by BIAs, the 'extensive travel and time spent away from home' and the potential 'cost to a healthy work–life balance'.

As mentioned in Chapter 7 regarding conducting research in this field, very little has been written in relation to the impact of repeatedly analysing the behaviour involved in heinous crimes. However, as highlighted in Chapter 8, the concept of potential vicarious victimization is recognized, as is the fact that chronic, long-term exposure to distressing material may impact individuals in a similar way to those faced with extremely disturbing one-off incidents (Clarke, 2013). Whilst it is true BIAs, analysts and the like may not have to deal directly with offenders or victims, attend post mortems or tell a family they have lost a loved one; they will read statements, watch interviews, look at photographs and attend crime scenes. Moreover, they have to digest every relevant detail of the offence interaction and therefore where possible utilize source data, such as watching the recorded victim interview, rather than relying on case summaries. This can be an arduous task, and can obviously involve long-term exposure to distressing information. It would be naïve to assume this would not impact the lives of those involved.

'Burnout' is defined as exhaustion and diminished interest in work (Freudenberger, 1974), which appears to result from occupational stress in combination with other factors. Research indicates high levels of such 'emotion work' correlate to risk factors associated with burnout (Amaranto et al., 2003). In addition, we are sure after a few months of exposure to rape material for example, researchers or practitioners are far less likely to walk alone late at night or get in an unmarked taxi, than they would have done previously or when compared with others in the general population. Added to this, most people have lives and responsibilities outside work, and it would be unrealistic to expect that our own day-to-day stresses, traumas and difficulties such as bereavement, divorce, moving house, paying bills and being carers for others, would not also have some impact at different stages of our career.

Some people do not like the nature of the work and either would not even consider a job in this field, or soon leave. Others recognize it as a rewarding experience and focus upon the positive aspects and satisfaction derived from working in such environments, with difficult clients or with distressing material (Clarke, 2013). Assessment centres and interviews are proactively designed so that both the employer can ascertain if they think the individual can work with such content, and the interviewee can glean a better understanding of what such analyses can entail (to inform them if they feel they could do the work). Other individuals, whilst they do not totally switch off, learn to focus professionally, so that when looking at the data they will consider only what it is they are looking for and the purpose of this. It also seems apparent that over the years individuals can habituate to the content of what they repeatedly see, although this can have both positive and negative effects, as outlined in Box 9.5.

Box 9.5   Terri Cole's reflection on habituation to offence content

A relatively new member of the team had been exposed to a variety of potentially disturbing offence information (statements, photographs etc.) but had recently been assigned to work on a child murder that had come into the office. She asked me to review some of her interpretation from the crime scene photographs and as we were talking she made a general remark about these cases being 'so awful'.

I took the potential cue, expanded the conversation, continued to oversee her work and discuss with her if/how she wanted to continue supporting such an investigation and what additional support she could obtain. *However*, what I did not anticipate was the impact that conversation had on me.

(Continued)

I had not even really thought about it. It was 'another' case to me, I had not even really considered it was a child, a victim, brutally murdered, and we were viewing and analysing the horrific detail of this. To me it was just another job; I knew my role and professionally assisted a colleague. What concerned me was that very fact. I did not even consider that it *was* potentially disturbing until someone reflected to me a 'normal' person would view it as such. How could I have become so 'hardened' as to not even notice? What sort of person did that make me? Some would label this an unconscious defence mechanism (I am sure I have others – I rarely remember victim names though can often recall police operation names or detail of offences), others may label it professionalism, or even being an objective scientist. Whatever the label, it made me think about the nature of the work and how it must affect us all even though we may be perfectly capable of 'getting on with it'.

There are means by which the work can be undertaken with hopeful minimal effect to well-being, but individuals and organizations need to have measures in place to promote the ability to cope, recognize difficulties (individual and organizational) and have appropriate methods in place to deal with problems as they arise. The concept of resilience is of note here, referring to potentially protective factors that insulate us from what we see and hear. Rather than focusing when things go wrong, this emphasizes how we can all stay well and how to stop turning pressure into stress. Clarke (2012) makes the analogy of building our own resilience to when in an impending air crash we have to ensure our own 'oxygen masks' are on first, before we can adequately assist others.

Some people engage in a professional distancing coping strategy. Laurence Alison mentioned this in his reflection (Box 7.2): 'There are few happy stories on either side. As such the work must stand separate from oneself. In that way, and however upsetting a case may be, when you meet the victims, the offenders or the falsely accused who are now directly going to be influenced by your work you know you've done the best you can by driving for an evidence-based approach to your thinking and that, quite rightly, any effect you have is a function of the science, of the evidence and not of your own world view or personal preference.'

It has been noted that both police and prison work are 'high-stress' occupations (Brough and Biggs, 2010) and in relation to moderation of job stress the importance of adequate support has been recognized (Brough and Frame, 2004; Johnson and Hall, 1988). In this environment, support needs to come from within the organization for which you work in the form of management, peer support and access to regular counselling and supervision. Regular peer and managerial contact specifically to discuss emotional experiences and stresses has been introduced for BIAs which is of particular importance for staff who may often work alone and travel a good deal.

The quality of such relationships, however, needs careful consideration as individuals may not disclose if, for example, they feel it may affect their career prospects or such information would not be treated in confidence.

Resilience can be enhanced by supporting yourself – recognizing why you do this work (it is interesting and can be rewarding), taking regular breaks, keeping yourself fit and healthy, maintaining a work–life balance, having other interests; and also in obtaining support from others – sharing general stresses with family and spending time with friends totally unconnected to work. It is vital therefore for individuals to actively search for their own well-being strategies, as well as having organizational support, as we have a duty of care to ourselves which we must take seriously (Clarke, 2013). There are highs and lows to any job, but work in this field can be particularly demanding and have somewhat unique challenges. Although for most it is not 'just a job', the trick is to recognize it is 'work', and as such should only be a part of our overall lives.

Box 9.6   Reflective exercise

1. Think about the items in your kitchen.

    a) Do they reflect your personality or how you feel about cooking?
    b) Do you possess a multitude of fresh ingredients, gadgets, cookery books, an array of knives, a huge fridge and tiny freezer? Or do you prefer to use a microwave and have a variety of take-away menus to hand? Does your fridge have a collection of beyond sell-by date jars of pickles and slimy vegetables?
    c) In the same way as your kitchen may reflect your approach and feelings towards cooking, can a crime scene reveal an offender's actions, motivation and thoughts?

2. Consider the following scenario. It's Christmas Eve and seasonally snowing. You have been called out to attend a potential crime scene, a sudden death report. What is your hypothesis when attending the scene where an elderly female is found with her nightie pulled up exposing her lower torso. She is in her own home, which is in a state of disarray with items knocked over. She lives alone so it is unclear what if anything has been stolen from the property, although she is known to frequently forget to lock her front door.

CONCLUSION

This chapter has outlined the current provision of behavioural investigative advice by defining its origins, theoretical underpinning and potential contribution to investigations. We have detailed some of the techniques used and issues relating to the evaluation of advice provision. Overall, articulation of the rationale underlying the advice seems to be improving, and satisfaction surveys indicate overall investigators are pleased with the contribution.

We have also highlighted the difference between historic profiling and current BIA practice, which is far broader and supplies reports to investigations that are far more pragmatically focused on investigative need. It also seems that future advice in relation to other areas such as cyber, organized and acquisitive crime could also be considered. In recognition of the investigators' need to account for their decision making, advice provision is also far more evidence-based, transparently using research, scientific method and expertise as its foundation. A useful checklist for consideration when writing reports is included, which can be adapted and added to for other forensic psychology reports. Finally, a summary of some of the things we have learnt is supplied, alongside pragmatic considerations such as how we can psychologically cope working in this field.

Finally, was one of your hypotheses in the reflective exercise hypothermia? Symptoms include clumsiness or lack of coordination, confusion and poor decision-making, such as trying to remove warm clothes. Beware jumping to conclusions or going further than the evidence justifies.

RESOURCES

Alison and Rainbow (2011) bring together both academics and practitioners in their edited collection *Professionalising Offender Profiling*. The book provides a unique description of the professional development and current service provision in relation to behavioural investigative advice.

Canter and Youngs (2009) outline the theoretical basis of the investigative psychology approach, which is then exemplified by means of application to different crime types.

In *The Forensic Psychologist's Casebook*, Alison (2007) provides an excellent overview of case studies and examples where forensic psychologists have provided advice to police investigations.

A formalized taxonomy and means by which the FBI classify offences together with typical offender characteristics are provided in detail in the *Crime Classification Manual* (Douglas et al., 2006).

Key journals

Journal of Homicide and Major Incident Investigation

Journal of Investigative Psychology and Offender Profiling

Journal of Police and Criminal Psychology

10

ASSESSMENT

KEY CONCEPTS

This chapter aims to provide the reader with an idea of the complexity of forensic assessment and what assessment involves. Beyond this, it also seeks to inform readers of the need to understand both the explicit and implicit messages we receive in undertaking assessments with those who have committed offences and to consider why more than a surface level interpretation is essential if assessment is to be meaningful and productive. Finally, it offers the opportunity to think about the impact of this work on practitioners.

Knowledge concepts	Practice considerations
Consent	Collateral information
Confidentiality	Expertise
False-positive errors	Formulation
Motivational Interviewing (MI)	Psychometric qualification standards
Multimodal process	Resistance, defensiveness, deception,
Reliability	dishonesty and malingering
Risk assessment	Vulnerability
Validity	

Questions addressed

What is the process of assessment?

What is the role of psychometric testing in assessment?

How do we manage resistance, defensiveness, deception, dishonesty and malingering in assessment?

How might we work with and respond to the challenge of the offender who is resistant and defensive in assessment?

(Continued)

How do we respond to our own issues of revulsion and disgust?

What are the possible outcomes of assessment?

What is the impact of this work on forensic psychologists?

INTRODUCTION

Offenders are a heterogeneous group, even within specific offence types, such as sexual offending or violent offending, and as such assessments are necessarily multimodal and complex as we try to gain an understanding of that person's offending behaviour. An assessment is a snapshot of that person at that time, in relation to the areas under assessment. Within this, forensic psychologists are asked to address the following in one way or another:

- to understand *why* the person committed the offence;
- the nature, level and management of *risk* the offender presents with;
- the treatment *needs* of that person;
- alongside the individual's *treatability and treatment readiness.*

The former two are closely related and the latter two ask us to consider what we can offer that may be effective for that person within current service provision. An individual formulation, arising from the assessment, aims to provide an understanding of the individual's specific offending behaviour and seeks further to identify maintenance factors in this behaviour, and in doing so has implications for future treatment and risk management. A formulation therefore serves to pull together disparate pieces of information into a whole and seeks to place them in a coherent framework that increases the psychological understanding of that person. It acts as a way of capturing a lot of information and presents it in a coherent manner.

Assessments are carried out at various stages of an offender's pathway through the legal, prison or secure psychiatric system. An assessment may be conducted pre-sentence, at admission, pre treatment, whilst in treatment, post treatment, follow-up, pre release and post release. Forensic psychologists should aim to embed assessment as an ongoing part of the entire journey through that offender's management and care. A gold standard description of the assessment process would portray a seamless pathway, with decision making based on comprehensive assessments informing appropriate management and treatment. It is important to be clear that assessment serves a function in the overall care and management of offenders as well as gaining an insight into and understanding of the offending behaviour and related factors.

WHAT IS THE PROCESS OF ASSESSMENT?

Assessments are multimodal and include elements of information gathering, engagement, collaboration, attending to the therapeutic relationship, psychometric testing, eliciting information, which sometimes entails asking difficult questions repeatedly in various guises, and feedback. In the reality of providing assessments in forensic settings we often complete such work in settings that are not ideal, with limited time, limited information beforehand and often with reluctant and defensive clients.

The first step in assessment, therefore, is to be clear as to the exact purpose of the assessment. What are the assessment questions to be addressed? This will be followed by a review of all existing information, upon which to base the assessment. This information may come from a variety of sources (e.g. police reports, victim statements, court documentation), and consideration of this material will often help guide how an assessment might be approached, identify what specific areas are to be addressed and the nature of psychometric tests to be used. Forensic psychologists should ensure that they consider all relevant third party information, for example probation reports, in the initial stages of an assessment. It is important that in using such information, consent is obtained from the information source to use the material in a particular assessment, and also in the subsequent reporting of this information in the assessment report. Austin (2002) suggests that different sources of collateral information may require greater levels of corroboration than others and urges forensic psychologists to consider the validity of any collateral information reviewed. Thus, third party information from a source independent of the offender, for example a probation officer, as opposed to the offender's partner, or co-defendant, may require less effort in terms of corroboration.

It is likely that an offender will enter into an assessment with preconceptions and possibly misunderstandings about the purpose and process. Part of the early stages of assessment will be to make clear to the offender the purpose of a particular assessment and to deal with preconceptions held by the offender. This is also a time to cover the issues of consent and confidentiality and to be clear about who will have access to the completed assessment and how it is to be used.

It is important to keep a full record of what has been said by the offender during the assessment, and also be aware of what is not said. One of the things forensic psychologists do in assessments is to go back over material several times, asking the same thing in different ways. This may well be irritating for the offender, as they will probably already have had this dialogue with several other professionals en route and they are likely to tell you just this, probably with a level of irritation.

However, it is important to be clear with the person you are assessing that whilst you may be asking similar questions to other professionals, your emphasis may be slightly different and what you will be considering is different. This reiteration of questions allows you not only to check the accuracy of information, but also to make an assessment of how that person is likely to cope with treatment and therapy-type questioning.

WHAT IS THE ROLE OF PSYCHOMETRIC TESTING IN ASSESSMENT?

There are many excellent chapters and papers on the role of psychometric testing in forensic assessment. Crighton (2010) writes comprehensively about the use of psychological tests in assessment and covers key areas relating to reliability and validity of tests. As such, this chapter will not seek to repeat what is written about with clarity elsewhere. However, as noted in (October 2014) *The Psychologist* 'Testing in forensic contexts – new qualification standards', forensic psychologists are required to be formally qualified in the use of psychometric tests. In 2009, the Division of Forensic Psychology (DFP) approached the BPS's Committee on Training Standards', because there was no formal training in the use of psychometric tests in forensic contexts. Therefore qualifications at two levels were established to enable test users

a) to acquire the necessary skills and knowledge and provide the user with a clear specification of what they need to know;
b) to be able to use tests effectively and ethically in different contexts;
c) to be able to demonstrate use against a set of competency standards; and
d) permit consultant psychologists to delegate some of the routine testing practices to assistant psychologists and feel confident that they are using tests properly.

It is important therefore that forensic psychologists make themselves aware of these requirements. The new qualifications are:

- assistant test user (test administration)
- test user (forensic).

There are two routes to this new qualification, each requiring different levels to demonstrate competence and training in the area of use of psychological tests in forensic contexts (see https://ptc.bps.org.uk/how-apply-packs/bps-forensic-testing-qualifications, for more details). Obtaining this qualification would allow the individual entry onto the *Register of British Psychological Society's Qualifications in Test Use* (RQTU). Entry onto the Register requires test users to conduct forensic testing in accordance with the *Code of Good Practice for Psychological Testing* alongside adherence to the *Rules for Membership of the Society's Register of Qualifications in Test Use*. This new qualification standard adds to the ongoing development of professional standards in forensic psychology and underpins the understanding that selection and use of psychometric testing in forensic assessment requires a high standard of practice as well as theoretical knowledge. These are critical when using psychometric tests in the course of an assessment and suitable tests need to be carefully chosen and carefully administered. Furthermore, this qualification aims to ensure:-

- that appropriate interpretation of measures is used;
- that tests are not misinterpreted or over-interpreted;

- that care in the presentation of results is attended to;
- that practitioners demonstrate a sound knowledge of the relevant literature underpinning each test utilized.

When reporting on tests, forensic psychologists must articulate any limitations to the testing within the assessment process, including reliability, validity and any problems with norms for the person tested.

RISK ASSESSMENT AS A PARTICULAR EXAMPLE OF FORENSIC ASSESSMENT

The history of risk assessment can be traced to the 1950s when there was a belief that forensic professionals could use clinical judgement alone to assess risk. However, in the 1960s and 1970s evidence was mounting that demonstrated we were not good at predicting risk by this method, and the work of Steadman and Cocozza (1974) showed that we were, actually, very poor at predicting accurately future violent offending by clinical judgement alone. To continue our discussion from Chapter 5, key problems associated with what is known as first generation risk assessment (i.e. clinical judgement alone) are wide-ranging, from sources of error located within the individual practitioner relating to judgemental heuristics (see Table 5.1), gender effects of both offender and clinician (Elbogen et al., 2001) through to errors associated with prediction of rare events (Yang et al., 2010) and concomitant high frequency of false-positive errors.

The 1990s saw the rise of second generation actuarial/statistical assessment approaches. Actuarial Risk Assessment Instruments (ARAIs) are not psychological tests. ARAIs are designed to predict risk (Hart et al., 2007), whilst psychological tests are designed to describe and even to diagnose. Strong advocates for this methodology in assessing violent offenders are Harris and Rice (2010). They describe actuarial methods as providing more 'accurate' predictions than informal clinical judgement, experiences, or intuition. Harris and Rice cite the Violence Risk Appraisal Guide (Harris et al., 1993) as an early forerunner in the field of actuarial assessments. Other such tools subsequently include the STATIC-99 (Hanson and Thornton, 2000) and the Risk Matrix 2000 (Thornton, 2000).

The benefits of such instruments are clear, in that they eliminate the subjective errors present in clinical judgement; however, these instruments do not allow for the possibility of change in individuals and do little to help inform decisions about treatment domains to be addressed, nor do they allow for contextual factors to be considered. The field of risk assessment has subsequently seen the rise of what are known as third generation risk assessment instruments (structured professional judgement), which include dynamic, clinical and actuarial factors. Dynamic factors might include level of insight, relationship instability, attitudes held. These third generation instruments developed as an attempt to bridge the gap between actuarial risk assessment and clinical judgement alone. The HCR-20 (Webster et al., 1995, 1997) is an example of third generation risk assessment. Within the

HCR-20 a combination of actuarial factors is considered alongside dynamic variables, that is factors considered to be changeable (e.g. an offender's level of insight into his/her offence).

The popularity of these third generation structured professional decision making tools resulted from some forensic psychologists wanting the opportunity to use clinical judgement in light of good evidence to influence risk assessment (Doren, 2006). The benefits of third generation instruments are that they assist in the development of individual treatment and risk management plans, they help in identifying specific factors that increase or decrease risk and they allow for clinical override and address the weakness in actuarial assessments whereby 'unusual' risk factors in a particular case can be overlooked. Third generation risk assessments encourage us to complete this work alongside the offender, whilst actuarial risk assessments are often completed on and done 'to' the person being assessed. This fact alone has implications in our mind as to the ease with which we might develop a risk management plan that we would want the offender to engage with. Our understanding and experience is that completing risk assessments with a person results in far more meaningful and better adhered to risk management plans.

IS CLINICAL JUDGEMENT NO MORE THAN INTUITION?

Simon (1987) defined intuition in decision making as 'the situation has provided a cue, this cue has given the expert access to information stored in memory, and the information provides the answer. Intuition is nothing more and nothing less than recognition.' If this is so, are more experienced forensic practitioners better placed to use clinical judgement/override in risk assessments and how does one go about gaining this expertise?

'Expertise' is multifaceted and takes time to acquire. Klein (1999, in Kahneman, 2011) suggests that 'true experts know the limits of their knowledge'. Yet Kahneman believes that 'pseudo-experts' hold an 'illusion of validity'. That suggests that pseudo-experts do not know what they do not know, and gives rise to erroneous subjective confidence in their decision making. This is the Donald Rumsfeld uncertainty conundrum:

> as we know, there are known knowns; there are things we know we know. We also know there are known unknowns; that is to say we know there are some things we do not know. But there are also unknown unknowns – the ones we don't know we don't know. (US Defense Secretary Donald Rumsfeld at a news briefing, February 2002)

Both Kahneman and Klein agree that the degree of confidence a person holds in relation to their intuition is unreliable. Furthermore, Kahneman states (2011: 333) that highly irregular events and environments, such as the rare event of murder, lead to intuition being even less accurate at predicting outcomes.

When assessing events such as murder and rape we must recognize that the probability of these types of events occurring is often overestimated as a result of the confirmatory bias of memory. Overweighting of such events is increased when it attracts attention, is explicitly described, it results in people being overly concerned about it re-occurring and there are vivid portrayals of it and explicit reminders. It would seem that these conditions are routinely met when we consider serious offences and consequently the careful consideration of actuarial factors alongside clinical judgement is vital for even the most experienced practitioners in the field.

HOW DO YOU MANAGE RESISTANCE, DEFENSIVENESS, DECEPTION, DISHONESTY AND MALINGERING IN ASSESSMENT?

> That lying should be necessary to life is part and parcel of the terrible and questionable character of existence. (Nietzsche)

Grayling (2001) suggests that to lie is to be human and that without lies we would have no 'inner privacy'. Yet we assume that for much of the time people tell the truth in everyday life, or get by with only the occasional 'white lie'. When we work with offenders and we believe them to be lying how do we respond? Do we naturally assume that in doing so they are being dishonest to avoid punishment, or lessen the punishment they might receive? In some cases this may be the case.

In other instances, however, might the 'lies' we encounter in the process of assessing a person be an attempt by that individual to protect their sense of 'self', to maintain some remnants of dignity, or indeed, because they themselves are not ready to admit to themselves the full extent of the truth in that moment or lack the insight to provide a reasoned and logical account of their motives or behaviour. If in some cases this is correct, then we must embark on assessment with great sensitivity and skill, as in seeking the truth we might stumble upon frailties in the person that could be devastating if mismanaged. Or in approaching the quest for the truth without such sensitivity, might we push it further underground or alienate the offender from us to such a degree that they withhold important information, in which case the assessment and possible future treatment engagement is ruptured. This in itself could serve to increase an individual's risk, firstly by not being able to assess such risk fully we are unable to develop a sound risk management plan, but secondly, and as important, such a rupture may result in the offender's disengagement from necessary treatment.

This speaks to the point captured in the HCPC document in 'Standards of Proficiency – Practitioner Psychologists', in which the document makes clear for clinical psychologists that within professional relationships with clients clinicians must 'understand explicit and implicit communications in a therapeutic relationship'. The present author (Y.S.) considers this standard holds equally true for forensic psychologists and that the above may be an example of explicit and implicit communication that we are indebted to understand and manage in therapeutic encounters with forensic clients.

What else may influence how honest an offender may be? Here is an exercise to complete before you start this section of the chapter; it is adapted from workshop material used by Paul Gilbert (2009) when teaching about 'Compassion Focused Therapy and Compassionate Mind Training for Shame Based Difficulties'. It is designed to help participants recognize the complex nature of shame and demonstrates how we all have an intuitive knowledge of shame.

Box 10.1   Reflective exercise

Please consider something you are ashamed of, and write a couple of sentences about it now. It's assumed that it is just the one shameful thing; after all you are, or are trying to become, a reflective forensic psychologist!

How does thinking about this shameful event make you feel about yourself?

Please think about how it would feel to have to tell a stranger about this shameful event.

How do you think others would think and feel about you if they heard you talk about this shameful event?

What do you think you might do to your account of this shameful event if you had to tell another person about it?

How easy was that? Did you actually do it? Were you entirely honest? Now scrunch up the piece of paper you have written this on and either eat it, burn it or feed it to the dog, before one of your family, your partner or a friend finds it! You have the luxury of getting rid of the evidence; an offender does not. An offender also has to speak this out loud, not only to you, but also perhaps numerous times before and after the assessment with you. We might also be recommending that the offender join a treatment group work programme within which further detailed disclosure of offence material is expected. Should we really be surprised when many offenders present with hostility, irritability, anger, denial, dishonesty and general resistance during assessment?

Talking about shameful events in our lives makes us feel vulnerable. Making ourselves vulnerable is intensely unpleasant. See Box 10.2 for the dialogue between Brené Brown, a psychologist who specializes in shame and vulnerability research, and her therapist as they talk about Brown's personal experience of vulnerability (Brené Brown, 2012).

Box 10.2 Brené Brown on uncertainty

BB: I hate uncertainty. I hate not knowing. I can't stand opening myself to getting hurt or being disappointed. It's excruciating. Vulnerability is complicated. And it's excruciating. Do you know what I mean?

Therapist: What does it feel like?

BB: Like I'm coming out of my skin. Like I need to fix whatever's happening and make it better.

Therapist: And if you can't?

BB: *Then I feel like punching someone in the face.*

Therapist: And do you?

BB: No. Of course not.

Therapist: So what do you do?

BB: Clean the house. Eat peanut butter. *Blame people.* Make everything around me perfect. Control whatever I can ... Whatever's not nailed down.

Therapist: When do you feel most vulnerable?

BB: *When I'm in fear. When I'm anxious and unsure about how things are going to go, or if I'm having a difficult conversation, or if I'm trying something new or doing something that makes me uncomfortable or opens me up to criticism or judgment.*

(Italics are the author's own in the transcript above)

This is clearly a universally and quite 'normal' response to being confronted with one's vulnerability and when asked to consider shame-laden events in our lives. Assessment is made more complicated by this very human reaction. We expect a lot from those we assess, and we do so in a situation where that person is often experiencing significant stress as a result of being seen for a court appearance or in the stressful situation of being in a secure establishment with all the pressures that brings. At each and every step, there is a substantial investment on the part of the offender to make the best impression they possibly can. How difficult is that challenge going to be when they are being asked to disclose and elaborate on what is potentially the most shameful thing they have ever done. So this work is complicated both for us and for the offender.

In their research on residents experiencing a prison therapeutic community, Brown et al. (2014) describe the difficulties the offenders had in opening up and recounting their histories in their therapy groups. One resident commented 'disclosing to other people caused me a hell of a lot of grief' (p. 172). Another described how he had to build up trust before disclosing important things about his life and several talked about taking off a protective mask in order to get to a point of self revelation. The process is a hard thing to do. In part, learning to deal with not only their own emotional fall-out from their criminal behaviour was crucial to making therapeutic progress, but also being able to empathize in the damage caused to others. Taking responsibility and moving from an external to an internal attribution of blame was a mark of therapeutic progress.

The starting point with many we work with may well be one of shame about their offending behaviour. This shame may well be masked by more comfortable emotions such as anger and projected outward as blame. The experience of an offender blaming us or being angry with us should serve to alert us to the fact that they may be experiencing a quite different emotion, such as shame, and that this needs to be acknowledged and worked with. A conference presentation by Shell and Moore outlined encounters in an anger management group with young male offenders, all diagnosed with personality disorder, in a maximum security psychiatric hospital. What became apparent in conducting this year-long treatment programme was that men often turned to anger and violence in an attempt to regain power and that anger and violence provided a face-saving function. It also clearly demonstrated that increased self-awareness often exposed the individual to increased levels of shame and that these had to be managed by therapists in the group by neutralizing the person's intense fear of being humiliated, judged or perhaps even punished for their disclosure. This type of finding had previously been found by Gilbert and Andrews (1995), Gilligan (2003) and Linehan (1993) and is also illustrated in Brown et al. (2014).

So the potential for an offender to be dishonest, both wilfully and as a result of a desire to self-protect, seems obvious, both within an assessment interview and in completing self-report measures. Having as much information as possible, and having had time to consider it fully, prior to the assessment commencing allows the forensic psychologist to be in a better position to deal with potential deceit, avoidance or defensiveness when assessing an offender. Rogers (2008) strongly advises that an assessment of the offender's response style in forensic assessment is essential. It is clear that offenders will have a great investment in presenting in the most favourable light in forensic assessments, from having their very freedom at stake through to the type of disposal, length of disposal and also through to opportunities for treatment.

When making an assessment of the veracity of an account offered by an offender, the forensic psychologist also has to hold in mind the issue of mental health presentations (we know that offenders have a high rate of mental health problems), and the context of the assessment (i.e. prisons are stressful environments and impact significantly upon an individual). As such, the assessment task is complex and can be, as Ekman and O'Sullivan (2006) state, 'daunting'. In addition to this, we might not only be dealing with an individual denying or minimizing events on the one hand, we might also be having to consider the individual who is motivated to exaggerate or fabricate symptoms (i.e. malingering) and impairment in an attempt to influence decision making in regard to them. There are a number of psychometric tests that include within them an embedded measure of response style (e.g. MMPI, which has a built in measure of dissimulation). That is not to say that these are the only psychological tests that forensic psychologists should use. However, it is important that the psychologist is aware of those tests not having a response-style measure embedded within them and when using tests that do not include this that they are aware of the potential vulnerability to response style when interpreting results and reporting on these results.

HOW MIGHT WE WORK WITH AND RESPOND TO THE CHALLENGE OF THE OFFENDER WHO IS RESISTANT AND DEFENSIVE IN ASSESSMENT?

The spirit and techniques of Motivational Interviewing (MI), as outlined by Miller and Rollnick (2013), may be extremely useful in such instances. Motivational Interviewing is predominantly linked with the field of substance misuse. However, its techniques and the point of MI are of benefit to a much wider range of work arenas, including forensic work. MI was originally designed for working with people who are less ready to change, so who are presenting with ambivalence. It is defined as 'a collaborative conversation style for strengthening a person's own motivation and commitment to change'. The spirit of MI includes collaboration, acceptance, evocation and compassion. MI uses a set of simple techniques – open-ended questions, affirmations, reflections (simple and complex) and summaries – to work with individuals who are predominantly ambivalent about change and therefore considered to sit within the pre-contemplation or contemplation stages of change of the Prochaska and DiClemente (1983) trans-theoretical model.

These stages are defined as:

- Pre-contemplation – unaware/unconcerned by the problem
- Contemplation – acknowledgement but ambivalence about changing
- Action – change attempts in progress
- Maintenance – change consolidated and temptation to relapse diminishing.

Miller and Rollnick earlier, coined the term 'rolling with resistance' in dealing with ambivalence from clients. In more recent developments within MI there has been a move away from this term as it was seen to locate the difficulty within the individual client and to 'blame' them for resistance and for being 'difficult'. New developments in the field of MI have led to change from the terminology of resistance and the terminology now includes 'discord', and 'change' and 'sustain' talk by individuals. 'Discord' relates to the forensic psychologist's relationship in assessment with the client, whilst 'change 'and 'sustain' talk is

about the target behaviour of change. Discord therefore requires two participants: the psychologist and the offender. Miller and Rollnick offer the ideas that
in 'discord' we hear the voice of the person defending themselves by blaming,
minimizing, justifying; 'squaring off', which represents an oppositional stance;
interrupting by the client which might signal that the person does not feel
heard or understood; and disengagement from the assessment or conversation
taking place. Discord is not a sign that you are making progress and breaking
the person and their defences down. Rather it is a signal that the working alliance is being damaged. So, how should we respond to discord? Proponents
of MI indicate that a key response to discord in the therapeutic alliance is
through the use of reflections. They also suggest that therapists could apologize
when they have made assumptions/guesses leading to misunderstandings and
thereby created 'discord', or by pushing too hard and too fast. It might also help
to use affirmations to reduce defensiveness and discord. This might take the
form of an acknowledgement of how difficult the assessment task is, but recognition that the offender is still present in the room and attempting to explore
important themes. Whilst the above are offered as possible ways of responding
to discord, they are not the only way by any means.

HOW DO WE RESPOND TO OUR OWN ISSUES OF REVULSION AND DISGUST?

Some of the offences you will be privy to may be frightening or, quite
frankly, repellent. We discussed in a previous chapter the phenomenon of
vicarious stress whereby a professional over-identified with the trauma of a
victim. The situation we are describing here is its obverse – disgust and
revulsion in the events you are being told about. Lea, Auburn and Kibblewhite
(1999) identify this dilemma as the personal–professional dialectic. They
undertook detailed, semi-structured interviews with 23 key professionals
working with sex offenders. They identified a tension between a human
response to the crime and their professional responsibility of care for the
offender. Lea and colleagues found some of the professionals in their study
'shuttled' between these two sets of feelings whilst others tried to separate
the two. Brown and Blount (1999) found that the least experienced sex
offender treatment managers in their study, those who had been in post for
less than two years, were more likely than more experienced managers to
develop aversion towards the offender and experience heightened awareness
of personal danger, tensions with their own partners and a loss of confidence
in being around other people's children.

It would seem in light of the above that an acknowledgement of the potential for us, as practitioners working in forensic settings, to find ourselves at
times working with an individual whose behaviour/attitudes or beliefs we may
find abhorrent could occur. Knowing this, and being prepared for this as a
human response to hearing accounts of behaviour that is extreme, may help
the practitioner to manage their reaction to this event. If we give ourselves

permission as a profession to have this on the agenda as we work in such settings, it makes it considerably more likely that the individual practitioner will feel able to take these feelings to supervision and to feel supported in their ongoing engagement with the particular person, or indeed in requesting that someone else perhaps takes on the case. This should not be seen as a failure on the part of the practitioner, but rather it should be seen as serving the best interests of the offender. If on the other hand we do not acknowledge the above and we expect that practitioners should be able to deal with whatever is laid before them, then we do a disservice to practitioner, client and ultimately potentially wider society.

WHAT ARE THE POSSIBLE OUTCOMES OF AN ASSESSMENT?

Assessments are required of offenders for a wide variety of reasons at all stages of the legal process. At a very general level the outcome of any assessment will be to provide psychological opinion that can be used to inform decision making in regard to that individual, often balancing their needs against those of the wider community. With regard to treatment, forensic psychologists have to assess to see if an individual is suitable for treatment, the nature of the treatment required and its availability. It requires an understanding of the 'what works' literature and evidence base for treatment for offender populations. Alongside this, the psychologist will also be making an assessment about that person's treatment readiness.

Forensic psychologists need awareness that certain diagnoses/constructs identified during assessment may have a disproportionate influence on decision making, for example, consider psychopathy. The term 'psychopath' has fallen into routine usage within the general population. More often than not, if you asked a non-psychologist to tell you what a psychopath is you get a description of Hannibal Lecter. When forensic psychologists are in a position of making diagnoses such as these it is critical that they ensure that the diagnosis is accompanied by a clear description of what that means in relation to the particular individual being assessed. It is also critical that we make sure that in offering up such weighty diagnoses we use the best psychological assessment tools for this purpose, and that we make those in receipt of the findings of our assessment aware of the limitations of such tools.

WHAT IS THE IMPACT OF THIS WORK ON FORENSIC PSYCHOLOGISTS?

Rilke (cited in Grayling, 2001), in his 'Letters to a young poet', suggested that we need 'courage for the most strange, the most singular and the most inexplicable that we may encounter'.

We may feel anxious about assessment of certain types of offenders, particularly. We have a complex task that is demanding of us both personally and professionally on occasion. It is critical that the emotional impact of the work of forensic psychologists is considered. It would be unusual if the nature of what forensic psychologists are exposed to did not carry with it an emotional weight that resonated as shock, upset and anger for example, particularly when new to the area. More experienced practitioners on the other hand need to have an awareness of the possibility of becoming 'numbed' to hearing offence accounts, which is equally worthy of attention. And so, no matter what stage you are at in your career as a forensic psychologist, the nature of this work carries with it a weightiness that can have both a professional and personal impact, and we are professionally bound to ensure that we seek support and supervision to allow us to reflect upon and attenuate that impact upon us.

CONCLUSION

Forensic psychologists bear a heavy responsibility in completing any forensic assessments, particularly risk assessments, as our findings can have a significant impact on others' lives. We must therefore ensure that we maintain high standards of competence in this role. Forensic psychologists must remain aware of new developments in the field and incorporate these into their practice. It is vital when conducting any assessment that the tests and instruments forensic psychologists use are reliable and valid, and are the current tools most appropriate for the individual offender being assessed. The new qualification in psychological testing is welcomed in the field as it serves to further lend weight to the professionalization of forensic assessment and forensic psychology as a whole. Poor assessments may result in poor decision making and potentially catastrophic consequences. This not only discredits the individual practitioner, but also calls the profession into disrepute.

It is important in conducting assessments that we are clear about the distinction between what the person has done and the person as an individual. This relies on us to be professional in our approach to assessments, and we have a responsibility to the client, underpinned by our professional Codes of Conduct (BPS and HCPC) and the Human Rights Act to enter into assessments in this spirit. Therapist behaviours are very important in assessment and we must demonstrate respect and a desire to make sense of the offender and their behaviours, attitudes and beliefs that have led them to be in this situation. Undoubtedly, forensic psychologists are sometimes confronted with behaviours by individuals that can be upsetting, create feelings of disgust or anger etc., and so this work is also demanding on the individual practitioner at both a professional and personal level. It is essential that forensic psychologists seek appropriate support and supervision to manage these 'normal' reactions to some of the material they are exposed to. It is also critical that we are aware of the impact of assessments on the offender and that we acknowledge how difficult this process may be for that person. We need to be aware of distinguishing between genuine and distorted reports and to have an understanding of the rationale for distortions as a psychological defence as opposed to lying to avoid a consequence of offending behaviour. In recognizing this vulnerability and therefore courage in our clients it should make us attend to the power imbalance that is evident in all therapeutic relationships, but that comes with an additional layer of meaning in forensic contexts.

RESOURCES

There are now a number of edited collections that between them cover much relevant material e.g. Leam Craig, Theresa Gannon and Louise Dixon's *What Works in Offender Rehabilitation* (2013); Tony Beech, Leam Craig and Kevin Browne's *Assessment and Treatment of Sex Offenders* (2009); Clive Hollin's *Handbook of Offender Assessment and Treatment* (2001); and Caroline Logan and Lorraine Johnstone's *Managing Clinical Risk* (2012).

Key journals

Assessment

British Journal of Clinical Psychology

Journal of Consulting and Clinical Psychology

Psychological Assessment

Sexual Abuse - A Journal of Research and Treatment

11
TREATMENT AND REHABILITATION

KEY CONCEPTS

This chapter aims to provide an overview of the current status of treatment and rehabilitation of those who have committed offences and the central issues to be considered in provision of these services. The reader is introduced to key approaches in the field and is exposed to research and theories originating from other domains that are thought to be useful in understanding the current status of the field and to assist in thinking about future service provision and policy.

Knowledge concepts	Practice considerations
Desistance	Good Lives Model (GLM)
Peer mentoring	Managing hope and expectations
Rehabilitation	Motivational Interviewing (MI)
Therapeutic communities	Risk-Need-Responsivity (RNR) model
Treatment	Therapeutic alliance
'What works'	Transtheoretical model of the stages of change
	Understanding desistance as a process

Questions addressed

What are and what should be our treatment targets?

What happens within treatment?

What should the length of treatment follow-up be?

What is the value of peer mentor schemes?

What are the problems of treating offenders with co-morbidity?

What is the role of the forensic psychologist in treatment provision?

What can therapeutic communities offer?

Box 11.1   Reflective exercise

Please consider the following brief hypothetical scenario and answer the questions as well as you can. Take the time to give the situation careful consideration.

You apply for a new job that you are keen on getting. You are pleased to have been offered an interview and that your prospective employer has asked for references to be taken up. Sadly, the impetus for your move has been as a result of considerable disagreement with your senior manager at your present place of work about working practices.

You attend the interview and at first all seems to be going well until the panel start to ask you questions about your team work, ability to delegate and how you respond to criticism. You find yourself reacting defensively.

You are offered the job but you feel that your reference from your current employers has been negative in tone and that this is information your new employers are now privy to. You do not have sight of this reference and you are unsure whether you should ask to know what was said in it. In the interim you have started your new job. In light of the above please answer the following questions:

1. How will you feel knowing that others will have received a potentially negative reference about you?
2. How might these feelings impact on how you approach your new role?
3. How would you want your new employer and immediate staff and colleagues to treat you as you take up your new position?
4. What do you hope for in the new job?
5. What do you fear?

How difficult was it to imagine trying to establish yourself in this new role as a result of the above? The task might have generated some emotional reaction. You might have been worried about whether you were going to be given a chance to show your worth, what you could offer or concerned that this might be tainted by negative reports from your previous employer. It would undoubtedly have raised feelings of discomfort. Try to hold on to this learning as you consider the remainder of this chapter.

INTRODUCTION

An interest in and desire to address, and effectively reduce, offending behaviour has long been an ideal that policy makers and treatment providers have aspired to. Currently treatment for those convicted of crime can take many forms; for example, through individual work, collectively, as in therapeutic communities, and large-scale manualized programmes on offer within both forensic settings and the community. This was not always the case, however. The seminal paper by Martinson in 1974 led to therapeutic nihilism in the eyes of policy makers of the day, as his findings contributed to the doctrine of 'nothing works' in offender rehabilitation. There remained, however, voices that held on to the belief that for some offenders some things work some of the time, and the challenge became one of 'what works' in reducing reoffending.

In the 1980s, Martinson's 'nothing works' position was heralded as a 'misinterpretation' or indeed a 'misrepresentation' (McGuire, 2010) of the rehabilitation evidence, which had led to the provision of rehabilitation for offenders being significantly undermined and diminished. More recent investigations into treatment efficacy with offender populations has gone a considerable way to redressing the therapeutic despair that arose from the Martinson position in the 1970s. Now there is a cautious optimism about interventions to address reoffending, particularly if those interventions/programmes adhere to certain principles. The principles that held the ascendancy for over a decade were those comprehensively proposed through the work of Andrews and colleagues in the 1990s, and became known as the Risk–Need–Responsivity model (discussed in Chapter 6). This model has been viewed by many as the 'premier' model in the assessment and treatment of offender groups (Andrews and Bonta, 1994; see also Andrews et al., 2011). More recently, however, there have been a number of new kids on the block in the field of treatment and rehabilitation, namely the Good Lives Model of Tony Ward and his colleagues, supported by work from the field of positive psychology, and research originating from criminology in the area of desistance. This chapter will seek to extend our discussion of the current debate occurring within the field of treatment and rehabilitation, considering the research evidence and extensive wisdom of the key players who currently star in this arena.

WHAT ARE AND WHAT SHOULD BE OUR TREATMENT TARGETS?

> If you treat an individual as he is, he will stay as he is, but if you treat him as if he were what he ought to be and could be, he will become what he ought to be and could be. (Johann Wolfgang von Goethe)

There are many interested parties in the field of rehabilitation and the fact is that treatment targets are sometimes influenced to a degree by factors external to the individual offender and treatment providers. By this, we mean the social and political agendas of the day carry a weight that is often influential in dictating outcome targets at some level. That is not to say that those providing treatment would necessarily disagree with such treatment targets, however, if such influence can become problematic if this exerts an overriding focus of treatment (see as an example the earlier discussion on dangerous and severe personality disorder).

The current focus on risk assessment and management and criminogenic needs is considered by some (Laws and Ward, 2011) to fail to address at an individual level the wider issues that are likely to lead to better opportunities for the development of offence-free lives. Clinicians such as Laws and Ward are raising questions at a fundamental level about how we should approach the area of treatment and rehabilitation for those who have committed offences. These clinicians, alongside other colleagues, are urging us to think more widely about rehabilitation, using evidence from desistance research, and also taking an ethical standpoint with regard to the philosophical position, beliefs and values we take with us into this work (Ward, 2011).

From clinical psychology, within the field of treatment of substance misuse, the approach urged by Ward and colleagues has already begun to develop a strong footing and following. Within this arena there is an understanding that it is essential to consider wider 'recovery' for the individual with an addiction problem. This wider 'recovery' incorporates ideas of the 'spirit', in which those working in addictions enter into treatment provision. What do we mean by the word 'spirit' as used in this area? Miller and Rollnick (2013) talked of the 'spirit' of Motivational Interviewing (MI) as involving both a 'mind-set' and a 'heart-set'. Arising from their work came four key related concepts:

- Partnership/collaboration – we work 'with' a person and 'for' them and not do 'unto' them.
- Acceptance – we acknowledged the person's inherent value and potential; however this does not mean that we have to approve of the behaviour that person has engaged in.
- Compassion – we show compassion for the person we are working with and in doing so seek to promote their best interests and general well-being.
- Evocation – we draw out existing motivation and aim to strengthen this in working alongside the individual.

From the field of substance misuse the clear message is that fuller reintegration into the individual's community, alongside purposeful and meaningful lives for those in treatment, are consistent and necessary goals to achieve an addiction-free future. It is also acknowledged that stopping use of alcohol or drugs is the easier part of the process; of greater difficulty is maintaining abstinence from substance misuse. It is understood that long-term maintenance requires a treatment approach that pays due attention to wider 'recovery' and 'recovery capital' for the individual with substance misuse problems. The terms 'recovery' and 'recovery capital' are embedded firmly in the fields of both substance misuse and mental health (Best and Laudet, 2010; Deegan, 1998). The idea of 'recovery capital' is a construct created to refer to the sum of resources necessary to initiate and sustain recovery (Best and Laudet, 2010: 3). The idea of recovery capital originally emerged from the field of sociology (Bourdieu, 1980) and was later championed by Granfield and Cloud (2001, 2006) for use in the field of addictions and referring to 'social capital'. Within this field it is recognized that both the quality and quantity of recovery capital an individual has can have an influence on recovery. Cloud and Granfield (2009) further developed the notion of recovery capital to include:

- social capital – the sense of belonging and sense of support a person obtains from social groups that they belong to, including partnerships, families and friends;
- physical capital – tangible assets (e.g. a home);
- human capital – a person's health and their personal resources (e.g. intelligence); and
- cultural capital – encompasses values, beliefs and attitudes that make the individual able to participate in shared values of their community.

It is suggested here that these concepts offer interesting and pertinent ideas for the field of offender treatment and rehabilitation. As readers continue with this chapter they will perhaps recognize that these notions described above sit comfortably with the desistance research and the Good Lives Model of Ward and colleagues we discussed earlier. The ideas from the fields of mental health and substance misuse services which robustly state that recovery, in its truest sense, is a lived experience and that treatment programmes will play only a small part in this are important for us in the field of forensic psychology to consider.

Those who commit offences are a diverse group. The act of offending, of any type, is the end point of a long causal chain, involving complex interactions between social, biological, behavioural, affective and cognitive processes. It involves a complex set of interactions in relationships and within various environments. So offending exists as a dynamic state, fluid within the offender and also fluid within the context in which the offence occurs as well as the interaction between the two. This means that an understanding of the offending behaviour, for that person, requires an individual formulation of all these factors if it is to be both meaningful and useful in directing treatment focus and indicate pertinent treatment goals.

With this in mind, the questions for forensic psychology to consider would seem to be these:

- Is a narrow focus on offence-specific behaviours enough to result in reducing offending?
- Should treatment targets not only be wider ranging than just consideration of risk and criminogenic need but also include the generating of wider 'recovery capital' for the individual offender in an attempt to increase the possibility of establishing an offence-free, fulfilled and meaningful life within society?
- Are risk reduction and addressing criminogenic need incompatible with releasing recovery capital, or are all required in order for the full and meaningful rehabilitation of offenders?

Our discussion of this debate began in Chapter 6 in our consideration of theory and we extend this into the practice arena in this chapter. In doing this it is acknowledged that the approaches outlined are mainly those of large-scale treatment programmes and the theories and models that underpin them. It is important to recognize that this does not do justice to the wider array of excellent clinical approaches to offender treatment and rehabilitation work that operate on a daily basis elsewhere within the criminal justice field. The focus in this chapter on these particular models informs us of their significant importance in the current treatment and rehabilitation field and as such it is important for readers to have some appreciation of them. There is not scope in this chapter to discuss the range of other treatment provision nor particular programmes available in practice today. Should readers wish to pursue further reading in this area there are a number of excellent texts on the matter, and that edited by McGuire (2002) would be a good starting point.

RISK–NEED–RESPONSIVITY MODEL

The Risk–Need–Responsivity (RNR) model arose like a phoenix from the flames of the Martinson burnt wasteland (Andrews et al., 1990; see also Andrews and Bonta, 1994; Andrews and Dowden, 2006, 2007). RNR has been the dominant model in the design and development of treatment programmes in the UK for over a decade (Andrews et al., 2006). The three principles for effective rehabilitation were described as follows:

- Risk principle (match level of program intensity to offender risk level; intensive levels of treatment for high-risk offenders and minimal intervention for low-risk offenders)

- Need principle (target criminogenic needs or those offender needs that are functionally related to criminal behaviour)

- Responsivity principle (match the style and mode of intervention to the offender's learning style and abilities)

(Andrews et al., 2011)

Research has demonstrated that attention in treatment to these three components has a greater overall effect in reducing reoffending than paying attention to only one of the components (Andrews et al., 2011).

As well as developing these theoretical underpinnings, Andrews and colleagues have also provided a family of instruments to support the assessment and treatment phases of offenders subjected to RNR practice. Such instruments include:

- the Youth Level of Service Inventory (Andrews et al., 1984);
- the Level of Service Inventory-Revised (Andrews and Bonta, 1995), which aims to assess risk level and criminogenic needs;

- the Youth Level of Service/Case Management Inventory Manual and Scoring Key (Hoge and Andrews, 2002);
- the Level of Service/Case Management Inventory (Andrews et al., 2004);
- Level of Service: Risk–Need–Responsivity (Andrews et al., 2008).

The RNR model has been highly influential in the development of policy, theory and delivery of effective treatment provision (Ogloff and Davies, 2004; Ward et al., 2007), and RNR-style treatment programmes have been adopted as the preferred model for treatment provision for offenders within the criminal justice setting resulting in the implementation of large-scale treatment programmes both in prisons and through probation services at a national level. These programmes, based on cognitive behavioural intervention methods, are heavily manualized. It is perhaps worth briefly stating that manualized programmes seek to ensure that there is adherence to the treatment focus and aim to provide for maintenance of programme quality and integrity, guarding against programme 'drift' (a diversion from the treatment focus) and in doing so hope to result in greater effect size in outcomes. However, disappointingly, the outcome studies in relation to the implementation of these large-scale interventions in the UK produced poorer results in terms of reoffending than anticipated. It is considered that this is likely to have been partly as a result of problems with implementation and concerns around quality of programme provision, delivery fidelity and treatment integrity (Goggin and Gendreau, 2006; Young, 2010).

Critics of the RNR model (Ward and Maruna, 2007) argue that it is not the content of the RNR model per se that they take issue with, rather it is what it fails to include in what it is trying to achieve, and consequently they claim its treatment focus is too narrow. They take the position that the RNR model is a deficit/weakness model of the offender and because of that it fails to attend to the strengths or personal needs of that individual, or indeed their broader needs and therefore the fuller recovery and reintegration of the individual into their community and construction of a future non-offending identity. Fortune, Ward and Polaschek (2014: 2) declare that in their view RNR 'runs the risk of conflating social needs with therapeutic goals', which potentially could be both self-defeating and unethical. They say the alternative Good Lives Model as a strengths-based approach avoids these mistakes because it explicitly seeks to enhance offender well-being as well as engaging dynamic risk factors.

GOOD LIVES MODEL

This empirically and theoretically grounded rehabilitation approach has undoubtedly been considered a response to the view that RNR models are too narrow in their focus. The GLM (Ward and Stewart, 2003; Ward and Maruna, 2007) is a 'strengths'-based approach within which the former propose that treatment and rehabilitation in the criminal justice field should turn its attention more widely to offenders' lives, not just the offence-specific behaviours, and promote attainment of broader life goals in pro-social ways. The argument is made that this in turn will reduce offenders' need to continue to engage in crime because they are working towards achieving personal fulfilment. The GLM pays considerable attention to the human rights of offenders to be treated with respect and dignity (Ward and Birgden, 2004; Ward and Willis, 2010). It has also striven to emphasize concepts of offender motivation and the role of personal identity (Ward et al., 2007), and the instillation of hope and an inculcation of belief in the possibility of embracing pro-social, non-criminal identities in the future.

Whilst the GLM was originally developed to be used in the treatment of sex offenders, its application is suggested to be equally pertinent to all offender groups. It is described by Laws and Ward (2011: 220) as a theoretically grounded rehabilitation approach, with applications in assessment and treatment, which further tries to locate the process of change within the individual with a grounding in an understanding of human motivation.

The GLM draws heavily from other fields, including criminology and work in the area of desistance, positive psychology and law (as enshrined in the Human Rights Act 1983). Polaschek (2010: 448) argues that the GLM 'provides an important humanistic counterweight to pressure on some programmes to integrate politically driven punitive agendas into their practices.'

GLM and desistance models fit comfortably together, with the GLM proposing that 'effective treatment should aim to provide alternative means for achieving human goods' (Ward and Marshall, 2007: 297) and that 'assisted' desistance may encourage and support naturally occurring desistance. Together they can confront barriers to community reintegration and improve treatment efficacy thereby leading to longer periods of desistance being maintained. This is a fundamental shift from the RNR approach and is supported by the work of Attrill and Liell (2007). They found that offenders experience the emphasis on risk assessment, as in RNR models, as demotivating. Getting the balance between addressing necessary risk factors whilst also acknowledging and working with offenders' resilience and personal strengths would seem to be an essential cornerstone in assisting desistance.

Both the GLM and RNR models are examples of current approaches to the treatment of offenders. The two approaches encompass similar themes and ideas but there is a significant difference between them in terms of their underlying philosophies. Their different starting positions affect practice, the balance and emphasis of programme treatment targets and consideration of how psychological treatment is positioned within a broader rehabilitation agenda for the individual. For RNR the emphasis is on risk management and criminogenic need, with less weight offered to wider issues, whilst for the GLM the balance is shifted, not ignoring those elements strongly promoted in the RNR model but with a stronger emphasis on the wider recovery and rehabilitation and reintegration of the individual offender undertaking treatment, with the hope of ex-offenders developing meaningful and productive lives in time to come. Laws and Ward (2011: 11–12) identify the key differences between the RNR Model and the GLM as the extent to which they fit with desistance concepts. The RNR

Model is a rehabilitation framework constructed from empirical analysis of the effectiveness of various treatment programs and is strongly based on outcome data. The GLM is built around the concept of good lives and is concerned with providing offenders with the psychological and social capital to fashion ways of living that are personally endorsed and that result in offending. GLM looks beyond the treatment setting into the current and post release environments with an emphasis on offender agency.

Thus, RNR predicts that interventions based on its principles are more likely to result in risk reduction and lower recidivism rates compared to programmes that do not incorporate RNR principles. The GLM seeks to incorporate desistance concepts by focusing on identity construction and the social ecology of offending.

There has been, and remains, strong critique and debate between these two models, critiques that highlight the relative merits of both, and rejoinders from either side defending the emphasis each has taken and why. Some flavour of this ongoing debate was offered in Chapter 6 on theory and here we further develop the argument.

In response to critique from GLM proponents, Andrews and colleagues hold firm to the RNR model and uphold the primary focus on targeting criminogenic need. They strongly refute the suggestion by proponents of GLM that the RNR model fails to attend to the well-being of offenders, but argue that this should not be at the expense of attending to risk and criminogenic need. Andrews and colleagues further raise concerns with regard to the emphasis on the strengths-based approach of the GLM as potentially giving rise to the possibility of criminogenic need and risk being overlooked. Andrews and Dowden (2007) express concern at what they see as the GLM focus on wider domains of human needs, when it remains a difficult task to provide effective treatments for addressing criminogenic need alone. They argue that criminal justice services should retain their focus on addressing the public safety imperative through attention to the offender's criminogenic need as primary and suggest that concern with the wider needs of offenders in terms of what the GLM calls 'primary goods' (e.g. meaningful employment, leisure, relationships) should be addressed by other services, such as mental health service and education for example. In response, the proponents of GLM argue that forensic psychologists should not consider themselves to be the primary treatment providers for offenders, and further impress upon forensic practitioners that as we engage with and work alongside offenders in treatment, we understand that offending is but one aspect of the person who is sitting with us. The GLM asks that we are mindful and respectful in how we look to motivate and harness hope in those who have committed offences, and impresses on us the need to use the widest possible strategies to assist that person begin the considerable challenge to change and move away from a criminal self to becoming a non-criminal pro-social member of society. Thus part of the treatment facilitator's role is to assist the individual offender to make use of and indeed promote wider opportunities, rather than to

return the offender to the context and ways of life in which they remain potentially marginalized, quickly demotivated and faced with limited choices, which
in turn may lead them to make the choice to return to old identities, as support
and resilience to develop new ones fail to arise or are withdrawn.

DESISTANCE RESEARCH

The evidence base for the process of desistance from crime comes from both
academic research and directly from narratives collected from 'desisters' and
those involved with working, managing, treating and living with 'desisters'.

Identified within the desistance literature are factors, both internal/psycho-
logical factors and external/social factors that may impact upon an individual's
desistance course. These factors include:

- getting older and concomitantly achieving increased levels of maturity;
- family and relationships – within this there appear to be a number of ways
  in which positive intimate relationships can impact upon desistance, for
  example having children may make a person think twice about the prospect
  of returning to prison;
- substance misuse;
- employment – meaningful and satisfying work;
- hope and motivation, on the part of the offender about their opportunity and
  ability to change;
- giving back and contributing to society;
- sense of belonging to a non-criminal social group;
- not assuming a criminal identity;
- having others encourage and believe in them as non-criminals.

In addition to these, the desistance literature provides evidence about the
process of desistance from crime and identifies a range of principles that are
useful in informing criminal justice practice and, within that, treatment
programmes. These are summarized by McNeill et al. (2012) as:

- an acknowledgement of the complexity and difficulty of the 'process' of
  desistance;
- the need to have bespoke plans to support change;
- a necessary focus on both building and sustaining motivation and hope
  (see also Farrall and Calverley, 2006);
- recognizing, affirming and developing a person's strengths;
- respecting and fostering agency (or self-determination);
- working with and through relationships (both personal and professional);
- developing social as well as human capital;
- recognizing and celebrating progress.

For desistance researchers, the issue is about more than criminal justice; rather, it requires greater engagement with communities, families, civil society and the state itself and all these parties are necessarily important for effective rehabilitation.

The study of desistance makes much of the language that we use when working with those persons who have committed offences, and asks those of us in the field to support and promote the establishment of new identities, for example from today's young offender to tomorrow's champion footballer. Recently there has been a media storm over the case of 25-year-old Ched Evans, a professional footballer who was convicted of rape and subsequently served a prison sentence. On his release, Evans, who has continued to protest his innocence, was offered a two-year contract with his former football club. The public outcry and media coverage relating to his release and his offer was considerable. *The Times* newspaper printed a substantial article in October 2014 relating how the well-known female patron of the football club threatened to resign her position should Evans return to the club. There was further reporting of TV personalities, who had supported Evans' right to return to life as a footballer being subjected to unpleasant abuse via the internet and there was widespread criticism of their support publicly. It is, in our view, a concern that it is the voice of celebrities that are heard and reported upon in such matters and that the reasoned voices of policy makers or, dare we suggest, forensic psychologists, are not considered to offer balanced comment upon such matters. The *Times* article also cited a poll by YouGov on 16th and 17th October which found that only 27% of those under the age of 25, and 39% of those aged between 26 and 60, thought Evans should be allowed to return to his former career as a footballer. How will this type of media coverage and public outcry encourage offenders and those involved in this work to maintain hope and a belief in the potential to establish an identity other than that of an offender? The use of labels that are damaging and static should be carefully considered in the language we use in discussing rehabilitation and those we are seeking to assist in desistance from crime.

WHAT HAPPENS WITHIN TREATMENT?

It is not possible within the scope of this chapter to review individual treatment programmes currently available, but we suggest that readers may wish to look at chapters in the handbook edited by Brown and Campbell (2010) for discussions of details in relation to programmes to address a variety of offence-specific behaviours currently available. However, in a more overarching way we hold to the view that therapy serves the function of potentially unlocking and promoting processes that provide the landscape for individual change (Roth and Fonagy, 2006).

Treatment itself is a process in which many complex aspects interact, including factors from the individual offender being offered treatment and also the dynamic that is introduced into this by external agencies (i.e. the treatment agent, treatment setting, family, friends, communities, and political and social agendas). Thus, evidence-based treatment programmes, such as those for sexual offenders in the UK, do not provide treatment to a homogeneous group of people, even if convicted of the same offence type. No two rapists, child sex offenders, or sexual murderers are the same. This requires treatment providers to use assessment for treatment to arrive at a bespoke formulation of that person's offending behaviours. The consequence of this understanding is that group work treatment programmes are providing treatment for a group of clients who will have different origins of their offending behaviour and differing maintenance factors, alongside varying levels of treatment readiness and motivation and different repertoires of personal resilience and strengths to approach the difficult and often daunting task of therapeutically engaging in change.

Alongside this sits the knowledge that no two therapists, or group facilitators are the same. We enter into the therapeutic domain with our own personal style, personality, attitudes, biases, beliefs, experience, motivation and hope/belief in the possibility of change for the person undergoing treatment. We are all also better, or worse, at remaining boundaried, maintaining programme integrity and we offer treatment in a variety of settings that will differ in the level of support for the programmes undertaken by those in treatment, and indeed the support we ourselves have available to us. All these things impact on the efficacy of treatment provision and outcomes for those attending these treatments.

It is perhaps not particularly in vogue to talk about vulnerability of offenders as they undertake treatment. If the emphasis of treatment is upon looking primarily at deficits without also encouraging, supporting and validating strengths and opportunities then we potentially do a disservice to offenders and more widely to society, as the ability to grasp change in such negative, fear-inducing and vulnerable states must certainly be reduced. In treatment we demand courage from our clients and particularly from those who have committed certain crimes (e.g. sex offenders) and who feel alienated from their families and communities. Courage is an act of bravery in the face of being afraid. It is human to feel fearful about major change in our lives and it is human and decent to offer support and respect for those who attempt to work toward this in the criminal justice system. As Plato said, 'courage is a kind of salvation'. As such, as mentioned earlier, those providing treatment for offenders should do so in the spirit of working *with* offenders and not *on* them (McCulloch, 2005; McNeill, 2006). It is our view that treatment is not something we do *to* someone, rather it is something we do *alongside* someone.

The notion of offender vulnerability is perhaps particularly highlighted when we consider, as mentioned in Chapter 8 of this text, there are a proportion of offenders who will themselves have been victims (Jennings et al., 2012; McGrath et al., 2011). It is not possible within this chapter to discuss at length the particular needs or the impact of victim experiences for this offender group having the dual experiences of victimization and offending behaviour. But it is vital to recognize, acknowledge and consider why this is important when we think about provision of psychological treatment for offenders for a variety of reasons, including the following.

1. In the assessment and the subsequent individual formulations of a person's offending behaviour, factors such as their own victim experiences may be highly salient in improving an understanding of the offender and the offending behaviour and give vital information about treatment need and direction as to how treatment should be offered for that person.

2. Once identified, there may of course be a need for this area to be specifically addressed with the individual offender in therapy, such work being aimed at working on the offender's personal narratives about victimization and the sequelae of these experiences.

3. The timing of this intervention may need to be thought about carefully in terms of the overall treatment pathway for that person.

4. More widely, victim experiences may also affect how that individual offender is willing, or indeed able, to engage in treatment directly addressing their offending behaviour; one might imagine that this might particularly be so when the focus of such work may turn to the impact of their offending on their victims, as in victim empathy work.

5. As practitioners in the field we may encounter strong resistance and defensiveness as barriers to full engagement as a consequence of prior experiences of victimization and it is important that we have an understanding of why that resistance may exist as this may allow us to sensitively work with it to a favourable conclusion.

Additional considerations arising from the challenges of working with an individual with dual experiences of being both victim and perpetrator relate to 'who' should offer such treatment with regard to an offender's victim experiences? Should it be the person/team that is to later provide treatment directed at the individual's offending behaviour? Indeed, in some circumstances there is no opportunity to offer therapy in relation to victim experiences of offenders. Further complicating matters is the knowledge that to undertake such therapeutic work in some secure settings (e.g. prisons) may not feel possible for the offender, as in such settings 'survival' on a daily basis requires of that individual a persona of invulnerability and there is a belief that the very environment they exist within does not provide the support and psychological, emotional and sometimes physical safety, in which to think about making oneself vulnerable in such a way. These are complex matters, and as said at the start of this paragraph, we do not have the luxury to discuss these weighty matters in depth here. However, forensic psychologists should be aware and hold this knowledge in mind when involved in the assessment and treatment of offenders, as an understanding of such things is critical to the provision of effective treatment for the individual.

And so the learning we can take from criminology tells us that desistance from crime is not an event, an 'either–or' scenario, but rather a 'process'. Offenders seldom just decide to quit a life of crime, in the same way as a person may decide to quit eating meat (Maruna, 2010). Indeed, the literature base on desistance conceives that cessation from crime is difficult and often involves several attempts before it is negotiated well. This process has elements common to those identified in the trans-theoretical model of the stages of change by Prochaska and DiClemente (1983), originating in the field of clinical psychology.

This model conceptualizes the process of change as being a fluid one, a process where a person can move both forward and backwards, and one that is open to being influenced by therapist qualities and interventions. This model identifies the stages of change as being Pre-Contemplation, Contemplation, Decision Making (preparation), Active Change, Maintenance. Notions of lapse/relapse and hopefully exit at some point from existing ways of being into new ways of being, new self-identities, are also held in mind in this model.

The desistance literature embraces this understanding as a process of moving away from crime, recognizing it not as a discrete event, but as an evolving sequence in which treatment, and therapist qualities, have a role to play. Those providing treatment and rehabilitation for offenders must therefore understand this process and also what stage the individual is at, at any given time within that process. The therapist should be helping to manage difficulties and setbacks constructively and with the knowledge that desistance is an individualized and subjective process, and that a one-size-fits-all model will not work (Weaver and McNeill, 2010). This way of working quite naturally lends itself then to the inclusion of the practice of Motivational Interviewing (MI) as a treatment modality and the 'spirit' of MI is clearly strongly aligned with the 'spirit' of the GLM and desistance work. Miller in reflecting on his work with people experiencing alcoholism, in Miller and Rollnick (2013: 8) makes explicit his learning that 'clients' openness versus defensiveness, change talk versus sustain talk, is very much the product of the therapeutic relationship. Resistance and motivation occur in an interpersonal context'. We, the present authors, believe that it is useful to hear the wisdom of Miller's considerable experience in working with those who have high levels of ambivalence and resistance in the face of change. Those working with offenders will experience resistance, defensiveness and ambivalence as the fear of change is confronted and it is helpful to understand this and use the knowledge and skills established in the work of those such as Miller to assist in the work we undertake.

Maruna (2010) sees a value in offender treatment programmes that address internal/psychological factors to the offender which can assist with desistance by generating a 'blueprint' for change. Maruna also recognizes the therapeutic relationship as a vehicle for addressing issues of motivation, hope and modelling of pro-social and appropriate relationships.

WHAT SHOULD THE LENGTH OF TREATMENT FOLLOW-UP BE?

There are those who argue that extended follow-up should be the norm. However, offending behaviour is notoriously difficult to measure, and because official records are not necessaily reliable, follow-up periods have tended to be rather short term (two years or less) and long-term follow-up studies have not occurred routinely There are many questions around the idea of extended follow-up. Perhaps one of the most difficult to address is the fact that as time elapses between treatment and offending, and as ex-offenders reintegrate into their communities and re-establish their lives, it becomes very difficult to attribute change as a direct result of the original treatment. There are many factors available in the lives of the individual that might impact upon their desistance from re-engaging in a criminal lifestyle, for example, employment (whether in a job or remaining unemployed), family (whether stable and supportive or chaotic), health (whether well or ill), to name but a few. At some point does follow-up data become meaningless because we simply cannot disaggregate cause and effect? Additionally if we take only recidivism as our measure of treatment success, what of those people who have committed undetected offences, of which there may be many, or those whose offending is less serious than their original index offence that led them into treatment? How can we possibly hope to capture and record this information? It would appear that we do not have a sophisticated system that allows for these vagaries at present, nor perhaps more depressingly the demand to understand such issues from policy makers and purse holders. (see Brown et al., 2014: 247–50 for some further discussion of these points.)

WHAT IS THE VALUE OF PEER MENTOR SCHEMES?

The advent of peer mentoring is fashionable in a host of different services currently, from mental health, substance misuse and criminal justice services. The idea is of peer mentors acting as 'recovery champions' alongside holders of expert knowledge via lived experience and thereby able to offer visible examples of successful recovery. In doing so they can instil hope and inspire those who have yet to undertake the process of desistance and change.

Positive examples of peer mentoring within the criminal justice field can be found but it would appear that there remain significant barriers to acceptance of peer mentoring in forensic settings. These barriers perhaps further highlight the 'broader tension between punitive and rehabilitative ideals' (Buck, 2014). In her PhD research Buck discovered that the narratives of peer mentors highlighted the difficulties they experienced in making the transition from an identity as past offender to current pro-social citizenship, in the perceptions of others. Succinctly put, these reformed peer mentors continued to find themselves constrained by their 'risk-defined past' rather than accepted by their 'self-defined present'. Buck's findings begs the question of how we can support peer mentoring schemes positively and also poses the conundrum of how we might address the apparent rupture that appears to exist between the ideal of wider rehabilitation and what the reality is of those living it. The ideal of welcoming reformed members of society, as opposed to limited acceptance or ongoing marginalization, must be addressed at every level if true rehabilitation is to have the chance to flourish and within that for those with past criminal histories to find a useful and fulfilling role within society and local communities.

As yet, the narratives of criminal justice peer mentors suggest that we have a considerable way to go to achieve this aim, a finding that is exemplified in the case of Ched Evans cited earlier in this chapter.

WHAT ARE THE PROBLEMS OF TREATING OFFENDERS WITH CO-MORBIDITY?

Evidence tells us that there is a significant percentage of offenders in secure settings presenting with dual or multiple diagnoses. That is, within prison populations we recognize that a significant proportion of the population will have both substance misuse difficulties alongside mental health difficulties and probably personality disorders of some description. This reality results in greater complexity of treatment needs and, unless well managed, may in turn lead to poorer outcomes. Y.S.'s experience of working alongside this population is that clinical complexity is the norm and not the exception, a finding already touched upon in Chapter 10 of this book in quoting the finding that 90% of prisoners had one or more psychiatric/substance misuse disorders (Bradley Report, 2009). Whilst there have been some attempts to establish a limited number of evidence-based, manualized treatment programmes in the field of offender treatment programmes, for example the Sex Offender Treatment Programme Becoming New Me (adapted for those who have social or learning difficulties), these programmes are not going to be able to offer a service to the substantial number of those men and women presenting with complex needs and dual or multiple diagnosis issues.

WHAT IS THE ROLE OF THE FORENSIC PSYCHOLOGIST IN TREATMENT PROVISION?

The role of forensic psychologists in treatment settings may vary, depending on the treatment context. Generally, what we have seen is that the role of the forensic psychologist has evolved and developed over recent years. Whilst there is usually still involvement of trainee forensic psychologists in direct provision of treatment programmes, experienced and suitably qualified forensic practitioners are more likely to hold programme manager and treatment consultant roles in such programmes. Also, with this development has come the advent of other professionals being utilized as treatment facilitators; this might include prison or probation officers in delivery of treatment. The role of the forensic psychologist in this instance is to provide direct supervision and/or management to programme facilitators so as to ensure that programme integrity is maintained and that the prescribed treatment protocols are strongly adhered to. However, there are a number of concerns with this as briefly outlined below:

1. The concern that non-psychologists acting as programme facilitators may impact negatively upon quality of programme delivery and treatment efficacy (as discussed within this chapter).
2. Offenders who present with any significant level of complexity may not be allowed to access treatment programmes, as they are less likely to be

viewed as suitable candidates for treatment along with considerations of treatment readiness. This may mean that programme selection is in fact 'cherry-picking' good bets for treatment provision, especially to achieve performance targets (a situation potentially exacerbated by payment by results regimes). If this is the case then this will skew results and potentially lead to a false interpretation of overall programme effectiveness in the treatment of offenders.

3. Rigid adherence to heavily manualized treatment programmes constrains treatment providers and stifles creativity and flexibility in responding to the complexity of even the least complicated cases.

From treatment programmes in healthcare settings, Garfield (1994) found that 'therapy as planned' requires a coordination of effort between the therapist and client. Within this, Garfield suggested that the following factors were associated with greater positive outcomes: the person's

- capacity to think about their difficulties;
- readiness for treatment;
- motivation; and
- general adjustment.

All of the above are pertinent to the engagement and treatment of offenders and it requires treatment facilitators in forensic contexts to be mindful of these factors both in assessment and treatment, and to hold an awareness of barriers to treatment and treatment engagement and to maintain a watchful eye on the therapeutic alliance. This is a highly nuanced and skilled undertaking that is difficult to attend to fully when you are the direct programme facilitator. As a programme manager, overseeing provision of treatment programmes by staff from a range of disciplines and varying backgrounds is increasingly difficult and requires significant expertise and excellent supervisor qualities.

The instilling and holding of hope and belief in the possibility of change in people is critical. If those who provide treatment feel it is hopeless, even if this is not explicitly communicated, such an attitude will impact upon treatment outcome (Lambert, 1983). The lack of both hope and belief in change may well be internalized by the client and will correspondingly reduce their motivation to either consider or make changes (Snyder, 2000). Beech and Fordham (1997) found that instilling hope in sex offenders undergoing group treatment was linked to treatment change. To be hopeful, we need to believe in the programmes that we are delivering and also have a confidence in our ability to respond to issues as they arise in treatment, that are not prescribed in a manual. We require a comprehensive understanding of both the process of change and the theoretical underpinnings of these models as well as acknowledging the barriers faced by each individual as they confront this most daunting of tasks. Maintaining a good therapeutic alliance between therapist and client is critical to these considerations (Horvath, and Luborsky, 1993).

Andrews, Bonta and Wormith (2011) state that perhaps the single most valuable contribution the GLM has been able to offer clinicians who practise in the field is a model that is invigorating when they find themselves practising in negative or pessimistic environments, offering a 'safe, respectful, and honourable camp from which the clinician may operate'. However, Andrews et al. (2011) also report an impatience with what they see as the rather 'passive' approach to helping offenders lead pro-social lives offered by desistance proponents. As a clinician, Y.S. finds the GLM model sits more comfortably with her values and approach to offender assessment and treatment, i.e. the notion of individual formulations guiding personalized treatment planning being paramount and also an acknowledgement that the therapeutic relationship, as a vehicle for change in itself, is identified as critical alongside the spirit in which we enter into the therapeutic process of accompanying someone on the process of change. If the GLM can redress this balance and widen the focus of treatment to include these critical factors, that is to be applauded. However, many would see the GLM as offering far more than just this, and consider that this critique does not do justice to the wider implications of the model.

WHAT CAN THERAPEUTIC COMMUNITIES OFFER?

Of course, it is not only large-scale treatment programmes that are of value in treating offenders. There are other therapeutic approaches that offer opportunities for offenders to turn their lives around. One other such approach is that of therapeutic communities (TCs). These have held a long tradition in provision of services for offenders, in units such as Grendon Underwood and Dovegate (see Genders and Player, 1985, for an account of the former and Brown et al., 2014, for an account of the latter). Box 11.2 gives a first-hand account of a man who underwent treatment in a TC and his realization that he needed help. This is included because it illustrates the ideas of respect, hope and the process of change as he made a conscious decision to work for and adopt a pro-social, good life.

Box 11.2   Setanta O'Kelly's story

Mid-July 2006, I was arrested on a shoplifting charge which then involved getting questioned about a number of street robberies. I was remanded into HMP Brixton. To tell you the truth I was glad, as my life was a living hell. I remember just before I was arrested going into a police station and trying to hand myself in for breaching bail conditions that were set due to some shoplifting matter. I was meant to be signing on at this police station and had failed to do so. But it wasn't noticed or recorded so there was no warrant out for my arrest. Just my luck.

(Continued)

After that I just went off-key. I was up to all sorts. Shoplifting by day and street robberies by night. So really it was just a matter of time before I got nicked.

I spent a year in Brixton prison and saw it as a disbursal prison the average stay being 3-4 months. I became one of the longer-serving prisoners there and that meant I knew more or less the runnings of the prison and whatever wing I was on. I knew which screws were okay and which ones to keep away from. The same applied to prisoners. I had some really good mates there and I never ever had any bother.

I got sentenced to 5 years imprisonment in March 07 after a week's trial. I was a bit relieved as I thought I was going to get 7 years. I remember the night I got sentenced lying on my bunk and thinking to myself 'You are going to be 40 years of age any day now, you can't return home to Ireland, because you will be shot or at least sentenced to another 5-7 years. You have two daughters who don't know you. You have torn your family's hearts out and you have aged your Mum. You have nowhere to live, you have no money, you look like a junkie, you are a junkie and you are just starting a 5-year prison sentence. But still tonight you were running around the wing looking for a bit of gear. You owe out more or less all your canteen as well. Also the only friend you have in this country is the people in this prison. How sad is that to say you have no friends outside of these walls. How much more can you take before you realize that this will eventually kill you. Have you not had enough. It is not fun anymore. It's time to stop. Really it's time.'

So once again I had a realization that I need to stop using. But without really knowing it. I didn't know how to stop. I hadn't got a habit as such but I had something because as soon as I cleared my debts it wouldn't be long before I would be back to score again. So the cycle continued. I had the same cell-mate for about 10 months. He used to be pissed off when he realized I was stoned. I would go to NA [Narcotics Anonymous] and I would come back into my cell all motivated up and be saying 'That's it, I finished with the drugs.' My cell-mate would just ignore me, because he knew in a day or two I would be stoned again. He could always tell because I would be too hyper and the cell would be spotless.

But as fucked up as it was, I did notice that after I was at NA, I did manage to not use for a day or two. That struck something within me to realize that if I could sort of get something like that every day well then I could give myself a chance of maybe getting clean. I was really lucky as I had a CARAT [Counselling, Assessment, Referral, Advice and Throughcare] worker who sort of seemed to go out of her way with me. Or at least that's how it seemed. She was always honest with me and would constantly challenge me, as to whether I was using or not. She even used to get me tested and then tell me it was her who requested that I was tested. Anyway, the thing was we got on, and I was telling her my plans for my future as I was now sentenced and it wouldn't be too long before I was transferred to another prison so the best thing was for me to try and initiate my own transfer so at least I wouldn't be caught by surprise.

Most of my friends that were moving on were going to a prison called The Mount. I was told that they did some sort of RAPt [Rehabilitation for Addicted Prisoner Trust] course there and that if I wanted to go there I should put my name down, as there was a waiting list. I was telling my CARAT worker about this and I said something like I would be able to sort my head out if I go there as there is a RAPt course there that I could attend. She told me that if I was really serious about sorting my head out that she knew of a place down in Devon, at a prison called Channings Wood. They have a place there which is called a TC. She then went on to explain about the concept of a therapeutic community. I was intrigued as the idea of a peer-led community appealed to me and in a way it sounded a bit exciting. So I explained to my cell-mate what a TC was and he said that even though he would love me to be transferred to the same prison as him he felt I would not stay off the drugs there and I really need to give this TC a try.

Fortune et al. (2014) suggest that there is a 'natural fit' between the GLM and TCs as the similarity between them is that both highlight the importance of the quality of relationships, emphasize the centrality of capacity building and the necessity of taking a holistic view of the offenders' needs. Both too are infused and enthused by the belief that the environment has to be supportive of the development and practise of skills, that there has to be an emphasis on personal responsibility in achieving a positive offence-free life. Both TCs and the GLM value the criticality of providing offenders with the necessary skills that can be generalized to a wide range of environments (work, social, leisure) such that the offenders can successfully manage all aspects of their life after release.

CONCLUSION

It would seem that over the last couple of decades there have been useful developments in the field of effective rehabilitation after the pessimism of 'nothing works'. Within this there has been a debate about what the balance and priority goals should be for treatment of offenders. At the time of writing, the GLM is certainly gaining a substantial following, and is offering thought-provoking ideas from within the positive psychology and desistance fields as theoretical underpinnings for its wider approach to offender rehabilitation. The RNR model remains at this time in the ascendancy, not least because the bulk of research has evaluated this approach. Its proponents have acknowledged some of the insights of the GLM and have replied to critiques from the GLM proponents by emphasizing the broader base of RNR than a model purely focused on offender deficits, risk and criminogenic need (Wormith et al., 2012). The big batters on both sides continue to slog it out, but we detect a more productive engagement as Wormith and colleagues state that the interchange between the two camps should not descend into 'a we-said/they-said exchange, which serves to alienate readers who otherwise seek if not a resolution at least some guidance in developing their own research and practice' (Wormith et al., 2012: 111). In having a more constructive debate our attention is drawn to the importance of looking from as many angles as possible at the idea of positive rehabilitation and full reintegration of individuals who have committed crimes into full citizenship within their communities, and to the hopeful position of leading pro-social and fulfilling lives.

What is obvious as an observer to this ongoing debate is that there are presently models in the field of offender treatment and rehabilitation that have and continue to demonstrate that some things work for some offenders some of the time. However, there are a number of considerations that are potentially useful in relation to the two models. Firstly, in times of austerity, with services being commissioned in a highly competitive playing field, it is right that we continue as a profession to insist on the treatment programmes and rehabilitation approaches that are not just 'best buys' in terms of monetary value, but rather, we hold out for approaches that are theoretically and ethically sound, not with an eye on our purchasers, but with an attention to those entering the services we offer, and communities and society beyond that. Within this debate, we must ask ourselves the difficult question of whether we offer a strong enough voice as a challenge to policy-driven decisions around programme provision and must rightly confront adherence to certain approaches when we recognize they have an element of commercial interest and personal and professional investment.

On another note, we have to acknowledge that in providing services of offender treatment we have to make ourselves open to learning from other disciplines and to acknowledge that we offer but one part of the broader process of rehabilitation and reintegration for those who have histories of criminal behaviour. Laws and Ward (2011: 6) believe that treatment programmes should be considered as only one part of the desistance process for an individual offender, and 'not necessarily the most important one at that'. Maruna (2010) supports this position and states that just undertaking a treatment programme alone will not be enough to support desistance, but that consideration of critical external factors in desistance, as outlined above, is pivotal in rehabilitation success. If we fail to accept this and fail to promote to policy holders, commissioners and communities the reality of this then in all likelihood, no matter what efforts we put into psychologically informed treatment programmes, we will be setting those individuals up to fail, as they learn that new self-identities encouraged and formed in treatment go unrecognized in society and communities. It is taken as a truism that hope is essential to life. How would life be if there were no hope, to anticipate only rejection and failure? It is hard to bear the thought of disappointments when hopes are denied, and beyond that to think of the waste of a return to past identities, not through proactive choice from a number of options, but to return because the individual feels there is limited choice, or indeed no choice. Those who offer the GLM must be mindful of instilling hope in those offered treatment, and that this hope is not then dashed upon return to a community and society that rejects and continues to marginalize them. This would seem both to be cruel and may well increase a person's identification with criminal subgroups, making future engagement with treatment services more difficult in the face of the death of hopes, thus escalating potential risk.

A further note of caution is offered to the enthusiastic forensic psychologist eager to instil hope and provide help to establish a 'good life' for the person they are working alongside. Unexamined assumptions about what constitutes a good life may be unhelpful at best. To assume that a person we are working with will share our perception and therefore wish to obtain a 'good life' as described in the GLM may be naïve. We cannot impose our belief and ideal of a good life on another. A 'good life' is a social and moral construct. What a 'good life' looks like in our current culture and era may well be markedly different from what constituted a good life even 20 years ago, and also what it would look like in 20 years' time.

Not all law-abiding citizens manage to obtain the 'goods' as detailed by Ward and colleagues because it is a perplexing task to find a fulfilling and meaningful life at times in the often-challenging nature of daily living. What if, for that person, this is not the moment for them to make a decision to step into this change? What if they never choose this model of a good life? Well, that is their choice, and if they continue to make that choice then other areas of the criminal justice system, police, courts and secure services will necessarily deal with them in due course. What if they come from a different social class or culture whose values and aspirations are not shared by a mainstream white middle class? It is not wise, and actually is impossible, to impose change upon another. It is possible to sit with someone and assist them to consider, and bear witness to their decision about the potential to change and identify the steps required to do so. And also within this, to make explicit the costs of remaining in a criminal lifestyle. This is not a passive observation of the process, but an active, participative one on the part of the therapist, as they work with the individual in their choices to undertake this process, or not.

And finally, forensic psychology needs to be open to learning from literature and evidence in a broader context than forensic psychology alone. And so consideration of what is known about therapy and therapist characteristics and supervision models of reflective practice alongside theories of practice to do with Motivational Interviewing and stages of change should be considered as standard, learning that wider issues relating to recovery capital from the field of substance misuse are useful to consider. This, alongside work from positive psychology and research from the criminology field, further informs those involved in the design and development of programmes that to increase treatment efficacy attention to culture, context and other factors should also be addressed. The list is probably never ending, but it seems that to match the complexities of offender rehabilitation we must look more widely at what informs our practice in this arena.

RESOURCES

The edited collections recommended as further reading in Chapter 10 are also relevant for this chapter: Leam Craig, Theresa Gannon and Louise Dixon's *What Works in Offender Rehabilitation* (2013); Tony Beech, Leam Craig and Kevin Browne's *Assessment and Treatment of Sex Offenders* (2009); Clive Hollin's *Handbook of Offender Assessment and Treatment* (2001); and Caroline Logan and Lorraine Johnstone's *Managing Clinical Risk* (2012). Also, Sarah Brown (2005) has a very accessible account of sex offender treatment programmes. Laws and Ward's book *Desistance from Sexual Offending* (2011) articulates the philosophy and objectives of the Good Lives Model whilst Andrews, Bonta and Wormith present a spirited defence of RNR. Several chapters in the Sheldon, Davies and Howells' *Research in Practice for Forensic Practioners* (2011) illustrate evaluation methods used in treatment regimes.

Key journals

Aggression and Violent Behaviour

Clinical Psychology Review

Criminal Behaviour and Mental Health

International Journal of Forensic Mental Health

Journal of Substance Abuse Treatment

Personality and Individual Differences

12
REPORT WRITING

KEY CONCEPTS

This chapter seeks to outline some of the central tenets underpinning legislation and professional guidelines in the field of forensic report writing. It encourages forensic psychologists to remain invigorated by discussions around ethics and professional conduct and to increase their awareness of the personal attributes and biases that they inevitably bring to the process of report writing.

Knowledge concepts	Practice considerations
Confidentiality Consent Objectivity Professional versus personal dialectic	British Psychological Society (BPS) Feedback Health Care Professions Council (HCPC) Legislation and speciality guidance Language (verbal and written) Supervision and reflective practice Personal biases and decision making heuristics

Questions addressed

Why should we write reports?

Why do we need so much legislation and guidance in this area?

Why is the language we use to interview offenders and use in reports important?

Why should we share our reports with offenders?

How do others view/experience our reports?

What is the balance between the personal and professional dialectic?

INTRODUCTION

There is a plethora of guidance and textbooks with chapters on forensic report writing, or indeed some texts entirely devoted to the specific subject (Greenfield and Gottschalk, 2009). These texts and guidelines are essential for forensic psychologists to consider informing good practice and for continued professional development.

So, in what way will this chapter add to the already large body of work available on the subject of forensic report writing? Well, in writing this chapter Y.S. has spent time reflecting on her 20 years of practice as a forensic clinical psychologist and has thought about what she has learnt about report writing during that time. In considering this, she acknowledges that the 'nuts and bolts' of report writing are both well documented, and complex. Furthermore, to do well, forensic psychologists must be aware of all the critical documentation (e.g. the Mental Health Act 2007) and professional practice guidance (e.g. Health Care Professions Standards of Proficiency, 2009), and must keep up to date with such material. Forensic psychologists, both during training and when newly qualified, must be able to achieve a high standard of professional practice in this area, and this is of course entirely attainable once you know what you need to know and what is expected of you! In addition, Y.S. has also learnt over the years that, alongside developing an understanding of professional practice issues and requirements, and increasing her knowledge about offenders and offending behaviour, the complexity of working in this field appears greater all the time. At a personal level Y.S. has consequently always sought a level of good supervision, and more recently peer support and review, to ensure ongoing development of her practice. Alongside this is the fact that as you become a more experienced practitioner you will necessarily be required to widen the scope of the types of reports that you write, such as expert witness work and risk assessments, and there is often an expectation or requirement for the utilization of a broader range of psychometric tests, their sophisticated interpretation and inclusion of these findings, or your interpretation of these findings, into reports (see the discussion in Chapter 10 about now having to qualify in the use of psychometric testing). Such psychological information has to be communicated in an understandable way to the person who has commissioned the report, and indeed it must ultimately be understandable to the person about whom the report is written.

This chapter will explore and encourage a greater understanding of the complexity that also increases as you begin to appreciate and reflect upon the process of report writing in forensic settings in the wider sense. By this is meant an awareness of what we personally bring to the task of report writing and the inherent vulnerability that this brings, as well as consideration of the obligations we have to offenders in terms of their human rights in consenting to engage in the process of having a report written about them. In addition, there is the potential for the biases and the heuristics we discussed in Chapter 5, often not consciously, and an acknowledgement of the influence they may have upon how we go about decision making, opinion formation and hence the recommendations made, which are then presented in forensic psychology reports. This chapter considers how we might ensure that, through high-quality supervision, peer review and continuing professional development, we have the space to reflect on the issue of our own 'humanness' which may influence our dealings with offenders and in particular in this instance our report writing. Professor Graham Towl touched on this in his introduction to a co-edited book entitled *Forensic Psychology*. Towl states:

> It is not good enough merely to provide a scientifically accurate report in the forensic domain; there is an ethical responsibility for the psychologist to ensure that their report is also a just report. (2010:11a)

The practice of accurately and fairly, or as Towl describes it, 'justly', reporting in written form about an individual requires us therefore to be aware, and to address, what we bring at both a personal and professional level to these tasks. Not to do so is at best remiss and at worst unethical, and may in turn lead to us contravening not only professional guidance and legislation but more fundamentally an offender's human rights. This in turn reflects badly on the forensic psychologist at an individual level and potentially more widely upon the entire field of forensic psychology, bringing practice and practitioners into disrepute.

Before you get into the body of the chapter, we again invite you to do a short reflective exercise.

Box 12.1   Reflective exercise

Please consider the following brief hypothetical scenario and answer the questions as well as you can. Take the time to give the situation careful consideration.

You are going to see a medical doctor (your GP) about a serious health concern that will require surgery. She has written a report following her detailed examination, which also included the results of various tests for purposes of advising a surgeon on the next steps in the management of your care.

You ask to see the report.

Your GP tells you it is confidential, was meant only for the surgeon, who can be trusted to carry out any necessary procedures.

How would this make you feel?

You persist in your request.

(Continued)

The GP tells you the report is in technical language that you won't understand and she has not time to explain it to you.

How would you react to this?

You insist on seeing the report:

1. What would you want to see covered in the report?
2. How would you want the report to refer to you?
3. As the process of getting to see the report was difficult how might this influence

    a) your relationship with your GP?
    b) how you approach your future treatment?

Please hold in mind your responses in this exercise as you read the remainder of this chapter. Consider how you felt and what you imagined the impact of this scenario might have been for you as an individual.

WHY SHOULD WE WRITE REPORTS?

Well, at the most basic level the very immediate answer to this question is: because there is an increasing demand for report writing by forensic psychologists in an increasing range of arenas. This reflects the establishment of this field as providing a useful function to, amongst others, courts, prisons and mental health services. Currently the demand for the services of forensic psychologists shows little evidence of abating.

There is a wide span of topics that forensic psychologists are routinely asked to comment upon. This might include:

- offering an opinion on an individual's capacity to stand trial;
- assessing the risk they present to harming themselves or others;
- their mental state at time of offence;
- the role of other factors such as PTSD (post-traumatic stress disorder) or substance misuse;
- or providing a psychological autopsy, which is an assessment of a person's state of mind in the circumstances of an equivocal death.

Indeed, the wide-ranging nature of forensic psychologist reports is illustrated by the 1997 Office for National Statistics (ONS) *Survey on Psychiatric Morbidity among Prisoners* (published in 1998). This document outlines the prevalence of psychiatric problems among male and female, remand and sentenced prisoners, and thus the type of assessment and subsequent report a forensic psychologist may be tasked with undertaking. Key findings from this survey are documented in the Bradley Report (2009), a review of people with mental health problems or learning disabilities in the criminal justice system. This document reported that the ONS survey found:

- over 90% of prisoners had one or more of the five psychiatric disorders studied (psychosis, neurosis, personality disorder, hazardous drinking and drug dependence);
- remand prisoners had higher rates of mental disorder than sentenced prisoners; and
- rates of neurotic disorder in remand and sentenced prisoners were much higher in women than in men.

It is therefore no surprise that forensic psychologists are asked to offer an opinion, in written form, on a wide range of issues regarding offenders at each and every stage of the criminal justice process. Indeed, the source of requests for reports has expanded in recent times, with requests from defence solicitors, the Crown Prosecution Service, parole boards, mental health review tribunals and family courts, to name but a few.

It is important to understand the position of responsibility forensic psychologists assume in undertaking the provision of such reports. Reports have the ability to influence decisions about the disposal of an individual to prison, secure psychiatric provision or the community and to influence decisions regarding level of security, and indeed release from secure institutions. Forensic psychology reports may also impact upon what that individual is subsequently offered in terms of therapeutic intervention once they arrive at their destination, and at a more individual level may impact upon how the person who the report is written about is perceived by receiving establishments, and how that individual may feel about themselves and their future engagement in treatment following the experience of assessment and report writing. The powerful influence of a forensic psychologist's written report should not be underestimated and therefore is not a task to be undertaken without due regard to the above. It is also important to recognize that what we write today about an offender will remain in that person's record for all time, following that person as they progress, or not, through whichever system they find themselves within. Such reports also have the power to influence the offender's life more widely, and may continue to have an impact upon that person, and decision making in regard to them, beyond the moment of submitting the report and within the immediacy of the situation in which the report is undertaken.

With the above in mind, why should we write reports? There are a number of reasons why forensic psychologists should engage in report writing:

- It is *important* to record a psychological understanding of an individual and for this psychological information/evidence to be conveyed articulately and helpfully to those who are involved in decision making in relation to the individual being reported upon.

- A report serves a *useful* function, it is helpful in decision making regarding legal processes, disposal/detention and therapeutic opportunities offered, as well as at an individual level in engagement and increasing motivation of the individual being reported upon, and in some instances it is useful at a wider community/societal level.
- Report writing is *fascinating*. We are offered the privileged position of working in an intellectually interesting and complex field that has the ability to offer a constantly changing landscape.
- It is absolutely *necessary* because we have something to offer that is unique.

Greenfield and Gottschalk (2009) also cite as reasons for writing reports that it is 'beautiful' and 'fun'. The notion that forensic psychology as an area of work is 'fun' should not diminish the significant responsibility and weightiness of this task, which can, as outlined above, have a significant part to play in serious decisions with far-reaching consequences for individuals and society. However, Y.S. has on occasion experienced a deep sense of satisfaction on completion of a report that has been considered carefully by those in receipt of it, and from which positive outcomes have occurred. Of course, a report author's idea of a positive outcome in such an instance may be contrary to how others perceive that outcome.

WHY DO WE NEED SO MUCH LEGISLATION AND GUIDANCE IN THIS AREA?

Whilst we want this chapter to offer something a little different from other contributions on the same subject, we would not be serving the reader well if we did not provide a section on the legislative requirements. That there is a considerable amount of material available in the form of legislation and guidance serves to reinforce the 'complexity' of undertaking this task to a high standard and also underlines the responsibility we have when undertaking the role of report writer. As such we should perhaps not be surprised by the amount of literature available to provide a comprehensive framework for this task, and rather than feeling dismay at the amount we need to be aware of and to 'know', we should be grateful for its existence in offering guidance and thereby ensuring that we provide reports of a consistently high standard.

It is not possible to consider all of this material within one chapter, but it is important to mention a number of essential documents that should be read at source. Some of this documentation is specific to provision of reports, whilst other documents are more general and require a working knowledge of their contents. The documentation below is not offered in any particular order of priority or importance. In addition to legislation and guidance identified below, it is beholden on the forensic psychologist to make themselves aware of more general legislation, such as the Data Protection Act 1998, and also policies and procedures that are in place within the organizations/services in which the individual forensic psychologist practices.

PROFESSIONAL GUIDELINES

Both the British Psychological Society (BPS) in 2008 and 2009, and the Health and Care Professions Council (HCPC, previously HPC) in 2008, provide Codes of Ethics, Practice and Conduct for psychologists, and forensic psychologists should make themselves familiar with these specifications. It is neither necessary, nor possible, to outline in depth all the guidelines here, however, there are a number of aspects relating to forensic practice and forensic settings specifically that warrant greater exploration. These are issues covering ethics and standards of conduct relating in particular to confidentiality and consent. If these words result in sighs of boredom from prospective readers (rather like the weary announcements of stewards on airplanes requiring prospective travellers to heed the often-repeated safety instructions), we ask you to read the following paragraphs with fresh eyes, and that you remain open to hearing the intricacies that exist with regard to consent and confidentiality in a forensic setting.

CONFIDENTIALITY

We quite clearly have a duty to inform offenders when report writing with regard to the purpose of the report, who the report will be shared with and from where the report is requested. In addition to this, we should be frank about the limitations of confidentiality to be offered and the grounds upon which confidentiality may be breached (see discussion of Tarasoff in Chapter 7 for additional details). There is clear direction for this in guidance available above for practitioners. The standard line presented is that as forensic psychologists we must ensure we alert the offender at the outset that there is limited confidentiality and the grounds upon which this confidentiality will necessarily be broken.

In other texts there is an emphasis on issues such as duty to warn and conflict of interests in working with an offender population in relation to confidentiality, and these areas are of course important and rightfully highlighted.

In addition to the above, how often have you heard forensic psychologists saying that their client is not 'only' the person sat in the room with them, and that they also consider wider society to be their client, a notion that is influenced by the social and political context in which we practise. As this chapter is being written there is a storm brewing in the social and political world about the Human Rights Act, and the UK's adherence to judgments of the European Court of Human Rights (Grayling, 2014). There have previously been strong reactions to the use of human rights legislation in relation to offenders. In 2011 a Supreme Court ruling forced the UK government to reluctantly draw up new rules in relation to serious sex offenders and the Sex Offenders Register. The headlines around this read 'Human rights victory for rapists and paedophiles', and resulted in outspoken commentary from MPs. Indeed, Priti Patel, a Conservative MP at that time, said that the court ruling lent weight to the need for the Human Rights Act (HRA) to be reformed and stated 'Sex offenders are vile criminals. Why are these people allowed to use human rights laws to protect themselves? What about their victims?' There have been resulting calls to amend the HRA, the latest (Grayling, 2014) being current Lord Chancellor Chris Grayling's paper, in which he considers it to be unfit for purpose in the current world climate. As you hold that thought in mind, we ask you to consider the ideas presented by Ward (2011). Ward considers the implications of rights-based thinking in assessments, with results often reflected in subsequent report writing. The HRA includes guidance on the rights of offenders and indicates that it is beholden of public authorities, which would include our work as forensic psychologists, to understand that they have a clear 'obligation' to an offender's 'well-being'. The HRA demands of us that we enter into our work with an awareness that to be treated with dignity is a basic right of us all and that we must embrace the spirit of this. It may be that in assessment and report writing a forensic psychologist acknowledges the existence of conflicting interests, whereby on balance the rights of the offender are considered against those of the victim, or more widely of community/society, and that an outcome is achieved in which the interests of all concerned are fairly reached. It is sometimes difficult to satisfy these differing entitlements and decisions are made according to factors such as needs, or risks for example. This is not an uncommon dilemma for forensic psychologists to be confronted with, and in considering each case on an individual basis the forensic psychologist's role is to balance those competing demands, i.e. the rights of the individual offender and the wider interests of the community, to enable the report to represent the most just and fair outcome for all parties. This is perhaps particularly the case when completing risk assessment reports, in which the forensic psychologist's reports can carry significant sway.

We exist in what has been described as a risk-averse culture (Evershed, 2013) and as such we must be cognizant of this fact, and how we go about ensuring that we fairly reach our conclusions and report our findings, providing evidence that supports the recommendations in our reporting. Thus an awareness of the current generation of risk assessment tools, such as the HCR-20 and the evidence base supporting such tools is vitally important, alongside an understanding that risk assessment also has elements of personal and social construction that require attention if we are to complete report writing in a responsible manner. This should result in outcomes for offenders that are 'just'; this in turn would mean that an offender is dealt with to a degree that their punishment is no 'greater or more severe than is necessary', whilst ensuring that the rights of the community/society are not endangered in dealing with the offender in this way. As Ward so succinctly puts it:

> The balancing of offenders' entitlements and obligations with those of the rest of the community is a complex and subtle task and requires careful thought and due consideration. (2011: 110)

This article and another by Tony Ward (2008) are well worth reading in full as they present a detailed argument defining human rights and addresses the balance alluded to in the quotation and also the rights of victims discussed in Chapters 5 and 8.

CONSENT

Establishing true informed consent in forensic settings has been the subject of much discussion. Can an individual be said to be able to offer informed consent in the truest sense, when not to do so will undoubtedly be viewed negatively by some? In such instances the power imbalance inherent in the relationship between the psychologist and offender is played out overtly. It is critical that forensic psychologists establish with the offender the purpose of the report to be written and that they are frank about its use, who will have sight of it and the potential 'costs and benefits' for the person as a result of agreeing, or declining, to engage in this process. If an offender declines to engage it is very important that we try to make sense of why this has happened and that we clearly state our understanding of this in the report. We should take the time to offer as rich a description as possible as to the reason for the offender's refusal to participate in this task. White (1997) talks of 'thin' versus 'thick' descriptions to enhance our understanding of events, terms he took from the work of the cultural anthropologist Clifford Geertz (1973). Geertz described 'thin' descriptions as those that 'exclude the interpretations of those who are engaging in these actions'. It is the same for an offender declining to participate in an interview for a report: a 'thick' as opposed to a thin description may look something like this:

- 'XXX declined to take part in the interview for this report' (thin description).
- 'XXX declined to participate in the interview for this report. It is my understanding that the venue in which the interview was scheduled to take place was not ideal and resulted in XXX feeling anxious, and indeed fearful, at what other inmates might see or hear' (thick description).

The latter richer description adds a greater understanding surrounding the context of the assessment and to the resultant motive for the person declining to participate, such that their reason for doing so is seen more fully. In some instances we might be able to gain further insight from information held elsewhere, for example the offender may have suffered an assault from another prisoner. Box 12.2 gives an account offered by a man who found himself in this situation.

Box 12.2   An offender's experience of having a forensic psychologist's report written about him

This brief account is of an offender who was asked to be interviewed for a forensic psychology report for a court appearance. The offence was a violent one and the victim was a child. The account offered here is a historical one, but of interest to note is that the man was able to recall strongly the event and the feelings that accompanied it, despite this having taken place nearly 30 years ago.

(Continued)

The interview took place in a large and busy London remand prison, on a prison landing in a landing observation office, and so was little more than a set of four reinforced glass walls. The man in question recalls feeling acutely anxious about being in a 'glass box' and that his file was open on the desk throughout the interview. He recalled how worried he had felt about other inmates being able to read the details of the offence he had been charged with.

The man recalled how the female forensic psychologist spent less than 20 minutes with him in total for the purpose of the report.

Her whole demeanour, attitude and body language made me not trust her. She had my personal file open in front of her in an open office and I just wanted the interview over as I was worried that other prisoners could read it. I remember just feeling fear. That whole setting diminished me as a person. Why is privacy of less value in prison? I felt of less value or no value.

When I was being interviewed I wasn't going to be truthful because I didn't trust the person in front of me. Nobody ever wanted to get my trust. I've never met anyone that hasn't let me down. This was about survival for me. What was being asked of me in that situation was too hard, too difficult, and it was easier to reject.

I knew it was a complete waste of time. Why open up? The person assessing me for a report for court was giving me nothing to help with my survival. She should have been asking me, 'What's the best way to get out? Explain to me why you're here?' I had none of that.

It was a 20-minute interview for a court report. I knew that the key to my survival was being smarter than the others around me, including professionals. This was about my very survival, both physical and psychological.

I was released in the Court of Appeal 19 months after my conviction and all charges against me were quashed. I have almost no memory for the physical assaults experienced in prison, they were all forgettable. But the psychological burden and stress, well, I thought I had coped better with it. But I have had to put things away to cope. I don't like opening that box now. This is hard, doing this. The psychological scars have healed largely, I think, but I'm not sure.

Before this life event this person had been an international athlete. He has since gone on to run a successful business, has married and had two children who have both gone to university. On reflection about this event in his life he said, 'I had to put this image up in the interview, because that's how you survive.'

In keeping with the 'spirit' of the professional practice guidance offered here, Y.S. met with this man after transcribing what he had said in interview, to discuss with him if he still consented to its inclusion in this book and also if he wanted to amend or add anything further to the piece of written work. During this process the man was able to acknowledge that his initial claim that he had 'no memory' of the physical assaults perpetrated against him whilst a prisoner was in fact untrue. He said that in reality he could recall every one of them, but that he had not wanted to admit this in the earlier discussion, even to himself. He felt that it was only in being offered the opportunity to read back and discuss his account that he had been able to admit to this. This is an example of why we must share our written reports with the individual we are writing about. The power of seeing an account in written form, and the chance to then discuss it, can allow for greater understanding and improved engagement in the process.

There are clearly implications for an offender should they decline to participate in an assessment for the purpose of a report for a tribunal hearing or court for instance. However, how easy is it for an offender to refuse this task, as they too will be aware of these implications? The imbalance of power in such scenarios is significant and one we need to be constantly mindful of. The issue of truly informed consent in such instances, with offender populations, must be considered. Towl (2010c: 67) eloquently writes about the power relationships in the work of forensic psychologists with offenders and the importance of the individual responsibility and accountability we hold as practitioners when such a power imbalance exists. Towl acknowledges that the professional in such circumstances must be mindful not only of the organizational and professional guidelines to inform their work but also at a more personal level that they accept responsibility for their accountability for both their actions and inactions.

How might these issues impact how honest an individual is likely to be in disclosing information that they consider is not in their favour in the course of an interview for a report? The notion of malingering and deception by offenders is well recognized. Indeed, in a standard reference in the field, edited by Richard Rogers (2008), the clinical assessment of malingering and deception is thoroughly explored and best practice guidelines are offered to forensic psychologists to maximize the accuracy of their psychological evaluations. However, what is particularly important to recognize is that the desire to dissimulate in a psychotherapeutic encounter is not solely the domain of the offender. Indeed, Rogers introduces the book he edited by stating:

> Complete and accurate self-disclosure is a rarity in the uniquely supportive context of a psychotherapeutic relationship. The most involved clients may intentionally conceal and distort important data about themselves. (2008: 3)

We should perhaps not be surprised by this when offenders, where they perceive full disclosure may have significant negative consequences for them in terms of their future disposal or management, choose to be selective in their accounts. Indeed, on the contrary we might have other interpretations of over-disclosure in such instances, for example an interpretation of why someone might want to present in a particularly negative light might be worthy of consideration in such instances.

THE MENTAL HEALTH ACT (2007)

The Mental Health Act (MHA) provides significant guidance that a forensic psychologist should be conversant with. With regard to report writing in particular, it is clear about when a case may be made for non-disclosure of a report to an individual. And so, whilst it notes how reports written about an individual must under normal circumstances be disclosed, it adds that the exception to this arises if it is deemed that to do so would have an adverse impact upon that individual or that doing so might place a third party at increased risk. This is important information for a forensic psychologist to know, as it might arise in the course of their work whereupon they have a need to invoke this guidance for the well-being of the offender or a third party.

THE MENTAL CAPACITY ACT (2005)

It is vital for those in a position of assessing capacity to be fully informed of the Mental Capacity Act (MCA) and understand fully the definition of capacity as outlined in this important document. The following text is from that legislation, which states:

> A person should be considered unable to make a decision if he is unable to do any of the following steps in decision-making:
>
> * understand the information relevant to the decision;
> * retain that information;
> * use or weigh that information as part of the process of making the decision;
> * communicate his decision (whether by talking, sign language or other means).

The fact that a person is able to retain information relevant to a decision for a short period only does not prevent him from being regarded as able to make a decision.

ASSESSMENT OF CAPACITY IN ADULTS: INTERIM GUIDANCE FOR PSYCHOLOGISTS (BPS, 2006)

This document recognizes that the guidance is relevant to applied psychologists throughout the UK and furthermore that the demand for assessment of capacity, that is, to assess an individual's capacity to make legally significant decisions, is likely to increase demands upon psychologists in this area. This guidance acknowledges that 'the legal position in relation to decision making for adults who lack capacity is complex'. With this in mind, forensic psychologists need to make themselves aware of this documentation in relation to the area of capacity to stand trial (fitness to plead).

This guidance makes explicit the approaches to assessing capacity, and proposes that a functional approach is the preferred method. There is the understanding that it may at times be possible to impact upon a person's decision making capacity, for example by simplifying language used in court and so on. The guidance outlined at p. 62 give the five criteria for judging capacity to stand trial in England and Wales i.e.

- Ability to plead
- Ability to understand evidence
- Ability to understand the court proceedings
- Ability to instruct a lawyer
- Knowing that a juror can be challenged.

Various studies have considered reports and their inclusion of the above five criteria in terms of capacity to stand trial (Grubin, 1991; James et al., 2001; Mackay and Kearns, 2000). The findings of these studies demonstrate at best partial consideration of these criteria in the reports is given and James et al. found that some elements of the court process were easier to understand than others.

PSYCHOLOGISTS AS EXPERT WITNESSES: GUIDELINES AND PROCEDURE FOR ENGLAND AND WALES (BPS, 2010)

Expert witness reports require considerable experience and this area of work has its own set of guidance that underpins it. It is often said that to be a good expert witness one needs experience not only in report writing at this level, but also in court room skills. It is possible to be expert in one but not in the other. This particular area is not one that all forensic psychologists are comfortable in and the level of professional skill required is reflected in the fact that there are now available specific training courses/CPD events on expert witness work.

Documents worth consulting prior to submitting a report for the purpose of criminal proceedings are:

- Criminal Procedure and Investigations Act 1996 (CPIA)
- Criminal Justice Act 2003
- Revised Code of Practice
- CPS Guidance Booklet for Experts (May 2010)

Within this set of documentation is the regime set out by the CPIA and the Code in relation to disclosure of information. There is clear guidance about how to manage material that is generated during the assessment that is unused, and stipulates that whilst this material is unused it may still be relevant to the case and must be retained. It is clearly stipulated that it is not the forensic psychologist's decision as to whether material generated is relevant or not. It is therefore essential that when completing a report for court as a forensic psychologist that you take the following steps:

- Retain (everything, until otherwise instructed)
- Record (from the moment you receive your instruction)
- Reveal (you are required to reveal everything you have recorded).

There are three ways in which to reveal material to the prosecution. These are:

- within the report itself;
- statements; and
- the Index of Unused Material.

All the above aim to ensure that there is a fair system in relation to disclosure of unused material. The intention is to enhance the expert's credibility and increase confidence in their role within the prosecution process.

There are adverse consequences for non-compliance with guidance in disclosure. Such consequences may include a prosecution being halted or delayed, a conviction being found unsafe, your professional credibility being questioned, affecting future work in this area, and finally there could be potential action taken by your professional body in light of non-compliance leading to loss of accreditation and a potential for civil action by the accused against you.

Box 12.3   Suggested essential headings for inclusion in a court report

1. Cover page, to include:

   - *Date of report*
   - *Specialist field of psychologist*
   - *Report completed on instruction of whom*
   - *Subject matter*
   - *Psychologist name*
   - *Psychologist contact address and details*

2. Contents page
3. Introduction, to include:

   - *Details on report authors' qualifications and experience*
   - *Instruction details*

4. Issues to be addressed and Statement of Instructions
5. Methods of assessment, to include:

   - *Description of case material reviewed*
   - *Note of material requested and not forthcoming*

6. Background information
7. Psychological assessment, to include:

   - *Presentation of person during assessment*
   - *Psychometric tests undertaken*

8. Conclusion and opinion, to include:

- *Distinction between factual evidence pertaining to the case as opposed to opinion offered by the expert*

9. Statement of truth

- *I confirm that I have made clear which facts and matters referred to in this report are within my own knowledge and which are not. Those that are within my own knowledge I confirm to be true. The opinions I have expressed represent my true and complete professional opinions on the matters to which they refer.*

10. Declaration, which might be stated as follows:

- *I understand that my duty is to help the court to achieve the overriding objective by giving independent assistance by way of objective, unbiased opinion on matters within my expertise, both in preparing reports and giving oral evidence. I understand that this duty overrides any obligation to the party by whom I am engaged or the person who has paid or is liable to pay me. I confirm that I have complied with and will continue to comply with that duty.*

WHY IS THE LANGUAGE WE USE TO INTERVIEW OFFENDERS AND USE IN REPORTS IMPORTANT?

Using respectful language in the process of interviewing an offender for the purpose of the report is self-evident. Darwell (2006) reminds us that demonstrating respect for offenders, no matter what the nature of their offence, does not equate with us minimizing the offence, nor the harm perpetrated by that individual. The language we use, however, can demonstrate respectful engagement and this in turn is likely to promote greater collaboration, thus providing the forensic psychologist and the offender with the opportunity for a qualitatively better report.

Furthermore, the language used to report findings is critical to how our findings are received and acted upon. Language can alter how people see things and readers are referred to the idea mentioned earlier in this chapter on 'thin' as opposed to 'thick' or rather rich and meaningful descriptions. This does not mean that our reports need be very lengthy; indeed, those in receipt of them would rather they were not. What it does require of us is to be concise in our formulations and descriptions, but to make them meaningful about the person reported on. A further point with regard to language in reports is the need to be aware of the impact of the use of highly emotive language and how this can affect how those reading the report perceive what has been written. So, writing that it was 'a frenzied and senseless attack' is different from writing that 'the attack suggested a degree of loss of control, as a result of ...' (a rich description) on the part of the offender.

Kahneman (2011) points out that the brains of humans give priority to bad news, 'threats are privileged above opportunities'. What does this mean in the area of report writing? The brain responds quickly to graphic emotionally laden words, and negative terms, such as 'frenzied' and 'killing spree' attract our attention more rapidly than do happy words (e.g. love, flower). Paul Rozin, who specializes in the concept of disgust, concludes that the negative wins out over the positive in many ways and he describes a 'broad negativity dominance' as being present in humans. And so, when we write about hurtful and harmful events, using emotionally charged language, it has a greater impact and is more thoroughly processed than positive information. This is significant and we should be mindful of this in our report writing and be alert to terminology as a result of this knowledge.

The language we use in the report itself must of course be understandable to all those who will potentially read it. Therefore, we should try to avoid psychological jargon that is incomprehensible to others. It is also vital that when reporting psychometric test results we do so in a way that is meaningful and does not lead to potential confusion, or misinterpretation, and subsequently inappropriate action and/or decision making. A very good example of the influence exerted by how we might present our findings in reports is offered by Kahneman (2011). Kahneman talks about the overweighting of unlikely outcomes and how 'emotion and vividness influence fluency, availability and judgments of probability – and thus account for our excessive response to the few rare events that we do not ignore'. What this essentially tells us is that people, including forensic psychologists, overestimate the probability of unlikely events and that they overweight these unlikely events in their decisions. These two processes are distinct but involve the same psychological mechanisms, those of focused attention, confirmation bias and cognitive ease. This has implications for forensic psychologists as they often are requested to report on unlikely and rare events, for example, murder. In the experiment conducted by Kahneman, professionals were asked to evaluate if it was safe to discharge a patient, with a history of violence, from a psychiatric setting. The assessment offered was supposedly an expert's assessment of the patient's risk and the risk posed was reported in one of two ways, as demonstrated below:

> Patients similar to Mr Jones are estimated to have a 10% probability of committing an act of violence against others during the first several months after discharge.

> Or

> Of every 100 patients similar to Mr Jones, 10 are estimated to commit an act of violence against others during the first several months after discharge.

The findings from this study demonstrated that the professionals shown the frequency format were almost twice as likely to deny discharge than those shown the probability format, 41% as opposed to 21% in fact. The learning from this is that how we present our findings in reports can be significantly influential.

At this point it is important to remind ourselves that as expert witnesses and forensic psychologists providing reports to courts and tribunals, we should at all times be objective and act independently of whoever has instructed us to provide the report. As such, we need an increased awareness of the impact of how we report findings. Also, Kahneman highlights how obsessive concerns about the likelihood of a rare event (a situation we might imagine as we report on the risk of an individual charged with murder or violence and future risk), the weight this carries for us in terms of getting a risk assessment wrong and an offender being released and going on to commit further serious offences, all contribute to overweighting, something we are not immune to even when we know of its existence. Kahneman states, 'When it comes to rare probabilities, our mind is not designed to get things quite right.'

Villejoubert, Almond and Alison (2009) note that there is a large body of decision-making literature that examines the interpretation of probabilities expressed in words or numbers. Studies find that whilst people prefer to communicate uncertainty in words – for example probable, possible, unlikely – they actually prefer to receive the information numerically. Decision makers were more likely to think they would make accurate inferences if probability was expressed as a percentage. There is wide variation in the ways people interpret verbally expressed probability and over 282 different terms have been located that express different degrees of uncertainty. Villejoubert and colleagues also observe that context also affects interpretation of probability words. Thus a higher numeric probability was assigned to the statement 'it is likely to snow in Aspen Ski resort, USA next December' than to the statement 'it is likely to snow in Liverpool, UK next December'. Verbal qualifiers also affect the interpretation of an occurrence or non-occurrence. Thus an outcome 'is probable' or 'has a small chance of occurring' have what is termed positive directionality and our attention is focused on a possible occurrence. Alternatively terms such as 'doubtful' or 'not quite certain' focus our attention to a possible non-occurrence.

WHY SHOULD WE SHARE OUR REPORTS WITH THE OFFENDER?

It is good practice to share your report with the person it is written about. 'Sharing' a report is more than just letting the person read what you have written. Notwithstanding that a number of offenders might have literacy problems, it is important that there is an opportunity to consider the written report with the offender, as it provides a platform for further discussion and exploration. Although this is not always possible, as on occasion as forensic psychologists we see an offender for court and do not have the luxury of returning to feed back the findings and opinions that we have made as a result of the assessment. In such instances, we should anticipate that the offender may in all likelihood have sight of the report we have written at some point in the future and we should be confident that what we have written is an accurate reflection of our understanding of the individual and is written in a manner that will allow that person to take forward and learn from the report.

However, whenever possible, we should aim to disclose and discuss the report and its findings with the person we have written about, as it can prove a powerful tool through which to elicit greater understanding for the person assessed of their difficulties, resilience/strengths and implications for later intervention. Such a dialogue can help significantly with engagement of the individual in future work and sets the scene for a more positive collaboration with services involved in the person's care and detainment subsequently (Mann and Shingler, 2001). At a more practical level, it offers the opportunity to check our understanding of material offered by the offender during assessment and interview and to check its accuracy, and it also allows us to consider the offender's response to receiving the feedback. Finally, if this stage of the process is managed well, it will lead to the offender perhaps feeling more positively about engagement with future assessment and treatment if appropriate.

HOW DO OTHERS VIEW/EXPERIENCE OUR REPORTS?

And so, what do the recipients of forensic psychology reports think of our psychological formulations, recommendations and opinions offered in forensic psychology reports? In relation to expert witness reports there is the sense that mental health professionals, as expert witnesses, are becoming the subject of increasing criticism. In the adversarial system that exists in the criminal court system in England and Wales, in which opposing experts can often be found to reach different opinions and conclusions, psychologists and psychiatrists have been described as 'hired guns' representing the views favourable to the side that instructed them, despite that when undertaking the role of the expert witness it is the expert's place to offer an impartial and objective opinion, to the court. Otto (1989) found some support for the proposition that mental health professionals' testimony may vary depending on the side they were retained by. This has led to expert testimony being described as 'an embarrassment to the law of evidence' (McElhaney, 1992). Appelbaum (1997) provides this neat observation with regard to the need for objectivity on the part of the expert and their reports: 'Justice is the trumping virtue in the ethics of the Expert and attention to truth and objectivity are essential.' Evershed (2013: 86) in discussing report writing states that:

> Reports have to inform, explain and frequently persuade a variety of different readers and assist them to reach a well-researched and well-argued conclusion.

The forensic psychologist's role in report writing should indeed inform and explain psychological evidence to different readers. However, we should not be seeking to 'persuade' report readers about the evidence presented in the body of the report. The ethics of that are unsound and go against Appelbaum's objectivity principle; persuasion is not in our remit as a professional. It is an example of the necessity of understanding the limits of our professional input and not stepping beyond. It is a fact that what we write may well influence the reader toward a particular course of action, but to set out to do so is not our role and should not be the intention when we are writing reports on an individual.

WHAT IS THE BALANCE BETWEEN THE PERSONAL AND PROFESSIONAL DIALECTIC? (ON THE NATURE OF BEING HUMAN)

And so we come to the nub of it. How do we practise in a way that means that the reports we are providing are what we say they are? That is, objective, evidence-based writing that reflects fairly and justly the assessment of an individual, holding in mind his or her rights alongside those of the community/society. Is this indeed possible in light of the above? Consider the extract in Box 12.4 from Professor Gisli Gudjonsson's early career. This formative experience subsequently led him to develop a Suggestibility Scale which has been used to raise doubts about confession evidence and potential miscarriages of justice (Gudjonsson, 1997).

Box 12.4 Extract from Gisli Gudjonsson (2014): How I got started

My interest in false confessions commenced whilst serving as a detective with the Reykjavik Criminal Investigation Police in the 1970s. The year of 1975 was a turning point when I became aware of the risk of false confession. The case involved a man with a history of alcoholism and memory blackouts. After I had confronted him with the allegations against him he immediately accepted that he must have committed the crime even though he had no recollection of having done so. Unknown to both of us at the time, no crime had actually been committed. Whilst reflecting on the false confession I had unwittingly elicited, I became aware of how a gentle challenge can lead to a distrust of memory in a vulnerable person after genuine failure to recollect the material event and uncritical acceptance of false allegation.

The first thing that we must ensure is that we undertake specialist training, study and gain supervised experience to a standard that equips us with the necessary knowledge base and skills by which to undertake the type of assessment and report writing that we are being asked to provide. This clearly comes under the BPS and HCPC guidance on competence. Furthermore, we must ensure that we are competent not only in content, but in process, that is in the actual 'doing' of report writing. We must, as forensic psychologists, continue to inform ourselves of all necessary legislation and guidance that exists within the field in which we are practising. Beyond these factors, we have to be mindful of the critical areas relating to power imbalances, confidentiality and consent in working with an offender population and that we remain aware that whilst we have to take a wider view of 'who is the client', we have an ethical and legal responsibility to the individual whom we are writing a report about, underpinned by the Human Rights Act. As in the Gudjonsson example, defendants, suspects or offenders who are the subject of our reports are often vulnerable individuals; they may also be manipulative and untruthful.

The above may seem pretty self-evident. What this chapter has also sought to introduce is the idea that we as individuals offering a service as forensic psychologists need to be aware of the personal dialectic we introduce into our everyday work with our fellow human beings; how this is influenced by our own personal biases and those imposed upon us by our histories, society and political agendas. Towl states:

> self-reflection is an important element of informing ethical decision making, particularly in relation to a reflection upon one's own values and how they impact upon decision making. In short we need to periodically challenge our own ethical practice and its biases. (2010c: 68)

We suggest that rather than periodically challenging our own values and biases, this should be routinely considered as part of monthly supervision for each and every one of us involved in this work.

Mahzarin Banaji (2007), in a foreword to a book entitled *Beyond Common Sense: Psychological Science in the Courtroom*, comments 'modern psychology provides at least two clear messages: our minds and behaviour are fallible; our minds and behaviour are malleable'. This important message reminds us to understand the care we must take in our role as a forensic psychologist, particularly as we are providing assessments and reports that have significant implications for outcomes for individuals and/or wider society. It would be naïve for a forensic psychologist to consider that their report is an entirely objective document, unaffected by their own biases in direction, interpretation and opinion. To this end, it is critical that we acknowledge this in our practice and use the platform of good supervision to continually reflect on how we approach the work we are engaged in, to consider our personal biases and potential errors in our thinking. This requires a considerable investment of effort and an acceptance of the courage to be open, potentially experiencing discomfort as we make ourselves vulnerable in our attempt to improve our practice, decision making and opinion formation. Reflective practice must quite literally be just that and perhaps should be included as a central tenet of forensic psychologist training courses. Kahneman (2011), considering the human nature of biases and thinking errors, offers the understanding that despite having a considerable understanding and insight into such matters his thinking has '[i]mproved only my ability to recognize situations in which errors are likely' and that 'I have made much more progress in recognizing the errors of others than my own.'

Supervision and peer review for the forensic psychologist are critical, alongside an openness to vulnerability and a supervisor/peer who is adequately trained and also aware of what it means to be human in this type of work and of the distinction between the professional and personal dialectic.

With this in mind, we warn that there are known and established limits on the human ability for introspection, such limits being set by our own previous experience/history and by the nature of the situations we exist within for example. It is important that we acknowledge this and aim to embrace vulnerability in supervision, peer review and CPD events, with openness to being challenged in this forum. After all, this is the place for such challenges. Rather here than in the courtroom. It takes professional courage to be open to such challenge and in this arena this author (Y.S.) believes that forensic psychology could learn from the rigorous use of supervision within clinical psychology, where it is generally understood by trainees in the field that supervision requires one to be open and in doing so it brings about better practice alongside professional and personal growth. However, as Rogers (2008) notes, 'Most individuals, including mental health professionals, are selective about how much they share with others; their concealments may be either passive omissions or active distortions.' This way of engaging in our professional lives requires significant effort and courage, but in the present author's view, this effort makes for good professional practice and practitioners.

CONCLUSION

Forensic report writing is a skilful and nuanced task, supported by a robust framework of legislation and professional guidance. This chapter argues that it is essential for forensic psychologists to keep updated on fundamental literature and guidance in the area of report writing, as well as developing a thorough understanding of the moral and ethical obligation, enshrined in law under the Human Rights Act 1998, to treat those we are writing reports about with respect and dignity, with the aim of providing a fair and just report, whilst balancing these factors alongside the rights of the wider community. This is neither at the expense of the victim nor the offender whose behaviour has resulted in them being in their current position. This chapter also sought to make forensic psychologists aware of the use of language in report writing and the significant impact our use of words can have upon how our work is received. Also, the role of supervision to reflect on what we personally bring to our work, the biases we may need to be vigilant for, and the decision making heuristics we personally use alongside an awareness of the impact of social and political agendas that prevail and influence the climate in which we practise at both a professional and personal level was discussed. We seek in this chapter to encourage forensic psychologists, of all levels of experience, to be open to challenges within the framework of supervision. This will require on occasion the need to embrace vulnerability as our practice comes under scrutiny, including what biases we personally bring to the process. This may, potentially, require a relinquishing of old views/understandings and ways of doing things, if they are found to be no longer useful or appropriate. This is a challenge for all forensic psychologists, and perhaps particularly so for the more experienced practitioner as we can all become 'stuck' in old ways of being and doing and change is at times uncomfortable and difficult. Yet embrace it we must if we wish to provide a high standard of professional practice in the area of forensic report writing.

RESOURCES

The Academy of Experts (TAE) has a website with a number of helpful resources, including details of the declarations required for expert reports. See www.academyofexperts.org.

Gumpert, Linblad and Grann's (2009) article on the quality of written expert testimony in alleged child sexual abuse is a useful read.

Goldfinger and Pomerantze's (2014) book on psychological assessment and report writing is a comprehensive treatise and well worth consulting.

Key journals

Civil Justice Quarterly

Expert Evidence

Journal of Professional Psychology Research and Practice

Psychiatry Psychology and Law

13

RE-IMAGINING FORENSIC PSYCHOLOGY

KEY CONCEPTS

This chapter provides an overview of the status of forensic psychology. We adopt the utility test to assess the assets and debits of forensic psychology's achievements. We also discuss future prospects by drawing together ideas from public criminology, critical and political psychology.

Knowledge concepts	Practical considerations
Cognitive revolution	Behavioural science and law project
Dystopia	Civic virtues
Procedural justice	Discipline raider
Social justice	Rendezvous discipline
Suggestibility	Special measures
	User as expert

We hope the discussion we present in this chapter stimulates a conversation challenging the future development of forensic psychology – what it is about, what it is for and where it is going. We also hope the ideas allow you space to reflect on the kind of forensic psychologist you would like to be and any research you might like to do.

Questions addressed

How can we assess the status of forensic psychology?

What is the status of forensic psychology as a discipline?

What is the utility of forensic psychology?

What are the future prospects for forensic psychology?

INTRODUCTION

Stanley Cohen wrote a remarkable book called *States of Denial* (Cohen, 2001), in which he analyses how people respond to injustice. The question he posed in the preface to the book (p. x) is this: 'What do we do with our knowledge about the suffering of others, and what does this knowledge do to us?' As human beings we feel, we mind, hopefully we care, we are elated, disappointed, irritated, disgusted and we celebrate successes and are presented with setbacks with which we cope to a greater or lesser extent. These human responses are as much the experiences of those who offend as they are ours. Rather than being emotionless scientists who eliminate such knowledge when they step into work, we suggest being aware of our own histories, what we bring to our professional roles and how we reflect in order to connect to our various clients, are important considerations when engaging in humane and 'just' forensic psychology research and practice.

We have sought in this book to persuade our forensic psychology colleagues and new students to engage in some wider reading than possibly the more limited recommended sources on typical university reading lists. We wanted to get beyond the 'what is assessed is read' mindset. To that end we have drawn on the writings and thinking of criminologists and also tapped into less widely read areas of psychology, particularly political and critical psychology. The purpose has mainly been to expose ideas that would not normally surface in standard core forensic psychology texts. We did this because we think the realities of our contemporary world should feature in our professional lives. When we were writing this book, the Ebola crisis was engulfing countries of Africa. There is continuing turmoil in the Middle East. In recent years radical protest has revolted against corporate greed and global policies that protect the wealthiest. Capitalism itself is under threat. As Michelle Fine rather eloquently puts it:

> The world today is plagued by growing and hardening inequalities gaps; the explicit protection of elite power; a psychic numbing to crisis; oppression and violence; an ideological valorization of individualism and freedom tithed to a cumulative sense of powerlessness. People are 'flooded' with 'science' and facts, much of it purchased by corporations and think tanks. Critical voices for democracy, independence, racial justice, solidarity movements, public radio television and public science are severely underfunded and thereby muted. (2012: 419)

What Fine is promoting in her essay is the case for critical psychology. Like political psychology, critical psychology presents a radical critique of the mainstream. Cromby and Willis (2013) suggest we in the UK are at a particularly interesting time to test our disciplinary boundaries and check our values. They say:

> The coalition government elected in 2010 is implementing privatization initiatives and spending cuts to health, education, welfare and benefits that are in the words of the Environment Minister Greg Barker, 'on a scale that Margaret Thatcher in the 1980s could only have dreamed of'. (2013: 934)

Later in their article (p. 947) they describe the threats being experienced by many, including psychologists, that spending cuts and privatization are imposing. For academics, careers and futures are less secure (a position as we have shown in Chapter 4 that also besets CJS practitioners). In the present market economy, all must compete as never before, becoming leaner, meaner, more focused, more ruthless and more determined. Additional administrative and bureaucratic demands require us to work harder, faster, longer with fewer resources and less reward. Students and clients are more demanding, our performance is monitored and the public's satisfaction with services is measured. We have stretch targets that we have to hit, deadlines to meet and be paid by results.

Vera Baird, the current Police and Crime Commissioner for Northumbria, chairs the Women's Safety Commission and in a review published in December 2014 concluded that 31% of the funding to the domestic violence and sexual abuse sector was cut between 2010/11 and 2011/12 resulting in shortfalls in support and counselling as well as pressure on places for perpetrator violence programmes. Nearly half of those surviving domestic violence do not have the prescribed forms of evidence that would entitle them to access legal aid.

Fine (2012: 422) completes this rather dystopian picture with a view that suggests in a world dichotomized into 'the haves' and 'have nots', we (psychologists) are being funded to study how the latter cope, collapse or develop into threatening individuals that society has to be protected from. The danger of all of this, she fears, is that the disadvantaged and marginalized are scapegoated as 'other' and abandoned by the state, alienated from communities and punished. Scholarship is being constrained by our own institutions and political imperatives, which focus on individual failings and turn away from the complex messiness of people's lived realities. At worst, Fine argues:

> we are being recruited to help build a science that supports neo-liberalism, by naturalizing intergroup conflict, prejudice, and identity threat and not solidarity; that fetishes the autonomous individual or artificial group as if angling free from history and context; a science that privileges internal validity over external validity; a science easily deployed in applied settings to test single variable interventions, confirm the null hypotheses of 'no effect' and legitimize the decision to 'cut waste', maximize efficiency, weed out corruption and greed and 'improve' outcomes. (2012: 424)

She is especially critical of the methodological narrowing and 'triumphalism' of the randomized controlled trial as *the* preferred method to evaluate manualized programmes. As we showed earlier in Chapter 5 with the work of Raynor (2004, 2008), government can turn on the RCT evaluators if the results do not demonstrate success and perversely insist on evidence-based practice rather than practice-based evidence.

This may be giving the impression that we are yielding to a counsel of despair. We are not. But we do think that forensic psychology is potentially at a cross roads, with some critical choices to be made about its future development.

We indulge in a 'what if' hypothetical scenario: what if forensic psychology were to become more radical? By this we mean become involved more audibly in public debate, tackling inhumane policies and more actively by visibly engaging in social justice issues. That is the path we would like forensic psychology to take. First we pause to look at forensic psychology past and take stock on what it has achieved in the last several decades.

HOW CAN WE ASSESS THE STATUS OF FORENSIC PSYCHOLOGY?

When Loader and Sparks (2012) reviewed the current state of criminology, they took an approach that might helpfully be applied to chart the status of forensic psychology. They started with the late Stan Cohen's seminal analysis (Cohen, 1981) as a marker against which to assess progress. They used broad themes to explain the growth in criminology, such as the greater prominence given to crime by politicians; the presence of controversy; and the nature of disciplinary boundaries. Drawing on these, they took a critical look at a variety of political and socio-economic influences contributing to the shaping of their discipline and asked some key questions: what is criminology interested in, who consumes criminological research and to what effect? With reference to the situation in the UK, Loader and Sparks explained (2012: 4) that Cohen's review was published 'on the cusp of significant change'. Politically, Britons were entering the period of a huge shake up in the institutions of justice initiated by Margaret Thatcher's Conservative administration. Academically, then 'it was possible to read *everything* that was produced in the modest criminological literature that existed' (original emphasis). What followed was a closer attention given to crime within the political domain and an expansion in criminological activity within academia.

We have similarly seen an expansion in forensic psychology research, as well as in pedagogic and clinical activities. There are now numerous courses at masters levels in the UK and postgraduate training in the United States (Heilbrun and Brooks, 2010), Canada (Helmus et al., 2011) and Australia (Packer, 2008) has followed a similar pattern. Crighton and Towl (2008: 30) observed that funding for psychologists directly employed by public sector prisons in the UK rose from £12 million in 2000 to over £30 million by 2005. Notwithstanding this growth, by and large, those producing forensic psychology texts have paid little analytic attention to broader external factors that have contributed to those increasing numbers or influenced the kind of work done. Needs (2010b: 77), for example, suggests that it was the injection of funding into accredited rehabilitation programmes in prisons in the UK that was instrumental in the significant increase in prison-based forensic psychologists. He also argues that the managerialist emphasis on targets and auditing has actually shrunk the forensic psychologist's role in some respects. His reflection in Box 13.1 suggests he thinks forensic psychology is ready for its next iteration.

Box 13.1   Adrian Needs on developing forensic psychology

One of the things that attracted me to join the Prison Service in 1983 was that the area (no one really used the term 'forensic psychology' then) seemed under-developed. There was clearly scope for initiative and creativity in contributing to its further development as well as playing a part in helping people's lives. At the same time, the work could be extremely varied.

These were the days before CBT [cognitive behavioural therapy] was fully on, let alone dominating the map. This gave substantial freedom to draw upon other approaches; I found personal construct theory especially useful. Innovations included use of 'laddering' as a technique, for exploring elusive motivational aspects of offences and the 'Way Of Me Behaving And Thinking' (WOMBAT) framework for engaging prisoners in a collaborative process of personal change. Recently I was asked if the material I developed over 20 years ago on working with personality disorders could be re-issued. It might be objected that such work wasn't supported by large-scale studies and as such wasn't 'evidence-based'. On the other hand, in the case of problems in institutional behaviour and adjustment, whether it was effective or not tended to be evident rather quickly.

There was also a strong tradition of psychologists working as consultants at the organizational level. Sometimes this was very high profile and could mean that, as in the more clinical areas, the knowledge, practical experience and integration gained by psychologists working in prisons was often second to none. Versatility tended to be valued by senior managers. Although some staff specialized according to local demands there could be a synergistic, holistic quality to psychologists' work and, horror stories about certain individuals apart, there could be a great deal of trust from prisoners and staff alike.

The massive expansion in employment of psychology staff after I left (I don't think there was a connection!) was accompanied by a narrowing of roles around programmes and risk assessment. This was compounded by an attempt to recruit psychologists from other backgrounds to undertake work that previously had been performed by what were now identified as 'forensic' psychologists. The speed of expansion meant that some rapidly promoted individuals had little experience outside of this model of working, the operation of which was heavily influenced by the 'managerialist' ethos of the public sector. I hesitate to refer to all this as a Faustian pact but there have been adverse consequences as well as some benefits (Gannon and Ward, 2014). Trainees, in particular, were hit hard by the reduced opportunities for demonstrating Stage 2 competencies and this wasn't helped by the overly bureaucratic way that Stage 2 was administered and interpreted for several years after its implementation (see Needs, 2010a).

(Continued)

On a more personal note, I spent many years working with the extreme end of the prison population, sometimes in particularly challenging situations. (The more you did it, the more you were asked to do it.) I could accept exposure to violence and so forth as part of the job; I suppose I have tried to live up to notions of duty, integrity and compassion that some might see as rather old-fashioned. The problem is, whilst we cannot expect others to see things as we do, in any organizational context there are likely to be a few individuals, including those who might be expected to know better, who are prepared to act when it suits them as if they haven't even heard of such values. Professional ethics shouldn't just be a matter of what we do with clients or research participants. Looking back over a long and varied career, it is this that saddens and disturbs me most. Then again, it has given me insights into a range of areas, from organizational failures (Needs, 2010b) to my current work with military veterans that incorporates a reformulation of PTSD [post-traumatic stress disorder]. I also look back with great fondness on the many decent individuals who have a congruent outlook. For some reason these are often the people who have the keenest sense of humour!

There are also signs that the field of forensic psychology is set for another phase of development, characterized by reflection and drawing once again from innovation and a range of areas. In personal construct theory terms, as part of the 'creativity cycle' it is time to move once more from 'preemption' to 'circumspection'. As such, the scope for further development is as great as ever. Let's get contextual influences (and influencing contexts) right this time.

So using Loader and Sparks' (2012) template we can identify some key marker papers that can be used as a benchmark against which to judge progress of forensic psychology. Emeritus Professor Ron Blackburn provides us with a starting point that locates developments in the UK. His cogent review of forensic psychology (Blackburn, 1996) incidentally appeared in the first issue of *Legal and Criminological Psychology*, the BPS's specialist forensic psychology journal.

WHAT IS THE STATUS OF FORENSIC PSYCHOLOGY AS A DISCIPLINE?

In our discussion in Chapter 6 we drew attention to the German psychologist Wilhelm Wundt as an early exponent of scientific experimental psychology. A student of Wundt's, Hugo Münsterberg, travelled to the United States and, at the invitation of William James, set up Harvard University's psychological laboratory in 1892 (Wrightsman, 1999). Here he applied psychological laboratory-based knowledge to the real world of education and work as well as crime. So from its origins, forensic has been an applied psychology. Forensic shares with other areas of application – ideas from mainstream psychology, namely the biological

bases of behaviour, learning theories, cognitive concepts such as memory, attention and perception and information processing, developmental processes such
as attachment and maturation, and attitudes, attribution and group process and
their influence on decision making drawn from social psychology (Harrower,
1998–9). In addition, psychodynamic and humanist approaches are also drawn
upon in that these discuss needs and motivation as well as the uniqueness of an
individual's experiences (Bekerian and Levey, 2005).

There have been intellectually inspired changes from the mainstream that
have been influential in shaping forensic psychology. During the 1970s a discernible paradigm shift took place in social psychology (Backman, 1979).
Disillusioned with the experimental method and the topics looked at, there was
a revolution in thinking that located research in the 'real' world with the
requirement to ask the primary participants directly about their experiences
and behaviours. This spawned a movement towards qualitative methodologies
and notions of the active meaning maker 'participant' replacing notions of the
passive experimental 'subject'. With reference to law and psychology, Nagel
(1983: 17) proposed that as an 'outgrowth of social psychologists' self-reflection
on the failure of their discipline to advance social policy [which] was an
explicit rejection of the academically effete nature of much social psychology
curiosity … an attempt [was made] to become more action oriented.'

There was a discernible break with the experimental tradition. Focus shifted
to real-world settings with studies having greater ecological validity. Whilst
laboratory controls enable much groundwork to be done to understand the
processes involved, a field setting contains much greater complexity.

Another influence towards more qualitative methods was the increasing
acknowledgement of the recipient's perspective in their treatment. Thus the
idea of the 'user as expert' began to feature in evaluations whereby patients
and prisoners were asked to explain, in their own terms, their experiences of
an intervention (see, e.g., a study of Broadmoor patients by Tapp et al., 2013).

Another shift was as a consequence of 'the cognitive revolution' (Hollin, 2012).
This changed the focus from behavioural perspectives and distinguished between
the impersonal cognitive activities such as problem solving and the inter-personal,
that is, how we think about ourselves and others. A number of conceptual ideas
were incorporated into theories of crime, such as locus of control whereby people
believe their behaviour is entirely due to their own volition or they attribute it to
some external cause. Hollin notes concepts such as empathy and perspective taking abilities and moral reasoning were other aspects of social cognition that came
to be associated with criminal behaviour. We have also 'borrowed' the idea of
social information processing from mainstream cognitive psychology. This is a
model of stages whereby people are said to firstly encode and interpret social
cues, then establish goals in reference to their understanding of the information
processed. Thereafter they decide how to respond – often drawing on past experiences – consider possible alternatives, then they perform actions they think best
able to attain their goals. More sophisticated models were developed, as was the
research base, although as Hollin points out (p. 99), cognitive factors alone were
not, in and of themselves, going to offer a full explanation of offending.

As previously explained, the retreat from the 'nothing works' evaluation of interventions with offenders and the emergence of 'what works' (McGuire, 1995, 2013) and 'what helps' (Ward and Maruna, 2007) approaches saw the development of RNR (Risk–Need–Responsivity) and the GLM (Good Lives Model) (Wakeling and Travers, 2010). The GLM in particular was an advocate for a human rights perspective and seeks a value-driven, tailored, strength-based model of change.

Forensic psychology may be considered a 'rendezvous' subject (a term coined by David Downes (1998) to describe criminology) in that it is a field organized round, for the most part, the problems of crime and is at the intersection between psychology, law and criminology, as Figure 13.1 illustrates.

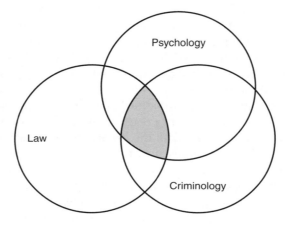

Figure 13.1   Intersection of psychology, law and criminology

We have described above gleanings from other areas of psychology and are happy to support the notion that forensic psychology is a 'raider,' in Loader and Sparks' (1998) use of the term, from both mainstream psychology and criminology, to great effect. In Box 13.2 Clive Hollin describes the waxing and waning of the relationship between psychology and criminology.

Box 13.2   Clive Hollin on the interface between psychology and criminology

Academics like nothing better than dividing the world into discrete disciplines in an attempt to bring order into our everyday lives. However, some topics irritatingly refuse to fall into line with academic niceties consequently leaving several disciplines laying claim to a particular area. This point is particularly true when it comes to crime, a topic where criminology and psychology (not to mention law and sociology among several others) have claimed academic pre-eminence. The claims and counter-claims to the academic ownership, as it were, of crime have passed through several phases.

Phase 1, 1879–1967: Spot the difference

If we take the academic discipline of psychology as beginning in 1879 when Wilhelm Wundt (1832–1920) established a psychological laboratory at Leipzig, then from that date two ground rules emerged: (1) psychology would be a science using experimental methods; (2) psychology's central concern would be the individual. Thus, the early psychological theories of criminal behaviour, such as William Sheldon's (1898–1977) constitutional theory, incorporated genetics, intelligence and psychological functioning. Similar topics also occupied the attention of the early forerunners of criminology, such as Cesare Lombroso (1835–1909) and Richard Dugdale (1841–1883), who emerged from a background of anthropology rather than laboratory experimentation.

Phase 2, 1967–mid 1980s: No common ground?

As psychology evolved, particularly with regard to social influences on the individual, so criminology became increasingly aligned with sociology. In 1973 the publication of *The New Criminology* by Ian Taylor, Paul Walton and Jock Young drew a stark divide between criminology and psychology. In a direct challenge to the theory of criminal behaviour expounded by the psychologist Hans Eysenck (1916–1990), the new criminology criticized psychology's emphasis on the individual rather than the social and its favouring a scientific, positivistic approach rather than political analysis. A line was drawn and there could be little or no point of contact between criminology and psychology. As psychology entered its next theoretical phase it did not follow criminology in turning outwards to look for social accounts for behaviour, rather it turned inwards to search for cognitive and biological explanations for human action. It becomes increasingly difficult to find any point of contact between psychology and criminology during this period.

Phase 3, 1990s to present day: Cordial relations?

In the 1990s several strands within American criminology returned to thinking about the individual offender, partly influenced by the notion of the 'reasoning criminal'. In the UK the 'what works' crime reduction initiative, heavily influenced by Canadian researchers such as Don Andrews and Paul Gendreau, and later the focus of a project aimed at reducing violent offending led by Joel Dvoskin on behalf of the American Psychology–Law Society, led to an increase

(Continued)

in evidence-based practice with offenders. This development resulted in several multidisciplinary collaborations between psychologists and criminologists in the design, implementation and evaluation of 'what works' programmes. This collaboration continues to bear fruit not only in an applied sense but also in publications and other forms of scholarship.

We are arguing for a rapprochement not with any old criminology but with 'public criminology' in order to offer forensic psychology a way to think about responding to contemporary socio-economic and political context. Turner (2013) proposes our present political and socio-economic circumstances represent a serious threat to truth and that one role for a public criminology is to fight for truth. By this she means opposing the interpretations of those with ideological axes to grind which may be supporting inhumane policies. Capital, for example, a proposal not to rescue illegal immigrants crossing to Europe from North Africa in rickety boats in order to deter this illicit trade. Turner proposes it is not enough to do research but that findings must be assertively promoted as an antidote to the apparent side-lining of inconvenient evidence by government (which we discussed in Chapter 5). The implication is that forensic psychologists get off the neutral observer fence and take sides in public debate so that principled positions are argued that may contribute to better policies, as did Don Andrews in his criticism of the Canadian Sentencing Commission (Andrews, 1990). This is not to argue for a naïve evangelism, as research and practice-based evidence cannot necessarily settle disputes, but at least articulate, alternative voices should be heard. But actually academics in particular are not very good at communicating with politicians, policy makers and the public (Rock, 2014). Paul Rock declares of criminology (but which can equally be applied to forensic psychology) that it is overshadowed by the 'titans' of the criminal justice system – the judiciary, the police and the Bar.

The interface between forensic psychology and law is complicated (Blackburn, 1996; Carson 2003; Haney, 1980). Haney proposed a three-way classification: *in, and* and *of* law. Blackburn's reading of these distinctions is that psychology *in* law denotes specific applications such as witness testimony reliability, competence of an accused or capacity of parents in child custody cases. Psychology *and* the law is the subject matter of psycho-legal studies. Psychology *of* the law concerns why some laws are obeyed and others are flouted or public attitudes towards punishment. Carson (2003) continues this discussion of the relationship between the two disciplines and argues sorting this out is key to the autonomy of the discipline of forensic psychology. This is also discussed on the other side of the Atlantic (Hess, 2006). He describes psychology *in* the law and gives the example of researching in prisons and psychology *by* the law, in other words where legal codification prescribes behaviour, for example the duty to warn a third party if a client presents a threat to their life or well-being (the Tarasoff judgment). Finally he talks about psychology *of* the law which is an examination of psycho-legal issues, and he cites by way of example mock jury studies to determine how jurors calculate the size of civil injury claims. So we see here some different interpretations and emphasis between the United States and the UK.

The question then to ask is whether there are sufficient degrees of separation to conclude that forensic psychology is an autonomous field of study. Ogloff and Finkelman (1999: 13) delineate differences between psychology and law as follows:

- psychology emphasizes creativity, and the law emphasizes conservatism, i.e. psychology looks for the novel whilst the law operates on the past through the notion of precedent of prior judgments;
- psychology is empirical and the law is authoritative, i.e. the former relies on the accretion of evidence through continual testing whilst the latter has a hierarchical system whereby a lower court is bound by the judgment of a higher court;
- psychology relies on experimentation while the law relies on the adversarial process, i.e. understanding is enlarged by objective investigation whereas in the adversarial context it is winning the case that establishes precedent;
- psychology is descriptive and the law is prescriptive, i.e. the law pronounces about what should happen whilst psychology attempts to describe what actually happens;
- law is idiographic and psychology is nomothetic, i.e. in legal cases the behaviour is specific to that case whereas psychology tries to develop generalizations;
- the law emphasizes certainty and psychology probability – i.e. in law the defendant is either guilty or not guilty (or the case is not proven in Scotland), psychological findings are often based on statistical probability, i.e. their occurrence is less likely attributable to chance (the law has particular difficulty in handling statistical probabilities);
- psychology is proactive and the law reactive – i.e. the law has to deal with what it is presented with whilst psychologists can chose what to study.

Mark Brown rehearses an argument suggesting that, at its heart, the difference between law and psychology arises from the theory of knowledge and what is potentially knowable and where lawyers and psychologists attempt to 'grapple with two views of what is apparently the same phenomenon' (Brown, 1997: 221). This is because 'the lawyer and the behavioural scientist have different backgrounds, disciplines, methods and goals' (Carson, 2003: 21). Carson with respect to psychology and law (like Hollin with respect to psychology and criminology) calls for 'a project' that crosses the disciplinary divide in the interest of 'more effective and efficient justice'. But what if we uncoupled ontologically and epistemologically from law? The legal arena is where we work, and where we do, of course, need to communicate effectively but our discipline, as shown above, is not a joint enterprise. As we outlined in Chapter 1, 'Legaland' and 'Mentaland' have different cultures, languages and goals (Eastman, 2000). The law, and more broadly the criminal justice system, presents us with 'rooms', for example the courtroom, the crime room and the treatment room, where we have a distinct role to look at things differently from the judiciary and criminal justice professionals (Bekerian and Levey, 2005).

WHAT IS THE UTILITY OF FORENSIC PSYCHOLOGY?

ASSETS

Blackburn (1996) makes a crucial point about the utility of forensic psychology. This permits us to ask the question, what use has it all been? Where, if at all, has forensic psychology made a difference, in Carson's terms, to the efficiency and effectiveness of justice and in answering Loader and Spark's query of criminology, how has the discipline contributed to better politics of crime and its regulation? To put this another way: has forensic psychology contributed to the public good? Do forensic psychologists possess civic virtues, for example participating in the creation of well-being, contributing to social justice, actively engaging in influencing policy?

In Quinsey's (2009) assessment, some areas of forensic psychology have made great strides whereas in others progress has been non-existent. In particular, he thinks advances in technology and statistical sophistication have greatly enhanced data collection and computation. Certainly, better measurement techniques have helped to move us from the pessimistic 'nothing works' position that there is little point to rehabilitative interventions, to a more encouraging 'what programmes work' (and how) position (McGuire, 2013). From the research reviewed in Craig, Dixon and Gannon (2013) it is evident that hundreds of prisoners have materially gained from programmes designed to improve their cognitive and emotional skills whilst meta analyses (e.g. Farrington and Welsh, 2003) show early intervention can have an impact on preventing delinquency.

In Chapter 5 we discussed the concept of new punitiveness. This has seen the drift towards harsher sentencing and longer periods of incarceration. Andrews and Bonta (2010) suggest that 'even in Canada', where rehabilitation has been part of sentencing and correctional policy, the physical conditions and confinement within prison has hardened. They note the strain that harsher sentencing has had on correctional budgets and the devaluing of psychological interventions in favour of 'get-tough' policies. Whilst they lay some of the ascendancy of get-tough policy on the Martinson review and the 'nothing works' movement, this was not to say that efforts in developing rehabilitation initiatives stopped. The Risk–Need–Responsivity approach was developed during the 1990s. Tony Ward and colleagues have been instrumental in developing a human rights perspective into interventions assessment, treatment and monitoring of offenders (Ward and Birgden, 2007). This has been one of the core strands in the development of the Good Lives Model as a strengths-based approach to rehabilitation (Ward and Maruna, 2007). As this approach gains currency, evaluations are demonstrating its promise (e.g. Gannon et al., 2012; Harkins et al., 2012). We think this is absolutely on the right track and resonates the critique of mainstream psychology offered by both critical and political psychologies.

Investigative interviewing has also made a significant contribution. Development of the cognitive interview and its modifications sensitizing it to children, the elderly and those with learning disabilities, has been a major achievement of forensic psychology (see meta-analysis by Memon et al., 2010).

In particular, forensic psychologists have looked at vulnerable suspects and defendants, as well as vulnerable witnesses (Bull, 2004; Gudjonsson, 2010). Gudjonsson (2010: 161) states that determining the credibility of victims, witnesses and suspects is 'one of the most challenging tasks facing the criminal justice system'. In particular, Gudjonsson (2003b) provides examples of forensic psychology expertise being brought to bear on miscarriages of justice, particularly through false confessions made by vulnerable suspects. The Gudjonsson Suggestibility Scale was first accepted in the Court of Appeal in the UK in 1991. This was on behalf of Engin Raghip, one of the 'Tottenham Three' who were indicted for the murder of Police Constable Colin Blakelock on the Broadwater Farm estate during disturbances in 1985. Analysis by Gudjonsson showed Mr Raghip suffered significant intellectual impairment, and was illiterate and abnormally suggestible. The Court accepted the psychological findings and the conviction was quashed. The use of Gudjonsson's Suggestibility Scale has since been more widely accepted in the US and Scandinavian courts.

The work of Ray Bull and colleagues has contributed to the development of special measures such as screens, live TV links, video recording of evidence in chief and intermediaries to help vulnerable witnesses in court (Bull, 2010). Bull also made a significant contribution to the original 2002 guidance on achieving best evidence ('ABE') for vulnerable and intimidated witnesses (Her Majesty's Government, 2002). An early memorandum had been based on work commissioned from Bull and, as he says, this original 1992 Memorandum (see Box 13.3) was probably a world's first and was largely informed by psychological evidence.

Box 13.3   Reflection by Ray Bull

My journey into forensic psychology 'began' when I was studying for my BSc in Psychology (with Mathematical Statistics and Pure Mathematics) at the University of Exeter, where the Psychology Department then shared a building with the Faculty of Law. Surprisingly, given my later interests in applying psychology to legal and policing settings, at that time this sharing had no apparent effect on me, even though some of the law students were good university friends of mine.

(Continued)

After six years at Exeter I moved to London to a lectureship in experimental psychology specializing in attention, perception, memory, and advanced design/ statistics. There I was approached by the Home Office enquiring whether I would provide an 'independent review' of the research literature on honest but mistaken eyewitness identifications of faces and persons. This I did, and when the review was completed I realized that I now had some chapters that could become part of a book and some sections that could be expanded into chapters. At this time I was sharing an office with Brian Clifford, who also lectured on cognitive psychology, and he agreed to join with me in writing it. The resulting proposal was rejected by two publishers, not on academic grounds but on 'likely low sales'! The book was eventually published in 1978 with the 'weak' title of *The Psychology of Person Identification*. Covering all the relevant literature turned out to be a major development in my career.

Later (in the 1980s) events in London, particularly the Brixton riots in 1981, led the Metropolitan Police to be criticized for the behaviour of junior patrol officers. Partly in response to this the London Police (the 'Met') decided to expand its recruit/probationer training to incorporate 'Human Awareness' (i.e. interpersonal skills, self-understanding and cultural awareness). This required considerable investment and the 'Met' decided to have the new train- ing independently evaluated. I was asked in 1981 to conduct this 12-month evaluation. The recommendations in my report were adopted and I was asked to continue this work for another four years. I was especially pleased that the outcome of this long project was a major change nationally in police training.

I moved in the late 1980s to take up the Headship of a Psychology Department in Glasgow, Scotland. At the instigation of Dr Rhona Flin we applied for and obtained a research grant from the Scottish Home and Health Department to conduct a large study of child witnesses testifying in criminal trials in Glasgow. Such complex and sensitive research had not been attempted before and its findings had a major impact on policy in the UK in terms of new legislation regarding how best to assist children present their testimony. At this time I was also asked by the Crown Office (in Scotland) to write a substantial guidance document for Scottish Law Officers on how to interview witnesses with 'mental handicaps' about what they had experienced, and this report too is said to have had a major effect on subsequent legislation in the UK and perhaps beyond.

In 1990 I moved back to England to develop a Psychology Department in Portsmouth. In 1992 the government in England and Wales brought in legisla- tion to allow video-recorded interviews with child witnesses conducted by police officers/social workers to act as their evidence in chief in criminal trials. At that time few other countries had yet done this and there was widespread concern about its effectiveness. Together with an academic lawyer, I was asked by the Home Office to write the 'first full working draft' of what became the *Memorandum of Good Practice on Video Recorded Interviews with Child*

Witnesses for Criminal Proceedings, which was published by Her Majesty's Stationery Office in 1992. This 'applied psychology' document had a lasting impact in a surprising variety of countries and its successor (the 'ABE' – see below) proved to be another milestone in my career.

In the mid-1990s I was fortunate enough to receive many invitations from UK police forces to assist them in improving the training of officers who interview witnesses, victims and suspects. As a result of this I decided to write a comprehensive book on this topic with a former PhD student, Becky Milne. The book, entitled *Investigative Interviewing: Psychology and Practice* (Milne and Bull, 1999) applied cognitive psychological research and theory to the practice of police interviewing, and is reputed to have influenced police interviewing in many countries. (A second edition is currently being written.)

At the turn of the millennium I was invited by the Home Office to be a member of the small team (led by Graham Davies whose work and wide influence I had for long admired) commissioned to write the substantial official document *Achieving Best Evidence: Guidance for Vulnerable and Intimidated Witnesses, Including Children* ('ABE') (Her Majesty's Government, 2002), in which I wrote the new large section on interviewing vulnerable adults.

DEBITS

Blackburn (1996) himself raised a number of concerns on the debit side, including the issue of court preparedness. He was critical of the courtroom-unfamiliar psychologist who 'does not understand the adversarial system or the role of the expert witness, is fearful, over-technical and muddled'. Concerns remain about the quality of some expert witnesses. Jane Ireland looked at assessments presented to family courts and concluded there was 'wide variability in report quality with evidence of unqualified experts being instructed to provide psychological opinion' (Ireland, 2012).

Blackburn similarly raised the spectre of the inadequacy of scientific rigor and identified three areas that particularly concerned him:

1. the claims of psychological offender profiling;
2. the limits of assessment instruments to address all the questions that the law may address to forensic expertise; and
3. the reliability and validity of predicting dangerousness.

Offender profiling, or behavioural investigative advice in a later reincarnation, still attracts considerable debate (Brown, 2015). As we detailed in Chapter 9, Almond, Alison and Porter (2007) looked at 47 offender profiling reports written in 2005, which were found to contain a total of 805 claims. Some 96% of the claims contained grounds for their claim but only 34% had any formal support or backing. In terms of confirmability, 70% of the claims were verifiable. However, only 43% were falsifiable, in that they could be objectively measured post conviction. Alison and Rainbow (2011: xv–xviii) also looked at the reputational damage caused by the controversy of offender profiling advice that led to the dismissal of the case against Colin Stagg for the murder of Rachel Nickell on the grounds of entrapment. (See Chapter 3 for further discussion of this case.)

With respect to his second concern, Blackburn was comfortable that some assessment, such as measuring the extent of a head injury, can satisfactorily be answered by established psychological tests. Other legal questions go beyond the power of the instrument, for example measures of intelligence and adjustment used to assess parenting capacity actually have little predictive validity. Some work has been accomplished since to establish better protocols in parental assessment. Puckering (2010), for example, describes the adoption of a framework in England and Wales for the assessment of children in need and their families, and in Scotland an integrated assessment framework and good practice dictates that the use of structured measurement instruments is accompanied by detailed observations. Coid et al. (2011), however, remain exercised about the reliability of structured risk assessments because there is a ceiling effect beyond which instruments are unlikely to improve and there is also a degree of 'shrinkage' of results when instruments are applied to populations on which they were not originally standardized. Another problem lies in the use of aggregate scores. Since few studies provide information on the predictive ability of individual items, it is possible that certain items within these instruments do not have predictive ability, and that bi-variate correlations with violence as an outcome are merely the result of a strong correlation with other items, which are truly predictive. They conclude:

> clinicians should be aware of the limitations and be critical when using either an actuarial, structured clinical risk assessment instrument, or a personality disorder assessment instrument, if the intention is to carry out a comprehensive assessment of risk on which to base subsequent risk management or treatment interventions. (2011: 16)

A related concern was expressed by Quinsey (2009). This has to do with the disposition of mentally ill offenders. He says the persistence of controversies about how the mentally ill criminal should be treated is 'astonishing'. He concluded:

> [B]eliefs concerning punishment, free will and criminal responsibility, all part of our common folk psychology pertaining to moral reasoning, are poorly mixed with the technological issues of promoting community safety and deterrence in the insanity defence. I do not mean the phrase 'folk psychology' in any pejorative sense – our evolved theory of mind

and its attendant notions of causal agency and blame are central to human sociality. The problem is that these slippery quasi-theoretical ideas are fatal to conceptual progress and prevent straightforward application of prediction and intervention technologies. (2009: 17)

We are pessimistic about possible technological fixes, in part because of the limitations Coid and colleagues point out and in part the febrile nature of the punitive–rehabilitative debate, which we pick through in Chapter 5.

Finally, in relation to the reliability and validity of predicting dangerousness, Blackburn (2000) discusses the disposal of the dangerous personality-disordered offender. He was concerned about trying to clearly demarcate a category of 'dangerous psychopaths' or 'severe personality disorders'. He thought this was regressive as it represented 'a disease entity approach' which is grossly over-simplified and at worst 'a demonic stereotype'. He was against the segregation of those designated DSPD. As a consequence of a political decision to detain and compulsorily treat those designated with DSPD, three high secure prisons and two secure hospitals began running DSPD programmes and did so for the next decade spending in the order of £500 million by 2009. In December 2010 the newly elected Conservative–Liberal Democrat Coalition issued a government Green Paper entitled 'Breaking the Cycle' (Ministry of Justice, 2010b) to reshape the DSPD programme, in the face of contradictory evidence as to effi-cacy of the intervention (O'Loughlin, 2014). By and large forensic psychologists were pretty invisible and mute in this debate.

We hope to have demonstrated in the preceding sections, that the story of forensic psychology is fashioned from a more complex seam of influences than simply the accumulation of a corpus of knowledge from within itself. There have been successful applications of forensic psychology, and 'raids' from mainstream psychology have been used to develop methodologically and widen our thinking about cognitive processes. In addition, other related social sciences such as criminology offer useful concepts and analyses.

WHAT ARE THE FUTURE PROSPECTS FOR FORENSIC PSYCHOLOGY?

We think there needs to be a clearer articulation of the elements that forensic psychology draws up to create a more coherent and integrated account of the discipline. Hence what is required is a more detailed mapping of what we can draw from core sub-disciplines of psychology and our applied sister disciplines illustrated in Figure 13.2. This would entail a project to delineate those ele-ments of these sub-disciplines that contribute to areas of concern of forensic psychologists.

Thereafter we might conceive of a matrix in which an integrated forensic psychology co-exists with aspects of public criminology within the context of legal settings, as illustrated in Figure 13.3.

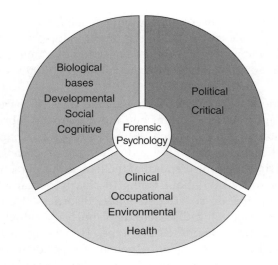

Figure 13.2 Areas that forensic psychology can draw upon

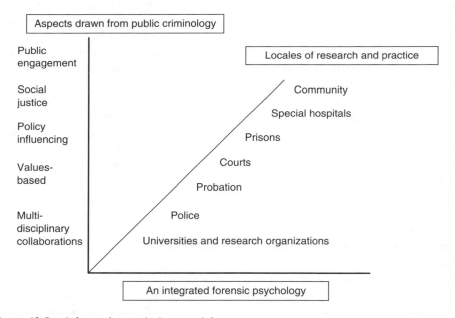

Figure 13.3 A forensic psychology matrix

The work of Jacqueline Wheatcroft and Sandra Walklate (Wheatcroft and Walklate, 2014) is an example of more radical forensic psychology. This presents analysis of an important social issue, false rape allegations, from a values perspective and is a collaboration between a psychologist and criminologist. They are also seeking to create greater public awareness and engage policy makers.

In terms of research methodologies, Howells et al. (2011) suggest an agenda for the future:

- effort should be directed at local initiatives and be conducted by research practitioners who are embedded in the services under scrutiny;
- the scientist practitioner model should be further developed so that the skill set should be integrated rather than bifurcated;
- research methods need to be located within a broader philosophical and theoretical base and not confined and restricted by positivist scepticism, in particular engagement with and development of mixed methods approaches;
- protecting the dignity and moral status of all research participants, particularly offenders, should be paramount;
- approaches to risk assessment should be further developed and integrated with risk management.

As for underdeveloped content knowledge, Chapter 5 draws attention to the lack of forensic psychological interest in why crime rates are dropping, whilst Chapter 8 implies that more can be done to understand the relationships of being both a victim and an offender. Howells et al. (2011) suggest there is potential for studying situational factors and also the impacts of environments, particularly regimes in custodial institutions. Justickis (2008) proposes forensic psychology should extend its areas of interest into every branch of law. She lists 20 distinct areas, such as environmental protection, intellectual property and commercial law, stating that legally regulated behaviour:

- involves a chain of psychological events involving perception, thinking, memory, emotion and motivation (if any link in the sequence fails this poses psychological questions to provide an answer);
- can affect an individual's person, i.e. involvement in the legal system is often highly stressful and potentially endangers psychological well-being;
- should endorse the legitimacy of the law and its institutions.

There is also scope for philosophical development and encouragement given to creating a 'vibrant theoretical research culture' (see Box 13.4). David Carson (2003: 21) suggested there should be a behavioural science and law 'project' which is grounded in the pursuit of justice with a value base. He argues whether as a researcher, teacher or practitioner, forensic psychologists can research, teach or practice in isolation of the broader context and ignore justice but that 'a disinterest in the promotion of justice will damage the disciplines and professions involved as much as a disinterest in methodology'. Carson believes the work achieved on restorative justice and therapeutic jurisprudence represents a start in such a project. As we described in Chapter 8, restorative justice expresses concerns about the interests of victims, witnesses and affected communities. Therapeutic jurisprudence 'is a perspective and a research agenda with law reform and the reform of practice as a principal objective' (King and Wexler, 2010: 126). Such a project chimes with the promotion of human rights as discussed above and there has been some coming together of these as a principled approach to interventions with prisoners (see, for example, Birgden and Perlin, 2009).

Anthony Beech and Tony Ward in Box 13.4 below explain why it is so critical to develop the theoretical basis that underpins our work.

Box 13.4   Anthony Beech and Tony Ward on why a theoretical basis is so important, both when conducting research and also underpinning interventions

There is nothing more practical than a good theory. (Lewin, 1952)

Theories are conceptual structures formulated to explain why certain phenomena exist and persist, and this usually involves a reference to underlying causes. However, a major problem in our field is that there is a widening gap between the current focus on risk assessment and management of offenders, and the accurate modelling of the causal processes generating offending and their associated problems. In our view, unless this gap is bridged, the future of theory development is murky and likely to ultimately channel the criminological psychology field into ill-informed practice and research dead ends.

Hence, a vibrant theoretical research culture is a necessary element of scientific and clinical success. We do not need to remind people that without this, this approach ultimately does not mean a less harmful world. We would really stress that theories are essential cognitive tools for clinicians and researchers because of their ability to guide case formulations and to streamline and boost the effectiveness of treatment. We build theories in order to understand why certain problems have occurred, how they develop and what the distal and proximal causes are that create and maintain them. In a nutshell, clinicians need to be theoretically literate.

We think that the past record of colleagues such as Ray Bull and Gisli Gudjonsson, and developments by Tony Ward and others in developing the Good Lives Model, as illustrated above, do demonstrate that forensic psychologists have engaged social injustices. We want more of this. Tyler and van der Toorn call for a 'subjective' approach to justice because this

[e]xplores the influence of whether people evaluate decisions and policies as consistent with or discrepant from their judgments about what is right or wrong. This psychological approach can be contrasted to a philosophical approach in which scholars define objective criteria for evaluating the justice or injustice of authorities and institutions and their policies and practices. Such criteria are often based upon a philosophical normative analysis of factors that shape fairness. (2013: xx)

We have, in Chapter 4, discussed the impacts of neo-liberalism and its manifestation in New Public Management. We presented an analysis of new punitiveness in Chapter 5 and the politicization of law and order. We talked about a discourse of popularism guiding political decision making and the political obsession with risk or rather risk aversion. Taken together with the age of austerity we currently find ourselves in, this has resulted in the dystopian analysis of the critical psychologists. There is an understandable coping strategy of battening down the hatches, keeping our heads below the water line, rendering our dues in five-star journal publications and generating the required amounts in research revenues or hitting our recidivism targets. Cohen (2001) muses about how some simply do not see what others see or else see nothing wrong or just do not care. But it does not have to be like this. Cohen argues for 'acknowledgement', that is to say, when people are actively aroused through thinking, feeling and acting, responding both psychologically and morally to what they know. When they see a problem that requires attention, Cohen asks that people do something – they intervene, help, become committed.

Robert Reiner, in a wonderfully cogent critique of neo-liberalism (Reiner, 2006, 2012, 2013), says it undermines the legal and ethical constraints aimed at holding individuals and corporations to account (Reiner, 206: 332). He prognosticates that the fruits of neo-liberalism will intensify injustices (Reiner, 2013: 176). Earlier we asked how we can square inhumane policies, such as withdrawing air–sea rescue help to immigrants who come to grief trying to cross the Mediterranean from North Africa. Robert Reiner reminds us of Stan Cohen's pithy encapsulation in the following story:

> A fisherman sees a body floating down stream, and jumps in to rescue it. The same happens a few minutes later, and then again, and again. Finally, the fisherman ignores the tenth body and starts running upstream. 'Why aren't you rescuing that poor man?' shouts an observer. The fisherman replies he's going to find out how to stop these poor people getting pushed into the water in the first place. (Cohen, 1985: 236)

Political psychology offers an alternative to denial and self-interest. The work of Tom Tyler and his associates (see Tyler and van der Toorn, 2013) draws attention to procedural justice. This is an idea that proposes that rather than gaining compliance through exertion of power or threat of punishment, people may align themselves to institutions that act fairly. They write persuasively that actually most people are not primarily motivated to maximize their personal or group-based self-interest, rather they have a powerful desire to be treated fairly and provide others with justice.

In terms of our practice in working alongside forensic populations, assessing, providing treatment and the notion of wider rehabilitation, we are strongly of the view that there is a need for us to enter into this complex and challenging work with humility and humanity, and to hold a hope and belief in the possibility of change for the individual before us. Beyond this, we need to offer this voice to policy makers, in an effort to promote recovery beyond psychological treatment programmes and interventions into communities, embracing the understandings of our colleagues from the field of criminology and clinical psychology.

It is interesting, as demonstrated in Chapter 6 of this book, that the voice of a celebrated playwright was offered in support of the wider rehabilitation of an individual in the community, not that of a professional or policy maker. Whilst one may consider this to reflect society's love of celebrity culture, it perhaps more alarmingly suggests that there is a vacuum into which celebrities step. We would argue that it should be the voice of those working in the field who should be stepping into and filling this void, with opinions based on knowledge and experience, offered fairly and kindly, and thereby supporting and encouraging a reduction in the difficulties experienced by the marginalization and alienation of those with past histories of offending.

There is, in our view, an increasing impetus for change in the field of forensic psychology; a call for innovation in practice and for practitioners that move us away from operating as neutral experimenters, providing nailed-down accredited programmes that feel suffocating of creativity. We recall the words of Mary McMurran and others who have bravely contributed to this book, and reflect on the stifling of innovation experienced by many in the field in recent years. We personally grieve the loss of these opportunities for those new to the field. The risk in this, to our minds, is that those forensic psychologists with a desire to work more imaginatively will not tolerate the restrictive working practices in some areas (by this we mean the accredited programmes in the criminal justice system) and we are in danger of losing future innovators and thinkers from the field. It is, in our view, time to take off the blinkers and pull back the covers so that we can breathe more freely and infuse the field of forensic psychology with vitality once again.

RESOURCES

The work of Stan Cohen is definitely worth, reading especially *States of Denial* (2001).

Ian Loader and Richard Sparks' account of public criminology is outlined in detail in their book, and there is a shorter review article (Loader and Sparks, 2010a, 2010b).

Jacqueline Wheatcroft and Sandra Walklate's (2014) research on thinking differently about false rape allegation is a good illustration of new ways of working.

Clive Hollin's (2007) chapter in the *Oxford Handbook of Criminology* presents a more detailed argument for a rapprochement between criminology and psychology.

Key journals

Applied Psychology in Criminal Justice

Criminology and Public Policy

International Journal of Criminology and Psychology

International Journal of Law and Psychiatry

Journal of Criminal Psychology

Psychiatry, Psychology and Law

Psychology, Public Policy and Law

REFERENCES

ACPO (Association of Chief Police Officers) (2005) *Practice Advice on Core Investigative Doctrine*. Wyboston: National Centre for Policing Excellence.

ACPO (Association of Chief Police Officers) (2006) *Murder Investigation Manual*. Wyboston: National Centre for Policing Excellence.

Adhami, E. and Browne, D.P. (1996) *Major Crime Enquiries: Improving Expert Support for Detectives*. Special Interest Series: Paper 9. London: Home Office.

Adler, J. and Gray, J. (eds) (2010) *Forensic Psychology: Concepts, Debates and Practices*, 2nd edn. Cullompton: Willan.

Adshead, G. (2002) 'Three degrees of security; attachment and forensic institutions', *Criminal Behaviour and Mental Health*, 12(2): 31-45

Ainsworth, P. (1995) *Psychology and Policing in a Changing World*. Chichester: Wiley.

Ainsworth, P. (2001) *Offender Profiling and Crime Analysis*. Cullompton: Willan Publishing.

Aitken, C., Connolly, T., Gammerman, A., Zhang, G. and Oldfield, D. (1995) *Predicting an Offender's Characteristics: An Evaluation of Statistical Modelling*. Special Interest Series: Paper 4. London: Home Office.

Ajzen, I. (2005) *Attitudes, Personality and Behaviour*, 2nd edn. Milton Keynes: Open University Press.

Akers, R.L. and Jennings, W.G. (2009) 'The social learning theory of crime and deviance', in M.D. Krohn, A.J. Lixotte and G. Penly Hall (eds), *Handbook on Crime and Deviance*. London: Springer. pp. 103-20.

Alison, L. (2005) 'From trait-based profiling to psychological contributions to apprehension methods', in L. Alison (ed.) *The Forensic Psychologist's Casebook* Cullompton: Willan Publishing. pp. 3-22.

Alison, L. (ed.) (2005) *The Forensic Psychologist's Casebook*. Cullompton: Willan Publishing.

Alison, L., Bennell, C., Mokros, A. and Ormerod, D. (2002) 'The personality paradox in offender profiling: a theoretical review of the processes involved in deriving background characteristics from crime scene actions', *Psychology, Public Policy and Law*, 8 (1): 115-35.

Alison, L. and Eyre, M. (2009) *Killer in the Shadows: The Monstrous Crimes of Robert Napper*. London: Pennant Books.

Alison, L., Goodwill, A. and Alison, E. (2005) 'Guidelines for profilers', in L. Alison (ed.), *The Forensic Psychologist's Casebook*. Cullompton: Willan. pp. 235-77.

Alison, L., Goodwill, A., Almond, L., Heuvel, C. and Winter, J. (2010) 'Pragmatic solutions to offender profiling and behavioural investigative advice', *Legal and Criminological Psychology*, 15 (1): 115-32.

Alison, L., McLean, C. and Almond, L. (2007) 'Profiling suspects', in T. Newburn, T. Williamson and A. Wright (eds), *Handbook of Criminal Investigations*. Cullompton: Willan. pp. 493-516.

Alison, L. and Rainbow, L. (eds) (2011) *Professionalising Offender Profiling*. Oxford: Routledge.

Alison, L., Smith, M.D., Eastman, O. and Rainbow, L. (2003) 'Toulmin's philosophy of argument and its relevance to offender profiling', *Psychology, Crime and Law*, 9 (2): 173-83.

Alison, L., Smith, M.D. and Morgan, K. (2003) 'Interpreting the accuracy of offender profiles', *Psychology, Crime and Law*, 9 (2): 185-95.

Alison, L. and Stein, K. (2001) 'Vicious circle: accounts of stranger sexual assault reflect abusive variants of conventional interactions', *Journal of Forensic Psychiatry*, 12: 515-38.

Alison, L., West, A. and Goodwill, A. (2004) 'The academic and the practitioner – pragmatists' views of offender profiling', *Psychology, Public Policy and Law*, 10 (1/2): 71-101.

Almond, L., Alison, L., Eyre, M., Crego, J. and Godwill, A. (2008) 'Heuristic and biases in decision making', in L. Alison and J. Crego (eds), *Policing Critical Incidents: Leadership and Critical Incident Management*. Cullompton: Willan. pp. 151-80.

Almond, L., Alison, L. and Porter, L. (2007) 'An evaluation and comparison of claims made in behavioural investigative advice reports compiled by the National Policing Improvements Agency in the United Kingdom', *Journal of Investigative Psychology and Offender Profiling*, 4 (2): 71-83.

Amaranto, E., Steinberg, J., Castellano, C. and Mitchell, R. (2003) 'Police stress interventions', *Brief Treatment and Crises Interventions*, 3: 47-53.

American Psychology-Law Society (1991) 'Specialty guidelines for forensic psychologists', *Law and Human Behavior*, 15: 655-65.

Amick-McMullan, A., Kilpatrick, D. and Veronen, L. (1989) 'Family survivors of homicide victims: a behavioural analysis', *Behavior Therapist*, 12: 75-9.

Anand, D. (2014) *Review of Standards for Stage 1 and Stage 2 Training*. Forensic Update 114: April, 58-60.

Anderson, D.A. (1999) 'The aggregate burden of crime', *The Journal of Law and Economics*, 42 (2): 611-42.

Anderson, I. and Doherty, K. (2008) *Accounting for Rape: Psychology, Feminism and Discourse Analysis in the Study of Sexual Violence*. New York: Routledge.

Andrew, J. (2007) 'Prisons, the profit motive and other challenges to accountability', *Critical Perspectives on Accounting*, 18: 877-904.

Andrews, D.A. (1990) 'Some criminological sources of anti-rehabilitation bias in the report of the Canadian Sentencing Commission', *Canadian Journal of Criminology*, 32: 511-24.

Andrews, D.A. and Bonta J.L. (1994) *The Psychology of Criminal Conduct*. Cincinnati, OH: Anderson.

Andrews, D.A. and Bonta, J.L. (1995) *LSI-E The Level of Service Inventory-Revised*. Toronto: Multi-Health Systems.

Andrews, D.A. and Bonta, J. (2010) 'Rehabilitating criminal justice policy and practice', *Psychology, Public Policy, and Law*, 16: 39-55.

Andrews, D.A., Bonta, J. and Wormith, J.S. (2004) *The level of service/case management inventory. LS/CMI*. Toronto, ON: Multi-Health Systems.

Andrews, D.A., Bonta, J. and Wormith, S.J. (2008) *The Level of Service/Risk-Need-Responsivity (LS/RNR)*. Toronto, ON: Multi-Health Systems.

Andrews, D.A., Bonta, J. and Wormith, J.S. (2011) 'The Risk–Need–Responsivity (RNR) model: does adding the Good Lives Model contribute to effective crime prevention?', *Criminal Justice Behavior*, 38: 735-55.

Andrews, D. and Dowden, C. (2006) 'Risk principles of case classification in correctional treatment: a meta analytic investigation', *International Journal of Offender Therapy and Comparative Criminology*, 50: 88-100.

Andrews, D.A. and Dowden, C. (2007) 'The Risk-Need-Responsivity model of assessment and human service in prevention and corrections: crime prevention jurisprudence', *Canadian Journal of Criminology and Criminal Justice*, 49, 439-64.

Andrews, D.A., Robinson, D. and Hoge, R.D. (1984) *The Youth Level of Service Inventory: Manual and Scoring Guide. A Report of the Laboratory for Research and Evaluation in the Human Services*. Ottawa, Ontario: Carleton University.

Andrews, D.A., Zinger, I., Hoge, R., Bonta, J., Gendreau, P. and Cullen, F. (1990) 'Does correctional treatment work? A clinically relevant and psychologically informed meta-analysis', *Criminology*, 28: 369-404.

Annison, H. (2014) 'Interpreting the politics of the judiciary: the British senior judicial tradition and the pre-emptive turn in criminal justice', *Journal of Law and Society*, 41: 339-66.

Appelbaum, P. (1997) 'A theory of ethics for forensic psychiatry', *Journal of the American Academy of Psychiatry and the Law Online*, 25: 233-47.

Ashmore, Z. and Shuker, R. (2014) *Forensic Practice in the Community*. Abingdon: Routledge.

Attrill, G. and Liell, G. (2007) 'Offender's views on risk assessment', in N. Padfield (ed.), *Who to Release/Parole, Fairness and Criminal Justice*. Cullompton: Willan.

Audit Commission. (1989) *The Probation Service: Promoting Value for Money*. London: HMSO.

Ault, R.L. and Reese, J.T. (1980) 'A psychological assessment of crime profiling', *FBI Law Enforcement Bulletin*, 49: 22-5.

Austin, W.G. (2002) 'Guidelines for using collateral sources of information in child custody evaluations', *Family Court Review*, 40: 177-84.

Backman, C. (1979) 'Epilogue: a new paradigm', in G.P. Ginsburg (ed.), *Emerging Strategies in Social Psychological Research*. Chichester: Wiley. pp. 289-303.

Badcock, R. (1997) 'Developmental and clinical issues in relation to offending in the individual', in J.L. Jackson and D.A. Bekerian (eds), *Offender Profiling: Theory, Research and Practice*. Chichester: Wiley. pp. 9-41.

Baldwin, J. (1992) *Video-taping Police Interviews with Suspects - An Evaluation*. London: Home Office.

Banaji, M.R. (2007) 'Foreword: The moral obligation to be intelligent', in E. Borgida and S.T. Fiske (eds), *Beyond Common Sense: Psychological Science in the Courtroom*. Oxford: Wiley-Blackwell. pp. xxi-xxvi.

Bandura, A. (1977) *Social Learning Theory*. Englewood Cliffs, NJ: Prentice Hall.

Barnes, S. (2013) 'Victims of crime', in J. Clarke and P. Wilson (eds), *Forensic Psychology in Practice*. London: Palgrave Macmillan. pp. 205-19.

Barnett. G. (2014) 'Working with Sex Offenders'. Input delivered to Division of Forensic Psychology Annual Conference, Glasgow, 26 June 2014.

Barnett, J., Lazarus, A., Vasquez, M., Moorehead-Slaughter, O. and Johnson, W. (2007) 'Boundary issues and multiple relationships: Fantasy and reality', *Professional Psychology: Research and Practice*, 38: 401-10.

Barret, G.V. and Morris, S.B. (1993) 'The American Psychology Association's amicus curiae brief in Price Waterhouse v Hopkins', *Law and Human Behavior*, 17: 201-11.

Bartol, C. and Bartol, A. (1987) 'History of forensic psychology', in I. Weiner and A. Hess (eds), *The Handbook of Forensic Psychology*. Los Angeles: Sage. pp. 2-32.

Bartol, C. and Bartol, A. (2008) 'Introduction and overview', in C. Bartol and A. Bartol (eds), *Introduction to Forensic Psychology: Research and Application*, 2nd edn. Los Angeles: Sage. pp. 2-32.

Beech, A. and Fordham, A. (1997) 'Therapeutic climate of sexual offender treatment programmes', *Sexual Abuse: A Journal of Research and Treatment*, 9: 219-37.

Beech, A., Craig, L. and Browne, K. (2009) *Assessment and Treatment of Sex Offenders*. Chichester: Wiley.

Beech, A. and Ward, T. (2004) 'The integration of etiology and risk in sexual offenders: A theoretical framework', *Aggression and Violent Behaviour*, 10: 31-63.

Bekerian, D.A. and Jackson, J.L. (1997) 'Critical issues in offender profiling', in J.L. Jackson and D.A. Bekerian (eds), *Offender Profiling: Theory, Research and Practice*. Chichester: Wiley. pp. 209-20.

Bekerian, D. and Levey, A. (2005) *Applied Psychology: Putting Theory into Practice*. Oxford: Oxford University Press.

Bell, E. (2013) 'Punishment as politics: the penal system in England and Wales', in V. Ruggiero and M. Ryan (eds), *Punishment in Europe: A Critical Anatomy of Penal Systems*. Basingstoke: Palgrave Macmillan. pp. 58-85.

Bennell, C. and Jones, N.J. (2005) 'Between a ROC and a hard place: a method for linking serial burglaries by modus operandi', *Journal of Investigative Psychology and Offender Profiling*, 2: 23-41.

Bennell, C., Mugford, R., Ellingwood, H. and Woodhams, J. (2014) 'Linking crimes using behavioural clues: current levels of linking accuracy and strategies for moving forward', *Journal of Investigative Psychology and Offender Profiling*, 11: 29-56.

Berlins, M. and Dyer, C. (2000) *The Law Machine*, 5th edn. London: Penguin.

Bersoff, D.N., Goodman-Delahunty, J., Grisso, J., Thomas, J., Poythress, V.P., Norman, G. and Roesch, R.R. (1997) 'Training in law and psychology: models from the Villanova conference', *American Psychologist*, 52: 1301-10.

Best, D. and Laudet, A. (2010) *The Potential of Recovery Capital*. London: Royal Society for the Arts.

Bickley, J.A. and Beech, A.R. (2002) 'An investigation of the Ward & Hudson pathways model of the sexual offense process with child abusers', *Journal of Interpersonal Violence*, 17: 371-93.

Bieneck, S. and Krahé, B. (2011) 'Blaming the victim and exonerating the perpetrator in cases of rape and robbery: is there a double standard?', *Journal of Interpersonal Violence*, 26: 1785-97.

Birgden, A. and Ward, T. (2009) 'Where the home in the valley meets the damp dirty prison: a human rights perspective on therapeutic jurisprudence and the role of forensic psychologists in correctional settings', *Aggression and Violent Behaviour*, 14: 256-63.

Black, T. (2013) 'Broadmoor Hospital: a unique facility', *The Psychologist*, 26: 908-10.

Blackburn, R. (1971) 'Personality types among abnormal homicides', *British Journal of Criminology*, 11: 14-31.

Blackburn, R. (1993) *The Psychology of Criminal Conduct: Theory, Research and Practice*. Chichester: Wiley.

Blackburn, R. (1995) 'Psychopaths are they mad or bad?', in N.K. Clark and G.M. Stephenson (eds) *Issues in Criminological and Legal Psychology*, 22: 97-103. Leicester: British Psychological Society.

Blackburn, R. (1996) 'What is forensic psychology?', *Legal and Criminological Psychology*, 1: 3-16.

Blackburn, R. (2000) 'Treatment or incapacitation? Implications of research on personality disorders for the management of dangerous offenders', *Legal and Criminological Psychology*, 5: 1-2.

Blumstein, A., Farrington, D.P. and Moitra, S. (1985) 'Delinquency careers: innocents, desisters and persisters', in M. Tonry and N. Morris (eds), *Crime and Justice*, vol. 6 Chicago: University of Chicago Press. pp. 187-219.

Bohner, G., Eyssel, F., Pina, A., Siebler, F. and Viki, G.T. (2009) 'Rape myth acceptance: cognitive, affective and behavioural effects of beliefs that blame the victim and exonerate the perpetrator', in M.A.H. Horvath and J.M. Brown (eds), *Rape: Challenging Contemporary Thinking*. Cullompton: Willan. pp. 17-45.

Bonta, J., Jesseman, R., Rugge, T. and Cormier, R. (2006) 'Restorative justice and recidivism: promises made, promises kept?', in D. Sullivan and T. Toffit (eds), *Handbook of Restorative Justice: A Global Perspective*. Abingdon: Routledge. pp. 108–20.

Boon, J. (1997) 'The contribution of personality theories to psychological profiling', in J.L. Jackson and D.A. Bekerian (eds), *Offender Profiling: Theory, Research and Practice*. Chichester: Wiley. pp. 43–59.

Bornstein, B. and Hamm, J. (2012) 'Jury instructions on witness identification', *Court Review: Journal of the American Judges*, 48: 48–53.

Bourdieu, P. (1980) *The Logic of Practice*. Cambridge: Polity Press.

Bowling, B. and Phillips, C. (2002) *Racism, Crime and Justice*. Harlow: Longman.

Bradley, L.K. (2009) *The Bradley Report: Review of People with Mental Health Problems or Learning Disabilities in the Criminal Justice System*. London: COI for the Department of Health.

Breakwell, G. (1995) 'Research; theory and method', in G. Breakwell, S. Hammond and C. Fife-Schaw, (eds), *Research Methods in Psychology*. London: Sage. pp. 5–35.

Breakwell, G. (2007) *The Psychology of Risk*. Cambridge: Cambridge University Press.

Breakwell, G. and Rose, D. (2000) Research; theory and method in G. Breakwell, S. Hammond and C. Fife-Schaw, (eds), *Research Methods in Psychology*, 2nd edn. London: Sage. pp. 5–40.

Breakwell, G., Smith, J. and Wright, D. (2012) *Research Methods in Psychology*, 4th edn. London: Sage.

Brigham, J. (1999) 'What is forensic psychology anyway?', *Law and Human Behaviour*, 23: 273–98.

British Psychological Society (BPS) (2006) *Assessment of Capacity in Adults: Interim Guidance for Psychologists*. The British Psychological Society, Professional Practice Board: Assessment of Capacity Guidelines Group. Leicester: BPS.

British Psychological Society (BPS) (2007) *Statements on the Conduct of Psychologists Providing Expert Psychometric Evidence to Courts and Lawyers*. Leicester: BPS.

British Psychological Society (BPS) (2008) *Generic Professional Practice Guidelines*. Leicester: BPS.

British Psychological Society (BPS) (2009) *Code of Ethics and Conduct*. Leicester: BPS.

British Psychological Society (BPS) (2010a) *Guidelines on Memory and the Law*, Rev. edn. Leicester: BPS.

British Psychological Society (BPS) (2010b) *Psychologists as Expert Witnesses: Guidelines and Procedure for England and Wales*, 3rd edn. Leicester: BPS.

British Psychological Society (BPS) (2010c) *Professional Practice Board/Social Care Institute for Excellence Audit Tool for Mental Capacity Assessments*. Leicester: BPS.

British Psychological Society (BPS) (2014) 'Testing in forensic contexts – new qualification standards', *The Psychologist*, 14, no. 10.

Britton, P. (1992) *Review of Offender Profiling*. London: Home Office.

Britton, P. (1997) *The Jigsaw Man*. London: Bantam Press.

Brogden, M. and Ellison, G. (2013) *Policing in an Age of Austerity: A Postcolonial Perspective*. Abingdon: Routledge.

Brough, P. and Biggs, A. (2010) 'Occupational stress in police and prison staff', in J.M. Brown and E.A. Campbell (eds), *The Cambridge Handbook of Forensic Psychology*. Cambridge: Cambridge University Press. pp. 707–17.

Brough, P. and Frame, R. (2004) 'Predicting police job satisfaction, work well-being and turnover intentions: the role of social support and police organisational variables', *New Zealand Journal of Psychology*, 33: 43–52.

Brown, B. (2012) *Daring Greatly: How the Courage to be Vulnerable Transforms the Way We Live, Love, Parent and Lead*. Harmondsworth: Penguin Books.

Brown, J. (2000) 'The psychology of policing', in J. Hartley and A. Branthwaite (eds), *The Applied Psychologist*. Buckingham: Open University Press. pp. 60-76.

Brown, J. (2002) 'Researching equality', in I. McKenzie and E. Bull (eds), *Criminal Justice Research: Inspiration, Influence and Ideation*. Aldershot: Dartmouth/Ashgate. pp. 79-98.

Brown, J. (2011) 'Facet theory and multi-dimensional scaling methods in forensic psychology', in K. Sheldon, J. Davies and K. Howells (eds), *Research in Practice for Forensic Practitioners*. London: Routledge.

Brown, J. (ed.) (2014) *The Future of Policing*. Abingdon: Routledge.

Brown, J. (ed.) (2015) *Forensic Psychology: Critical Concepts on Psychology*, vols 1-4. Abingdon: Routledge.

Brown, J. and Anderson, K. (2000) 'Police experience of vicarious stress', *Forensic Update*, 62: 6-11.

Brown, J. and Blount, C. (1999) 'Occupational stress in sex offender treatment managers', *Journal of Managerial Psychology*, 14: 108-20.

Brown, J. and Campbell, E. (eds) (2010) *The Cambridge Handbook of Forensic Psychology*. Cambridge: Cambridge University Press.

Brown, J., Fielding, J. and Grover, J. (1999) 'Distinguishing traumatic, vicarious and routine operational stressor exposure and attendant adverse consequences in a sample of police officers', *Work and Stress*, 13: 312-25.

Brown, J., Miller, S., Northey, S. and O'Neill, D. (2014) *What Works in Therapeutic Prisons: Evaluating Psychological Change in Dovegate Therapeutic Community*. Basingstoke: Palgrave.

Brown, M. (1997) 'Varieties of truth; psychology-law discourses as a dispute over the forms and content of knowledge', *Legal and Criminological Psychology*, 2: 219-45.

Brown, S. (2005) *Treating Sex Offenders: An Introduction to Sex Offender Treatment Programs*. Cullompton: Willan.

Brunswig, K.A. and Parham, R.W. (2003) 'Psychology in a secure setting', in W. O'Donohue and E. Levensky (eds), *Handbook of Forensic Psychology: Resource for Mental Health and Legal Professionals*. Amsterdam: Elsevier. pp. 851-71.

Brussel, J. (1968) *Casebook of a Crime Psychiatrist*. New York: Bernard Geis Associates.

Bucholz, J. (2002) *Homicide Survivors: Misunderstood Grievers*. Amityville, NY: Baywood.

Buck, G. (2014) 'Civic re-engagement amongst former prisoners', *Prison Service Journal*, Issue 214.

Budd, T. (1999) *Burglary of Domestic Dwellings*. London: Home Office.

Bukhanovsky, A.O., Hempel, A., Ahmed, W., Meloy, J.R., Brantley, A.C., Cuneo, D., Gleyzer, R. and Felthous, A.R. (1999) 'Assaultive eye injury and enucleation', *Journal of American Academy of Psychiatry Law*, 27: 590-602.

Bull, R. (2004) 'Legal psychology in the twenty-first century', *Criminal Behaviour and Mental Health*, 14: 167-81.

Bull, R. (2010) 'The investigative interviewing of children and other vulnerable witnesses: psychological research and working/professional practice', *Legal and Criminological Psychology*, 15: 5-23.

Bull, R., Valentine, T. and Williamson, T. (2009) *Handbook of Psychology of Investigative Interviewing: Current Developments and Future Directions*. Chichester: Wiley.

Bullock, H. and Limbert, W. (2009) 'Class', in D. Fox, I. Prilleltensky and S. Austin (eds), *Critical Psychology: An Introduction*, 2nd edn. London: Sage. pp. 215-32.

Bullock, K. (2014) 'Intelligence-led policing and the national intelligence model', in J. Brown (ed.), *The Future of Policing*. London: Routledge. pp. 287-98.

Burgess, A.W., Hartman, C.R., Ressler, R.K., Douglas, J.E. and McCormack, A. (1986) 'Sexual homicide: a motivational model', *Journal of Interpersonal Violence*, 1 (3): 251-72.

Butler, G. (1994) 'Commercial burglary: what offenders say', in M. Gill (ed.) *Crime at Work: Studies in Security and Crime Prevention*. Leicester: Perpetuity Press. pp. 29–41.

Butterworth, D. (1997) 'Behavioural consistency and change in serial rape', PhD thesis, University of Cambridge.

Byrom, N. (2013). 'The state of the sector: the impact of cuts to civil legal aid on practitioners and their clients', *Centre for Human Rights in Practice, University of Warwick*. Available at http://www2. warwick. ac. uk/fac/soc/law/chrp/projects/legalaidcuts/153064_statesector_report-final. pdf

Cabinet Office (1983) *Financial Management in Government Departments*. Cm. 9057. London: HMSO.

Campbell, E. (1994) 'Vicarious traumatisation'. Paper presented to the BABCP (British Association for Behavioural and Cognitive Psychology) conference, July.

Campbell, E. (2010) 'Expert witnesses in civil cases', in J. Brown and E. Campbell (eds), *The Cambridge Handbook of Forensic Psychology*. Cambridge: Cambridge University Press. pp. 766–72.

Campbell, R. (2002) *Emotionally Involved: The Impact of Researching Rape*. New York: Routledge.

Cann, J., Friendship, C. and Gozna, L. (2007) 'Assessing crossover in a sample of sexual offenders', *Legal and Criminological Psychology*, 12: 149–63.

Canter, D. (1994) *Criminal Shadows: Inside the Mind of Serial Killers*. London: Harper Collins.

Canter, D. (2000) 'Offender profiling and criminal differentiation', *Legal and Criminological Psychology*, 5: 23–46.

Canter, D. (2010) *Forensic Psychology: A Very Short Introduction*. Oxford: Oxford University Press.

Canter, D. (2013) 'The myths of offender profiling'. www.socialsciencespace. com/2013/02/the-myths-of-offender-profiling/ (accessed 11 February 2015).

Canter, D. (2014) *Psychology and Crime*. Oxford Bibliographies. Oxford: Oxford University Press.

Canter, D. and Alison, L. (2003) 'Converting evidence into data; the use of law enforcement archives as unobtrusive measurement', *Qualitative Report*, 8: 151–76.

Canter, D. and Heritage, R. (1990) 'A multivariate model of sexual offence behaviour: developments in offender profiling', *Journal of Forensic Psychiatry*, 1: 185–212.

Canter, D. and Wentink, N. (2004) 'An empirical test of Holmes and Holmes' serial murder typology', *Criminal Justice and Behaviour*, 31: 489–515.

Canter, D. and Youngs, D. (2009) *Investigative Psychology: Offender Profiling and the Analysis of Criminal Action*. Chichester: Wiley.

Canter, D.V., Alison, L.J., Alison, E. and Wentink, N. (2004) 'The organized/disorganized typology of serial murder – myth or model?', *Psychology, Public Policy and Law*, 10: 293–320.

Carlen, P. (1976) *Magistrates' Justice*. London: Martin Robertson.

Carlin, M. (2010) 'The psychologist as expert witness in criminal cases', in J. Brown and E. Campbell (eds), *The Cambridge Handbook of Forensic Psychology*. Cambridge: Cambridge University Press. pp. 773–82.

Carson, D. (2003) 'Psychology and the law: a subdiscipline, an interdisciplinary collaboration or a project?', in D. Carson and R. Bull (eds), *Handbook of Psychology in Legal Contexts*, 2nd edn. Chichester: Wiley. pp. 1–27.

Carson, D. (2012) 'Reviewing reviews of professional risk-taking decisions', *Journal of Social Welfare & Family Law*, 34: 395–409.

Carson, D. and Bull, R. (eds) (2003) *Handbook of Psychology in Legal Contexts*, 2nd edn. Chichester: Wiley.

Chifflet, P. (2014) 'Questioning the validity of criminal profiling: an evidence-based approach', *Australian & New Zealand Journal of Criminology* [E-pub ahead of print 12 May 2014] doi:0004865814530732.

Chivite-Matthews, N. and Maggs, P. (2002) *Crime Policing and Justice: The Experience of Older People.* London: Home Office.

Choudry, S. (1996) *Pakistani Women's Experience of Domestic Violence in Great Britain.* Home Office Research Findings No. 43: 1-4. London: HMSO.

Christmann, K. (2012) *Preventing Religious Radicalisation and Violent Extremism: A Systematic Review of the Research Literature.* Youth Justice Board.

Chung, M. and Hyland, M. (2012) *History and Philosophy of Psychology.* Chichester: Wiley–Blackwell.

Clarke, J. (2012) 'The resilient practitioner', in J. Clarke and P. Wilson (eds), *Forensic Psychology in Practice: A Practitioner's Handbook.* London: Palgrave Macmillan. pp. 220-39.

Clarke, J. and Wilson, P. (eds) (2012) *Forensic Psychology in Practice: A Practitioner's Handbook.* London: Palgrave, Macmillan.

Clarke, R. and Felson, M. (eds), (1993) *Routine Activity and Rational Choice.* London: Transaction.

Clarke, T. (1999) '"It was a perverted … ritual thing". What is offender signature and does it exist?' Unpublished BSc dissertation, University of Plymouth.

Clear, T. and Rose, D. (1998) 'Incarceration, social capital and crime: implications for social disorganization theory', *Criminology*, 36: 471-9.

Cloud, W. and Granfield, W. (2009) 'Conceptualising recovery capital: Expansion of a theoretical construct', *Substance Use and Misuse*, 42: 1971-86.

Cohen, L. and Felson, M. (1979) 'Social change and crime rate trends: a routine activity approach', *American Sociological Review*, 44: 588-608.

Cohen, S. (1981) 'Footprints on the sand: a further report on criminology and the sociology of deviance in Britain', *Crime and Society: Readings in History and Theory.* London: Routledge & Kegan Paul.

Cohen, S. (1985) *Visions of Social Control.* Cambridge: Polity Press.

Cohen, S. (2001) *States of Denial: Knowing about Atrocities and Suffering.* Cambridge: Polity Press.

Coid, J.W. (1994) 'The Christopher Clunis Inquiry', *Psychiatric Bulletin*, 18: 449-52.

Coid, J. W., Kahtan, N., Gault, S., Cook, A. and Jarman, B. (2001) 'Medium secure forensic psychiatry services', *British Journal of Psychiatry*, 178: 55-61.

Coid, J.W., Yang, M., Ullrich, S., Zhang, T., Sizmur, S., Farrington, D. and Rogers, E. (2011) 'Most items in structured risk assessment instruments do not work', *Journal of Forensic Psychiatry and Psychology*, 22: 3-21.

Cole, T. and Brown, J. (2011) 'What do Senior Investigating Police Officers want from Behavioural Investigative Advisers?', in L. Alison and L. Rainbow (eds), *Professionalising Offender Profiling.* Oxford: Routledge. pp. 191-205.

Cole, T. and Brown, J. (2012) 'When is it best to seek assistance from a Behavioural Investigative Adviser?', *Journal of Homicide and Major Incident Investigation*, 8: 61-75.

Cole, T. and Brown, J. (2013) 'Behavioural investigative advice: assistance to investigative decision-making in difficult-to-detect murder', *Journal of Investigative Psychology and Offender Profiling* [E-pub ahead of print 23 July 2013] doi:10.1002/jip.1396.

Cole, T. and Gudjonsson, G. (2013) 'Audit and Evaluation Criteria for UK Behavioural Investigative Advisers'. Internal report to the Association of Chief Police Officers.

Colman, A.M. and Mackay, R.D. (1993) 'Legal issues surrounding the admissibility of expert psychological and psychiatric testimony', in N.K. Clark and G.M. Stephenson (eds), *Children, Evidence and Procedure* (Issues in Criminological and Legal Psychology, No. 20). Leicester: British Psychological Society. pp. 46–50.

Cooke, C.A. and Woodhams, J. (2009) 'Auto-ethnography as a method for examining vicarious traumatisation'. 19th European Association of Psychology and Law, Sorrento, Italy.

Cooke, D. (2010) 'Psychopathy', in J. Brown and E. Campbell (eds), *Cambridge Handbook of Forensic Psychology*. Cambridge: Cambridge University Press. pp. 292–8.

Copson, G. (1995) *Coals to Newcastle? Part 1: A Study of Offender Profiling* (Paper 7). Police Research Group Special Interest Series. London: Home Office.

Copson, G., Badcock, R., Boon, J. and Britton, P. (1997) 'Articulating a systematic approach to clinical crime profiling', *Criminal Behaviour and Mental Health*, 7: 13–17.

Corbett, C. and Maguire, M. (1988) 'Value and limitations of victim support schemes', in M. Maguire and J. Pointing (eds), *From Victims of Crime: A New Deal?* Bristol: Open University Press. pp. 26–39.

Craig, L.A., Dixon, L. and Gannon, T.A. (eds) (2013) *What Works in Offender Rehabilitation: An Evidence Based Approach to Assessment and Treatment*. Chichester, Wiley-Blackwell.

Crego, J., Alison, L., Roocroft, J. and Eyre, M. (2008) 'Emotions in policing: the emotional legacy of homicide investigations', in L. Alison and J. Crego (eds), *Policing Critical Incidents: Leadership and Critical Incident Management*. Cullompton: Willan. pp. 181–200.

Cresswell, J. (2003) *Research Design: Qualitative, Quantitative and Mixed Methods Approaches*, 2nd edn. Thousand Oaks, CA: Sage.

Crewe, B., Bennett, J. and Wahidin, A. (2008) 'Introduction', in J. Bennett, B. Crewe and A. Wahidin (eds), *Understanding Prison Staff*. Cullompton: Willan. pp. 1–13.

Crighton, D. (2010) 'Assessment', in G. Towl and D. Crighton (eds), *Forensic Psychology*. Oxford: BPS Blackwell. pp. 244–59.

Crighton, D. and Towl, G. (eds) (2005) *Psychology in Probation Services*. Malden, MA: Blackwell.

Crighton, D. and Towl, G. (2008) *Psychology in Prisons*, 2nd edn. Oxford: Blackwell.

Cromby, J. and Willis, M. (2013) 'England's dreaming? UK critical psychology, 2011', *Annual Review of Critical Psychology*, 10: 932–51.

Crown Prosecution Service (2014) *Prostitution and Exploitation of Prostitution*. [Online] www.cps.gov.uk/legal/p_to_r/prostitution_and_exploitation_of_prostitution/ (accessed 26 February 2014).

Cullen, E. and Mackenzie, J. (2011) *Dovegate: A Therapeutic Community in a Private Prison and Developments in Therapeutic Work with Personality Disordered Offenders*. Hook: Waterside Press.

Darwell, S. (2006) *The Second-Person Standpoint: Morality, Respect and Accountability*. Cambridge, MA: Harvard University Press.

Davies, A. (1997) 'Specific profile analysis: a data-based approach to offender profiling', in J.L. Jackson and D.A. Bekerian (eds), *Offender Profiling, Theory, Research and Practice*. Chichester: Wiley. pp. 191–207.

Davies, A., Wittebrood, K. and Jackson, J.L. (1998) *Predicting the Criminal Record of a Stranger Rapist*. Policing and Reducing Crime Unit Special Interest Series, Paper 4. London: Home Office.

Davies, G. (1996) 'Mistaken identification: where law meets psychology head on', *The Howard Journal*, 35: 232–41.

Davies, G. and Beech, A.R. (2012) *Forensic Psychology*, 2nd edn. BPS Textbooks in Psychology. Chichester: Wiley.

Davies, J., Sheldon, K. and Howells, K. (2011) 'Conducting research in forensic settings: philosophical and practical issues', in K. Sheldon, J. Davies and K. Howells (eds), *Research in Practice for Forensic Professionals*. Abingdon: Routledge. pp. 3–15.

Davis, D. (1997) 'The harm that has no name: street harassment, embodiment and African American women', in A. Wing (ed.), *Critical Race Feminism: A Reader*. New York: New York University Press. pp. 192–202.

Davis, D. and Follette, W.C. (2004) 'Jurors CAN be selected: Non-information, misinformation, and their strategic uses for jury selection', in W. O'Donahue and E. Levensky (eds), *Handbook of Forensic Psychology: Resource for Mental Health and Legal Professionals*. Amsterdam: Elsevier. pp. 782–807.

Dawes, R.M., Faust, D. and Meehl, P. (1989) 'Clinical versus actuarial judgement', *Science*, 2: 1668–73.

Dawson, S. and Dargie, C. (2002) 'New Public Management: a discussion with special reference to UK health', in K. McLaughlin, S.P. Osborne and E. Ferlie (eds), *New Public Management: Current Trends and Future Prospects*. London: Routledge. pp. 34–56.

Deegan, P.E. (1988) 'Recovery: the lived experience of rehabilitation', *Psychosocial Rehabilitation Journal*, 11: 11–19.

Deering, J. (2014) 'A future for probation?', *The Howard Journal*, 53: 1–15.

Department of Transport (2014) *Statistical Releases: Reported Road Casualties in Great Britain: Quarterly Provisional Estimates Q1 2014*. London: DoT.

Devery, C. (2010) 'Criminal profiling and criminal investigation', *Journal of Contemporary Criminal Justice*, 26: 393–409.

De Vries Robbé, M., de Vogel, V., Douglas, K. and Nijman, H. (2015) 'Changes in dynamic risk and protective factors for violence during inpatient forensic psychiatric treatment: Predicting reductions in postdischarge community recidivism', *Law and Human Behavior*, 39: 53–61.

Dhami, M. (2003) 'Psychological models of professional decision making', *Psychological Science*, 14: 175–80.

Dhami, M. (2008) 'On measuring quantitative interpretations of reasonable doubt', *Journal of Experimental Psychology: Applied*, 14: 353–63.

Diamond, B.L. (1956) 'Isaac Ray and the trial of Daniel M'Naghten', *American Journal of Psychiatry*, 112: 651–6.

Dick, P., Silvestri, M. and Westmarland, L. (2014) 'Women police: potential and possibilities for police reform', in J. Brown (ed.), *The Future of Policing*. Abingdon: Routledge. pp. 134–48.

Dignan, J. (2005) *Understanding Victims and Restorative Justice*. Maidenhead: Open University Press.

Doan, B. and Snook, B. (2008) 'A failure to find empirical support for the homology assumption in criminal profiling', *Journal of Police and Criminal Psychology*, 23: 61–70.

Dobash, R. and Dobash, R. (1979) *Violence Against Wives: The Case against Patriarchy*. New York: Free Press.

Doren, D.M. (2006) 'Recidivism risk assessments: making sense of controversies', in W.L. Marshall, Y.M. Fernandez, L.E. Marshall and G.A. Serren (eds), *Sexual Offender Treatment: Controversial Issues*. Chichester: Wiley.

Douglas, J.E. and Oleshaker, M. (1995) *Mindhunter*. London: Heinemann.

Douglas, J.E., Burgess, A.W., Burgess, A.G. and Ressler, R.K. (2006) *Crime Classification Manual*. San Francisco: Wiley.

Dowden, C., Bennell, C. and Bloomfield, S. (2007) 'Advances in offender profiling: a systematic review of the profiling literature published over the past three decades', *Journal of Police and Criminal Psychology*, 22: 44–56.

Downes, D. (1988) 'The sociology of crime and social control in Britain 1960–87', *British Journal of Criminology*, 28: 45–57.

Downes, D. and Morgan, T. (2012) 'Overtaking on the left? The politics of law and order in the "Big Society"', in M. Maguire, R. Morgans and R. Reiner (eds), *The Oxford Handbook of Criminology*, 5th edn. Oxford: Oxford University Press. pp. 182–205.

Doyle, M. (2011) 'Risk research', in K. Sheldon, J. Davies. and K. Howells (eds), *Research in Practice for Forensic Professionals*. Abingdon: Routledge. pp. 37–59.

Doyle, M. and Dolan, M. (2002) 'Violence risk assessment: combining actuarial and clinical information to structure clinical judgements for the formulation and management of risk', *Journal of Psychiatric and Mental Nursing*, 9: 649–57.

Eastman, N. (2000) 'Psycholegal studies as an interface discipline', in J. McGuire, T. Mason and A. O'Kane (eds), *Behaviour, Crime and Legal Processes: A Guidebook for Practitioners*. Chichester: Wiley. pp. 83–110.

Elbogen, E.B., Mercado, C.C., Tomkins, A.J. and Scalora, M.J. (2001) 'Clinical practice and violence risk assessment: Availability of MacArthur risk factors', in D. Farrington, C.R. Hollin and M. McMurran (eds), *Sex and Violence: The Psychology of Crimes and Risk Assessment* New York: Routledge. pp. 38–55.

Ellis, T., Pamment, N. and Lewis, C. (2009) 'Public protection in youth justice? The intensive supervision and surveillance programme from the inside', *International Journal of Police Science and Management*, 11: 393–412.

Ellison, L. (2002) 'Prosecuting domestic violence without victim participation', *The Modern Law Review*, 65: 834–58.

Ellison, L. and Munro, V. (2009) 'Turning mirrors into windows: assessing the impact of (mock) juror education in rape trials', *British Journal of Criminology*, 49: 363–83.

Ekman, P. and O'Sullivan, M. (2006) 'From flawed self-assessment to blatant whoppers: the utility of voluntary and involuntary behaviour in detecting deception', *Behavioural Sciences and the Law*, 24: 673–86.

Equality and Human Rights Commission (2009) *Positive Action Briefing Note*. London: The Commission.

Eschholz, S., Reed, M.D., Beck, E. and Leonard, P.B. (2008) 'Offenders' family members' responses to capital crimes', in C.R. Bartol and A.M. Bartol (eds), *Current Perspectives in Forensic Psychology and Criminal Behaviour*. London: Sage. pp. 177–88.

Evershed, S. (2013) 'Report writing', in J. Clarke. and P. Wilson (eds), *Forensic Psychology in Practice: A Practitioner's Handbook*. Basingstoke: Palgrave Macmillan. pp. 86–102.

Eysenck, H. (1987) 'Personality theory and the problem of criminality', in B. McGurk, D. Thornton and M. Williams (eds), *Applying Psychology to Imprisonment: Theory and Practice*. London: HMSO. pp. 29–58.

Eyssel F.A. and Bohner, G. (2008a) 'Modern rape myths: the Acceptance of Modern Myths about Sexual Aggression (AMMSA) scale', in M. Morrison and T.G. Morrison (eds), *The Psychology of Modern Prejudice*. Hauppauge, NY: Nova Science Publishers. pp. 261–76.

Eyssel, F.A. and Bohner, G. (2008b) 'Rape myth acceptance: a cognitive schema?' Paper presented to the XIII Workshop on Aggression, Potsdam, Germany.

Ezell, M. and Cohen, L. (2005) *Desisting from Crime: Continuity and Change in Long-Term Crime Patterns of Serious Chronic Offenders*. New York: Oxford University Press.

Farr, C., Brown, J. and Beckett, R. (2004) 'Ability to empathise and masculinity levels: comparing male adolescent sex offenders with a normative sample of non-offending adolescents', *Psychology, Crime and Law*, 10: 155–67.

Farrall, S. and Bowling, B. (1999) 'Structuration, human development and desistance from crime', *British Journal of Criminology*, 17: 252–67.

Farrall, S. and Calverley, A. (2006) *Understanding Desistance from Crime: Theoretical Directions in Resettlement and Reintegration*. Oxford: Oxford University Press.

Farrall, S. and Hay, C. (2010) 'Not so Tough on Crime? Why Weren't the Thatcher Governments More Radical in Reforming the Criminal Justice System?', *British Journal of Criminology*, 50 (3): 550–69.

Farrall, S. and Jennings, W. (2012) 'Policy feedback and the criminal justice agenda: an analysis of the economy, crime rates, politics and public opinion in post war Britain', *Contemporary British History*, 26: 467-88.

Farrall, S., Jackson, J. and Gray, E. (2009) 'Everyday emotion and fear of crime: preliminary findings from experience and expression'. Experience and Expression in Fear of Crime Working Paper no. 1.

Farrell, G., Tilley, N., Tseloni, A. and Mailley, J. (2010) 'Explaining and sustaining the crime drop; clarifying the role of opportunity-related theories', *Crime Prevention and Community Safety*, 12: 24-41.

Farrell, G., Tseloni, A., Mailley, J. and Tilley, N. (2011) 'The crime drop and security hypothesis', *Journal of Research in Crime and Delinquency*, 48: 147-75.

Farrington, D.P. (1986) 'Age and crime', in M. Tonry and N. Morris (eds), *Crime and Justice*, vol 7. Chicago: University of Chicago Press. pp. 189-250.

Farrington, D.P. (2004) 'Criminological psychology in the twenty-first century', *Criminal Behaviour and Mental Health*, 14: 152-66.

Farrington, D., Gottfredson, D., Sherman, L. and Welsh, B. (2002) 'The Maryland scientific methods scale', in L. Sherman, D. Farrington, B. Welsh and D. MacKenzie, (eds), *Evidence-based Crime Prevention*. London: Routledge.

Farrington, D.P. and Lambert, S. (1997) 'Predicting offender profiles from victim and witness descriptions', in J.L. Jackson and D.A. Bekerian (eds), *Offender Profiling, Theory, Research and Practice*. Chichester: Wiley. pp. 133-58.

Farrington, D.P. and Welsh, B.C. (2003) 'Family based prevention of offending: a meta-analysis', *Australian and New Zealand Journal of Criminology*, 36: 127-51.

Fattah, A. (1989) 'Victims and victimology: the facts and the rhetoric', *International Review of Victims and Victimology*, 1: 43-66.

Faulkner, D. (2010) 'The justice system in England and Wales', in G. Towl and D. Crighton (eds), *Forensic Psychology*. Chichester: BPS Blackwell. pp. 17-32.

Feeley, M. and Simon, J. (1992) 'The new penology: notes on the emerging strategy of corrections and its implications', *Criminology*, 30: 447-71.

Feist, A., Asche, J., Lawrence, J., McPhee, D. and Wilson, R. (2007) *Investigating and Detecting Recorded Offences of Rape*. Home Office Online Report 18/07. London: Home Office.

Felson, R.B. and Lane, K.J. (2009) 'Social learning, sexual and physical abuse, and adult crime', *Aggressive Behaviour*, 35: 489-501.

Figley, C. (1995) 'Compassion fatigue as secondary stress: an overview', in C. Figley (ed), *Compassion Fatigue: Coping with Secondary Traumatic Stress Disorder in Those Who Treat the Traumatised*. New York: Brunner Mazel.

Finch, E. and Munro, V.R. (2008) 'Lifting the veil? The use of focus groups and trial simulations in legal research', *Journal of Law and Society*, 35: 30-51.

Fine, M. (2012) 'Resuscitating critical psychology for "revolting" times', *Journal of Social Issues*, 68: 416-38.

Fisher, R. and Geiselman, R. (1992) *Memory-Enhancing Techniques for Investigative Interviewing: The Cognitive Interview*. Springfield, IL: C.C. Thomas.

Fishman, D. and Goodman-Delahunty, J. (2010) 'Pragmatic psychology', in J. Brown and E. Campbell (eds), *The Cambridge Handbook of Forensic Psychology*. Cambridge: Cambridge University Press. pp. 95-101.

Fiske, S., Bersoff, D., Borida, E., Deaux, K. and Heilman, M. (1991) 'Use of sex stereotyping research in Price Waterhouse v. Hopkins', *American Psychologist*, 46: 1049-60.

Fitzgibbon, W. and Lea, J. (2014) 'Defending probation: beyond privatisation and security', *European Journal of Probation*, 6: 24-41.

Fitzpatrick, B., Seago, P., Walker, C. and Wall, D. (2001) 'The courts: new court management and old court ideologies', in M. Ryan, S. Savage and D. Wall (eds), *Policy Networks in Criminal Justice*. Basingstoke: Palgrave. pp. 98-121.

Foot, P. (1967) 'The problem of abortion and the doctrine of the double effect', *Oxford Review*, 5: 1-5.

Fortune, C., Ward, T. and Polaschek, D. (2014) 'The good lives model and therapeutic environments in forensic settings', *Therapeutic Communities*, 35: 95-10.

Fox, B.H. and Farrington, D.P. (2014) 'Behavioral consistency among serial burglars evaluating offense style specialization using three analytical approaches', *Crime and Delinquency* [E-pub ahead of print 27 June 2014] doi: 0011128714540275.

Fox, C. and Albertson, K. (2011) 'Payment by results and social impact bonds in the criminal justice sector: new challenges for the concept of evidence based policy', *Criminology and Criminal Justice*, 11: 395-413.

Fox, D., Prilleltensky, I. and Austin S. (2009) 'Critical psychology for social justice concerns and dilemmas', in D. Fox, I. Prilleltensky and S. Austin (eds), *Critical Psychology: An Introduction*, 2nd edn. London: Sage. pp. 3-19.

Francis, B., Barry, J., Bowater, R., Miller, N., Soothill, K. and Ackerley, E. (2004) *Using Homicide Data to Assist Murder Investigations*. London: Home Office. (Retrieved 01/01/09 from www.homeoffice.gov.uk/rds/pdfs04/rdsolr2604.pdf.)

Francis, R.D. (2009) *Ethics for Psychologists*, 2nd edn. Chichester: Wiley.

Francks, R. (ed.) (2002) *Explanatory Power of Models*. New York: Springer-Verlag.

Freckelton, I. (2008) 'Profiling evidence in courts', in D. Canter and R. Zukauskiene (eds), *Psychology and Law: Bridging the Gap*. Aldershot: Ashgate. pp. 79-102.

Freudenberger, H.J. (1974) 'Staff burn-out', *Journal of Social Issues*, 30: 159-65.

Fritzon, K., Canter, D. and Wilton, Z. (2001) 'The application of an action systems model to destructive behaviour: the examples of arson and terrorism', *Behavioural Sciences and the Law*, 19 (5-6): 657-90.

Fritzon, K. and Watts, A. (2003) 'Crime prevention', in R. Bull and D. Carson (eds), *Handbook of Psychology in Legal Contexts*, 2nd edn. Chichester: Wiley. pp. 229-44.

Frost, N. (2010) 'Beyond public opinion polls: punitive public sentiment and criminal justice policy', *Sociology Compass*, 4/3: 156-68.

Gannon, T.A., Rose, M.R. and Ward, T. (2012) 'A descriptive offence process model of female sexual offending', in B. Schwartz (ed), *The Sex Offender* (vol. 7). Kingston, NJ: Civic Research. pp. 16.1-16.19.

Gannon, T.A. and Ward, T. (2014) 'Where has all the psychology gone? A critical review of evidence-based practice in correctional settings', *Aggression and Violent Behaviour*, 19 (4): 435-46.

Gannon, Theresa A., Waugh, Greg, Taylor, Kelly, Blanchette, Kelly, O'Connor, Alisha, Blake, Emily and O'Ciaedha, Caoiltr (2013) 'Women who sexually offend display three main offense styles: a re-examination of the descriptive model of female sexual offending', *Sexual Abuse: A Journal of Research and Treatment*, 26: 207-24.

Garfield, S.L. (1994) 'Research on client variables in psychotherapy', in A.E. Bergin and S.L. Garfield (eds), *Handbook of Psychotherapy and Behaviour Change*, 4th edn. New York: Wiley.

Garland, D. (2001) *The Culture of Control: Crime and Social Order in Contemporary Society*. Oxford: Oxford University Press.

Gavin, H. (2014) *Criminological and forensic psychology*. Los Angeles: Sage.

Geertz, C. (1973) '"Thick description": toward an interpretive theory of culture', in C. Geertz, *The Interpretation of Cultures*. New York: Basic Books.

Gekoski, A. and Gray, J.M. (2011) '"It may be true, but how's it helping?": UK police detectives' views of the operational usefulness of offender profiling', *International Journal of Police Science and Management*, 13: 103-16.

Genders, E. (2002) 'Legitimacy, accountability and private prisons', *Punishment and Society*, 4: 285–303.

Genders, E. (2003) 'Privatisation and innovation; rhetoric and reality: the development of a therapeutic community prison', *The Howard Journal*, 42: 137–57.

Genders, E. (2007) 'The commercial context of criminal justice and the perversion of purpose', *Criminal Review*, July: 513–29.

Genders, E. and Player, E. (1995) *Grendon: A Study of a Therapeutic Prison*. Oxford: Oxford University Press.

Gendreau, P. and Ross, R. (1987) 'Revivification of rehabilitation; evidence from the 1980s', *Justice Quarterly*, 3: 349–407.

Gendreau, P., Goggin, C., French, S. and Smith, P. (2006) 'Practicing psychology in correctional settings', in I. Weiner and A. Hess (eds), *The Handbook of Forensic Psychology*, 3rd edn. Hoboken, NJ: Wilet. pp. 722–50.

Ghetti, S., Schaaf, J. M., Quin, J. and Goodman, G.S. (2004) 'Issues in eyewitness testimony', in W. O'Donahue and E. Levensky (eds), *Handbook of Forensic Psychology: Resource for Mental Health and Legal Professionals*. Amsterdam: Elsevier. pp. 514–44.

Gilbert, P. (2009) 'Compassion Focused Therapy and Compassionate Mind Training for Shame Based Difficulties'. *Compassionate Mind Foundation*. www.compassionate mind.co.uk.

Gilbert, P. and Andrews, B. (1995) *Shame: Interpersonal Behaviour, Psychopathology and Culture*. Oxford: Oxford University Press.

Gilchrist, E. and Kebbell, M. (2010) 'Intimate partner violence: current issues in definitions and interventions with perpetrators', in J. Adler and J. Grey (eds), *Forensic Psychology: Concepts, Debates and Practice*, 2nd edn. Cullompton: Willan. pp. 351–77.

Gilligan, J. (2003) 'Shame, guilt and violence', *Social Research*, 70: 1149–80.

Gilmore, K. and Pittman, L. (1993) *To Report or Not to Report: A Study of Victim/ Survivors of Sexual Assault and Their Experience of Making an Initial Report to the Police*. Melbourne: Centre Against Sexual Assault (CASA House) and Royal Women's Hospital.

Glasser, M., Kolvin, I., Campbell, D., Glasser, A., Leitch, I. and Farrelly, S. (2001) 'Cycle of child sexual abuse: Links between being a victim and becoming a perpetrator', *The British Journal of Psychiatry*, 179: 482–94.

Gottfredson, M.R. and Hirschi, T. (1990) *A General Theory of Crime*. Stanford, CA: Stanford University Press.

Goggin, C. and Gendreau, P. (2006) 'The implementation and maintenance of quality services in offender rehabilitation programmes', in C. Hollin and E. Palmer (eds), *Offender Behaviour Programmes: Development, Application and Controversies*. Chichester: Wiley. pp. 209–46.

Goldfinger, K. and Pomerantz, A. (2014) *Psychological Assessment and Report Writing*, 2nd edn. Thousand Oaks, CA: Sage.

Goodey, J. (2005) *Victims and Victimology: Research, Policy and Practice*. London: Longmans.

Graham, J., Woodfield, K., Tibble, M. and Kitchen, S. (2004) *Testaments of Harm: A Qualitative Evaluation of the Victim Personal Statements Scheme*. London: National Centre for Social Research.

Granfield, R. and Cloud, W. (2001) 'Social Context and "Natural Recovery": The Role of Social Capital in the Resolution of Drug Associated Problems', *Substance Use and Misuse*, 36: 1543–70.

Gray, E., Jackson, J. and Farrall, S. (2011) 'Feelings and functions in the fear of crime', *British Journal of Criminology*, 51: 75–94.

Gray, W.R. (2001) *The Four Faces of Affirmative Action: Fundamental Answers and Actions* (No. 99). NJ: Praeger Pub Text.

Grayling, A.C. (2001) *The Meaning of Things: Applying Philosophy to Life*. London: Orion Books.

Grayling, C. (2014) 'Protecting human rights in the UK: The Conservative's proposals for changing Britain's Human Rights Law'. *The Guardian*, October.

Green, S. (2007) 'Crime, victimisation and vulnerability', in S. Walklate (ed), *Handbook of Victims and Victimology*. Cullompton: Willan. pp. 91-118.

Greenfield, D. and Gottschalk, J. (2009) *Writing Forensic Reports: A Guide for Mental Health Professionals*. New York: Springer.

Gregory, A. and Rainbow, L. (2011) 'Familial DNA prioritization?', in L. Alison and L. Rainbow (eds), *Professionalising Offender Profiling*. Abingdon: Routledge. pp. 160-77.

Gregory, J. and Lees, S. (1999) *Policing Sexual Assault*. London: Routledge.

Gresswell, D. and Hollin, C. (1994) 'Multiple murder: A review', *British Journal of Criminology*, 34: 1-14.

Groth, A.N., Burgess, A.W. and Holmstrom, L.H. (1977) 'Rape: power, anger and sexuality', *American Journal of Psychiatry*, 134: 1239-43.

Grubin, D. (1991) 'Unfit to plead in England and Wales, 1976-1988: a survey', *British Journal of Psychiatry*, 158: 540-8.

Grubin, D. (1995) 'Offender profiling', *Journal of Forensic Psychiatry*, 6: 259-63.

Grubin, D. (2008) 'The case for polygragh testing of offenders', *Legal and Criminological Psychology*, 13: 177-89.

Grubin, D., Kelly, P. and Ayis, S. (1997) *Linking Serious Sexual Assaults*. Police Research Group Technical Paper. London: Home Office Police Policy Directorate.

Gudjonsson, G.H. (1984) 'A new scale of interrogative suggestibility', *Personality and Individual Difference*, 5: 303-14.

Gudjonsson, G.H. (1997). *The Gudjonsson Suggestibility Scales*. Hove: Psychology Press.

Gudjonsson, G.H. (2003a) *The Psychology of Interrogations and Confessions: A Handbook*. Chichester: Wiley.

Gudjonsson, G. (2003b) 'Psychology brings justice: the science of forensic psychology', *Criminal Behaviour and Mental Health*, 13: 159-67.

Gudjonsson, G.H. (2008) 'Psychologists as expert witnesses: The 2007 BPS Survey', *Forensic Update*, 92: 23-9.

Gudjonsson, G. (2010) 'Psychological vulnerabilities during police interviews: why are they important?', *Legal and Criminological Psychology*, 15: 161-75.

Gudjonsson, G. (2014) 'How I got started: from memory distrust to false confessions', *Applied Cognitive Psychology*, 28: 809-11.

Gudjonsson, G. and Copson, G. (1997) 'The role of the expert in criminal investigation', in J.L. Jackson and D.A. Bekerian (eds), *Offender Profiling: Theory, Research and Practice*. Chichester: Wiley. pp. 61-76.

Gudjonsson, G.H. and Gunn, J. (1982) 'The competence and reliability of a witness in a criminal court', *British Journal of Psychiatry*, 141: 624-7.

Gudjonsson, G.H. and Haward, L.R.C. (1998) *Forensic Psychology: A Guide to Practice*. London: Routledge.

Gudjonsson, G.H. and Sartory, G. (1983) 'Blood injury phobia: a "reasonable excuse" for failing to give a specimen in a case of suspected drunken driving', *Journal of the Forensic Science Society*, 23: 197-201.

Gumpert, C.H., Linblad, F. and Grann, M. (2009) 'The quality of written expert testimony in alleged child sexual abuse: an empirical study', *Psychology Crime and Law*, 8: 77-92.

Haines, A. (2006) 'Criminal profiling use and belief: A survey of Canadian police officer opinion'. Unpublished Honours thesis, Memorial University of Newfoundland St Johns, Newfoundland, Canada.

Hakkanen, H. and Laajasalo, T. (2006) 'Homicide crime scene behaviours in a Finnish sample of mentally ill offenders', *Homicide Studies*, 10 (1): 33–54.

Haldenby, A., Majumdar, T. and Tanner, W. (2012) *Doing It Justice: Integrating Criminal Justice and Emergency Services Through Police and Crime Commissioners*. London: Reform.

Hale, C. (1996) 'Fear of crime: a review of the literature', *International Review of Victimology*, 4 (3): 79–151.

Hall, G. (2010) 'Clinical relevance of restorative justice', in J.M. Brown and E.A. Campbell (eds), *The Cambridge Handbook of Forensic Psychology*. Cambridge: Cambridge University Press. pp. 354–60.

Hall, M. (2009) *Victims of Crime – Policy and Practice in Criminal Justice*. Cullompton: Willan.

Hall, R. (2010) 'Risk management', in J. Brown and E. Campbell (eds), *The Cambridge Handbook of Forensic Psychology*. Cambridge: Cambridge University Press. pp. 410–15.

Hammond, S. (2000) 'Using psychometric tests method', in G. Breakwell, S. Hammond and C. Fife-Schaw (eds), *Research Methods in Psychology*. London: Sage. pp. 175–93.

Haney, C. (1980) 'Psychology and legal change: on the limits of factual jurisprudence', *Law and Human Behavior*, 4: 147–200.

Hansard (2014) 12th March: Written Statement Column 27WS.

Hanson, R.K. and Thornton, D. (1999) *STATIC-99: Improving Actuarial Risk Assessments for Sex Offenders* (User Report 99-02). Ottawa: Department of the Solicitor General of Canada.

Hanson, R.K. and Thornton, D. (2000) 'Improving risk assessment for sexual offenders: a comparison of three actuarial scales', *Law and Human Behaviour*, 24: 119–36.

Hare, R. (1998) 'The Hare PCL-R; some issues concerning its use and misuse', *Legal and Criminological Psychology*, 3: 99–119.

Hare, R., Cooke, D. and Hart, S. (1999) 'Psychopathy and sadistic personality disorder', in T. Millon, P. Blaney and R. Davies (eds), *Oxford Handbook of Psychopathology*. New York: Oxford University Press. pp. 555–84.

Harkins, L., Flak, V., Beech, A. and Woodhams, J. (2012) 'Evaluation of a community-based sex offender treatment programme using a Good Lives Model approach', *Sexual Abuse: A Journal of Research and Treatment*, 24: 519–43.

Harré, R. and Secord, P. (1972) *The Explanation of Social Behaviour*. Oxford: Blackwell.

Harris, G.T. and Rice, M. (2010) 'Risk and dangerousness in adults', in J. Brown and E. Campbell (eds), *Cambridge Handbook of Forensic Psychology*. Cambridge: Cambridge University Press. pp. 299–306.

Harris, G.T., Rice, M.E. and Quinsey, V.L. (1993) 'Violent recidivism of mentally disordered offenders: the development of a statistical prediction instrument', *Criminal Justice and Behaviour*, 20: 315–35.

Harrison, K. (2010) 'Dangerous offenders, indeterminate sentencing and the rehabilitation revolution', *Journal of Social Welfare and Family Law*, 32: 423–33.

Harrower, J. (1998) *Applying Psychology to Crime*. Coventry: Hodder and Stoughton.

Hart, S., Michie, C. and Cooke, D.J. (2007) 'Precision of actuarial risk assessment instrument', *British Journal of Psychiatry*, 190 (suppl. 49): s60–s65.

Harvey, D. (2005) *A Brief History of Neoliberalism*. Oxford: Oxford University Press.

Hazelwood, R.R. and Burgess, A.W. (eds) (1999) *Practical Aspects of Rape Investigation: A Multidisciplinary Approach*. Boca Raton, FL: CRC Press.

Hazelwood, R.R., Ressler, R.K., Depue, R.L. and Douglas, J.E. (1995) 'Criminal investigative analysis: an overview', in R.R. Hazelwood and A.W. Burgess (eds), *Practical Aspects of Rape Investigation: A Multidisciplinary Approach*. Boca Raton, FL: CRC Press. pp. 115–26.

Health Professions Council (HPC) (2008) *Standards of Conduct, Performance and Ethics*. London: HPC.

Health Care Professions Council (2013) *Fitness to Practice-Annual Report*. London: HCPC.

Health Care Professions Council (2014) *Fitness to Practice-Key Information 2014*. London: HCPC.

Healy, B. (2014) 'Towards a relational perspective: a practical and practice-based discussion on health and well-being amongst a sample of barristers', *QUR Law Review*, 14: 94–105.

Heidensohn, F. (1985) *Women and Crime*. London: Macmillan.

Heidensohn, F. (1992) *Women in Control*. Oxford: Clarendon.

Heilbrun, K. and Brooks, S. (2010) 'Forensic psychology and forensic science: a proposed agenda for the next decade', *Psychology Public Policy and Law*, 16: 219–53.

Helmus, L., Babchishin, K., Camilleri, J. and Olver, M. (2011) 'Forensic psychology opportunities in Canadian graduate programms: an update of Simourd and Wormith's (1995) survey', *Canadian Psychology*, 52: 122–7.

Her Majesty's Chief Inspector of Prisons for England and Wales (2014) *Annual Report 2012-13*. London: TSO. Available at www.justice.gov.uk/downloads/publications/corporate-reports/hmi-prisons/hm-inspectorate-prisons-annual-report-2012-13.pdf

Her Majesty's Government (2002) *Achieving Best Evidence: Guidance for Vulnerable and Intimidated Witnesses, Including Children*. London: Home Office.

Her Majesty's Government (2010) *The Coalition: Our Programme for Government*. London: Cabinet Office.

Her Majesty's Inspectorate of Constabulary (2014) *Crime-Recording: Making the Victim Count: The Final Report of an Inspection of Crime Data Integrity in Police Forces in England and Wales*. London: HMIC.

Herbert, C. (2010) 'Consent and capacity in civil cases', in J. Brown and E. Campbell (eds), *Cambridge Handbook of Forensic Psychology*. Cambridge: Cambridge University Press. pp. 596–601.

Herman, J. (2005) 'Justice from the victim's perspective', *Violence Against Women*, 11 (5): 571–602.

Heron, J. and Reason, P. (1997) 'A participatory inquiry paradigm', *Qualitative Inquiry*, 3: 274–94.

Hess, A. (2006) 'Defining forensic psychology', in I. Weiner and A. Hess (eds), *The Handbook of Forensic Psychology*, 3rd edn. Hoboken, NJ: Wiley. pp. 18–58.

Hirschfield, A., Christmann, K., Wilcox, A., Rogerson, M. and Sharratt, K. (2012) *Process Evaluation of Preventing Violent Extremism Programmes for Young People*. Youth Justice Board.

Hoge, R. and Andrews, D. (2002) *The Youth Level of Service/Case Management Inventory Manual and Scoring Key*. Toronto: Multi-Health Systems.

Hoge, R.D., Andrews, D. and Leschied, L. (1996) 'An investigation of risk and protective factors in a sample of youthful offenders', *Journal of Child Psychology and Psychiatry*, 37: 419–24.

Hollin, C. (2001) *Handbook of Offender Assessment and Treatment*. Chichester: Wiley.

Hollin, C. (2007) 'Criminological psychology', in M. Maguire, R. Morgan and R. Reiner (eds), *Oxford Handbook of Criminology*, 4th edn. Oxford: Oxford University Press. pp. 43–77.

Hollin, C. (2008) 'Evaluating offending behaviour programmes: does only randomisation glister?', *Criminology and Criminal Justice*, 8: 89–106.

Hollin, C. (2012) 'Criminological psychology', in M. Maguire, E. Morgan and R. Reiner (eds), *Oxford Handbook of Criminology*, 5th edn. Oxford: Oxford University Press. pp. 81–112.

Hollin, C. (2013) *Psychology and Crime: An Introduction to Criminological Psychology*, 2nd edn. Hove: Routledge.

Holmes, R.M. and Holmes, S.T. (1996) *Profiling Violent Crimes – An Investigative Tool*. London: Sage.

Holmstrom, L.L. and Burgess, A.W. (1978) *The Victim of Rape*. Hoboken, NJ: Wiley.

Homant, R.J. and Kennedy, D.B. (1998) 'Psychological aspects of crime scene profiling: validity research', *Criminal Justice and Behavior*, 25 (3): 319–43.

Hope, L. (2010) 'Jury decision-making', in: J. Brown, E. Campbell (eds), *The Cambridge Handbook of Forensic Psychology*. Cambridge: Cambridge University Press. pp. 675–82.

Hope, L. (2013) *Interviewing in Forensic Settings*. Oxford Bibliographies. Oxford: Oxford University Press.

Hope, T. (2005) 'Pretend it doesn't work: the anti-social bias in the Maryland Scientific Methods Scale', *European Journal of Criminal Policy and Research*, 11: 275–96.

Hope, T. (2009) 'The illusion of control; a response to Professor Sherman', *Criminology and Criminal Justice*, 9: 125–34.

Horvath, H.O. and Luborsky, L. (1993) 'The role of therapeutic alliance in psychotherapy', *Journal of Counselling and Clinical Psychology*, 61: 561–73.

Horvath, M.A.H. and Brown, J. (2006) 'Using police data for empirical investigation of rape', *Issues in Forensic Psychology*, 6: 49–56.

Hough, M., Allen, R. and Padel, U. (eds) (2006) *Reshaping Probation and Prisons: The New Offender Management Framework*. Bristol: Policy Press.

House of Commons Constitutional Affairs Committee (2007) *The Creation of the Ministry of Justice*. Sixth report of session 2006/7. HC 466. London: Stationery Office.

House of Commons Committee of Public Accounts (2014) Probation: Landscape Review. Fifty-eighth report of session 2013-14, HC 1114.

Howard League for Penal Reform [n.d.] *Collective Identity and Collective Exclusion*. www.urboss.org.uk/downloads/publications/HL_Life_outside.pdf (accessed 27 August 2014).

Howells, K. (2004) 'Anger and its link to violent offending', *Psychiatry Psychology and Law*, 11: 189–96.

Howells, K. and Day, A. (1999) 'The rehabilitation of offenders: international perspectives applied to Australian correctional system'. *Australian Institute of Criminology, Trends and Issues in Crime and Criminal Justice*, 112.

Howells, K. and Day, A. (2002) 'Grasping the nettle: treating and rehabilitating the violent offender', *Australian Psychologist*, 37: 222–8.

Howells, K., Krishnan, G. and Daffern, M. (2007) 'Challenges in the treatment of dangerous and severe personality disorder', *Advances in Psychiatric Treatment*, 13: 325-32.

Howells, K., Sheldon, K. and Davies, J. (2011) 'Conclusion', in K. Sheldon, J. Davies and K. Howells (eds), *Research in Practice for Forensic Practitioners*. London: Routledge. pp. 316-21.

Howitt, D. (2002) *Forensic and Criminal Psychology*. Harlow: Pearson Education.

Howitt, D. (2009) *Introduction to Forensic and Criminal Psychology*. Harlow: Pearson Education.

Howitt, D. (2011) 'Using qualitative methods to research offenders and forensic patients', in K. Sheldon, J. Davies and K. Howells (eds), *Research in Practice for Forensic Professionals*. Abingdon: Routledge. pp. 132-58.

Hoyle, C., Morgan, R. and Sanders, A. (1999) *The Victim's Charter – An Evaluation of Pilot Projects*. Research Findings No. 107. London: Home Office Research Development and Statistics Directorate.

Hudson, B. (2001) 'Punishment, rights and difference: defending justice in the risk society', in K. Stenson and R.R. Sullivan (eds), *Crime Risk and Justice: The Politics of Crime Control in Liberal Democracies.* Cullompton: Willan. pp. 144–72.

Huisman, W. and Nelen, H. (2014) 'The lost art of regulated tolerance? Fifteen years of regulating vices in Amsterdam', *Journal of Law and Society,* 41: 604–26.

Human Rights Joint Committee (2014) *Implications for Access to Justice of the Government's Proposals to Reform Judicial Review.* 13th report 2013/14. HL paper 174/HC paper 865. London: TSO.

Independent Police Commission (2013) *Policing for a Better Britain.* London: The Commission.

Indermaur, D. (1995) *Violent Property Crime.* Leichhardt, NSW: The Federation Press.

Ireland, C. and Fisher, M. (eds) (2010) *Consultancy and Advising in Forensic Practice: Empirical and Practical Guidelines.* Chichester: Wiley–Blackwell.

Ireland, J. (2012) *Evaluating Expert Witness Psychological Reports: Exploring Quality.* Preston: University of Central Lancashire.

Ishkanian, A. (2014) 'Neoliberalism and violence: the Big Society and the changing politics of domestic violence in England', *Critical Social Policy,* 34: 333–53.

Jackson, J.L., van den Eshof, P. and de Kleuver, E.E. (1997) 'A research approach to offender profiling', in J.L. Jackson and D.A. Bekerian (eds), *Offender Profiling: Theory, Research and Practice.* Chichester: Wiley. pp. 107–32.

James, A. (2013) *Examining intelligence-led policing.* Basingstoke: Palgrave.

James, D.V., Duffield, G., Blizard, R. and Hamilton, L.W. (2001) 'Fitness to plead: a prospective study of the inter-relationships between expert opinion, legal criteria and specific symptomatology', *Psychological Medicine,* 31: 139–50.

Jennings, M. (2003) 'Anger-Management Groupwork', in G. Towl (ed.), *Psychology in Prisons.* Oxford: Blackwell Publishing. pp. 93–101

Jennings, W.G., Piquero, A.R. and Reingle, J.M. (2012) 'On the overlap between victimization and offending: A review of the literature', *Aggression and Violent Behavior,* 17: 16–26.

Johnson, J. and Hall, E. (1988) 'Job strain, work place social support and cardiovascular disease: a cross-sectional study of a random sample of the working population', *American Journal of Public Health,* 78: 1336–42.

Jollife, D. and Farrington, D.P. (2004) 'Empathy and offending: a systematic review and meta-analysis', *Aggression and Violent Behavior,* 9: 441–76.

Jones, M. (2014) 'A diversity stone left unturned? Exploring the occupational complexities surrounding lesbian, gay and bi-sexual police officers', in J. Brown (ed.), *The Future of Policing.* Abingdon: Routledge. pp. 149–61.

Jones, S. (1986) *Policewomen and Equality.* London: Macmillan.

Jordan, J. (2001) 'Worlds apart? Women, rape and the police reporting process', *British Journal of Criminology,* 41: 679–706.

Jordan, J. (2004) 'Beyond belief? Police, rape and women's credibility', *Criminal Justice,* 4: 29–59.

Jordan, J. (2008a) 'Perfect victims. Perfect policing? Improving rape complainants' experiences of police investigations', *Public Administration,* 86: 699–719.

Jordan, J. (2008b) *Serial Survivors: Women's Narratives of Surviving Rape.* Sydney, NSW: The Federation Press.

Justickis, V. (2008) 'Does the law use even a small proportion of what legal psychology has to offer', in D. Canter and R. Zukauskiene (eds), *Psychology and Law: Bridging the Gap.* Aldershot: Ashgate. pp. 223–37.

Kahneman, D. (2011) *Thinking, Fast and Slow.* London: Penguin Books.

Kasperson, R., Renn, O., Slovic, P., Brown, H., Emel, J., Goble, R., Kasperson, J. and Ratick, S. (1988) 'The social amplification of risk: a conceptual framework', *Risk Analysis,* 8: 177–87.

Kebbell, M. (2010) 'Credibility', in J. Brown and E. Campbell (eds), *The Cambridge Handbook of Forensic Psychology*. Cambridge: Cambridge University Press. pp. 153–8.

Keegan, E. (2011) 'Putting torture in its place: a brief examination of the relationship between torture and human rights', *University College Dublin Law Review*, 11: 87–99.

Keeling, J.A., Rose, J.L. and Beech, A.R. (2006) 'A comparison of the application of the self-regulation model of the relapse process for mainstream and special needs sexual offenders', *Sexual Abuse: A Journal of Research and Treatment*, 18: 373–82.

Kelly, L. (1988) *Surviving Sexual Violence*. Cambridge: Polity Press.

Kelly, L. (2002) *A Research Review on the Reporting, Investigation and Prosecution of Rape Cases*. London: Her Majesty's Crown Prosecution Service Inspectorate.

Kemmis, S. and Wilkinson, M. (1998) 'Participatory action research in the study of practice', in B. Atweh, S. Kemmis and P. Weeks (eds), *Action Research in Practice: Partnerships for Social Justice in Education*. New York: Routledge. pp. 21–36.

Kenney-Herbert, J., Taylor, M., Puri, R. and Phull, J. (2013) *Standards for Community Forensic Mental Health Services*. London: Royal College of Psychiatrists Forensic Quality Network for Forensic Mental Health Services.

Keppel, R.D. (1998) *Signature Killers*. London: Arrow Books.

Kershaw, C., Chivite-Matthews, N., Thomas, C. and Aust, R. (2001) *The 2001 British Crime Survey: First Results, England and Wales*. London: Government Statistical Service.

King, M. and Wexler, D. (2010) 'Therapeutic jurisprudence', in J. Brown and E. Campbell (eds), *Cambridge Handbook of Forensic Psychology*. Cambridge: Cambridge University Press. pp. 126–32.

Klein, G. (1999) *Sources of Power: How People Make Decisons*. Cambridge, MA: MIT Press.

Knabe-Nicol, S. and Alison, L. (2011) 'The cognitive expertise of geographic profilers', in L. Alison and L. Rainbow (eds), *Professionalising Offender Profiling*. Abingdon: Routledge. pp. 126–59.

Knabe-Nicol, S., Alison, L. and Rainbow, L. (2011) 'The cognitive expertise of behavioural investigative advisers in the UK and Germany', in L. Alison and L. Rainbow (eds), *Professionalising Offender Profiling*. Abingdon: Routledge. pp. 72–125.

Kocsis, R.N. (2006) 'Validities and abilities in criminal profiling: the dilemma for David Canter's investigative psychology', *International Journal of Offender Therapy and Comparative Criminology*, 50 (4): 458–77.

Kocsis, R.N. and Hayes, A.F. (2004) 'Believing is seeing? Investigating the perceived accuracy of criminal psychological profiles', *International Journal of Offender Therapy and Comparative Criminology*, 48: 149–60.

Kocsis, R.N. and Heller, G.Z. (2004) 'Believing is seeing II: Beliefs and perceptions of criminal psychological profiles', *International Journal of Offender Therapy and Comparative Criminology*, 48: 313–29.

Kocsis, R.N., Irwin, H.J. and Hayes, A.F. (1998) 'Organised and disorganised criminal behaviour syndromes in arsonists: A validation study of a psychological profiling concept', *Psychiatry, Psychology and Law*, 5: 117–31.

Kocsis, R.N. and Palermo, G.B. (2015) 'Disentangling criminal profiling: accuracy, homology and the myth of trait-based profiling', *International Journal of Offender Therapy and Comparative Criminology*, 59 (3): 313–32.

Kocsis, R.N., Irwin, H.J., Hayes, A.F. and Nunn, R. (2000) 'Expertise in psychological profiling: A comparative assessment', *Journal of Interpersonal Violence*, 15: 311–31.

Köhnken, G., Milne, R., Memon, A. and Bull, R. (1999) 'A meta-analysis on the effects of the cognitive interview', *Special Issue of Psychology, Crime and Law*, 5: 3–27.

Kolb, D. (1984) *Experiential Learning*. Englewood Cliffs, NJ: Prentice Hall.

Koss, M. and Cleveland, N. (1997) 'Stepping on toes: social roots of date rape lead to intractability and politicization', in M.D. Schwartz (ed), *Researching Sexual Violence*

Against Women: Methodological and Personal Perspectives. Thousand Oaks, CA: Sage. pp. 4-21.

Kohlberg, L. (1984) *Essays on Moral Development: The Psychology of Moral Development*. San Francisco: Harper & Row.

Kovera, M. and Greathouse, S. (2008) 'Pretrial publicity; effects, remedies and judicial knowledge', in E. Borgida and S. Fiske (eds), *Beyond Commonsense: Psychology in the Courtroom*. Malden, MA: Blackwell. pp. 261-79.

Krakowski, M. (2003) 'Violence and serotonin: influence of impulse control, affect regulation and social functioning', *Journal of Neuropsychiatry and Clinical Neurosciences*, 15: 294-305.

Kuhn, Thomas S. (1962) *The Structure of Scientific Revolutions*. Chicago: University of Chicago Press.

Lacey, N. (2013) 'Punishment, (neo)liberalism and social democracy', in J. Simon and R. Sparks (eds), *The Sage Handbook of Punishment and Society*. London: Sage. pp 260-80.

LaGrange, R.L. and Ferraro, K.F. (1987) 'The elderly's fear of crime: a critical examination of the research', *Research on Aging*, 9: 372-91.

Lambert, M.J. (1983) 'Comment on "A case study of the process and outcome of time-limited counselling"', *Journal of Counseling Psychology*, 30: 22-5.

Langer, W. (1972) *The Mind of Adolf Hitler*. New York: Basic Books.

Langevoort, D. (1998) 'Behavioral theories of judgment and decision making in legal scholarship: a literature review', *Vanderbilt Law Review*, 51: 1499-540.

Latimer, J., Dowden, C. and Muise, D. (2005) 'The effectiveness of restorative justice practices: a meta-analysis', *The Prison Journal*, 85: 127-44.

Laub, J. and Sampson, R. (2001) 'Understanding desistence from crime', *Crime and Justice*, 28: 1-69.

Laws, D.R. and Ward, T. (2011) *Desistance from Sexual Offending: Alternatives to Throwing Away the Keys*. New York: Guilford Press.

Laycock, G. (2005) 'Defining crime science', in M. Smith and N. Tilley (eds), *Crime Science: New Approaches to Preventing and Detecting Crime*. Cullompton: Willan. pp. 3-24.

Lea, J. and Young, J. (1984) *What Is to Be Done about Law and Order?* Harmondsworth: Penguin.

Lea, S., Auburn, T. and Kibblewhite, K. (1999) 'Working with sex offenders: the perceptions and experiences of professionals and para professionals', *International Journal of Offender Therapy and Comparative Criminology*, 43: 103-19.

Leishman, F., Loveday, B. and Savage, S. (eds) (1996) *Core Issues in Policing*. London: Longmans.

Letherby, G., Williams, K., Birch, P. and Cain, M. (eds) (2008) *Sex as Crime?* Cullompton: Willan.

Levin, A. and Greisberg, S. (2003) 'Vicarious trauma in attorneys', *Pace Law Review*, 24: 245-52.

Lewin, K. (1952) *Field Theory in Social Science: Selected Theoretical Papers by Kurt Lewin*. London: Tavistock.

Lindsay, W.R., Stetoe, L. and Beech, A.R. (2008) 'The Ward & Hudson pathways model of the sexual offense process applied to offenders with intellectual disability', *Sexual Abuse: A Journal of Research and Treatment*, 20: 379-92.

Linehan, M.M. (1993) *The Skills Training Manual for Treating Borderline Personality Disorder*. New York: Guilford Press.

Lipscombe, S. and Beard, J. (2014) *The Rehabilitation of Offenders Act 1974*. House of Commons Briefing Paper.

Lipsey, M.W. (1992) 'Juvenile delinquency treatment: A meta-analytic inquiry into the variability of effects', in T.D. Cook, H. Cooper, D.S. Cordray, H. Hartmann, Larry V. Hedges, R.J. Light, T.A. Louis and F. Mosteller (eds), *Metaanalysis for Explanation*. New York: Russell Sage Foundation. pp. 83-128.

Loader, I. and Sparks, R. (2007) 'Contemporary landscapes of crime, order and control: governance, risk and globalisation', in M. Maguire, R. Morgan and R. Reiner (eds), *The Oxford Handbook of Criminology*, 4th edn. Oxford: Oxford University Press. pp. 78-101.

Loader, I. and Sparks, R. (2010a) *Public Criminology*. London: Routledge.

Loader, I. and Sparks, R. (2010b) 'What is to be done with public criminology?', *Criminology and Public Policy*, 9: 771-81.

Loader, I. and Sparks, R. (2012) 'Situating criminology: on the production and consumption of knowledge about crime and justice', in M. Maguire, R. Morgan and R. Reiner (eds), *The Oxford Handbook of Criminology*, 5th edn. Oxford: Oxford University Press. pp. 3-38.

Loftus, E. (1986) 'Ten years in the life of an expert witness', *Law and Human Behavior*, 10: 241-63.

Logan, C. and Johnstone, L. (eds) (2012) *Managing Clinical Risk: A Guide to Effective Practice*. Abingdon: Routledge.

Lombroso, C. (1911) *Crime, Its Causes and Remedies*. Boston, MA: Little, Brown.

Lösel, F. (2003) 'The development of delinquent behaviour', in R. Bull and D. Carson (eds), *Handbook of Psychology in Legal Contexts*, 2nd edn. Chichester: Wiley. pp. 244-67.

Lösel, F. and T. Bliesner (1994) 'Some high risk adolescents do not develop conduct problems: A study of protective factors', *International Journal of Behavioural Development*, 17: 753-77.

Loveday, B. (1996) 'Crime at the core', in F. Leishman, B. Loveday and S. Savage (eds), *Core Issues in Policing*. Harlow: Longman. pp. 73-100.

Luthar, S. and Latendresse, S. (2005) 'Comparable "risks" at the socioeconomic status extremes: pre-adolescents' perceptions of parenting'. *Developmental and Psychopathology*, 17: 207-30.

Lyall, M. (2014) 'Understanding parricide', *Journal of Forensic Psychiatry and Psychology*, 25 (4): [E-pub ahead of print 8 May 2014] doi: 10.1080/14789949.2014.916474.

Lyons, E. (2000) 'Qualitative data analysis; data display model', in G. Breakwell, S. Hammond and C. Fife-Schaw (eds), *Research Methods in Psychology*, 2nd edn. London: Sage. pp. 269-80.

Lynn, L. (1998) 'The new public management as an international phenomenon: a sceptical viewpoint', in L. Jones and K. Schedler (eds), *International Perspectives on the New Public Management*. Greenwich, CT: JAI Press.

Macdonald, S. (2007) 'ASBOS and control orders; two recurring themes two apparent contradictions', *Parliamentary Affairs*, 60: 601-24.

Mackay, R.D. and Kearns, G. (2000) 'An upturn in unfitness to plead? Disability in relation to the trial under the 1991 Act', *Criminal Law Review*, July: 532-46.

Maddock, S. (1999) *Challenging Women: Gender Culture and Organisation*. London: Sage.

Maden, A. (2007) 'Dangerous and severe personality', *British Journal of Psychiatry*, 190: s8-s11.

Maguire, M. (2012) 'Criminal statistics and the construction of crime', in M. Maguire, R. Morgan and R. Reiner (eds), *The Oxford Handbook of Criminology*, 5th edn. Oxford: Oxford University Press. pp. 206-44.

Mahoney, B., Davies, M. and Scurlock-Evans, L. (2014) 'Victimization among female and male sexual minority status groups: Evidence from the British crime survey 2007-2010', *Journal of Homosexuality*, 61: 1435-61.

Mair, G. and Burke, L. (2012) *Redemption, Rehabilitation and Risk Management: A History of Probation.* London: Routledge.

Malleson, K. and Moules, R. (2010) *The Legal System*, 4th edn. Oxford: Oxford University Press.

Mann, R.E. and Shingler, J. (2001) 'Collaborative risk assessment with sexual offenders'. Paper presented at the National Organisation for the Treatment of Abusers, Cardiff, Wales.

Marcus, B. (1982) 'Psychologists in the prison department', in D. Canter and S. Canter (eds), *Psychology in Practice: Perspectives on Professional Psychology.* Chichester: Wiley. pp. 105-24.

Marogna, G. (2005) 'Can criminal antecedent history of a homicide offender be inferred from his crime scene behaviours'. Unpublished MSc thesis, University of Leicester.

Marshall, B.C. and Alison, L.J. (2007) 'Stereotyping, congruence and presentation order: interpretative biases in utilizing offender profiles', *Psychology, Crime and Law*, 13: 285-303.

Martin, S. and Davis, H. (2001). 'What works and for whom? The competing rationalities of "Best Value"', *Policy & Politics*, 29: 465-75.

Martinson, R. (1974) 'What works? Questions and answers about prison reform', *The Public Interest*, 35: 22-54.

Martinson, R. (1979) 'New findings, new views: a note of caution regarding sentencing reform', *Hofstra Law Review*, 7: 243-58.

Maruna, S. (2010) *The Great Escape: Exploring the Rehabilitation Dynamics Involved in Changing Tune: A Report.* Belfast: Queens University.

Maruna, S. (2011) 'Judicial rehabilitation and the "clean bill of health" in criminal justice', *European Journal of Probation*, 3: 97-117.

Maruna, S. (2013) *'What Works' and Desistence from Crime: Merging Two Approaches to Research: A Discussion Paper Prepared for the Correctional Services Accreditation and Advice Panel.* Belfast: Queens University.

Maruna, S. and King, A. (2009) 'Once a criminal, always a criminal?: "Redeemability" and the psychology of punitive attitudes', *European Journal of Criminal Policy*, 15: 7-24.

Matthews, R. (2009) 'Beyond "So What?" Criminology: Rediscovering Realism', *Theoretical Criminology*, 13: 341-62.

Matthews, R.A. (2010) 'The Construction of "So What?" Criminology: A Realist Analysis', *Crime, Law and Social Change*, 54: 125-40.

Matthews, R. (2014) *Realist Criminology.* Basingstoke: Palgrave Macmillan.

Mayhew, P. (2000) 'Researching the state of crime: local, national and international victim surveys', in R. King and E. Wincup (eds), *Doing Research on Crime and Justice.* Oxford: Oxford University Press. pp. 91-120.

McCold, P. (2003) 'A survey of assessment research on mediation and conferencing', in L. Walgrave (ed.), *Repositioning Restorative Justice.* Cullompton: Willan. pp. 67-120.

McCourt, W. (2002) 'New public management in developing countries', in K. McLaughlin, S.P. Osborne and E. Ferlie (eds), *New Public Management: Current Trends and Future Prospects.* London: Routledge. pp. 227-42.

McCulloch, T. (2005) 'Probation, social context and desistance: retracing the relationship', *Probation Journal*, 52 (1): 8-22.

McElhaney, J. (1992) The 1992 All-Angus Rules, 19 LrrG. 19, 21 (Fall 1992).

McGrath, R., Cumming, G., Burchard, B., Zeoli, S. and Ellerby, L. (2010) *Current Practices and Emerging Trends in Sexual Abuser Management: The Safer Society 2009 North American Survey.* Brandon, VT: Safer Society Press.

McGrath, S.A., Nilsen, A.A. and Kerley, K.R. (2011) 'Sexual victimization in childhood and the propensity for juvenile delinquency and adult criminal behaviour: A systematic review', *Aggression and Violent Behavior*, 16: 485-92.

McGuickin, G. and Brown, J. (2001) 'Managing risk from sex offenders living in communities: comparing police, press and public perceptions', *Risk Management: An International Journal*, 3: 47–60.

McGuire, J. (1995) *What Works: Reducing Reoffending: Guidelines from Research and Practice*. Chichester: Wiley.

McGuire, J. (ed.) (2002) *Offender Rehabilitation and Treatment: Effective Programs and Policies to Reduce Reoffending*. Chichester: Wiley.

McGuire, J. (2010) 'Rehabilitation of offenders', in J. Brown and E. Campbell (eds), *The Cambridge Handbook of Forensic Psychology*. Cambridge: Cambridge University Press. pp. 400–9.

McGuire, J. (2013) 'What Works to reduce reoffending: 18 years on', in L.A. Craig, L. Dixon and T.A. Gannon (eds), *What Works in Offender Rehabilitation: An Evidence Based Approach to Assessment and Treatment*. Chichester, Wiley–Blackwell.

McLaughlin, E. and Murji, K. (2001) 'Lost connections and new directions: neo-liberalism, new public management and the "modernisation" of the British police', in K. Stenson and R.R. Sullivan (eds), *Crime Risk and Justice: the Politics of Crime Control in Liberal Democracies*. Cullompton: Willan. pp. 104–22.

McLaughlin, K. and Osborne, S. (2002) 'Current trends and future prospects of public management: A guide', in K. McLaughlin, S.P. Osborne, E. and Ferlie, E. (eds), *New Public Management: Current Trends and Future Prospects*. London: Routledge. pp. 1–2.

McLaughlin, K., Osborne, S.P. and Ferlie, E. (eds) (2002) *New Public Management: Current Trends and Future Prospects*. London: Routledge.

McMurran, M. (2010) 'Theories of change', in J. Brown and E. Campbell (eds), *The Cambridge Handbook of Forensic Psychology*. Cambridge: Cambridge University Press. pp. 118–25.

McNeill, F. (2006) 'A desistance paradigm for offender management', *Criminology and Criminal Justice*, 6: 39–62.

McNeill, F., Farrall, S., Lightowler, C. and Maruna, S. (2012) 'Reexamining evidence-based practice in community corrections: beyond "A confined view" of what works', *Justice Research and Policy*, 14: 35–60.

Memon, A. (2008) 'Eyewitness research: theory and practice', in D. Canter and R. Zukauskiene (eds), *Psychology and Law: Bridging the Gap*. Aldershot: Ashgate. pp. 51–64.

Memon, A., Meissner, C. and Fraser, J. (2010) 'The cognitive interview: a meta analytic review and study space analysis of the past 25 years', *Psychology, Public Policy and Law*, 16: 340–72.

Mental Capacity Act (2005) www.legislation.gov.uk/ukpga/2005/9/contents.

Mental Health Act (2007) www.legislation.gov.uk/ukpga/2007/12/contents.

Merrington, S. and Stanley, S. (2000) 'Doubts about the what works initiative', *Probation Journal*, 47: 272–5.

Miller, W.R. and Rollnick, S. (2013) *Motivational Interviewing*, 3rd edn. New York: Guilford Press.

Millward, L. (2005) *Understanding Occupational and Organisational Psychology*. London: Sage.

Milne, D. (2007) 'An empirical definition of clinical supervision', *British Journal of Clinical Psychology*, 46: 437–447.

Milne, R. and Bull, R. (1999) *Investigative Interviewing: Psychology and Practice*. Chichester: Wiley.

Milne, R. and Bull, R. (2003) 'Interviewing by the police', in D. Carson and R. Bull (eds), *Handbook of Psychology in Legal Contexts*, 2nd edn. Chichester: Wiley. pp. 111–25.

Milne, R., Clare, I.C.H. and Bull, R. (1999) 'Using the cognitive interview with adults with mild learning disabilities', *Psychology, Crime and Law*, 5: 81–99.

Ministry of Justice (2010b) 'Breaking the Cycle: Effective Punishment, Rehabilitation and Sentencing of Offenders'. Green Paper presented to Parliament December 2010. www.justice.gov.uk/consultations/docs/breaking-the-cycle.pdf.

Modood, T. (1998) *Ethnic Minorities in Britain: Diversity and Disadvantage. The Fourth National Survey of Ethnic Minorities*. PSI Report. London: Policy Studies Institute.

Moffitt, T. (1993) '"Life-course persistent" and "adolescent-limited" antisocial behaviour: a developmental taxonomy', *Psychological Review*, 100: 674–701.

Mokros, A. and Alison, L. (2002) 'Is offender profiling possible? Testing the predicted homology of crime scene actions and background characteristics in a sample of rapists', *Legal and Criminological Psychology*, 7: 25–43.

Monahan, J. (2006) 'Tarasoff at thirty: how developments in science and policy shape the common law', *University of Cincinnati Law Review*, 75: 497–521.

Monahan, J., Steadman, H., Robbins, P., Appelbaum, P., Banks, S., Grisso, T., Heilbrun, K., Mulvey, E., Roth, L. and Silver, E. (2005) 'An actuarial model of violence risk assessment for persons with mental disorders', *Psychiatric Services*, 56: 810–15.

Moran-Ellis, J. (1996) 'Close to home: the experience of researching child sexual abuse', in M. Hester, L. Kelly and J. Radford (eds), *Women Violence and Male Power*. Buckingham: Open University. pp. 167–89.

Moran-Ellis, J., Alexander, V., Cronin, A. et al. (2006) 'Triangulation and integration: processes, claims and implications', *Qualitative Research*, 6: 45–59.

Morgan, S. and Palk, G. (2012) 'Pragmatism and precision: psychology in the service of civil litigation', *Australian Psychologist*, 48: 41–6.

Mulcahy, L. (2007) 'Architects of justice: the politics of court house design', *Social and Legal Studies*, 16 (3): 383–403.

Mulcahy, L. (2010) *Legal Architecture: Justice, Due Process and the Place of Law*. Abingdon: Routledge.

Mulcahy, L. (2013) 'Putting defendants in their place: why do we still use the dock in criminal proceedings?', *British Journal of Criminology*, 53: 1139–56.

Muller, D.A. (2000) 'Criminal profiling. Real science of just wishful thinking?', *Homicide Studies*, 4: 234–64.

Murji, K. (2001) 'Moral panic', in R. McLaughlin and J. Muncie (eds), *The Sage Dictionary of Criminology*. London: Sage. pp. 175–7.

Murphy, G. and Clare, I. (2003) 'Adults' capacity to make legal decisions', in D. Carson and R. Bull (eds), *Handbook of Psychology in Legal Contexts*, 2nd edn. Chichester: Wiley. pp. 31–66.

Myhill, A. and Allen, J. (2002) *Rape and Sexual Assault of Women: The Extent and Nature of the Problem. Findings from the British Crime Survey*. Home Office Research Study 237: London: HMSO.

Nagel, R.W. (1983) 'Tensions between law and psychology, fact myth or ideology?'. Paper presented at the meeting of the American Psychology-Law Society, Chicago, October.

Nagin, D., Piquero, A., Scott, E. and Steinberg, L. (2006) 'Public preference for rehabilitation versus incarceration of juvenile offenders: evidence from a contingent valuation survey', *Criminology and Public Policy*, 5: 627–52.

Nash, M. (2001) 'Influencing or influenced? The probation service and criminal justice police', in M. Ryan, S. Savage and D. Wall (eds), *Policy Networks in Criminal Justice*. Basingstoke: Palgrave Macmillan. pp. 55–75.

Natarajan, M. (2008) *Women Police in a Changing Society*. Aldershot: Ashgate.

NHS Commissioning Board (2013) 2014/15 NHS standard contract for high secure mental health services (adults). www.england.nhs.uk/wp-content/uploads/2013/06/c02-high-sec-mh.pdf (accessed 2 March 2015).

Nee, C. (2004) 'The offender's perspective on crime: methods and principles in data collection', in A. Needs and G. Towl (eds), *Applying Psychology to Forensic Practice*. Oxford: BPS and Blackwell. pp. 3–17.

Nee, C. and Taylor, M. (1988) 'Residential burglary in the Republic of Ireland: A situational perspective', *The Howard Journal of Criminal Justice*, 27: 105-16.

Nee, C.and Taylor, M. (2000) 'Examining burglars' target selection: Interview, experiment or ethnomethodology?', *Psychology, Crime and Law*, 6: 45-59.

Needs, A. (2008) 'Forensic psychology', in G. Towl, D. Farrington, D. Crighton and G. Hughes (eds), *Dictionary of Forensic Psychology*. Cullompton: Willan. pp. 75-7.

Needs, A. (2010a) 'Training in forensic psychology: a personal view', *Forensic Update*, 100: 36-41.

Needs, A. (2010b) 'Systemic failure and human error', in C. Ireland and M. Fisher (eds), *Consultancy and Advising in Forensic Practice: Empirical and Practical Guidelines*. Chichester: Wiley-Blackwell.

Needs, A. and Towl, G. (eds) (2004) *Applying Psychology to Forensic Practice*. Oxford: Blackwell.

Netto, N.R., Carter, J. and Bonell, C. (2014) 'A systematic review of interventions that adopt the "Good Lives" approach to offender rehabilitation', *Journal of Offender Rehabilitation*, 53: 403-32.

Newburn, T. (2003) *Crime and Criminal Justice Policy*. Harlow: Pearson Education.

Norman, P., Bennett, P. and Lewis, H. (1998) 'Understanding binge drinking among young people: an application of the theory of planned behaviour', *Health Education Research*, 13: 163-9.

Norris, F.H. and Kaniasty, K. (1991) 'The psychological experience of crime: a test of the mediating role of beliefs in explaining the distress of victims', *Journal of Social and Clinical Psychology*, 10: 239-61.

Norris, G. and Petherick, W. (2010) 'Criminal profiling in the courtroom: behavioural investigative advice or bad character evidence', *Cambrian Law Review*, 41: 39-54.

O'Donohue, W. and Levensky, E. (eds) (2004) *Handbook of Forensic Psychology: Resource for Mental Health and Legal Professionals*. Amsterdam: Elsevier.

Office for National Statistics (ONS) (1997) *Survey of Psychiatric Morbidity among Prisoners in England and Wales*. London: Department of Health.

Office for National Statistics (ONS) (2014) *Crime in England and Wales. Year ending March 2014*. Statistical Bulletin, 17 July 2014.

Ogelsby, C. (1997) 'Widow protests parole of mall killer', *Atlanta Journal and Constitution*, April 18, p. F8.

Ogloff, J. and Davis, N.R. (2004) 'Advances in offender assessment and rehabilitation: contributions of the risk-needs-responsivity approach', *Psychology, Crime and Law*, 10: 229-42.

Ogloff, J. and Finkelman, D. (1999) 'Psychology and law: an overview', in R. Roesch, S. Hart and J. Ogloff (eds), *Psychology and Law: The State of the Discipline*. New York: Kluwer Academic/Plenum. pp. 2-20.

Ogloff, J. and Otto, R. (1993) 'Psychological autopsy: clinical and legal perspectives', *St Louis University Law Journal*, 37: 607-46.

Oleson, J. (1996) 'Psychological profiling: does it actually work?', *Forensic Update*, 46: 11-14.

O'Loughlin, A. (2014) 'The offender personality disorder pathway: expansion in the face of failure?', *The Howard Journal*, 53: 173-92.

O'Rourke, M. (1999) 'Dangerousness: how best to manage the risk', *The Therapist*, 6 (2): 11-12.

O'Rourke, M. (2008) 'Risk assessment', in G.J. Towl, D.P. Farrington, D.A. Crighton and G. Hughes (eds), *Dictionary of Forensic Psychology*. Cullompton: Willan. pp. 160-1.

Osborne, S.P. and McLaughlin, K. (2002) 'The New Public Management in context', in K. McLaughlin, S.P. Osborne and E. Ferlie (eds), *New Public Management: Current Trends and Future Prospects*. London: Routledge. pp. 7-14.

Otto, R. (1989) 'Bias and expert testimony of mental health professionals in adversarial proceedings: a preliminary investigation', *Behavioral Sciences and the Law*, 7: 267-72.

Otto, R. and Heilbrun, K. (2002) 'The practice of forensic psychology: a look toward the future in the light of the past', *American Psychologist*, 57: 5-19.

Packer, I. (2008) 'Specialized practice in forensic psychology', *Professional Psychology: Research and Practice*, 39: 245-9.

Pain, R. and Gill, S. (2001) *Children, Crime Victimisation and Sources of Support: A Feasibility Study for Junior Victim Support*. Durham: Department of Geography, University of Durham.

Pakes, F. and Pakes, S. (2009) *Criminal Psychology*. Cullompton: Willan.

Palmer, E.J. and Hollin, C.R. (1998) 'A comparison of patterns of moral development in young offenders and non-offenders', *Legal and Criminological Psychology*, 3: 225-35.

Parole Board (2014) The Parole Board for England and Wales: Annul Report and Accounts 2013-14. HC 299. London: HMSO.

Partington, M. (2006) *The English Legal System*, 3rd edn. Oxford: Oxford University Press.

Pawson, R. and Tilley, N. (1998) 'Caring Communities, Paradigm Polemics, Design Debates', *Evaluation*, 4: 73-90.

Pearson, A., La Bash, H. and Follette, V. (2010) 'Post traumatic stress disorder', in J. Brown and E. Campbell (eds), *The Cambridge Handbook of Forensic Psychology*. Cambridge: Cambridge University Press. pp. 283-91.

Pearlman, L.A. and Saakvitne, K.W. (1995) *Trauma and the Therapist: Counter Transference and Vicarious Traumatization in Psychotherapy with Incest Survivors*. New York: Norton.

Pease, K. (2001) 'Rational choice theory', in E. McLaughlin and J. Muncie (eds), *The Sage Dictionary of Criminology*. London: Sage. pp. 235-6.

Peay, J. (1994) 'Mentally disordered offenders', in M. Maguire, R. Morgan and R. Reiner (eds), *The Oxford Handbook of Criminology*. Oxford: Oxford Univeristy Press. pp. 1119-60.

Penrod, S., Bull Kovvera, M. and Groscip, J. (2011) 'Jury research methods', in B. Rosenfeld and S. Penrod (eds), *Research Methods in Forensic Psychology*. Hoboken, NJ: Wiley. pp. 191-214.

Phillips, C. and Sampson, A. (1998) 'Preventing repeated racial victimization – an action research project', *British Journal of Criminology*, 38: 124-44.

Pinizzotto, A.J. (1984) 'Forensic psychology: criminal personality profiling', *Journal of Police Science and Administration*, 12: 32-40.

Pinizzotto, A.J. and Finkel, N.J. (1990) 'Criminal personality profiling: an outcome and process study', *Law and Human Behavior*, 14: 215-33.

Piquero, A.R. and Moffitt, T.E. (2010) 'Life course persistent offending', in J. Adler and J. Grey (eds), *Forensic Psychology: Concepts, Debates and Practice*, 2nd edn. Cullompton: Willan. pp. 201-22.

Pointing, J. and Maguire, M. (1988) 'Introduction: the rediscovery of the crime victim', in M. Maguire and J. Pointing (eds), *Victims of Crime: A New Deal?* Milton Keynes: Open University Press. pp. 1-13.

Polaschek, D., Hudson, S., Ward, T. and Siegert, R. (2001) 'Rapists' offense processes: A preliminary descriptive model', *Journal of Interpersonal Violence*, 16: 524-44.

Pollitt, C. (2000) 'Is the emperor in his underwear? An analysis of the impacts of public management reform', *Public Management*, 2: 181-200.

Powell, G. and Powell, C. (2010) 'Personal injury', in J. Brown and E. Campbell (eds), *Cambridge Handbook of Forensic Psychology*. Cambridge: Cambridge University Press. pp. 612-19.

Porter, L. and Alison, L. (2004) 'Behavioural coherence in violent group activity: an interpersonal mode of sexually violent gang behaviours', *Aggressive Behaviour*, 30: 449-68.

Posen, I. (1994) *Review of Core and Ancillary Tasks*. London: HMSO.

Poythress, N., Otto, R.K., Darkes, J. and Starr, L. (1993) 'APA's Expert Panel in the Congressional Review of the *USS Iowa* incident', *American Psychologist*, January, 8-15.

Pratt, J., Brown, D., Brown, M., Hallsworth, S. and Morrison, W. (2005) *The New Punitiveness: Trends, Theories and Perspectives*. Cullompton: Willan.

Prentky, R.A. and Knight, R.A. (1991) 'Identifying critical dimensions for discriminating among rapists', *Journal of Consulting Clinical Psychology*, 59: 643-61.

Prins, H. (2007) 'The Michael Stone Inquiry: a somewhat different homicide report', *Journal of Forensic Psychiatry and Psychology*, 18: 411-31.

Prochaska, J.O. and DiClemente, C.C. (1983) 'Stages and processes of self-change in smoking: towards an integrated model of change', *Journal of Consulting and Clinical Psychology*, 51: 390-5.

Proulx, J. (2014a) 'Pithers' relapse prevention model', in J. Proulx, E. Beauregard, E. Lussier and B. Leclerc (eds), *Pathways to Sexual Aggression*. Abingdon: Routledge. pp. 9-25.

Proulx, J. (2014b) 'Ward and Hudson's pathways and self regulation model', in J. Proulx, P. Beauregard, P. Lussier and B. Leclerc (eds), *Pathways to Sexual Aggression*. London: Routledge. pp. 26-48.

Puckering, C. (2010) 'Parental capacity and conduct', in J. Brown and E. Campbell (eds), *The Cambridge Handbook of Forensic Psychology*. Cambridge: Cambridge University Press. pp. 242-50.

Quinsey, V. (2009) 'Are we there yet? Stasis and progress in forensic psychology', *Canadian Psychology*, 50: 15-21.

Raaijmakers, E., Keijser, J., Nieuwhbeerta, P. and Dirkzwager, A. (2014) 'Criminal defendants' satisfaction with lawyers: perceptions of procedural fairness and effort of the lawyer', *Psychology Crime and Law* [E-pub ahead of print 2 September 2014] doi: 10.1080/1068316X.2014.951646.

Radford, J. (1992) 'Women's laughter: a licence to kill? The killing of Jane Asher', in J. Radford and D. Russell (eds), *The Politics of Killing*. Buckingham: Open University Press. pp. 253-66.

Rainbow, L. (2008) 'Taming the beast: the UK approach to the management of behavioural investigative advice', *Journal of Police and Criminal Psychology*, 23: 90-7.

Rainbow, L. and Gregory, A. (2011) 'What Behavioural Investigative Advisers actually do', in L. Alison and L. Rainbow (eds), *Professionalising Offender Profiling*. Abingdon: Routledge. pp. 18-34.

Raynor, P. (2004) 'The Probation Service "Pathfinders": finding the path and losing the way?', *Criminal Justice*, 4: 309-25.

Raynor, P. (2008) 'Community penalties and Home Office research: on the way back to "nothing works"?', *Criminology and Criminal Justice*, 8: 73-87.

Reiner, R. (1994) 'A truce in the war between police and academe', *Policing Today*, 1: 30-2.

Reiner, R. (2006) 'Beyond risk: a lament for social democratic criminology', in T. Newburn and P. Rick (eds), *The Politics of Crime Control*. Oxford: Oxford University Press. pp. 301-43.

Reiner, R. (2007) *Law and Order: An Honest Citizen's Guide to Crime and Control*. Cambridge: Polity Press.

Reiner, R. (2010) *The Politics of the Police*, 4th edn. Oxford: Oxford University Press.

Reiner, R. (2012) 'What's left? The prospects for social democratic criminology', *Crime, Media, Culture*, 6: 135-50.

Reiner, R. (2013) 'Who governs? Democracy, plutocracy, science and prophecy in policing', *Criminology and Criminal Justice*, 13: 161-80.

Ressler, R.K., Burgess, A.W., Depue, R.L., Douglas, J.E. and Hazelwood, R.R. (1985) 'Crime scene and profile characteristics of organized and disorganized murderers', *FBI Law Enforcement Bulletin*, 54: 18-25.

Ressler, R., Burgess, A. and Douglas, J. (1988) *Sexual Homicide*. Lexington, MA: Lexington.

Rinear, E. (1988) 'Psychosocial aspects of parental response patterns to the death of a child by homicide', *Journal of Traumatic Stress*, 1: 305-22.

Robson, C. (1973) *Experiment, Design and Statistics in Psychology*. Harmondsworth: Penguin Educational.

Rock, P. (1998) *After Homicide: Practical and Political Responses to Bereavement*. Oxford: Hart Publishing.

Rock, P. (2012) 'Sociological theories of crime', in M. Maguire, R. Morgan and R. Reiner (eds), *Oxford Handbook of Criminology*, 5th edn. Oxford: Oxford University Press. pp. 39-80.

Rock, P. (2014) 'The public faces of public criminology', *Criminology and Criminal Justice*, 14: 412-33.

Rodger, J. (2012) 'Rehabilitation revolution in a big society', in A. Silvestri (ed.), *Critical Reflections: Social and Criminal Justice Within the First Year of the Coalition Government*. London: Centre for Crime and Justice.

Roesch, R. and Rogers, B. (2011) 'Review of *The Cambridge Handbook of Forensic Psychology*', *Canadian Psychology/Psychologie Canadienne*, 52: 242-3.

Rogers, R. (ed.) (2008) *Clinical Assessment of Malingering and Deception*, 3rd edn. New York: The Guilford Press.

Rogers,T.P., Blackwood, N.J., Farnham, F., Pickup, G.J and Watts, M.J. (2008) 'Fitness to plead and competence to stand trial: a systematic review of the constructs and their application', *The Journal of Forensic Psychiatry & Psychology*, 19: 576-96.

Rosenfeld, B., Byers, K. and Galietta, M. (2011) 'Conducting psychotherapy outcome research', in B. Rosenfeld and S. Penrod (eds), *Research Methods in Forensic Psychology*. Hoboken, NJ: Wiley.

Rosenfeld, B. and Penrod, S. (eds) (2011) *Research Methods in Forensic Psychology*. Hoboken, NJ: Wiley.

Rosenfeld, E. (2008) 'Understanding homicide and aggravated assault'. Paper presented to the Causes and Responses to Violence conference, Arizona State University, April.

Roth, A. and Fonagy, P. (2006) *What Works for Whom: A Critical Review of Psychotherapy Research*, 2nd edn. New York: Guilford Press.

Rowe, M. (ed) (2007) *Policing beyond Macpherson: Issues in Policing, Race and Society*. Cullompton: Willan.

Rowe, M. (2014) 'Race and policing', in J. Brown (ed), *The Future of Policing*. Abingdon: Routledge. pp. 120-33.

Roycroft, M., Brown, J. and Innes, M. (2007) 'Reform by crisis: the murder of Stephen Lawrence and a socio-historical analysis of developments in the conduct of major crime investigations', in M. Rowe (ed), *Policing beyond Macpherson*. Cullompton: Willan.

Ryan, M. (2005) 'Engaging with punitive attitudes towards crime and punishment: some strategic lessons for England and Wales', in J. Pratt, D. Brown, M. Brown, S. Hallsworth and W. Morrison (eds), *The New Punitiveness: Trends, Theories and Perspectives*. Cullompton: Willan. pp. 139-50.

Salfati, C.G. (2000) 'The nature of expressiveness and instrumentality in homicide', *Homicide Studies*, 4 (3): 265-93.

Salfati, C.G. and Bateman, A.L. (2005) 'Serial homicide: an investigation of behavioural consistency', *Journal of Investigative Psychology and Offender Profiling*, 2: 121-44.

Salfati, C.G., Horning, A.M., Sorochinski, M. and Labuschagne, G.N. (2014) 'South African serial homicide: consistency in victim types and crime scene actions across series', *Journal of Investigative Psychology and Offender Profiling* [E-pub ahead of print 7 August 2014] doi: 10.1002/jip.1428.

Santtila, P., Junkkila, J. and Sandnabba, K. (2005) 'Behavioural linking of stranger rapes', *Journal of Investigative Psychology and Offender Profiling*, 2: 87-103.

Santtila, P., Pakkanen, T., Zappala, A., Bosca, D., Valkama and Mokros, A. (2008) 'Behavioural crime linking in serial homicide', *Psychology, Crime and Law*, 14 (3): 245-65.

Santtila, P., Runtti, M. and Mokros, A. (2004) 'Predicting presence of offender's criminal record from antisocial lifestyle indicators of homicide victims', *Journal of Interpersonal Violence*, 19 (5): 541-57.

Savage, S. (2007) *Police Reform: Forces for Change*. Oxford: Oxford University Press.

Savage, S. and Charman, S. (1996) 'Managing change', in F. Leishman, B. Loveday and S. Savage (eds), *Core Issues in Policing*. Harlow: Longman. pp. 39-53.

Scarr, H. (1973) 'Patterns of burglary', *Social Problems*, 20: 499-515.

Schlosser, E. (1997) 'A grief like no other', *Atlantic Monthly*, September: 37-76.

Schweitzer, N.J. and Saks, M.J. (2007) 'The *CSI* effect: popular fiction about forensic science affects the public's expectations about real forensic science', *Jurimetrics*, 47: 357-64.

Scrivner, E. (2006) 'Psychology and law enforcement', in I.B. Weiner and A.K. Hess (eds), *The Handbook of Forensic Psychology*, 3rd edn. Hoboken, NJ: Wiley. pp. 534-51.

Sentencing Council (2014) *Crown Court Sentencing Survey*. Annual Publication: January to December 2013, England and Wales. http//:sentencingcouncil.judiciary.gov.uk (accessed 7 September 2014).

Sheldon, K., Davies, J. and Howells, K. (eds) (2010) *Research and Practice for Forensic Professionals*. London: Routledge.

Shepherd, E. (ed.) (1993) *Aspects of Police Interviewing*. Issues in Criminological and Legal Psychology No. 18. Leicester: British Psychological Society.

Shepherd, J. (2013) *Professionalising the Probation Service: Why University Institutes Would Transform Rehabilitation*. London: Howard League for Penal Reform/London School of Economics Mannheim Centre for Criminology.

Silvestri, A. (ed.) (2012) *Critical Reflections: Social and Criminal Justice Within the First Year of the Coalition Government*. London: Centre for Crime and Justice.

Simon, H. (1987) 'Making management decisions: The role of intuition and emotion', *The Academy of Management Executive*, 1987-1989: 57-64.

Singleton, N., Meltzer, H. and Gatwaed, R. (1998) *Psychiatric Morbidity Among Prisoners in England and Wales*. London: Office of National Statistics.

Smith, C. (1993) 'Psychological offender profiling', *The Criminologist*, 17: 244-50.

Smith, D. (2001) 'Electronic monitoring of offenders: the Scottish experience', *Criminology and Criminal Justice*, 1: 201-14.

Smith, N., Smith, K., Knight, L. and Clarke, T. (1998) 'Evaluating the Content of Offender Profiles - Summary Report'. Unpublished internal report. Police Research Group, National Crime Faculty.

Smyth, E. and Mishra, V. (2014) 'Barrister gender and litigant success in the High Court in Australia', *Australian Journal of Political Science*, 49: 1-21.

Snook, B., Eastwood, J., Gendreau, P., Goggin, C. and Cullen, R.M. (2007) 'Taking stock of criminal profiling: a narrative review and meta-analysis', *Criminal Justice and Behavior*, 34: 437-53.

Snow, D.L., Grady, K. and Goyette-Ewing, M. (2000) 'A perspective on ethical issues in community psychology', in J. Rappoport and E. Seidman (eds), *Handbook of Community Psychology*. New York: Kluwer/Plenum. pp. 897-917.

Snyder, C.E. (ed.) (2000) *Handbook of Hope: Theory, Measures and Application*. San Diego, CA: Academic Press.

Spalek, B. (2006) *Crime Victims: Theory, Policy and Practice*. Basingstoke: Palgrave Macmillan.

Spohn, C. (1991) 'Decision making in sexual assault cases: do black and female judges make a difference?', *Women and Criminal Justice*, 2: 83-105.

Stafford, M., Chandola, T. and Marmot, M. (2007) 'Association between fear of crime and mental health and physical functioning', *American Journal of Public Health*, 97: 2076-81.

Stainton Rogers, W. (2009) 'Research methodology', in D. Fox, I. Prilleltensky and S. Austin (eds), *Critical Psychology: An Introduction*, 2nd edn. London: Sage. pp. 335-54.

Stanko, E. (1997) '"I second that opinion": reflections on feminism, emotionality and research on sexual violence', in M.D. Schwartz (ed), *Researching Sexual Violence against Women: Methodological and Personal Perspectives*. Thousand Oaks, CA: Sage. pp. 74-85.

Stanko, E.A. and Hobdell, K. (1993) 'Assault on men: masculinity and male victimization', *British Journal of Criminology*, 33 (3): 400-15.

Stanko, B. and Williams, E. (2009) 'Reviewing rape and rape allegations in London; what are the vulnerabilities of the victims who report to the police?', in M. Horvath and J. Brown (eds), *Rape: Challenging Contemporary Thinking*. Cullompton: Willan. pp. 207-25.

Steadman, H.J. and Cocozza, J.J. (1974) *Careers of the Criminally Insane: A Community Follow-up of Mentally Ill Offenders*. Chicago: University of Chicago Press.

Stern, V. (2010) *The Stern Review: A Report by Baroness Stern, CBE, of an Independent Review Into How Rape Complaints Are Handled by Public Authorities in England and Wales*. London: Government Equalities Office and the Home Office. www.equalities. gov.uk/pdf/Stern_Review_of_Rape_Reporting_1FINAL.pdf.

Stevens, J. (2005) *Not for the Faint-Hearted: My Life Fighting Crime*. London: Weidenfeld and Nicolson.

Stockton, W. and Crighton, D. (2003) 'Sex-offender groupwork', in G. Towl (ed.), *Psychology in Prisons*. Leicester: BPS Blackwell. pp. 64-73.

Stott, C. and Gorringe, H. (2014) 'From Sir Robert Peel to PLRs: adapting to liaison-based public order policing in England and Wales', in J. Brown (ed.), *The Future of Policing*. London: Routledge. pp. 239-51.

Strickland, P. and Garton Grimwood, G. (2013) *The Abolition of Sentences of Imprisonment for Public Protection*. House of Commons Briefing Note.

Svensson, R. (2002) 'Strategic offences in the criminal career context', *British Journal of Criminology*, 42: 395-411.

Tapp, J., Warren, F., Fife-Schaw, C. et al. (2013) 'What do the experts by experience tell us about "what works" in high secure forensic inpatient hospital service?', *Journal of Forensic Psychiatry*, 24: 160-78.

Taylor, J. and Lindsay, W. (2010) 'Intellectual disabilities and offending', in J. Brown and E. Campbell (eds), *The Cambridge Handbook of Forensic Psychology*. Cambridge: Cambridge University Press. pp. 195-201.

Taylor, I., Walton, P. and Young, J. (1973) *The New Criminology: For a Social Theory of Deviance* (International Library of Sociology). London: Routledge.

Thomas-Peter, B. (2006) 'The modern context of psychology in corrections, influences, limitations and values of "what works"', in G. Towl (ed), *Psychological Research in Prison*. Oxford: Blackwell. pp. 24-39.

Thompson, J. and Ricard, S. (2009) 'Women's role in serial killing teams: deconstructing a radical feminist perspective', *Critical Criminology*, 17: 261-75.

Thompson, M.P. (2007) 'Homicide survivors: neglected victims of crime', in R. Davis, A. Lurigio and S. Herman (eds) *Vicims of Crime*, 3rd edn. Newbury Park, CA: Sage. pp. 109-23.

Thornton, D. (1987) 'Treatment effects on recidivism: A reappraisal of the "Nothing Works" doctrine', in Barry McGurk, D. Thornton and M. Williams (eds) *Applying Psychology to Imprisonment: Theory and Practice*. London: Her Majesty's Stationery Office. pp. 181-89.

Thornton, D. (2000) *Scoring guide for Risk Matrix: 2000*. Unpublished manuscript.

Thornton, D. (2002) 'Construction and testing: a framework for dynamic risk assessment', *Sexual Abuse: A Journal of Research and Treatment*, 14: 137-51.

Tilley, N. (2009) 'Sherman vs Sherman; realism vs rhetoric', *Criminology and Criminal Justice*, 9: 135-44.

Tong, S., Bryant, R. and Horvath, M. (2009) *Understanding Criminal Investigation*. Chichester: Wiley-Blackwell.

Tonkin, M., Bond, J.W. and Woodhams, J. (2009) 'Fashion conscious burglars? Testing the principles of offender profiling with footwear impressions recovered at domestic burglaries', *Psychology, Crime & Law*, 15: 327-45.

Towl, G. (2003) *Psychology in Prisons*. Oxford: BPS and Blackwell.

Towl, G. and Crighton, D. (eds) (2010) *Forensic Psychology*. Oxford: BPS Blackwell.

Towl, G. (2010a) 'Context: introduction', in G.J. Towl and D.A. Crighton (eds), *Forensic Psychology*. Oxford: Blackwell. pp. 10-12.

Towl, G. (2010b) 'Suicide in prison', in J. Brown (ed.), *The Future of Policing*. London: Routledge. pp. 416-22.

Towl, G. (2010c) 'Ethical issues in forensic pschology', in G.J. Towl and D.A. Crighton (eds), *Forensic Psychology*. Oxford: Blackwell. pp. 62-69.

Towl, G. and Crighton, D. (2008) 'Psychologist in prisons', in J. Bennett, B. Crewe and A. Wahidin (eds), *Understanding Prison Staff*. Cullompton: Willan. pp. 316-29.

Towl, G., Farrington, D., Crighton, D. and Hughes, G. (eds) (2008) *Dictionary of Forensic Psychology*. Cullompton: Willan.

Trojan, C. and Salfati, C.G. (2011) 'Linking criminal history to crime scene behavior in single-victim and serial homicide: implications for offender profiling research', *Homicide Studies*, 15 (1): 3-31.

Tseloni, A., Mailley, J., Farrell, S. and Tilley, N. (2010) 'Exploring the international decline in crime rates', *European Journal of Criminology*, 7: 375-94.

Tunstall, O., Gudjonsson, G., Eysenck, H. and Haward, L. (1982) 'Professional issues arising from psychological evidence presented in court', *Bulletin of the British Psychological Society*, 35: 329-31.

Turner, E. (2013) 'Beyond "facts" and "values": rethinking some recent debates about the public role of criminology', *British Journal of Criminology*, 53: 149-66.

Turner, H., Finkelhorn, D. and Ormrod, R. (2006) 'The effect of lifetime victimization on the mental health of children and adolescents', *Social Science and Medicine*, 62 (1): 13-27.

Tutu, D. (1999) *No Future Without Forgiveness*. New York: Image Doubleday.

Tyler, T. and van der Toorn, J. (2013) 'Social justice', in L. Huddy, D. Sears and J. Levy (eds), *Oxford Handbook of Political Psychology*, 2nd edn. Oxford: Oxford University Press.

UK Statistics Authority (2014) *Assessment of compliance with the codes of practice for official statistics; statistics on crime in England and Wales (produced by the Office of National Statistics)*. Assessment Report 268. London: UK Statistics Authority.

Ullman, S. and Townsend, S. (2010) 'The investigation and prosecution of rape', in J.R. Adler and J.M. Gray (eds), *Forensic Psychology: Concepts, Debates and Practice*. Abingdon: Willan. pp. 74-92.

van Koppen, Peter J. and Lochun, Shara K. (1997) 'Portraying perpetrators: The validity of offender descriptions by witnesses', *Law and Human Behavior*, 21: 661-85.

van de Zandt, P. (1998) 'Heroines of fortitude', in P. Easteal (ed), *Balancing the Scales: Rape, Law Reform and Australian Culture*. Sydney: The Federation Press.

Villejoubert, G., Almond, L. and Alison, L. (2009) 'Interpreting claims in offender profiles: the role of probability phrases, base-rates and perceived dangerousness', *Applied Cognitive Psychology*, 23: 136-54.

Walby, S. and Allen, J. (2004) *Domestic Violence, Sexual Assault and Stalking: Findings from the British Crime Survey*. Home Office Research Study 276. London: Home Office.

Walker, L.E. (1977) 'Who are the battered women?', *Frontiers: A Journal of Women Studies*, 2: 52-7.

Walklate, S. (2001) 'The victim's lobby', in M. Ryan, S. Savage and D. Wall (eds), *Policy Networks in Criminal Justice*. Basingstoke: Palgrave. pp. 201-17.

Walklate, S. (2007) (ed.) *Handbook of Victims and Victimology*. Cullompton: Willan.

Walklate, S. (2013 [1989]) *Victimology: The Victim and the Criminal Justice Process*. London: Routledge [Unwin Hyman].

Walmsley, R. (2014) *World Prison Population List*, 10th edn. International Centre for Prison Studies, University of Essex.

Wakeling, H. and Travers, R. (2010) 'Evaluating offender behaviour programmes in prison', in J. Brown and E. Campbell (eds), *Cambridge Handbook of Forensic Psychology*. Cambridge: Cambridge University Press. pp. 820-9.

Ward, T. (2008) 'Human rights and forensic psychology', *Legal and Criminological Psychology*, 13: 209-18.

Ward, T. (2011) 'Human rights and dignity in offender rehabilitation', *Journal of Forensic Psychology Practice*, 11: 103-23.

Ward, T. and Beech, A. (2006) 'An integrated theory of sexual offending', *Aggression and Violent Behaviour*, 11: 44-63.

Ward, T. and Beech, A. (2014) 'Dynamic risk factors: a theoretical dead-end?', *Psychology Crime and Law* [E-Pub ahead of print 29 May 2014] doi:10.1080/1068316X.2014.917854.

Ward, T. and Birgden, A. (2007) 'Human rights and correctional clinical practice', *Aggression and Violent Behaviour*, 12: 628-43.

Ward, T. and Marshall, B. (2007) 'Narrative identity and offender rehabilitation', *International Journal of Offender Therapy and Comparative Criminology*, 3: 279-97.

Ward, T. and Maruna, S. (2007) *Rehabilitation: Beyond the Risk Paradigm*. London: Routledge.

Ward, T. and Stewart, C.A. (2003) 'The treatment of sex offenders: risk management and good lives', *Professional Psychology: Research and Practice*, 34: 353-60.

Ward, T. and Willis, G. (2010) 'Ethical issues in forensic and correctional research', *Aggression and Violent Behavior*, 15: 399-409.

Ward, T., Louden, K., Hudson, S.M. and Marshall, W.L. (1995) 'A descriptive model of the offense chain for child molesters', *Journal of Interpersonal Violence*, 10: 452-72.

Ward, T., Melser, J. and Yates, P.M. (2007) 'Reconstructing the Risk Need Responsivity model: a theoretical elaboration and evaluation', *Aggression and Violent Behavior*, 12: 208-28.

Ward, T., Yates, P. and Willis, G. (2012) 'The good lives model and the risk need responsivity model: a critical response to Andrews, Bonta and Wormith (2011)', *Criminal Justice and Behavior*, 39: 94-110.

Warr, M. (1987) 'Fear of victimization and sensitivity to risk', *Journal of Quantitative Criminology*, 3: 29-46.

Waters, I. (1996) 'Quality of service or paradigm shift?', in F. Leishman, B. Loveday and S. Savage (eds), *Core Issues in Policing*. Harlow: Longman. pp. 205-17.

Weaver, B. and McNeill, F. (2010) '"Travelling hopefully": desistance research and probation practice', in J. Brayford, F. Cowe and J. Deering (eds), *What Else Works? Creative Work with Offenders and Other Social Excluded People*. Cullompton: Willan.

Webster, C.D., Douglas, K.S., Eaves, D. and Hart, S.D. (1997) *HCR-20: Assessing Risk for Violence, Version 2*. Vancouver: Mental Health, Law and Policy Institute, Simon Fraser University.

Webster, C.D., Eaves, D., Douglas, K.S. and Wintrup, A. (1995) *The HCR-20 Scheme: The Assessment of Dangerousness and Risk*. Vancouver: Simon Fraser University and British Columbia Forensic Psychiatric Services Commission.

Wells, P. (2007) 'New Labour and evidence based policy making, 1997–2007', *People, Place and Policy*, [online] 1/1: 22–9.

West, A.G. (2001) 'From offender profiler to behavioural investigative advisor: the effective application of behavioural science to the investigation of major crime', *Police Research and Management*, 5: 95–108.

Wheatcroft, J.M. and Walklate, S. (2014) 'Thinking differently about "false allegations" in cases of rape: the search for the truth', *International Journal of Criminology and Sociology*, 3: 239–48.

Wherton, J. (2004) 'An exploratory study into gay homicides: predicting the victim-offender relationship using crime scene characteristics'. Unpublished BSc dissertation, University of Bath.

White, M. (1997) *Narratives of Therapists Lives*. Dulwich: Centre Publications.

White, R. and Haines, F. (2004) *Crime and Criminology: An Introduction*, 3rd edn. Melbourne: Oxford University Press.

Whittaker, M., Brown, J., Beckett, R. and Gerhold, C. (2006) 'Sexual knowledge and empathy: a comparison of adolescent child molesters and non-offending adolescents', *Journal of Sexual Aggression*, 12: 143–54.

Wijkman, M., Bijleveld, C. and Hendriks, J. (2010) 'Women don't do such things! Characteristics of female sex offenders and offender types', *Sexual Abuse: A Journal of Research and Treatment*, 22: 135–56.

Williams, P. (1997) 'Spirit-murdering the messenger: the discourse of finger pointing as the law's response to racism', in A. Wing (ed.), *Critical Race Feminism: A Reader*. New York: New York University Press. pp. 229–36.

Wilson, P. and Soothill, K. (1996) 'Psychological profiling: red, green or amber?', *The Police Journal*, 1: 12–20.

Wilson, P., Lincoln, R. and Kocsis, R. (1997) 'Validity, utility and ethics of profiling for serial violent and sexual offenders', *Psychiatry, Psychology and Law*, 4: 1–11.

Winkel, F.W. and Koppelarr, L. (1991) 'Rape victims' style of self-presentation and secondary victimization by the environment: an experiment', *Journal of Interpersonal Violence*, 6: 29–40.

Wolhuter, L., Olley, N. and Denham, D. (2009) *Victimology: Victimisation and Victims' Rights*. London: Routledge Cavendish.

Woodhams, J. (2012) 'Offender profiling and crime linkage', in G. Davies and A. Beech (eds), *Forensic Psychology – Crime, Justice, Law, Interventions*. Chichester: BPS and Wiley. pp. 173–87.

Woodhams, J., Hollin, C.R. and Bull, R. (2007) 'The psychology of linking crimes: a review of the evidence', *Legal and Criminological Psychology*, 12: 233–49.

Wormith, J.S., Gendreau, P. and Bonta, J. (2012) 'Deferring to clarity, parsimony and evidence in reply to Ward, Yates and Willis', *Criminal Justice and Behaviour*, 39: 111–20.

Wrightsman, L. (1999) *Judicial Decision Making: Is Psychology Relevant?* New York: Kluwer Academic/Plenum.

Wrightsman, L.S. and Fulero, S.M. (2005) *Forensic Psychology*, 2nd edn. Belmont, CA: Wadsworth.

Yang, M., Wong, S.C. and Coid, J. (2010) 'The efficacy of violence prediction: a meta-analytic comparison of nine risk assessment tools', *Psychological Bulletin*, 136: 740-767.

Young, J. (1994) 'Incessant chatter: recent paradigms in criminology', in M. Maguire, R. Morgan and R. Reiner (eds), *The Oxford Handbook of Criminology*. Oxford: Oxford University Press. pp. 69-124.

Young, S. (2010) 'Programmed interventions for offenders', in J. Brown and E. Campbell (eds), *Cambridge Handbook of Forensic Psychology*. Cambridge: Cambridge University Press. pp. 384-92.

Young, S., Chick, K. and Gudjonsson, G. (2010) 'A preliminary evaluation of reasoning and rehabilitation 2 in mentally disordered offenders (R&R2M) across two secure forensic settings in the United Kingdom', *The Journal of Forensic Psychiatry & Psychology*, 21: 336-49.

INDEX

Pages containing relevant tables and figures are indicated in *italic* type.